THE NEW EUROPEAN RURALITY

Ashgate Economic Geography Series

Series Editors:
Michael Taylor, Peter Nijkamp and Tom Leinbach

Innovative and stimulating, this quality series enlivens the field of economic geography and regional development, providing key volumes for academic use across a variety of disciplines. Exploring a broad range of interrelated topics, the series enhances our understanding of the dynamics of modern economies in the developed and developing countries, as well as the dynamics of transition economies. It embraces both cutting edge research monographs and strongly themed edited volumes, thus offering significant added value to the field and to the individual topics addressed.

Other titles in the series:

Creativity and Space:
Labour and the Restructuring of the German Advertising Industry
Joachim Thiel
ISBN 0 7546 4328 X

Proximity, Distance and Diversity:
Issues on Economic Interaction and Local Development
Edited by Arnoud Lagendijk and Päivi Oinas
ISBN 0 7546 4074 4

Foreign Direct Investment and Regional Development in
East Central Europe and the Former Soviet Union
Edited by David Turnock
ISBN 0 7546 3248 2

China's Rural Market Development in the Reform Era
Him Chung
ISBN 0 7546 3764 6

The Sharing Economy:
Solidarity Networks Transfroming Globalisation
Lorna Gold
ISBN 0 7546 3345 4

The New European Rurality
Strategies for Small Firms

Edited by

TERESA DE NORONHA VAZ
University of Algarve, Portugal

ELEANOR J. MORGAN
University of Bath, UK

PETER NIJKAMP
Free University, Amsterdam,
The Netherlands

ASHGATE

Published by
Ashgate Publishing Limited
Gower House
Croft Road
Aldershot
Hants GU11 3HR
England

Ashgate Publishing Company
Suite 420
101 Cherry Street
Burlington, VT 05401-4405
USA

Ashgate website: http://www.ashgate.com

British Library Cataloguing in Publication Data
The new European rurality : strategies for small firms. -
    (Ashgate economic geography series)
    1. Rural development - European Union countries 2. Small
    business - European Union countries
    I. Vaz, Teresa de Noronha II. Morgan, Eleanor III. Nijkamp,
    Peter
    307.1'412'094

Library of Congress Cataloging-in-Publication Data
The new European rurality : strategies for small firms / edited by Teresa de Noronha
    Vaz, Eleanor J. Morgan, and Peter Nijkamp.
        p. cm. -- (Ashgate economic geography series)
    Includes index.
    ISBN 0-7546-4536-3
    1. Agricultural industries--Europe. 2. Rural development--Europe. 3. Small
business--Europe--Management. I. Vaz, Teresa de Noronha. II. Morgan, Eleanor J.
III. Nijkamp, Peter. IV. Series.

HD9015.A2N49 2005
630'.68'4--dc22

                                                                    2005020511
ISBN 0 7546 4536 3

Contents

List of Tables

List of Figures

Editorial Preface

The position of rural areas appears to be problematic in an increasingly urbanised world. In the current debates on urban innovation poles, advanced technology areas and global command centres, there seems to be little place for rural regions. Their potential and the opportunities they offer are poorly recognised and their role has been largely neglected in these broader discussions.

Nevertheless, a significant part of the earth's surface is made up of rural areas which not only provide a home for nature but also are host to agriculture, tourism, and a great variety of leisure activities. These rural economic sectors do not stand alone; instead they interact closely with the urban world. They are influenced by the patterns of urban activity (through the effects on local ecological niches, for example) and they, in turn, offer resources such as agricultural products and environmental services to urban areas. An exploration of the potential of modern rurality is therefore a relevant and timely endeavour.

There is now an intensive debate on rural development, especially in Europe, with its transition to open borders and to a single market. This is particularly important in agriculture, especially with the current drive towards applying advanced forms of biotechnology in production. Protecting the interests of rural areas has even been recognised as one of the official goals ('the second pillar') of the Common Agricultural Policy. In this context, the position of agriculture itself is at stake, as past EU policy in this field has distorted free market competition and led to the unnecessary spending of large parts of the EU budget, undesirable overproduction and environmental decay. It is no longer certain that large parts of Europe's rural areas will always continue to be used for agriculture. As a consequence, rural areas are having to re-position themselves to take account of changing policies and competitive conditions.

What development opportunities are there for rural areas under such changing circumstances? Is there any potential for productive small-scale entrepreneurial activities? Should rural areas be turned into nature reserves? How can smaller rural firms best be encouraged, especially as regards the adoption of new technologies? Such questions are at the heart of this publication. It aims to bring together a variety of studies on modern rurality with the goal of demonstrating the feasibility of new entrepreneurial activities in rural areas. These may be of considerable relevance if a sustainable development of the rural economy is to be achieved, as sound economic motives seem likely to become necessary ingredients in a survival kit for the balanced development of Europe's rurality.

Teresa de Noronha Vaz, Eleanor J. Morgan and Peter Nijkamp

List of Contributors

Tessa Avermaete
Tüzin Baycan Levent
Shlomo Bekhor
Martine Boutary
Cristina Brasili
Giuseppina Carrà
Federica Cisilino
Mordechai Cohen
Andrew Copus
Nick Crawford
Efthalia Dimara
Anabela Dinis
Roberto Fanfani
Guillermina García Figueroa
Xavier Gellynck
Elena Georgoudaki
José Salas González
Edmundo Haro
Lois Labrianidis
Eveline S. van Leeuwen
Denise Mahon
Enno Masurel
M-Christine Monnoyer
Eleanor J. Morgan
Maria Manuela Santos Natário
Paulo Alexandre Neto
Peter Nijkamp
Teresa de Noronha Vaz
Rene Ochoa Ochoa
Iuri Peri
Eamonn Pitts
Felisberto Marques Reigado
Daniel Shefer
Dimitris Skuras
Jacques Viaene
Myriam Sagarnaga Villegas
Gabriella Vindigni

PART I

NEW PERSPECTIVES ON EUROPEAN RURALITY AND ENTREPRENEURSHIP

Chapter 1

Rural Europe and Small Firms: A Strategic Positioning and Synthesis

Teresa de Noronha Vaz, Eleanor J. Morgan and Peter Nijkamp

A New Rural Scene

The world is moving towards becoming urban in character, at least in terms of the proportion of people residing in urban areas. But it is still largely rural in geographical terms, taking into account the amount of non-urbanized land. At the same time, the traditional urban/rural divide is gradually vanishing; the economic, ecological and social footprint of cities now reaches far out into rural areas, while rural areas increasingly feature activities that were traditionally found in an urban economy. Consequently, rural areas can no longer simply be seen as the natural home of agricultural activity; sometimes 'rurality' refers to extended urbanity. In addition, rural areas are increasingly a part of the modern leisure industry, with mass tourism on the one hand and small-scale recreation on the other. Modern developments in information and communications technologies mean rural areas have a less peripheral character than before. As a result, rural areas currently find themselves at the interface of two sets of forces, namely local and regional developments occurring in their vicinity and global developments taking place at a distance.

Globalization is exerting a profound impact on the spatial features of European economic activity and this is particularly evident when the consequences for firms' location decisions and their organization and logistics are considered. The sustainable development of European rurality requires environmental conditions which are able to preserve rural characteristics but, at the same time, are still able to allow for entrepreneurial expansion. This implies difficult trade-offs between agricultural interests, the importance of rural pursuits, recreation and leisure activities, environmental quality and small-scale entrepreneurial activities that fit a rural landscape. How can the balanced and sustainable development of rural areas be achieved?

Four important issues deserve attention in exploring the possibilities for sustainable development of rural regions in the future. These are first, the specific characteristics of these rural areas and the types of economic activity featured; second, the effects of the predominance of small firms, with their vital links to the external production environment, on the potential for development; third, the nature of new – sometimes green – technologies in combination with the emergence of new models of industrial production and organization and, finally, the opportunities originating from various types of public policies which might promote sound rural development. The four issues will be briefly discussed to set the context for the aims and scope of the book presented in the next section of the chapter.

First, economic activity in rural areas is generally based on traditional sectors (such as agriculture and handicrafts) that tend to be less receptive to technical change and may therefore become vulnerable to global competition. Local development in the European periphery is mostly determined by the behaviour of small firms whose low investment levels, lack of access to knowledge bases and limited ability to absorb new technologies constitute major growth impediments. At the same time, the location of traditional industrial activities is changing as it becomes increasingly orientated towards segmented production modes, while specialized activities move towards those areas that can respond flexibly to the new market demands, both locally and globally. The likely result is an increase in the trade flows of goods and services, as well as of information and knowledge, which will tend to lead to intense interactions between those regions which manage to participate in the new developments.

In the second place, the strong links between small firms and their environments have led to the much discussed concept of 'embeddedness'. The importance of the concept is twofold, as it can be used to understand the socio-economic and cultural hindrances to entrepreneurial dynamism, while helping, at the same time, to explain the possible structural effects of regional policy in such regions.

Next, new modes of industrial organization are becoming more important. In particular, the adoption of new technologies has resulted in modular and more flexible forms of production emerging in place of large production units that were based on scale economies and integrated processes. Regions may be seen currently as competing among themselves in terms of their capacity to offer firms the best opportunities for decentralizing their productive processes and management.

Finally, the different types of public support and accompanying policies required to support the transition to a new type of sustainable rurality need to be distinguished. For example, the capability to learn is an important determinant of innovation, so that technological support appropriate to address the internal and external learning environment of firms needs to be addressed. Clearly, for each small firm, innovative activities and the ability to network externally are determinants not just of growth but also of survival. This calls for innovative public policies. How these can occur – in terms of driving forces, strategies and instruments – in rural areas (including lagging territories) is the main concern of this book.

Before describing the features of the book, some remarks are in order on the current European policy context. There are many reasons why economic and industrial structures vary between different regions in the European Union (EU). The European Commission has promoted a variety of programmes and regulations to reduce growth discrepancies among regions. While these have had some success, concerns about the persistent nature of regional differences have gradually turned into new policy perspectives on the reform of the structural funds. These allow more fine-tuning than previously to take account of specific regional attributes. This approach is based on the evidence of distinct and different development opportunities among the European regions and their economic actors, and suggests a higher level of flexibility as regards the integration of the different territories in the EU.

Although there are opportunities for technological development in rural areas and among firms engaged in more traditional activities, the EU has traditionally tended to focus on the most advanced regions and the so called high-tech industries in its technology (and specifically R&D) policies. The cohesion goals have led to considerable aid being given to scientific research outside the richer areas and financing from the Framework programmes for R&D has contributed to a catch-up by the cohesion countries. Technological gaps still remain, however, and these hinder moves to sustainable development in more peripheral parts of the EU. Uncertainty about the complex links between technological development and economic growth in such environments needs to be addressed and in particular, the conditions for effective technological policies in peripheral regions, including rural areas, need to be identified.

Against the above background, it is interesting to note that several theoretical approaches have been developed in recent years to help in understanding the complex nexus of entrepreneurship and its geographical setting. In general, these indicate the need for concerted actions linking the concepts of territories, knowledge and entrepreneurship (see Shane, 2003; Kizner, 1997; Davidsson, 2002; and Kent et al. 1982). The results of empirical studies show that some territorial systems in similarly classified rural areas have different economic and environmental dynamics. Furthermore, the factors responsible for growth and development in some rural areas may shift within short periods of time, creating unstable cause and effect relationships (EC, 2003). In the process of structural change in rural territories, the key role small firms may play in contributing to both regional income and employment stability has been clearly demonstrated. Also, in comparing different regions, there is evidence of sustained development in those areas where innovative small firms predominate. Unfortunately, several peripheral areas seem to be unable to participate in these competitive processes and are a long way from creating innovative environments independently of state investment in public support institutions. Despite this, private initiatives at the firm level are seen by some as the tool to improve development in such regions (Brüderl and Preisendörfer, 1998; Sullivan, 2000).

Aims and Contents

This book examines the conceptual, empirical and policy issues associated with new perspectives on rurality. It identifies and discusses the driving forces, new challenges, entrepreneurial responses and policy actions that impact on the rural economic landscape in Europe, particularly on small firms. It contains a set of original contributions that examine these features of rurality, drawing on empirical evidence from rural areas in many different countries and from a variety of rural activities. It examines why a more positive perspective on the possibilities for sustainable development in rural areas is needed and how this may be implemented. While suggesting the need for new strategies in rural regions, it also provides original evidence of the efforts made by various stakeholders to change the endogenous capacities of such peripheral areas. The following chapters illustrate the complexity to which rural areas are exposed in this era of globalization. They provide both qualititative and statistical evidence suggesting promising possibilities for change and growth. Indeed, a new concept of rurality is assumed in that processes based on a balanced introduction of technological innovation and change are seen as compatible with social inclusion and a high-quality living environment. This calls for a conceptual reconsideration and the book includes a novel analytical discussion of the new rurality as well as a set of empirical studies providing evidence of the strategies of different actors, particularly of small firms, in this environment.

The book is divided into four parts. Part I, entitled *New Perspectives on European Rurality and Entrepreneurship*, consists of two chapters that together provide a conceptual overview of the issues under consideration. Following this editorial introduction, Chapter 2 examines 'Entrepreneurship in small enterprises and local development'. This focuses on the osmotic linkages between entrepreneurs in small firms and their territorial environments. The chapter explores how the organizational capacities and efficiency of small firms may be a consequence of their local conditions while, at the same time, their own capacity to learn and innovate has a crucial influence on environmental change. The ability of some small firms to perform well in times of structural change may be partly explained by their past learning accumulated through specialization in traditional activities and also through complex interactions within production and innovation networks. The chapter characterizes the different roles of small firms in the light of their specific goals and their capacity to promote differentiated innovative activities. The role of institutions in either supporting or hindering smaller firms is also discussed.

The second part of the book identifies and examines *Determinants of Structural Change in Peripheral Regions*. It contains four chapters which are empirically based and together deal with emerging processes that may alter the usual expectations for lagging areas. Chapter 3, 'Accessibility, innovative milieu and the innovative activity of businesses in EU peripheral and lagging areas', is based on research carried out as part of a Framework Programme V project funded by the EU. The results derive from fieldwork in twelve lagging areas within six EU member states – Finland, Germany, Greece, Ireland, Spain and the U.K. The aim of the chapter is twofold. First, the twelve lagging areas are categorized into different types of innovative milieu using a two-dimensional classification process based on alternative classification criteria for innovative activity and the level of local synergies. The resulting innovative milieu classification is then related to the area's accessibility as measured by baseline peripherality indicators estimated for the twelve regions. Second, the factors influencing the innovative activity of individual firms are examined taking into account specific accessibility characteristics based on a survey carried out among 600 businesses in the twelve case study areas. Accessibility is shown to affect the innovative activity of businesses considerably while aspatial factors related to business networking and entrepreneurial specific factors ameliorate locational disadvantages.

Chapter 4 examines 'Human capital as the critical factor for the development of Europe's rural peripheral areas' and is also based on the results of an EU funded Framework V project. The fieldwork was conducted through two surveys, one carried out among the local population and the other among innovative firms in the chosen study areas within Germany, Greece, Poland, Portugal and the UK. The research investigates the development constraints facing rural peripheral areas in Europe and highlights the barriers to growth resulting from the limited entrepreneurship which often characterizes these areas. Dynamic rural firms are usually those that convert the perceived disadvantages of rural areas into sources of competitive advantage by emphasizing the local character of their products, or by being able to deal with the location disadvantages of rural areas through the development of highly developed co-operation networks. The author points out that the presence of entrepreneurs capable of rising to the challenge in rural peripheral areas should not be taken for granted as rural emigration tends to deprive these areas of the most dynamic individuals. Recently, however, certain rural areas in some European countries have exhibited a new dynamism, mainly due to a wave of in-migration of relatively affluent, former urban dwellers. These newcomers often have considerable management experience, as well as contacts and access to networks of information. The chapter also emphasizes that rural areas are very different between, as well as within, European countries and that there are also significant national differences in perceptions of rurality.

Chapter 5, 'Agri-food districts: theory and evidence', addresses the long standing debate about the survival and future evolution of industrial districts and possible impact of globalization in undermining the factors that have contributed to the success of local and regional development. This chapter first examines the literature relating to the theory of industrial districts. It is evident that, even where local and regional economies have become global in terms of market orientation, their production and innovation systems tend to remain primarily local. The authors then point to the recent interest in agri-food districts in the literature and emphasize the need to take a local approach to the analysis of Italian agri-food systems. The work presents a quantitative analysis of efficiency at the firm level in two sectors, meat and fruit and vegetables using firms drawn from two different Italian districts in each case. An economic and financial analysis is carried out by clustering firms into different groups according to whether or not they belong to specific food districts. The analysis shows firms inside the local systems performed better than the rest, especially in the meat industry. In the second stage of the analysis, the 'district effect' is again tested but this time using a stochastic frontier production function to assess the effect on technical efficiency due to the firm being located in a district area. This validates the previous results for the meat sector but shows a more limited effect in the fruit and vegetable sector. The statistical methods adopted in this study hold promise for future work on the relevance of the district effect.

'The embeddedness of small enterprises within the rural local economy of small and medium sized towns' is examined in Chapter 6. This assesses the local-regional/supra-regional orientation of small scale farms and firms in rural areas using data gathered in the Netherlands as part of a larger EU funded project. Particular attention is given by the authors to the role of local centres (villages and towns) in the functioning of rural areas. The degree of embeddedness of local firms in rural areas appears to be fairly high, so that fears of socio-economic erosion of rural areas appear not to be justified by the empirical facts.

Chapters 7, 8, 9 and 10, which together make up the third part of the book, are concerned with *New Strategies in Small Business Development*. These chapters focus on new strategic choices in the rural periphery and the impact of different strategies, many of which are related to innovative methods. The findings are drawn from a number of countries including France, Italy, the Netherlands and Portugal where such strategies have been detected.

The fierce competition that may be faced by local industries within the same region, especially as regards traditional products, is highlighted in 'Organizational success factors in local agri-food industries' (Chapter 7). Survival mechanisms may be based on learning principles and the use of organizational networks. This chapter summarizes the most important literature in the field and tests the above proposition by means of a study of local honey producers in Sicily. The analysis is based on a recently developed artificial intelligence method for nominal (linguistic) information based on decision tree analysis.

'The implementation of information and communication technologies in SMEs' (Chapter 8) investigates the reasons for the limited adoption of information and communications technologies (ICTs) in smaller firms. Previous literature has highlighted both the diversity of applications for which ICTs are introduced and the fact that in many cases these technologies are only used for local applications and so, even when adopted, their powerful tools tend to be under utilized. The research is based on a qualitative study of 21 firms carried out by a multidisciplinary team of six researchers. Four typologies are developed; two of them focus on the ICT adoption process and the other two focus on the functions assigned to the ICTs and on the business processes involved. The fieldwork observations confirm that the organizational changes involved in setting up ICTs in SMEs are as varied as the applications for which they are introduced. Some firms modify their organization first and then, to different degrees, change their strategy. Others have a strategic vision and only adapt their organization afterwards. The findings show the importance of segmenting the firms and appreciating their varied needs for ICTs before applying any particular public support policy.

Chapter 9 on 'Break-out strategies of ethnic entrepreneurs' investigates the significant shift in the labour market orientation of ethnic groups towards self employment observed in recent years. This movement is generally referred to as 'ethnic entrepreneurship' and is distinguished from 'normal' entrepreneurship by its orientation towards ethnic products, ethnic markets and customers or indigenous ethnic business strategies. The chapter examines the trends in 'break-out strategies' of ethnic entrepreneurs on the basis of a comparative evaluation of several empirical studies that have investigated their attitudes and behaviour. It shows that ethnic entrepreneurs have gradually moved beyond their own ethnic groups on the demand side to become a significant part of the local economy. Besides the diversity of the services that they provide in terms of their sectoral orientation and the different types of customers served, these entrepreneurs also bring employment opportunities to their own ethnic groups. Their successes have encouraged them to expand their fields of interest and, ultimately, their businesses and hence social status. However, this comparative evaluation also shows that ethnic entrepreneurs still tend to be fairly dependent on ethnic networks in terms of sources of capital and the labour force they employ.

The final topic covered in Part III is 'Rural entrepreneurship – an innovation and marketing perspective' (Chapter 10). Although entrepreneurship is generally seen as an important ingredient in rural development, some features of rural areas mean that entrepreneurship can be particularly challenging in the rural context. This chapter highlights the characteristics of the new global and information economy and the opportunity that this represents for small firms in peripheral rural areas. The chapter argues that, at the organizational level, niche marketing strategies are the most appropriate for rural firms, allowing them to be innovative and take advantage of the opportunities opened up by the new economy. This is illustrated by reference to some Portuguese examples, all of which relate to the introduction of traditional and heritage products into the global market. The examples illustrate different strategies adopted to move beyond traditional markets, including innovation in marketing methods and in organizational arrangements as well as in products themselves. The chapter ends with some conclusions for policy which emphasis the importance of stimulating the creation of network structures.

The fourth and last part of this book is a collection of *Case Studies*, most of which result from EU projects supported within the Framework Programme V. These empirical studies (which include statistical analyses as well as qualitative methodologies) examine the behaviour of firms and others who can influence the territorial dynamics of innovation. They mainly refer to Europe although one chapter demonstrates a method of projecting the economic outlook for a particular sector in the context of pig farmers in Mexico which has more general application.

Chapter 11 considers 'The adoption of information and communication technologies among smaller food firms in rural areas of Greece'. It is commonly believed that ICTs offer a new means of revitalizing rural economics as they diminish the impacts of distance and time, increase access to information and provide rural and remote enterprises with the opportunity to serve new markets. This study examines the reasons for a low rate of ICT adoption among rural SMEs in the light of the much discussed potential advantages of the new technologies. Rather than considering such firms as homogeneous economic agents, the research examines ICT adoption among differentiated clusters of rural SMEs. Following the literature review, the chapter presents the results of empirical research into the adoption and intensity of use of ICTs among food enterprises located in four lagging Greek regions. A 'worlds of production' framework is used to categorize the sample and analyse the reasons for differential rates of adoption and use.

Different factors are found to influence decisions regarding ICTs depending on the world in which each firm operates. The chapter concludes by examining the policy implications of the findings and suggesting appropriate strategies for policy makers.

The authors of Chapter 12, 'The allocation of public support to small food firms in Belgium, Ireland and the UK', present the results of a statistical study investigating factors affecting the receipt of public support. They analyse the impact of innovativeness, firm performance, information-searching capabilities and aims of the business on obtaining public support generally. More specifically, they also explore the extent to which these characteristics determine participation in innovation-oriented support programs. The research focuses on a sample of 177 small food and drink manufacturing firms based in six lagging and relatively rural regions of the EU, two in each of the three countries studied. The data, which was collected through face-to-face structured interviews with the top managers in these firms, is analysed using logistic regressions. The investigation indicates that the more innovative firms were more likely to obtain public support, especially those involved in product and process innovation. Firms with lower turnover and larger employment were more likely to obtain support for investment but R&D support was not related to these characteristics. Younger entrepreneurs were most likely to obtain public assistance and the objectives of the firm also had a significant influence.

Chapter 13 examines 'A medium term economic outlook for cyclical markets: a case study of Mexican pig farms' and introduces a planning perspective. It provides an evaluation of the competitiveness of pig farming in one of the main pork producing states in Mexico and an assessment of the future viability of pig production up to 2009 in different types of farms. Although this chapter does not address European rurality, its approach to considering the future of Mexican pig farming in order to assist in formulating a rescue plan is worth considering in a European context. The empirical estimates are based on a Farm Level Income and Policy Simulation Model with six producer panels providing technical information to simulate farms' activities. The projections of the economic viability of the representative farms investigated were made by applying price projections to input and output materials (sorghum and pork) and macroeconomic indicators (inflation and exchange rates). The results suggest that, under prevailing market conditions, only fattening farms and breeding farms are competitive. Integrated farms were generally not competitive. Profitability projections showed decreasing profitability through the planning horizon and this general trend was consistently found under the different technical scenarios analysed. If these conditions persist, some pig producers are likely to leave the industry thereby reducing employment and increasing Mexico's problems of migration, poverty and inequity.

Recently many researchers have dealt with questions relating to the spatial diffusion of innovation in manufacturing industries and its relationship to regional development. However, few past studies have considered diffusion processes in the agricultural sector. 'Adopting innovations in agriculture: an exploratory analysis using discrete choice models' (Chapter 14) investigates the determinants of the spatial diffusion of a new agricultural product as an important element in the economic development of a rural region. The research is based on a case study of a new variety of greenhouse tomato and considers two aspects of innovation diffusion, first, the selection of a specific tomato variety and second, the choice of fertilization technique. The data was gathered from two main sources – aggregate data on agricultural settlements and a survey conducted among 151 farmers from 21 agricultural communities. Both multinomial logit and nested logit models are used in the study. The results indicate that the choice of tomato variety is conditioned by the choice of fertilization technique and provides evidence of the influences – regional, local and individual – that have a bearing on the farmer's decision making processes.

Rural development largely depends on the ability of SMEs to stay competitive and this leads to the question of whether suitable local rural policies are in place to support their innovation efforts. The aim of the next chapter 'Assisting small and medium sized enterprises: technological innovation policies in rural areas' (Chapter 15), is to analyse the relationship between the development of SMEs through technological innovation and some specific policies designed to assist innovation in a rural context. The first part of the chapter presents a brief overview of the problems faced by smaller firms in the innovation process and the main regional tools to stimulate innovation among SMEs, with particular attention to the Rural Development Programme and to the Interreg Italy/Slovenia Programme. The second part aims to assess the importance of public policies to support innovation. The empirical work is based on information about rural policies together with data on Italian enterprises in Friuli-Venezia Giulia.

The final chapter, 'Attitudes to territorial innovation processes in Raia Central Ibérica', demonstrates that innovation is not an individual firm process but rather results from the involvement of a large set of participants with the capacity to influence the territorial dynamics of innovation. The aim of this study is to analyse the behaviour of participants in innovative initiatives promoting the competitiveness of the Raia Central Ibérica (RCI). The study looks at five sub regions of the RCI, three Portuguese and two Spanish. The sample for the quantitative analysis includes 166 companies and 46 institutions, among them educational institutions, public institutions and those set up to offer support and assistance to firms. The attributes included in the analysis of firms relate to the general characteristics of the organization, the top manager's characteristics, sources of innovation, networking, financial support, obstacles to innovation, future attitudes towards innovation and the dynamics of collective learning. Three different types of behaviour were distinguished among the firms through cluster analysis and the institutions and associations were also classified into three different behaviours. The characteristics of each cluster were then examined statistically. The profiles drawn up in this way allowed some inferences to be drawn about the conditions encouraging the best performance.

References

Brüderl, J. and Preisendörfer, P. (1998), 'Network Supports and the Success of Newly Found Business', *Small Business Economics*, Vol. 10, pp. 213-225.

Davidsson, P. (2002), 'What Entrepreneurship Research Can Do for Business and Policy Practice', *International Journal of Entrepreneurship Education*, Vol. 1(1), pp. 1-20.

European Commission (2003), *Entrepreneurship in Europe*, Green Paper, Enterprise Publication, Brussels.

Kent, C., Sexton, D. and Vesper, K. (eds) (1982), *The Encyclopaedia of Entrepreneurship*, Prentice-Hall, Englewood Cliffs.

Kirzner, I. (1997), 'Entrepreneurial Discovery and the Competitive Market Process', *Journal of Economic Literature*, Vol. 35, pp. 60-85.

Shane, S. (2003), *A General Theory of Entrepreneurship*, Edward Elgar, Cheltenham.

Sullivan, R. (2000), 'Entrepreneurial Learning and Mentoring', *International Journal of Entrepreneurial Behaviour and Research*, Vol. 6, pp. 160-175.

Chapter 2

Entrepreneurship in Small Enterprises and Local Development

Teresa de Noronha Vaz

Introduction

This chapter discusses the osmotic links between entrepreneurs in small firms and their territorial environments. If small enterprises are able to perform well during periods of structural change, they may create jobs and enhance knowledge, so encouraging market dynamism. The ability of small firms to perform well at such times may be partly explained by their past learning, accumulated through specialisation in traditional activities, and by complex interactions within production and innovation networks.

The different roles of small firms are characterised in this chapter in the light of their specific goals and their capacity to promote differentiated innovative activities. Later in the chapter, the role of institutions which may act as regulators and be supportive or obstructive, is discussed. It demonstrates why the organisational capacities and efficiency of small firms may be a consequence of their local conditions while, at the same time, their own capacity to learn and innovate has a crucial influence on environmental change. The remainder of this first section considers the recent increase in the attention given to small and medium sized enterprises (SMEs), noting both changes in theoretical approaches by economists and in political attitudes.

The dominant neoclassical theory in economics shows how decisions concerning supply originate at a firm level taking technology as given and perfectly known. The characteristic static approach to modelling these decisions meant that the adaptation processes, and their continuity, were ignored. Yet, the importance of processes like innovation (in its radical or incremental form) requires recognition of the discrepancy between the approach of strict neoclassical theory and the real world. Orthodox thought also tended to ignore the fact that production takes place in organisations (Lydall, 1998). This has hindered the development of research agendas in such areas for a long time and, in particular, created a gap regarding the role and functioning of SMEs in the economy. Phenomena related to the characteristics of knowledge, such as lack of appropriability, uncertainty, indivisibility, which result in the market failures highlighted by Arrow (1996) are still also far from being perfectly understood.

During the last fifteen years, economic theory has been paying much more attention to the actual behaviour of the firm. In this context, the concept of entrepreneurship within SMEs has aroused more interest even though it has not been clearly defined. Schumpeter, in his early work, stressed the role of the entrepreneur in the development of new industries, but later commented on the development of giant corporations and accompanying bureaucratisation of economic organisations which he saw as killing the entrepreneurial spirit (Schumpeter, 1934).

As mentioned previously, firm creation depends on the cultural context and on the ways in which the social order influences and changes the atmosphere surrounding business and the people contributing to their development. Therefore the emergence of entrepreneurs is encouraged by favourable economic and social conditions and political efforts may lead to increased opportunities for entrepreneurial activity (Lydall, 1988) even if this has not been specifically addressed as part of the objectives of industrial policies.

The concept of SME entrepreneurship has recently received more attention in the political sphere, when having observed that small firms play an important role in employment and in the diffusion of new technologies, new political attitudes took root in the 1990s. Policy makers recognised the potential power and influence that SMEs could exert in the European economy (Gabolde, 1998). Although the institutional framework acts to promote local relationships, and frequently the local level is the only context in which small firms have connections, small firms entrepreneurs have political and social concerns acting in an osmotic way with their territorial environment. However, the differentiated role of such firms in the various industries and their organisational links with local environments, on which they seem to be very dependent, have not been systematically studied and therefore have not been clearly identified. In order to address this question, it is necessary to use a theoretical framework in which institutions, rather than markets, act as the constraining and ruling forces.

Entrepreneurship and the Specific Goals of SMEs

Enterprise creation is mainly due to an individual decision to set up a small unit of production. This fact helps to explain why SMEs' goals may differ from those of large firms. Even if profits are required, there is a high probability that the small firm owner does not have the necessary know how to maximise them. Many reasons explain this weakness but a lack of managerial training and a lack of distinction between individual interests and firm objectives seem to be the most relevant factors.

The objectives pursued by SMEs are always constrained by the following four major characteristics of entrepreneurship, namely: personalisation, the drive to secure the survival of the enterprise, the need to create new market or technological opportunities (Julien, 1995) and the role of strategic thought related to the organisational configuration of the firm (Conti, 1991). Some comments on these aspects follow.

Taking the first characteristic, personalisation, the set of organisational and productive choices made by managers of the SMEs have been identified as 'itineraries' with a personal character in which the firm's objectives become inseparable from the economic, political, social and psychological objectives of their owners. Such identification is, however, based on an oversimplified definition of the firm. The usual links assumed between the SME's manager and the owner of the capital can be misleading in view of the complex nature of even smaller productive organisations. As is the case for large firms, SMEs have to build a collection of resources whose organisation brings together the necessary knowledge required to operate in the modern economy.

Another characteristic of the small firm results from its greater flexibility in organising new resources and adapting to constantly changing market conditions. The increasing instability and uncertainty in the market are dealt better thanks to the quick responses to the opportunities and challenges generated by market instability on the part of smaller firms. A high birth rate and high level of mortality are observed in the small firms' population, especially in times of structural turbulence.

A further point worth clarifying is the difference between the strategy and ultimate goals of the firm. Enterprise behaviour is oriented toward action but, instead of being determined by the opportunities resulting from pure market mechanisms, is based on subjective thought (Conti, 1995). This elaboration of strategic choices is related to the organisational configuration of the firm. Ultimate goals are deeply rooted in what can be called a unique moral personality. Because of bounded rationality, as described by Simon (1986), decision making is imperfect and behaviour is satisficing rather than maximising. Developing this behavioural approach, Nelson and Winter define firms as using routines in their operations but changing their techniques, procedures, policies or business strategies over time (Nelson and Winter, 1982). These capabilities are built through *searches* that are routine-guided and routine-changing processes. The firm is thus defined as an organisation with the capabilities needed to search for new markets, new resources, new technologies and new organisational configurations.

The stability of such a firm may be maximised when facing uncertainty (Hodgson, 1988). To respond effectively to changed market situations, capabilities are needed not only to find improved technical solutions but also to control the conduct of the organisation's members. These necessary capabilities are different in SMEs from those in large firms. Take, for example, innovative SMEs known as 'Schumpeterian pioneers' (Clarysse, 1997). These are young organisations inspired by a visionary leader, they have a real innovation culture, they retain control over all their value chain, but all their activities are informal. Such SMEs do not have the capacity to use all resources available in their environments and, in particular, are not skilled at searching for finance like large firms. This organisational deficiency of small firms hinders them, for example, in applying to the European Framework Programs for funding.

Institutional Support and Foundations

The external environment of a firm is primarily made up of political, social and economic institutions. They vary from country to country and represent a complex system within which economic activities may evolve quite differently. The nature of the environment can be quite crucial for the activities of SMEs. It can provide them with resources, particularly human capital and information and generate valuable contributions to reducing uncertainty. The external links established are not simply market relations but can be a vital network of contracting bonds. The management of such links at the firm's boundaries requires a sustained degree of trust between members. The functioning of the firm depends on the capacity to find common and cohesive interests and behaviours (Hodgson, 1988).

Institutions are devised by societies to create order and reduce uncertainty in exchange, define the choice set, and the profitability and feasibility of engaging in economic activity (North, 1991). They contribute to reducing the cost of producing and transacting, facilitate increasing specialisation by helping towards co-operative solutions and make defection more costly so that the potential gains from production and trade are possible. The main consequence of strong and effective institutions is that, based on intensive information management, the capability to predict and project within such extended complexity and uncertainty becomes possible (Hodgson, 1988). Important issues arise, however, from the political and social dimensions of institutions. If they are characterised by various levels of effectiveness, how are individuals or firms affected by weak or unequal effectiveness levels? In particular, if large firms obtain information about the application of policies more easily than others, the institutional environment will have uneven impacts on the transaction costs of firms. For example, there have been huge improvements in the provision and functioning of stock markets in many contemporary societies to the benefit of large firms' financing. There have, however, been no similar institutional changes favouring the activities of SMEs.

The Essence of the Firm

The external environment of the SMEs usually has a regional dimension in which each region represents a social context and provides a specific incentive structure for economic activities and entrepreneurship. This structure may be more precisely defined with the concept of a 'territorial complex' (Conti, 1995). In this view of the region, the formal aspects of relations between enterprises are represented by contractual and institutional networks that exist alongside informal relations consisting of inter-subjective information flows. The co-ordination devices are of two different types: those constituted by institutions regulating the firm, on one hand, and those institutions regulating the environment, on the other.

Alchian and Woodwood (1988) have discussed Williamson's analysis of transaction costs and questioned the institutional essence of the firm in this context. In this approach, the members of the firm's organisation are 'teamwork members' and their coalition represents the nexus of long-term contracts. They have a comparative advantage in working together because of the knowledge of one another's personal talents. It is a coalition among owners of separately owned resources, whose value depends on continued association (whereas ownership integration is the common ownership of the specific resources as a bundle). The value of specific resources depends on the performance of the team. Problems arise in the governance of the firm with incomplete integration, when some shareholders, creditors, employees, subcontractors or customers own specific resources not shared in common with other stakeholders. Conflicts are avoided by protecting against opportunism through credible commitments. Therefore a great number of different forms of commitments are utilised in corporate governance.

SMEs correspond to the U form, which has a unitary chief and no divisionalised functions. This form is more viable when the firm is relatively specialised horizontally and vertically. Does this mean that such a firm cannot get the specialised resources needed to deal with the organisational problems of a complex production system? There is a limitation that corresponds to the lack of searching capability previously discussed. This limitation is correctly identified by Williamson as an inability to collect and use all pertinent information necessary to create safeguards against opportunism (Williamson, 1985). The suggestion regarding the incapacity of SMEs to create solutions by forming contractual arrangements increasing trust, especially because their assets are mainly human capital and are not owned in common, requires more detailed discussion.

Trust and Commitment in SMEs

The previous section pointed out a major fragility of the small firm, namely its lack of self-defence mechanisms against opportunism. This leads to a consideration of whether the required trust is safeguarded by those parts of the external environment with which SMEs constantly deal.

How far SMEs can negotiate credible commitments and enforce them depends on the complex set of institutions created by capitalist economies, not only those based on law. In the firm, dependence generally occurs in complex ways enhanced through a large variety of arrangements. The institutional environment typically does not provide the strong support needed by SMEs to build suitable arrangements. Several cases can be cited to show the difficulties that small firms have to face in trying to negotiate credible commitments; this section focuses on technological change as the co-ordination of activities, functions and roles helps to determine performance in innovation.

In the area of technological change, where large firms often lead radical innovations, sometimes in co-operation with public organisations, there is the question of which types of arrangements will allow SMEs to be involved in the diffusion of the new technologies, in terms of appropriability, and the spread of information and learning. As Edquist and Johnson (1997) explained, innovative activities are typically related to behaviour patterns influenced by institutional phenomena like common habits, established practices or laws. Institutions shape the process of technological evolution globally and, as part of the external environment of the firm, determine its references in terms of understandings, visions and actions.

Both non-market and market relationships are important in explaining the processes of technology creation and commercialisation (Lynn, Reddy and Aram, 1996). Non-market organisations such as trade unions and regional tribunals have important impacts on the rules of markets and vertical channel relationships.

Lynn, Reddy and Aram (1996) suggest a distinction between two levels of institutional environments in structuring innovative activities: innovative communities and superstructures. In their view, the term 'innovative community' refers to the organisations directly and indirectly involved in the commercialisation of a new technology. It is a set of interacting populations embedded in a dense web of social and economic relationships including producers and distributors, trade associations, professions and state agencies. Variables of interest regarding the community are its size, diversity, stability and the boundary permeability of the community. In contrast, 'superstructure' organisations provide their members with collective goods and often specialise in co-ordinating flows of information or co-ordinating the activities of organisational substructures. This raises the question of the extent to which SMEs participate in innovative communities. If they do, the relevant question is related to their capacity to negotiate credible commitments within the permeable boundaries of the community. It is easy to imagine the problems that need to be solved when the innovative communities are affected by a systemic innovation (Langlois and Robertson, 1995).

Organisational Capacities Linked to Local Development

In face of the difficulties pointed out above, it seems that the greatest challenge that SMEs have to meet is how to gain organisational capabilities permitting their entrepreneurial role in the economy to flourish.

Environmental Handicaps for the Organisational Efficiency of the SME

Studies on organisations point out the dialectic interaction between organisation and environment (Guilhon, 1998). SMEs have some capacity for adaptation and growth in an evolving environment. How much the personality of the manager/owner matters in the process depends on the characteristics of the organisation. Organisational capacities result mainly from the firm's ownership, objectives and innovative activities. The management may have to change the organisational structure of the firm in order to keep its objectives and performance under control.

This general view of SMEs does not give any decisive picture of the links between organisational capacities and entrepreneurship. Can entrepreneurial SMEs exist in any type of environment?

In the less favoured regions (LFRs) of EU, there are few innovative SMEs. This observation highlights the constraints limiting organisational capacities and shows that there are problems which small firms cannot deal with by themselves. These relate to innovative activities, for example, where knowledge absorption depends on adequate human resources. The inter-regional technological gap is more than twice the cohesion gap between the developed and the less developed regions within the EU (Landabaso, 1997). This gap has several origins. For example, there are six times as many research staff as a proportion of workers in the more advanced compared with LFRs. Public assistance for innovation – mainly directed at small firms – is ten times higher per person in most advanced regions than in the less developed ones. There is also a relative lack of well developed systems to finance innovation. These problems compound the shortcomings of small firms, with their difficulties in identifying and addressing technological needs. As LFRs have a greater predominance of family firms and these tend to have weak links to both the international market and to science-technology systems they may be less well integrated into the needs and resources of the regional productive system.

Such handicaps have, in practice, resulted in various contradictions in the operational programmes conducted by regional authorities in LFRs. By ignoring the limitations of linear models of innovation, they have neglected the importance of the identification and structured expression of demand by small firms, the existence of bottlenecks in the innovation process and the need for interfaces between the scientific subsystem and the productive sector. As a result, the experience of European funds supporting innovation in Objective 1 regions shows that without a regional strategy for innovation able to provide an adequate environment for co-operation within the region, increasing public financial support will not generate significant contributions to regional development (Landabaso, 1997).

Positive Contribution of the Environment Towards the Organisational Efficiency of the SME

The qualities of the economic environment are a crucial factor in entrepreneurship among SMEs; an appropriate environment can allow them to learn by the combination of internal and external capacities (Lebas and Zuscovitch, 1993). They can intertwine themselves structurally with their environment in order to absorb all kinds of knowledge, information and capacities with which it is possible to identify problems and solutions through innovation. Technological learning is increasingly viewed as endogenously linked to industrial activities, giving organisational learning a more important place, both at individual and collective levels.

Organisational change may be orientated either along the lines of intra-firm co-operation or inter-firm co-operation. SMEs are more affected by solutions arising in the latter way, where complementary resources amongst different firms can be co-ordinated. In their case, 'organisational balance depends on the formation of quasi-rent, that is to say, the creation of specific resources at the scale of the collective, global organisation' (Foray, 1991, p. 401). This condition is satisfied with the creation of an inter-firm organisational architecture appropriate to the effective interaction of resources.

Several kinds of organisational changes are needed to promote inter-firm co-operation at the environmental level. These include innovative networks, where interactive learning creates various links between enterprises. This represents the results of organisational change that is frequently observed in the rich European regions but is quite rare in LFRs, partly due to a lack of appropriate economic and technology policies. They include the development of organisational learning that creates new competencies within small firms. In addition, public intervention can help through the better use of European regulations and national controls and through the creation of other indirect incentives for co-operative behaviour to help transform the local environment.

Organisational Learning and Networking in Peripheral Areas

The extreme heterogeneity of strategies, managerial behaviour and ways of competition among firms is increased by differences between their local environments. In the lagging regions, SMEs have to cope with poor external resources. The primary question about possible changes in their learning capabilities is to know how they can be improved at the level of the local environment, both through collective learning and by interfacing their resources through new industrial organisations.

An approach to the learning process in SMEs cannot be limited to a managerial definition of the firm, in which the manager/owner secures changes in its intra-organisational structure without corresponding changes in the environment.

Organisational learning takes place at both the environmental level and firm level, requiring a need for coherency among the internal accumulation of knowledge and changes in the environmental context. Results of this accumulation, in terms of routines, norms and rules, contribute to the strategic connection of decisions if firms keep closely intertwined with their environment.

SMEs can be divided into different groups according to their different strategies in terms of their intentions to innovate linked to their environmental system. In the classification offered by Clarysse et al. (1997), each of the three behavioural types corresponds to a different organisation/environment interaction:

1) 'Schumpeterian pioneers' are young organisations pursuing a clear growth strategy to become dominant, offering a totally new concept of product and service, and generally seem to interact well with their local environment.
2) 'Porterian innovators' intend to be world-wide technological leaders in their specific market segments. It is important to observe that not all innovative SMEs are dependent on a locally limited environment.
3) The most dynamic SMEs set up their organisation in a strong interactive evolution with the local development of a wealthy region offering a lot of complementarities with other small or large companies.

Learning and Networking among SMEs

Some empirical studies have provided evidence of the role played by the environment in the decisions of small firms. However, how these firms address the problem of learning given the changing characteristics of their environments is a different issue. Small firms do not have the capacities needed to modify their whole industrial context. Their adaptation to a changing environment requires them to face competition with a dynamic vision of their industry and markets. These firms are unfamiliar with co-operative routines, however, and many observations show their reluctance to co-operate locally (Wig and Wood, 1997).

The challenge is to build up new routines outside their normal opportunistic behaviour allowing the productive association of internal and external resources. Freel (1998) defines these routines as the essence of the firm's accumulated knowledge. Once it is accepted that the routines resulting from searching are different in small firms from those existing within big ones, it is necessary to find suitable ways of sharing knowledge in small firms, mainly using previous experiences, in order to start the learning process (Freel, 1998).

It is now largely agreed that once SMEs manage to incorporate learning processes, they increase their probability of success in innovative activities. Evidence based on the European Community Survey (CIS) established that knowledge creation is increasingly the result of a process taking place through networking rather than through hierarchies and markets (Gabolde, 1998). Lundvall and Borrás (1997) suggest that networks of SMEs improve their innovative performance if supported by the different areas of knowledge which relate to regional and local interests. This is quite important in helping to understand why SMEs meet special problems in LFRs. If the environmental context has no positive inputs of knowledge to supply, networking can hardly fertilise innovative ideas.

Evidence about this organisational gap is given by the Keeble report into the long term competitiveness of small firms, innovation and regional development in UK during the 1990s (Keeble, 1997). The statistical evidence from a survey of SMEs emphasises differences between innovative activities in core and peripheral regions. It appears that in the core regions, SMEs operate in a more competitive and open environment, have competitive advantages associated with specialised expertise and product design through collaborative partnerships and networks with other firms and organisations. In contrast, firms in peripheral regions have few opportunities to co-operate and are closed to external influences whether competing or not. These statistical differences establish the consequences of the organisational gap existing in the peripheries. The weakness of networking and co-operative systems leads to a technological gap. The organisational gap also affects the differences observed earlier between the LFRs and advanced regions in terms of human capital and public assistance for innovation.

Co-ordinated Strategies and Interfaces among Different Learning Organisations

Technological change needs to be discussed in a context of the interface between institutional interaction, including the knowledge base and improvement in organisational methods, and historical local development (the learning process). The advantages resulting from eventual interchanges lead to innovative processes. In other words, besides the intrinsic capacity of the enterprise to innovate, the appropriate environmental conditions need to exist to allow this to happen. Small enterprises are particularly sensitive to uncertainty and are therefore very dependent on their external conditions. An information-rich and synergistic local environment is among the set of factors that can help to reduce their uncertainty.

SMEs are Learning Organisations

The most difficult environments in which SMEs manage to survive could be viewed as providing experimental conditions to analyse a small learning organisation. Such a study could be biased since survival may be simply due to the lack of an elimination process in the absence of suitable competition. This appears to be one reason for many lagging tendencies of certain less favoured European regions. SMEs are organisations whose members work together with knowledge of one another's personal talents but without good searching capabilities, partly because they do not successfully co-ordinate the learning activities of their members. They may be characterised by an inability to collect and utilise all pertinent information to make good decisions related to external conditions and they are highly dependent on the political and economic institutions created by capitalist economies.

It should be emphasised that institutional environments are relatively stable in peripheral areas. Therefore innovative communities or 'innovative milieux' cannot simply be created through political decisions. They need some public assistance to support innovative activities, but these activities are essentially private and result from learning within firms. SMEs do not start learning activities just because universities exist nearby. Indeed situations have been observed where an agglomeration of manufacturing SMEs failed to transform geographical proximity into an innovative milieu, in spite of apparently favourable environmental conditions such as the presence of R&D facilities (Kalantaridis et al., 1999). Potentially important impediments that could explain this failure relate both to internal and external learning.

Organisational Learning and the Phenomena of Rural Development

The learning capability of SMEs must be perceived as part of co-ordination strategies and in a context of structural change in which firms and non-market organisations need to learn through interfaces. SMEs' activities to be favoured may only occur through an important shift in the outlook of society. The interfaces needed require social legitimacy at various levels: economic, social, legal and political.

To take an example, the agro-food sector has continuously had to face new uncertainties (such as the health consequences of new technologies and the legal identification of ingredients incorporated in food) during the last thirty years. In this sector of 'closely linked formal environments', small enterprises employ more external sources than internal ones in their innovative activities (Nicolas and Hy, 2000). Various interfaces have been created, helping them to combine sources of technical know-how and information. Sometimes, local institutional networks help by creating cohesion or a favourable context for innovation that may be represented as depending on a proximity which is more cultural and social than geographical. This is not far from the concept of innovative milieu.

As (rural) areas of peripheral regions are characterised by quite low industrial growth. High tech industries are not present to any extent, and an interactive environment fails. The requirements of economic growth in these areas mean that their traditional industries first need to close their technological gap. These industries must continue in their use of existing competencies in order to maintain the cohesion of the social establishment while, at the same time, renewing their technologies continuously, as in the case of agricultural production.

The final conclusion relates to the discussion of local economic environments in LFRs. In this context, an important aim of this book is to examine the possible achievement of local development through technological learning in traditional industrial sectors of the LFRs, such as the agro-food sector. Rural areas of the EU depend upon agriculture as the basis of their production structure. In addition, considering the huge technological and economic transformations occurring globally in the primary sector, the book draws attention to the need for new policies and the development of new competencies in these areas. Organisational learning becomes more urgent then ever in such contexts and new concepts of exchanges are called for at both firm level and in the local society.

In brief, the accumulation of technological expertise in SMEs located in LFRs depends on institutional change. To go from their present environments towards interactive environments, rural areas of peripheral regions need to overcome their organisational learning gap. Camagni, (1991) introduced the idea of an innovative milieu as a complex network of informal social relationships situated in a geographical area. He argued that such contexts were able to define attributes necessary to promote innovative capability at local level as well as incentives for collective learning processes.

It is clear in viewing the developments from this starting position to the recent efforts to understand the learning process at local level that much has been achieved. As Dosi and Marengo (2000) argue, the complexity of learning is enormous, and it is not possible to reduce it to simple information arrangements. Agents participate in the choice of the exchanges which they wish to engage in as means of defining their path and of discovering important regularities that can be used to improve their processes and decisions.

References

Alchian, A. and Woodwood, S. (1988), 'The Firm is Dead. Long Life to the Firm', *Journal of Economic Literature*, Vol. XXVI, pp. 65-79.

Arrow, K.J. (1996), 'Technical Information and Industrial Structure', *Industrial and Corporate Change*, 5 (2), pp. 645-652.

Camagni R. (1991), *Innovation Networks: Spatial Perspectives*, Belhaven Press, London, pp. 121-144.

Clarysse, B., Muldur, U. and Dirdonck, R. (1997), 'Strategic Differences of Innovative SMEs', *Working Paper*, University of Gent.

Conti, S. (1991), 'Les Conditions Territoriales du Developement de la PME: La Leçon Theorique du Modèle Italien', in C. Fourcade (ed.), *Petite Entreprise et Development Local*, Editions ESKA, pp. 155-177.

Conti, S. (1995), 'Four Paradigms of the Enterprise System', in S. Conti, E. Malecki and P. Oinas (eds), *The Industrial Enterprise and its Environment: Spatial Perspectives*, Avebury Press, Aldershot, pp. 59-97.

Dosi, G. and Marengo, L. (2000), 'Some Elements of an Evolutionary Theory of Organizational Competences', in G. Dosi (ed.), *Innovation, Organization and Economic Dynamics*, Edward Elgar, Cheltenham.

Edquist C. and Johnson, B. (1997), 'Institutions and Organisations in Systems of Innovation', in C. Edquist (ed.), *Systems of Innovation*, Pinter, London, pp. 41-63.

Foray D. (1991), 'The Secrets of Industry are in the Air: Industrial Cooperation and the Organizational Dynamics of the Innovative Firm', *Research Policy*, Vol. 20(5), pp. 393-405.

Freel, M. (1998), 'Evolution, Innovation and Learning: Evidence from Case Studies', *Entrepreneurship & Regional Development*, Vol. 10 (2), pp. 137-149.

Gabolde, J. (1998), *Second European Report on S&T Indicators*, European Commission, Brussels, Annex.

Guilhon, A. (1998), 'Vers une Nouvelle Définition de la PME à Partir du Concept de Controlabilité', in O. Torrês (ed.), *PME, de Nouvelles Approches*, Economica, Paris, pp. 55-67.

Hodgson, G. (1988), *Economics and Institutions*, Polity Press, Cambridge (UK).

Julien, P-A. (1995), 'Economic Theory, Entrepreneurship and New Economic Dynamics', in S. Conti et al. (eds), *The Industrial Enterprise and its Environment: Spatial Perspectives*, Avebury, Aldershot.

Kalantaridis, C. and Pheby, J. (1999), 'Processes of Innovation among Manufacturing SMEs: the Experience of Bedfordshire', *Entrepreneurship and Regional Development*, Vol. 11(1), pp. 57–78.

Keeble, D. (1997), 'Small Firms, Innovation and Regional Development in Britain in the 1990s', *Regional Studies*, Vol. 31(3), pp. 281-293.

Landabaso, M. (1997), 'The Promotion of Innovation in Regional Policy: Proposals for a Regional Innovation Strategy', *Entrepreneurship & Regional Development*, Vol. 9(1), pp. 1-24.

Langlois, R.N. and Robertson, P.L. (1995), *Firms, Markets and Economic Change*, Routledge, London and New York.

Lebas, C. and Zuscovitch, E. (1993), 'Apprentissage Technologique et Organisation', *Economie et Société, série W (5)*, pp. 153-195.

Lundvall, B-A. and Borrás, S. (1997), *The Globalising Learning Economy: Implications for Innovation Policy*, European Commission TSER Program, Brussels.

Lydall, H. (1998), *A Critique of Orthodox Economics, an Alternative Model*, Saint Martin's Press, New York.

Lynn, L.H., Reddy, N.M. and Aram, I.D. (1996), 'Linking Technology and Institutions: the Innovation Community Network', *Research Policy*, Vol. 25, pp. 91-106.

Nelson, R.R. and Winter, S.G. (1982), *An Evolutionary Theory of Economic Change*, Harvard University Press, Cambridge MA.

Nicolas, F. and Hy, M. (2000), 'Apprentissage Technologique et Innovation en Agro-alimentaire', *Économie Rurale*, No. 257, pp. 1-16.

North, D.C. (1991), 'Institutions', *Journal of Economic Perspectives*, Vol. 5(1), pp. 97-112.

Schumpeter, J.A. (1934), *The Theory of Economic Development*, Harvard University Press, Cambridge.

Simon, H. (1986), 'On the Behavioural and Rational Foundations of Economic Dynamics', in R. Day and G. Eliasson (eds), *The Dynamics of Market Economics*, North-Holland, Amsterdam.

Wig, H. and Wood, M. (1997), 'What Comprises a Regional System of Innovation?', *Regional Policy and Development*, Vol. 18, pp. 66-98.

Williamson, O.E. (1985), *The Economic Institutions of Capitalism: Firms, Markets, Relational Contracting*, The Free Press, New York.

PART II

DETERMINANTS OF STRUCTURAL CHANGE IN PERIPHERAL REGIONS

Chapter 3

Accessibility, Innovative Milieu and the Innovative Activity of Businesses in EU Peripheral and Lagging Areas

Andrew Copus and Dimitris Skuras

Introduction

This chapter is based on results derived from fieldwork in twelve lagging areas located in six EU member states (Finland, Germany, Greece, Ireland, Spain and the UK). It was carried out as part of an EU funded research project entitled 'Aspatial Peripherality, Innovation and the Rural Economy' (AsPIRE – QLK5-2000-00783). AsPIRE, which was funded under the EU's Fifth Framework Programme, is concerned with the changing nature of peripheral disadvantage. 'Aspatial peripherality' is the term used to describe a range of processes that are increasingly emerging to compound or distort the handicaps conventionally associated with remote locations.

The aim of the present chapter is twofold. First, an attempt is made to place the twelve lagging areas into categories of innovative milieu using alternative classification criteria for innovative activity and the level of local synergies. This innovative milieu categorization is then related to the areas' accessibility, as measured by baseline peripherality indicators estimated for the twelve regions.

Secondly, the factors influencing the innovative activity of individual firms are examined taking into account accessibility specific characteristics. This is based on a business survey carried out among 600 businesses in the twelve case study areas which gathered data, among other things, on business specific characteristics, various types of innovative activity and business networking. Accessibility as a major spatial factor is shown to affect the innovative activity of businesses considerably while aspatial factors related to business networking and entrepreneurial specific factors ameliorate locational disadvantages.

Background

The resurgence of regional economies has challenged conventional economic wisdom which suggests that highly accessible locations will enjoy higher rates of growth and prosperity. Certain peripheral and less accessible regions exhibit high levels of economic growth despite their disadvantaged locations. The relatively low correlation of peripherality indicators with economic indicators has shown the limitations of conventional peripherality indicators based on transport costs (Copus et al., 2003). It has also been demonstrated that accessibility is only one of several transport and non-transport factors determining regional economic performance. Various regional economies under perform or over perform the level of economic development that might be expected given the location of the region. Factors other than location may be (and have been) employed to explain regional growth or, conversely, poor performance. Figure 3.1 depicts the main idea behind aspatial peripherality.

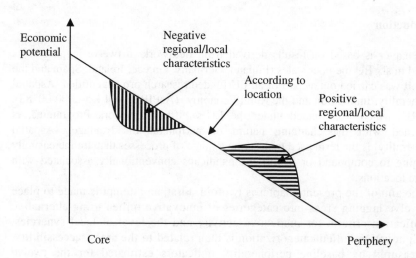

Figure 3.1   The basic aspatial peripherality concept

A review of formalized, conventional models of peripherality shows that these models have generally focused on two causal elements from the broader set of elements comprising the concept of peripherality, namely distance costs and lack of agglomerative economies (Copus, 2001). This simplification means that such models are probably of limited value as a basis for regional policy design. For instance, whilst proof that agglomeration can take place on the basis of physical linkages alone may be of considerable theoretical significance, the process is far more complex in reality, and is probably not amenable to mathematical modelling. Furthermore, inertia or 'path dependency' plays an important role, potentially 'locking out' areas from the benefits of agglomeration or accessibility, even after transport networks have been improved. Peripheral areas need policies that 'unwind' this complex process. The ability to develop an effective response will almost certainly be enhanced by taking account of the full range of observed effects, including many that cannot at present be modelled in a rigorous quantitative manner.

In this chapter, we look for evidence to explain this phenomenon of development which is currently not explained by spatial factors (Spiekermann et al., 2002). The concept of 'innovative milieu' offers a useful analytical tool. Innovative milieu may emerge independently of location and accessibility and be supported by non-spatial factors. However, the concept of innovative milieu is difficult to operationalize and quantify. We attempt to measure the emergence of innovative milieu in regional economies by quantifying the two major concepts that characterize an innovative milieu, namely innovative and synergistic activity. Evidence shows that, despite conventional expectations, less accessible areas tend to have features indicating the existence of innovative milieu, while more accessible areas may not. We then proceed with our analysis exploring the factors influencing innovative activity at firm level and find that innovative activity is negatively affected by location, but local synergies (and the consequent action of cooperative networks) ameliorate this negative effect.

Case Study Areas and Data

Twelve areas in six European Union countries were selected for study under the AsPIRE project of which this research forms part. In each country, the two areas consist of one area that is characterized by proximity to major urban centres and markets and one that is considered to be less accessible. The less accessible regions show higher levels of economic development and are generally more dynamic economically. Details of the sampling frame and sampling methods, as well as more general discussion of the AsPIRE project, are available on the project's website given in the references.

The two case study areas in Scotland are the Northern Isles and East Ayrshire. The Northern Isles comprise the island group known as Shetland, approximately 1,000 kilometres from London. Economically, the Northern Isles outperform both similar peripheral regions in Scotland and other more central locations. The East Ayrshire area is located 40 kilometres from Glasgow, 80 kilometres from Edinburgh and about 500 kilometres from London and has access to very good transportation networks. The area has experienced decades of decline especially in the coal mining, iron and steel and textiles industries. All that is left in the area now are a few niche market, specialist companies associated with engineering, and some tourism related, craft companies.

In Finland, the two areas are Keski-Suomi and Satakunta. Keski-Suomi is located in the middle of Finland, approximately 300 kilometres from Helsinki. Keski-Suomi has poor access to transportation networks and the journey to

Helsinki is relatively slow and expensive. Jyväskylä, the central town of Keski-Suomi, has successfully attracted telecommunications, electronics and graphics industries and has a highly educated workforce. Satakunta is located on the west coast of Finland approximately 240 kilometres from Helsinki. Satakunta's economic performance is not as good as might be expected in view of its relative accessibility and significant industrial production in the energy, metal and machinery sectors.

The Spanish regions chosen are L'Alcoia and El Camp de Morvedre. L'Alcoia is one of the less accessible locations of Comunidad Valenciana and is characterized by poor communication infrastructures and a lack of energy and raw materials. It is, nevertheless, one of the most dynamic areas with its economic activity being focused on traditional home-textiles, toys, metal industries and transportation equipment. El Camp de Morvedre is a flat coastal area located 26 kilometres north of Valencia. Despite being fairly accessible to the main economic centres in Spain, the level of economic development is relatively low.

The German regions are Rottal-Inn and Bitburg-Prüm. Rottal-Inn is located on the Austrian border of South-East Germany and is part of the state of Bavaria. Despite its peripheral location, Rottal-Inn has evolved to one of the economically most successful rural counties in Germany. The growth of Rottal-Inn is attributed to the rapid expansion of the service sector, especially tourism. Bitburg-Prüm directly borders Luxembourg and Belgium and is located close to large urban agglomerations. The economy of the area is weak, however, and its GDP per capita is only 72 per cent of the national average.

The two study areas in Greece are Evrytania and Kalavryta. Evrytania is one of the most disadvantaged and peripheral areas of the whole of EU according to official Eurostat indicators. The main town, Karpenisi, is located almost 250 kilometres from Athens, but travel time is relatively long due to the rather poor condition of the road system and the lack of rail or air connections. The prefecture of Evrytania, nevertheless, exhibits a dynamic local economy centred around a dispersed tourism sector and a high quality local food industry. The area of Kalavryta is situated close to the town of Patras (the third major urban agglomeration in Greece). The road network is relatively good bringing the travel time from Athens down to two hours, a fact that makes Kalavryta attractive for day or weekend travellers from Patras and Athens. The tourism sector of the area is concentrated around the town of Kalavryta and owes much to the development of a ski resort in the area.

In Ireland, the two study areas are the counties of Wexford and Clare. County Clare is within the Mid-West region, and situated on the west coast. It is probably unique in being relatively remote from the national capital, Dublin, but having strong international links for historical reasons. Shannon airport and the surrounding development zone are associated with a dynamic service sector, focused particularly on internationally traded services and international tourism. Wexford is in the South-East of Ireland. Although much closer to Dublin, the quality of the road network means that the drive time from Wexford is still about three hours. It lacks an international airport and its economy is generally more dispersed, indigenous and slower growing.

A survey of 50 businesses was carried out in each case study area. A two-stage, (quota, then representative stratified) sampling procedure was devised. The sample of 50 businesses in each area was first divided into two sub-samples (25 each) to be drawn from the manufacturing and service sectors (as defined by the NACE Divisions). Each sub-sample was proportionately stratified to reflect the distribution of micro, small, medium and large firms in each case study area. The business questionnaire was designed to be administered face to face with the manager of the firm. The majority of the questions were closed, simply requiring the interviewee to give a choice from a series of options or a response within an attitudinal scale which could be ticked or, in other cases, a figure.

Innovative Milieu and Cooperation Networks

An innovative milieu may be defined as the set, or the complex network of mainly informal relationships in a limited geographical area, often determining a specific external 'image', internal 'representation' and sense of belonging, which enhance the local innovative capability through synergetic and collective learning processes (Camagni, 1991). This term has been widely used in subsequent work to describe a particular type of environment as an innovative milieu (Neely and Hii, 1998; Mole and Worrall, 2001; Maillat and Lecoq, 1992; Maillat, 1998).

The elements of an innovative network or milieu are individuals and institutions (actors) participating in an innovation process and the formal and informal relations that they develop for this purpose. The informal relations are mainly between customers, suppliers, and public and private actors, and result in the transfer of tacit knowledge through mobility and inter-firm imitation. The formal relations are usually trans-territorial and concern vocational training, technological development or infrastructure (Camagni and Capello, 1999; Perrin, 1991; Bramanti and Senn, 1991).

Camagni (1995) describes four regional types according to how far they present the characteristics of an innovative milieu. In the first, there is no innovation and no milieu. The second regional type has no milieu, but there is innovation. The third shows some evidence of a milieu through synergies and some innovation, but only to a limited extent. Finally, in the fourth type, the innovative milieu is observed. Knowledge and learning in an innovative milieu are transmitted with the help of mechanisms such as relationships and links between firms, suppliers, customers, collaboration with universities and laboratories, and the mobility of highly skilled workers (Keeble and Wilkinson, 1999). Figure 3.2, which was adapted from Shefer and Frenkel (1998), shows these four regional types.

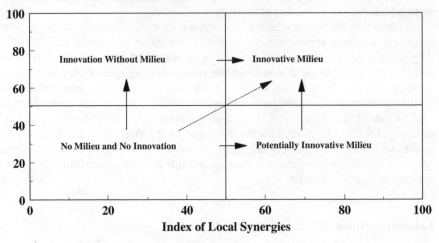

Index of local Innovativeness

Source: Adapted from Schefer and Frenkel (1998)

Figure 3.2   The four regional types of innovative milieu

The extent of local innovativeness may be proxied by the percentage of firms presenting some signs of innovative activity. A broad definition of innovativeness was initially used here, given by the percentage of firms reporting the introduction of a product new to the firm. An indicator of local synergies, in the sense of business cooperation, is given by the percentage of firm reporting access to at least one, spatially defined, horizontal network. A firm is assumed to access at least one horizontal network if more than 50 per cent of its transactions for either inputs or outputs are carried out with the same firms which are located in the same geographical area as the business under consideration.

Figure 3.3 depicts the four types of innovative milieu by using the previously mentioned indices of innovativeness and local synergies. It is evident that three of the six less accessible areas are in the innovation milieu type or very close to it (L'Alcoia, Keski-Suomi and the Northern Isles). In Greece, Evrytania, the less accessible area, ranks higher in terms of the percentage of firms accessing horizontal networks and reporting innovation than does Kalavryta, the more accessible area.

Percentage of Firms Reporting a New to the Firm Product

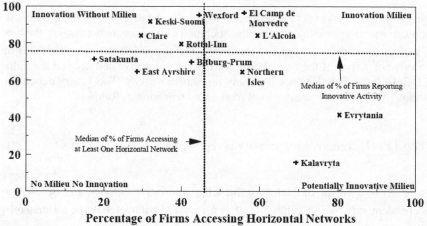

Percentage of Firms Accessing Horizontal Networks

✚ More Accessible Region

✘ Less Accessible Region

Figure 3.3   Innovative milieu and horizontal cooperation networks

The analysis was repeated using a much narrower measure to capture local innovativeness, i.e. the percentage of firms reporting a totally new product. Again, one of the less accessible areas (Northern Isles) falls clearly into the innovation milieu type with Keski-Suomi (the less accessible area in Finland) being very close to it and two more accessible areas (Satakunta and East Ayrshire) fall clearly into the no innovation no milieu type. In this subsequent analysis, synergy was also captured by a more complex measure than before, and was based on the percentage of firms having a simultaneous access to at least one horizontal and one vertical network. A firm is assumed to access at least one vertical network if more than 50 per cent of its transactions for either inputs or outputs are carried out with the same firms which are located outside the geographic area where the firm under consideration is located. If this index of synergies is drawn against the simple index of innovativeness, namely the percentage of firms reporting the introduction of product at least new to the firm, the same picture is revealed. On the one hand, the less accessible area of L'Alcoia falls in the innovation milieu type and two other less accessible areas (Keski-Suomi and Rottal-Inn) are very close to it. On the other hand, two more accessible areas (East Ayrshire and Bitburg-Prüm) are clearly away from the innovation milieu type. These results indicate that some less accessible areas of our sample are close to developing an innovative milieu while some accessible areas are in the innovation without milieu or in the no innovation no milieu type, with the distinct exception of the Spanish area of El Camp de Morvedre.

Factors Affecting Innovative Activity

The aim of this section is to assess econometrically the extent to which businesses' innovative activity is influenced by the operation of business networks, i.e. the type of various networks accessed by enterprises. The dependent variable, Y, takes on the value of 1 (j=1) if the firm shows any kind of innovative activity and the value of 0 (j=0) if the firm does not show any innovative activity. This binary dependent variable is investigated using a logit model for estimation as follows:

$$\text{Pr}\,ob\,\left(Y=1,\text{ if innovative activity is reported}\right)=\frac{e^{\beta' x}}{1+e^{\beta' x}}=\Lambda\left(\beta' x\right) \qquad (1)$$

where $\mathbf{x}$ is a vector of factors influencing innovative activity and denoted as independent variables in Table 3.1, β is a vector of parameters to be estimated by the model and $\Lambda(.)$ indicates the logistic cumulative distribution function.

Table 3.1 Variable definitions and descriptive statistics

Variable Name	Definition	Mean (S.D)
INNOVATION	Dummy variable, 1=firm claims innovative activity, 0=firm does not claim any innovative activity	0.705 (0.456)
ACCESSIBILITY	National accessibility indicator	73.583 (20.727)
GDP1999	GDP per capita in 1999 in '000 euros	16.790 (52.730)
HORIZONTAL	Dummy variable, 1=firm accesses at least one horizontal network for inputs or outputs, 0=otherwise	0.525 (0.460)
SECTORS	Dummy variable, 1=business is in manufacturing, 0=business is in services	0.55 (0.498)
FIRM'S AGE	Firm's age in years	20.111 (25.770)
HUMAN CAPITAL	Dummy variable, 1=entrepreneur raised in entrepreneurial environment, 0=otherwise	0.378 (0.485)
EDUCATION	Dummy variable, 0=entrepreneur has completed secondary school, 1=entrepreneur has higher education	0.602 (0.490)
METHOD OF ACQUISITION	Dummy variable, 1=the business created by the present owner, 0=the business was acquired by any other method	0.665 (0.472)

The log-likelihood function for the logit model in equation (1) is estimated as:

$$\ln L = \sum_{j} \left[Y_{j} \ln \Lambda\!\left(\beta'\mathbf{x}\right) + \left(1 - Y_{j}\right)\ln\!\left(1 - \Lambda\!\left(\beta'\mathbf{x}\right)\right) \right] \tag{2}$$

Parameter estimates are shown in Table 3.2. Parameter estimates of the logit model indicate the direction of the effect of each explanatory variable on the response probability but do not directly represent the actual probability changes. By differentiating equation (1), we find the marginal effects at the sample mean of the regressors on the probabilities (see Greene, 1997):

$$\frac{\partial P_{Y=1}}{\partial \mathbf{x}} = P_{Y=1}\left[\beta - \sum_{Y=0}^{Y=1} P_{Y}\beta \right] = \Lambda\!\left(\beta'\mathbf{x}\right) - \left[1 - \Lambda\!\left(\beta'\mathbf{x}\right)\right] \tag{3}$$

A goodness of fit measure based on the likelihood ratio test statistic, usually reported as McFadden's ρ^{2} measure (Maddala, 1983), is:

$$\rho^{2} = 1 - \frac{\log L_{\Omega}}{\log L\omega} \tag{4}$$

where L_{Ω} is the maximum of the likelihood function when maximized with respect to all parameters and L_{ω} is the maximum when the likelihood function is maximized with respect to the constant term only, i.e. setting all the βs equal to zero. The marginal effects reported in the far right column of Table 3.2 show how much the probability that a firm will claim an innovative activity, expressed in percentages, will change if the independent (explanatory) variable changes by a marginal amount from its sample mean. The marginal effects for dummy independent variables are estimated as a difference between the variable's two values, 0 and 1 (Greene, 1997). The interpretation of the marginal effects is, thus, straightforward.

The accessibility and the economic development of the firm's location positively affect the probability of innovative activity in the firm (INNOVATION). Thus, between two firms that have similar characteristics at the sample's mean, 10 degrees more in the level of the relative national accessibility indicator is associated with a 5 per cent increase in the probability that this is an innovative firm. Similarly, for each thousand Euros higher per capita income, the corresponding probability of innovative activity increases by 2.4 per cent. Accessing at least one horizontal (in spatial terms) network increases the probability of innovative activity by 7.6 per cent. Thus, while accessibility and economic development increase the probability that firms will be more innovative, the operation of horizontal networks may offset accessibility and development

Table 3.2 Coefficient estimates and marginal effects of logit model

Independent Variables	Coefficient Estimate	Asymptotic t-value	Marginal Effect
Constant	-3.682	-6.299**[a]	---
ACCESSIBILITY	0.027	5.436**	0.005
GDP1999	0.126	6.393**	0.024
HORIZONTAL	0.413	1.763*[b]	0.076
SECTORS	0.636	2.780**	0.119
FIRM'S AGE	-0.005	-1.186	---
HUMAN CAP.	0.559	2.432**	0.104
EDUCATION	0.547	2.566**	0.108
METHOD OF ACQUISITION	0.336	1.394	---

Summary Statistics

N			548.000
$\log L_{\Omega}$			-280.430
$\log L_{\omega}$			-332.690
$-2[\log L_{\omega} - \log L_{\Omega}]$			104.54**
McFadden's ρ^2			0.157
% correct predictions			77.00

a: two asterisks indicate significance at the 5 per cent level
b: one asterisk indicates significance at the 10 per cent level

disadvantages in less accessible regions. In other words, firms that are located in less accessible disadvantaged regions may also have the same (or higher) probability of being innovative, depending on their access to horizontal networks. The operation of horizontal business networks may support an innovative milieu and advance a lagging area to a 'learning region' where regional competitiveness is bound up with the local business network's ability to absorb, disseminate and effectively utilize technical and market intelligence (Morgan, 1997; Asheim, 1996; Hallin and Malmberg, 1999; Keeble et al., 1999).

The sector of economic activity also plays a very important role in innovation (holding all other variables constant). Firms in the manufacturing sector show a 10.4 per cent higher probability of being innovative than their services counterparts. Two human capital characteristics play an important role in offsetting the disadvantages of location and of lower economic development. Comparing entrepreneurs owning enterprises with the same characteristics, the results show that those raised in an entrepreneurial environment will have 10.4 per cent higher probability of owning an innovative enterprise. In addition, those with more than secondary level education will also have 10.8 per cent higher probability of owning an innovative business.

Conclusions

This chapter attempted to provide empirical evidence supporting the argument that the resurgence of remote regional economies may be due to the concurrent action of innovative activity and cooperation networks and the wider existence of the so called 'innovative milieu'. Further investigation of the factors influencing innovative activity among firms revealed the significant role of cooperation networks. Access to networks with other local firms greatly increases the probability that firms will exhibit some type of innovative activity.

Two directions are suggested for future work. Firstly, alternative measures of innovative and synergistic activity may be examined. Our definitions of innovative activity are convenience definitions and might be refined with access to other data such as public and private expenditure on research and development or patent registrations. Defining the existence of synergies as percentage of firms accessing various types of business networks is also restrictive because it ignores a large part of the informal networks linking businesses to the wider social capital and institutions. Links of entrepreneurs with the wider regional social capital and the institutional environment may also facilitate knowledge spillovers, enhance tacit knowledge and increase the ability to innovate.

The second direction suggested for future work is to focus on firm specific processes and the concurrent role of the entrepreneur as a network manager and an innovator (Nijkamp, 2003). The mechanism by which network operation influences innovation is still not clear in the literature. Moreover, the processes usually assumed in this type of research have been described as fuzzy and work investigating this area has been heavily criticized for its lack of strict scientific methodology (Markusen, 2003). How knowledge flows in networks and how this is transformed into innovation need further careful investigation.

References

Asheim, B. (1996), 'Industrial Districts as Learning Regions: A Condition for Prosperity', *European Planning Studies*, Vol. 4(4), pp. 379-400.

Aspatial Peripherality, Innovation and the Rural Economy QLK5-2000-00783 (AsPIRE) (http://www1.sac.ac.uk/management/External/Projects/AspireExternal/).

Bramanti, A. and Senn, L. (1991), 'Innovation, Firm and Milieu: A Dynamic and Cyclic Approach', in R. Camagni (ed.), *Innovation Networks: Spatial Perspectives*, GREMI, Belhaven Press, London, pp. 89-104.

Camagni, R. (1991), 'Introduction: From the Local Milieu to Innovation through Cooperation Networks', in R. Camagni (ed.), *Innovation Networks: Spatial Perspectives*, GREMI, Belhaven Press, London, pp. 1-9.

Camagni, R. (1995), 'The Concept of Innovative Milieu and its Relevance for Public Policies in European Lagging Regions', *Papers in Regional Science*, Vol. 74(4), pp. 317-340.

Camagni, R. and Capello, R. (1999), 'Innovation and Performance of SME's in Italy: the Relevance of Spatial Aspects', in M. Fischer, L. Suarez-Villa and M. Steiner (eds), *Innovation, Networks and Localities*, Springer, Berlin-Heidelberg-NY, pp. 181-214.

Copus, A. (2001), 'From Core-Periphery to Polycentric Development; Concepts of Spatial and Aspatial Peripherality', *European Planning Studies*, Vol. 9(4), pp. 539-552.

Copus, A., Skuras, D., Goudis, A. and McLeod, M. (2003), 'Accessibility, Innovation and Performance of SMEs in Europe's Lagging Areas', Paper presented to the 2nd *Hellenic Workshop for Productivity and Efficiency Measurement* (2nd HEWPEM), Patras, Greece. (accessible at : http://hewpem.econ.upatras.gr).

Greene, W. (1997), *Econometric Analysis*, Prentice-Hall, Upper Saddle River, NJ.

Hallin, G. and Malmberg, A. (1999), 'Attraction, Competition and Regional Development in Europe', *European Urban and Regional Studies*, Vol. 3(4), pp. 323-337.

Keeble, D. and Wilkinson, F. (1999), 'Collective Learning and Knowledge Development in the Evolution of Regional Clusters of High Technology SME's in Europe', *Regional Studies*, Vol. 33(4), pp. 295-303.

Keeble, D., Lawson, C., Moore, B., and Wilkinson, F. (1999), 'Collective Learning Processes, Networking and "Institutional Thickness" in the Cambridge Region', *Regional Studies*, Vol. 33(4), pp. 319-332.

Maddala, G.S. (1983), *Limited Dependent and Qualitative Variables in Econometrics*, Econometric Society Monographs, Cambridge University Press, Cambridge.

Maillat, D. (1998), 'Interactions between Urban Systems and Localized Productive Systems: An Approach to Endogenous Regional Development in Terms of Innovative Milieu', *European Planning Studies*, Vol. 6(2), pp. 112-131.

Maillat, D. and Lecoq, B. (1992), 'New Technologies and Transformation of Regional Structures in Europe: the Role of the Milieu', *Entrepreneurship and Regional Development,* Vol.4, pp. 1-20.

Markusen, A. (2003), 'Fuzzy Concepts, Scanty Evidence, Policy Distance: the Case for Rigour and Policy Relevance in Critical Regional Studies', *Regional Studies*, Vol. 37(6/7), pp. 701-717.

Mole, K. and Worall, L. (2001), 'Innovation, Business Performance and Regional Competitiveness in the West Midlands: Evidence from the West Midlands Business Survey', *European Business Review*, Vol. 13(6) pp. 353-364.

Morgan, K. (1997), 'The Learning Region: Institutions, Innovation and Regional Renewal', *Regional Studies*, Vol. 31(5), pp. 491-503.

Neely, A. and Hii, J. (1998), *Innovation and Business Performance: A Literature Review*, The Judge Institute of Management Studies, University of Cambridge.

Nijkamp, P. (2003), 'Entrepreneurship in a Modern Network Economy', *Regional Studies*, Vol. 37(4), pp. 395-405.

Perrin, J.C. (1991), 'Technological Innovation and Territorial Development: an Approach in Terms of Networks and Milieu', in R. Camagni (ed.), *Innovation Networks: Spatial Perspectives*, GREMI, Belhaven Press, London, pp. 35-54.

Shefer, D. and Frenkel, A. (1998), 'Local Milieu and Innovations: Some Empirical Results', *The Annals of Regional Science*, Vol. 32, pp.185-200.

Spiekermann, K., Wegener, M. and Copus, A. (2002), Review of Peripherality Indices and Identification of Baseline Indicator, Deliverable 1. AsPIRE QLK5-2000-00783. (accessible at:
http://www1.sac.ac.uk/management/external/Projects/AspireExternal/Documents/)

Chapter 4

Human Capital as the Critical Factor for the Development of Europe's Rural Peripheral Areas[1]

Lois Labrianidis

Introduction

The main objective of this chapter is to enhance our understanding of the underdevelopment of European rural peripheral areas and to show that this could be partly attributed to the existence of limited entrepreneurship in these areas. This limited entrepreneurship might be explained by a plethora of reasons, such as the small size of local markets and the difficulties of accessing wider markets, or by the lack of finance. The most important reason, however, appears to derive from the characteristics of the human capital in these rural areas (such as the older age structure, conservatism, and lack of education) with the most dynamic elements of rural societies usually being the most likely to migrate to an urban area.

At this stage, it is important to note that this research addressed the issue of the lack of entrepreneurs and not of businessmen and women. It dealt with the entrepreneur who is assumed to possess several unique characteristics, such as superior foresight, alertness, a will to succeed for the sake of it and not for the fruits of success, creativity, leadership, independence, tolerance of ambiguity and uncertainty, resourcefulness and optimism. The literature focusing on the role of the entrepreneur in economic development is very extensive and has been developed by Cantillon, Say, Knight, Schumpeter, Kirzner, Casson and Baumol, among others. It is usefully reviewed, for example, in Binks and Vale (1991), Martinelli, (1994) and Kalantaridis (2004).

There is considerable variation in the answers given to the central question of what determines the incidence of entrepreneurship. On the one hand, it is argued that features of the market environment (e.g. market opportunities, risk, availability of labour, capital and raw materials) are the prime factors. On the other hand, the importance of an appropriate social climate (affording legitimacy and recognition to innovative behaviour) and cultural characteristics, as well as the role of social and institutional actors, are seen as important influences on the extent and nature of entrepreneurial behaviour.

Peripherality is viewed here as a four dimensional concept (Ferrao and Lopes, 2004). First, peripherality is understood as *distance* from a given point of reference, from a space that is central in terms of access to markets, information and communication. Second, it is seen as *dependency* (deriving from theories of circular causation and Marxist unequal exchange theory), whereby the region is dependent and therefore underdeveloped. Third, it is seen as *difference*, acknowledging the uniqueness, shaped by history, of each region whose specific characteristics are viewed as positive, locally differentiating factors. The existence of 'authentic' landscapes and cultural traditions allows the development of strategies for their exploitation. Finally, it is seen as *discourse*, emphasizing the importance of the specific character of each region, not only regarding its individual characteristics in objective terms but, rather, on the basis of the social meaning attributed to them (how the content of space is created through discourse). The use of all four dimensions enables an effective understanding of the multitude of impacts caused by the peripheral location of a region.

This chapter is based on an EU funded research project (Labrianidis et al., 2002). The field work (comprising 4,939 questionnaires to the general population, 996 questionnaires to successful entrepreneurs and more than 150 interviews with key informants) was carried out in ten case study areas in five countries (Germany, Greece, Poland, Portugal and Britain). These countries have different levels of development with Germany and Britain being more developed, Portugal and Greece being less developed and, finally, Poland chosen to represent a (then) pre-accession country.

The selected case study areas were Nordwes-Mecklenburg and Waldshut (Germany); Kilkis and Lesvos (Greece); Bialostockosuwalski (Bialystock) and Zielonogorski (Poland); Oeste and Baixo Alentejo (Portugal), and Cumbria and the two counties of Devon and Cornwall in Britain. They have a higher share of GDP from agriculture than the national average and a greater proportion of employment in agriculture than the national average (the only exception seems to occur in Poland but this must be attributed to the gross distortion due to the huge contribution of the black economy); a population density lower than the national average, (the only exception being Oeste), and lower GDP per capita than the national average (the only exceptions being Cumbria and Kilkis). Each of the following sections in turn addresses one of the main findings from the research carried out in these areas.

Diversity of Rurality in Europe

A precise demarcation of rural areas in Europe, although very important, is anything but an easy task due to the changing character of rural areas as well as their varied and heterogeneous structures. The longstanding axioms defining rural areas as the non-urban space, or the domain where agriculture and physical landscape are important, are inadequate to describe today's complex reality. They have been vigorously questioned during the past decade during which the distinction between urban and rural areas has become increasingly blurred.

The increasing complexity of the pattern of economic organization, which underlies the urban/rural distinction, has undermined this same distinction. Using the terms loosely, England, for example, is in physical terms predominantly 'rural' but in socio-economic terms it is overwhelmingly 'urban'. This fuzziness of the urban/rural distinction has important implications for methods of delimiting urban and rural areas in practice. No single approach can provide the whole answer; different approaches, stressing different characteristics, fit different purposes and the distinction is only partially achievable through reliance on quantitative indicators.

Thus, it may be more appropriate to suggest that there are a series of distinctions such as land cover, population characteristics and social organization. As society has evolved, these have changed. This sectoral – spatial approach directly connects rural space with agriculture and urban space with industry and services. Rural space is, however, no longer confined to agricultural activities and land uses, but also includes multi-sectoral activities. Small and medium towns integrated into the agricultural context, manufacturing and tourism activities, as well as coastal areas, are suitable for inclusion in rural areas. Despite significant dissimilarities between them, urban and rural areas are not autonomous and self-sufficient entities. On the contrary, they constitute a continuous space of interdependence and interaction (Saraceno, 1994).

These changes are associated with a broader debate regarding the dramatic changes currently underway in rural Europe. Over the past decade or so, the countryside has been socially and economically remoulded. As the post war agricultural modernization project has gradually and unevenly faded, new processes and actions associated with both public and private interests are at work and produce new patterns of diversity and differentiation within the contemporary countryside. The common trends affecting rural areas can be separated, according to Marsden (1998), into those affecting the entire society (i.e. globalization, the strengthening of free market ideology, the liberalization of international trade, and changes in cultural values) and those specific to rural locations (i.e. the decline in agricultural employment, emergence of environmentalism, and new uses of rural space). These processes have led to a consumerized countryside, one that exhibits a wide range of external relationships and is subject to wide-ranging demands.

European countryside is characterized by a diversity of historical trajectories, terrains, climates, landscapes and population densities that find their counterpart in the great variety of economic activities, types of agricultural production, problems and opportunities. As a result, there are several definitions of rural areas. Traditionally, rural areas have been defined as those areas given over to particular resource based economic activities, notably agriculture and forestry, and areas of natural open space such as moorlands and mountainous areas. Alternatively, rural areas can be defined in terms of a number of socio-spatial characteristics, such as population densities and distance from major cities (Cloke, 1977; Cloke and Edwards, 1986). More recent approaches define 'rural' more in terms of a social representation of reality, placing the emphasis upon the way people strive after a rural ideal and try to achieve this in their everyday lives (Hoggart et al., 1995). This approach is becoming more important as the traditional production functions of rural areas based on agriculture and forestry decline in importance and various consumption functions, such as recreation and leisure, become more significant, particularly in certain countries (Ilbery, 1998). The debate about what constitutes rurality is therefore symptomatic of the changes that are occurring to the economy and social composition of these localities in the European context.

The introduction of this multitude of criteria into a working definition is more than usually problematic. Therefore, the vast majority of national conventions focus upon rather simple measures of the size of the population in a locality and/or population density. Moreover, despite the limited reliability of quantitative criteria, international organizations (such as the OECD and EUROSTAT) usually adopt these for the definition of rural areas as they are particularly useful for inter-regional or inter-state comparisons. Population density has been traditionally used for the definition of rural areas in Europe perhaps due to the fact that two of the few attributes common to European rural areas are relatively low population densities and the significant role of agriculture in the local economy. The usefulness of the above classification is questionable since the criterion of population density is not sufficient even for a robust distinction between urban and rural areas. Low population densities are not always associated with rural populations; there are towns with large population and low densities (e.g. new towns in Britain). Neither do high population densities always suggest the existence of an urban population (Saraceno, 1994, p.457). This brings a need for more sophisticated methodologies for classifying European regions and these can be based on the increasing availability of socio-economic and demographic data at the regional level.

The effort described in the following paragraphs is by no means intended to produce a universal classification of European regions. In fact, we believe that such efforts – although undoubtedly useful – will never be able to provide more than a partial image for two reasons. The first is that secondary data at NUTS 3 or lower level are usually limited to a relatively small number of variables. The second, and probably most important reason, is that secondary data are neither capable of depicting the various processes at work nor the historical trajectories of each region. It therefore seems more appropriate to seek contextual and not universal classifications.

The approach followed here was a disaggregative one,[2] under which all regions are viewed as a single large group, which needs to be progressively split into sub-groups on the basis of a number of pre-selected discriminatory criteria. The first split was between predominantly urban (which were excluded from the analysis) and rural regions. We defined as urban those regions that contained a city with population larger than 500,000 inhabitants, or with more than 65 per cent of their total population living in conurbations with more than 10,000 inhabitants. The second step concerned the remaining regions, which were split into three sub-groups according to their accessibility (peripheral, semi-peripheral and accessible) on the basis of the travel time to the nearest of 52 important international agglomerations.[3]

The results of this country classification process are shown in Table 4.1. The countries with the highest proportion of peripheral areas are the Nordic ones, closely followed by the southern European countries. At the other end of the spectrum are the central European countries (Belgium, the Netherlands, Luxembourg and Germany), with most of their territories being classified as accessible rural.

Table 4.1 Share of area type by country

	Peripheral	Semi-peripheral	Accessible rural	Urban
Finland	85.9	8.4	2.3	3.3
Sweden	82.8	13.0	2.8	1.4
Greece	68.5	10.8	15.0	5.7
Denmark	62.0	16.7	21.0	0.2
Spain	54.2	12.4	11.6	21.8
Portugal	44.9	20.6	33.4	1.1
Ireland	37.6	24.6	36.4	1.3
Italy	34.5	19.4	26.8	19.3
France	29.3	29.6	29.0	12.1
Austria	27.5	38.9	30.8	2.8
Britain	27.2	31.9	33.9	7.0
Germany	6.4	27.7	58.1	7.8
Netherlands	3.3	11.5	78.5	6.7
Belgium	0.0	0.0	67.3	32.7
Luxembourg	0.0	0.0	100.0	0.0
TOTAL	49.4	19.4	22.4	8.9

Source: Ballas et al. (2003)

Peripherality was the first classification criterion, and three further variables were subsequently applied to each of the regions. These were economic performance (approximated by GDP per capita); competitiveness (expressed by the average number of patent applications for the years 1989-96), and dependence on agriculture (expressed as the percentage of employment in agriculture). The use of patent applications as a variable is one of the innovative features of this research. Regional innovation is becoming increasingly important, as economies become more complex and a greater variety of goods and ideas are patented (Ceh, 2001). However, we are also aware of the limitations of this indicator. Patents are not always a reliable indicator of competitive dynamics, particularly when dealing with rural spaces. Nevertheless, the inclusion of this variable in the analysis was decided because it simply is quite a good proxy of competitiveness. All three additional variables were not applied to all regions indiscriminately. For each type of peripherality, different thresholds were used, based on a set of relatively simple criteria (see Ballas et al., 2003). For example, the threshold for division of peripheral regions into advancing or lagging was 2.275 patent applications, while for accessible regions the respective figure was 14.4. The same approach was used for the other two classification criteria (see Table 4.2), ensuring that the variation within the three groups is relatively limited, giving more meaningful results.

Table 4.2 The disaggregation criteria

THEMES

1. Rurality/ peripherality	Peripheral TTIME > 135 minutes		Semi-peripheral TTIME < 135 minutes and TTIME > 82 minutes		Accessible rural TTIME < 82 minutes	
2. Dynamism/ competitiveness	Lagging PATENTS < 2.275	Advancing PATENTS > 2.275	High PATENTS > 8.3125	Low PATENTS < 8.3125	High PATENTS > 14.3625	Low PATENTS < 14.3625
3. Economic performance	Relatively high GDP per capita > 10379.1	Relatively low GDP per capita <= 10379.1	High GDP per capita > 13185.52	Low GDP per capita <= 13185.52	High GDP per capita > 14224.1	Low GDP per capita <= 14224.1
4. Role of agriculture	Very important EMPLA > 15.97%	Relatively limited EMPLA < 15.97%	Important EMPLA > 11.39%	Limited EMPLA < 11.39%	Important EMPLA > 8.41%	Limited EMPLA < 8.41%

Source: Ballas et al., 2003.

The combination of the criteria resulted in 25 types of regions being identified. The 'base' regions were peripheral and lagging, with relatively low economic performance and agriculture having a very important role (37 regions), while at the other end of the spectrum were accessible, dynamic regions with high economic performance and a limited agricultural sector (130 regions).

The countries which are dominated by the least competitive regions are Greece, Spain, Portugal, Ireland and Italy. Agriculture plays a relatively important role in most of these regions. It should be noted, though, that there are also several of the least competitive regions with low economic performance in Britain, Eastern Germany and Austria. However, in most of these regions the role of agriculture is much less significant than in their southern European counterparts and in Ireland. The countries having a majority of highly competitive regions with high levels of economic performance are found in central Europe (predominantly in Germany and North West France) and

Northern Europe (Netherlands and Denmark). Further, there are some regions of this type in the Scandinavian member states and in Britain. It is also noteworthy that the latter has a large number of regions that are highly competitive but attain relatively low levels of economic performance.

The suggested typology clearly shows the huge diversity of rural areas between, as well as within, countries. It proves quite a satisfactory typology since, unlike most other classifications, it manages to depict the various national differences quite well. In most other (aggregative) classifications these are often masked, particularly in the case of the smaller countries such as Greece or Portugal.

The Role of National Characteristics

A question that naturally arises is how one can compare the development of entrepreneurship among European rural areas as the attributes of rurality are so different and there are huge inequalities in the level of development of the various countries as measured by a variety of economic, institutional and social indicators. The results of our empirical research suggest that national characteristics influence key areas of the rural regions in a significant way. Indeed, the role of the particular national context is probably greater than other analytical categories, such as the spatial ones. The differences between the environments in which businesses operate are more significant between countries than between different degrees of rurality in the same country so the national framework component prevails over rural international diversity.

Perhaps the most important differentiating factor between countries originates from their radically diverging views of rurality. In fact, social representations of the rural vary considerably even within the developed world. They can be classified schematically – as Halfacree and Boyle suggest (1998, p.9) following Short (1991) – according to whether they regard the countryside as a backward relic of the past to be escaped from at all costs or whether they see it as a haven of sanity and security in a world where the city represents the uncertain mayhem of Babylon rather than the ordered progress of Jerusalem (see Williams, 1973, for the more pastoral vision of the countryside). A typical example of the first view might be the dominant attitude in Greece while the latter predominates in Britain.

The rural idyll, as Ilbery (1998 p.3) argues following Rogers (1993), portrays a positive image surrounding many aspects of rural lifestyle, community and landscape. In fact, the countryside represents an ideal society that is orderly, harmonious, healthy and peaceful and provides a refuge from modernity. It is characterized by mutual cooperation and support, self-help and voluntary commitment. Needless to say that not all people living in the countryside conform to this rural idyll; they behave in different ways, aspire to different goals and have unequal access to what they desire. As Little and Austin (1996) argue, the rural idyll is created by the wealthy for the wealthy and reflects particular power relations in society.

Finally, a very important differentiating factor between countries is related to the notion of trust. Economic action is inevitably social action and hence depends for its successful implementation on a supportive social context. The institutional context of society has a major role to play in fostering either cooperation or self-interest, traits common to individuals. Within this context, firms realize that they can profit not only through competition but also through cooperation. In addition, the wider environment of the firm (i.e. the social and political system in which it is embedded and with which it interacts) can play a vital role in facilitating or obstructing its learning capacity. Thus, the key issue is not the organizational form but what Cooke and Morgan (2000, p.17) call the 'associational capacity', i.e. the capacity to create and sustain a robust architecture for generating and using knowledge from a wide variety of sources, including employees, suppliers, customers and public bodies. As Cooke and Morgan (2000, p.30) argue, only a few social settings are wholly devoid of trust, hence it is best to speak of high-trust and low-trust relationships.

However, it appears that, in this respect too, there are quite significant differences between the countries of Southern Europe and those of Northern Europe, while developed transition economies (such as Poland) seem somehow to lie in the middle. Needless to say, this divide is not clear-cut and the argument is about degrees of difference rather than a sharp divide; moreover, there are 'niches' in all three groups. In particular, in the countries of Southern Europe, centralized state structures and a weak civil society lead to hierarchical, clientelistic political[4] networks inhibiting the building of social capital. Hence, 'civil society' can neither function as the arbitrator of market and non-market rules of conduct, nor act as the intermediary between the self-seeking individual and society. Thus certain factors are more frequently noticeable in Southern Europe: these include a non-cooperative stance towards other companies; a lack of willingness to participate in trade associations; a lack of willingness to 'invest' in their employees; an absence among entrepreneurs of long-term commitment and trust; a lack of trust/ acceptance of the social context, and a lack of professionalism.

Thus, on the one hand, in 'Northern' Europe people tend to cooperate and this gives them an immense market power. One typical such example is that of the 'Digital Peninsula Network' in South Cornwall. It is a cluster formed by very small businesses (many of whom were self-employed individuals working from their own homes) involved in IT and related activities. The cluster allowed these businesses to work on a project basis, building up 'alliances' to serve a particular market and to work on particular projects. Moreover, at least half of the businesses surveyed were generating a majority of their sales from outside the region, thereby demonstrating the feasibility for very small firms in these sectors of locating in the region. On the other hand, the lack of trust in 'Southern' Europe leads to lack of cooperation, even in cases where there are co-locations of firms belonging to the same sector. This is seen in Greece in the cases of ouzo firms in Plomari and of wine producing firms in Kilkis (Labrianidis, 2004).

Characteristics of Rural Entrepreneurship

Entrepreneurship is not an undifferentiated process and in rural areas we can identify a multiplicity of entrepreneurial processes at work. Some of these are locality specific, whilst others appear in more than one national context. It is interesting that the incidence of these processes does not follow national or spatial divides. These processes are evolving through time, with some declining or disappearing altogether, others in the process of transformation and new forms emerging. They are path dependent so they cannot readily be transposed from one context to another. The influence of the rural character of the location on entrepreneurship varies considerably and whilst some entrepreneurial processes are distinctly rural, others simply occur more or less incidentally in the countryside. As a result, the degree of embeddedness of each process within the local milieu varies significantly, with major implications for developing enterprise strategies. Undoubtedly, however, specific environments can be associated with the emergence of particular entrepreneurial processes. Thus, 'need driven' entrepreneurial processes are prevalent in the case of the two most hostile socio-economic regimes, namely Lesvos and Baixo Alentejo.

Throughout the ten case study areas, there appear to be five common factors stimulating rural entrepreneurship. These are the over-representation of males; younger age; the acquisition of higher education qualifications; parental entrepreneurial influences (through the provision of role models and inheritance of a family business) and previous experience of running a business. The consistent and invariably significant influence of these factors lends support to the thesis that out-migration deprives rural areas of individuals (young and well-educated) who can identify opportunities, and, on account of their (urban-university) experiences, break the mould of deprivation and produce change. There are also four factors that have a differential impact upon the propensity of individuals to engage in entrepreneurship in the ten case study areas. These are origin; unemployment prior to entrepreneurship; education prior to entrepreneurship, and occupational background. They provide us with a powerful reminder of the pervasive influence of local historical trajectories shaping entrepreneurial behaviour. Legal restrictions, namely the qualification requirements needed to become entrepreneurs, also appear to be an influence on the incidence of rural entrepreneurial ventures. This is manifested in a comparison between Germany, where strict rules exist that can act as barriers to entry, and Greece and Poland, where there are no such restrictions. Finally, there appear to be significant differences in the legitimacy afforded to entrepreneurship. A factor invariably affecting the general attitude is the existence of a history of social structures inhibiting the development of individualism. This is achieved through surprisingly diverse mechanisms, such as the latifundi organization in Baixo Alentejo, or the communist systems of Poland and the former GDR. The result is a suspicion of entrepreneurship or the entrepreneur.

Our research indicates that rural enterprises which display a significant degree of dynamism place a considerable weight upon product/service definition. These are enterprises that turn the perceived disadvantage of the rural environment into a source of competitive advantage through the emphasis on the local character of products, as discussed later, or are able to overcome it altogether through the development of collaborative arrangements. These collaborative arrangements involve either linkages with other enterprises or higher education institutions.

The Role of Human Capital

Europe's rural areas, with few exceptions, have failed to attract larger firms mainly due to the poor provision of tangible and intangible infrastructure and their small markets. This means that the pervasive influence of small and micro-scale firms conditions economic growth in rural areas. Hence, economic growth in rural areas is closely associated with the entrepreneurial talent of the local population. The supply of potential entrepreneurs to confront the threats and exploit the opportunities available in the countryside is, however, by no means guaranteed. This is because those who could reasonably have been expected to perform the entrepreneurial function may well have been the first to seek to out-migrate to the more inviting urban areas. Indeed, even the most developed rural areas suffer from the loss of young and dynamic people. Within this context, the question of how a critical mass of entrepreneurship is built is a key economic development issue for rural areas.

Two major currents of people have recently been moving into rural areas. First, there are economic immigrants. The number of immigrants that are employed in agriculture has increased significantly over the past fifteen years in Europe and especially in Southern Europe (EC, 2000, pp.3-4). These recent immigrants have located mainly in Southern Europe (Greece, Portugal, Spain and Italy) which has been transformed into a new immigration area due to a shift in its position within the international division of labour (King and Rybaczuk, 1993). A significant part of those immigrants settled, at first at least, in the countryside contributing to its revitalization and to the enhancement of the entrepreneurial activity there (for the case of Greece, see Labrianidis and Lyberaki, 2001).

Second, rural areas in some European countries (such as Britain, Portugal and Italy) have also more recently experienced a wave of in migration by relatively affluent, formerly urban dwellers. This urban-rural population flow has not been the result of a search for new employment opportunities but rather the pursuit of more desirable residential environments. Indeed, social and environmental problems within cities have prompted relatively affluent urban dwellers to relocate to the countryside (Clout, 1993). Also one must not forget the limited job creation in urban areas during the 1980s and 1990s. In other European countries (e.g. Greece), out-migration flows from rural areas have declined during this time and there has been a trend for return migration of economically active people to some semi-urban areas. Although accessible rural areas or areas with a trajectory of tourist development have been the main beneficiaries, many more rural locations have also experienced a halt or a reversal in their long-term population decline with the arrival of these new inhabitants. Their arrival has had significant economic consequences. They often possess considerable expertise in management and have information and contacts, as well as the finances necessary to initiate new venture formation. A significant minority of these new inhabitants, therefore, soon became involved in entrepreneurial activities, expanding the number of enterprises in rural areas.

The networks of social and professional contacts, established by entrepreneurs outside the region at some point in their lives, were shown to be essential to the emergence and growth of their enterprise ventures. The contexts that afforded entrepreneurs these networks were varied, such as study at a university or elsewhere; military service elsewhere; setting up as a migrant in another area/city; being newcomers to the area; setting up as an emigrant in another country, and employment in a multinational firm in another country. In all these cases, the contact with different socio-cultural realities also constitutes a source of new knowledge that enables entrepreneurs to break with local tradition and introduce discontinuity and change. Thus, we advance the thesis that those who possess experiences acquired outside the rural localities under investigation are better equipped (through both networks of contacts and different cognitive frameworks) to act as agents of change.

Overall, in-migration[5] appears to be a significant source of entrepreneurial capacity in all regions, since a third (33.8 per cent) of all business owners are in-migrants, while in some of the regions they spectacularly outnumber local business owners. The impact of in-migration on business activity seems to create a rather distinct pattern, since in-migration seems to be of extreme importance in some cases, while in others its impact is marginal. In general, in-migrants are relatively few in the southern case study areas and they tend to engage less in business ownership than locals (for example. 27.8 per cent of in-migrants in Lesvos are engaged in business ownership, while the respective share for locals is 31.6 per cent) while in three case study areas of northern countries (Nordwestmecklenburg, Bialystok and Cumbria) the rates of involvement of immigrants is almost double that of locals. The shares of in-migrants are slightly lower than those of locals in the remaining case study areas. In Devon and Cornwall, this might be attributed to a very high percentage of the retired among immigrants. Recent immigrants (i.e. those who arrived within the last decade) appear to be the most intensively involved segment of the population in six of the ten case study areas.

The absence (due to out-migration) of individuals who can introduce discontinuity and change is particularly apparent in some, mainly Southern European, case study areas, in terms of the absence of corresponding entrepreneurial groupings. Whilst in some areas (Kilkis and Oeste) this gap is filled by immigrants who frequently perform entrepreneurial roles, more localities (Lesvos and Baixo Alentejo) lack young and well-educated entrepreneurs who are willing to pursue new opportunities rather than reluctantly engaging in pre-existing family businesses.

Research on the factors which influence the incidence of entrepreneurial ventures has followed two distinct lines of enquiry. One school believes that economic stimuli through the market mechanism provide the best explanation (Baumol, 1995), whereas another, earlier tradition, argues that it is social and psychological features which are the most important (Wilken, 1979). To begin with, our aspiration was to combine these two traditions, which are not mutually exclusive, and explore the interaction between demand and supply side considerations in rural areas. Our findings, however, suggest otherwise. This is because, as we have already mentioned, the supply of potential entrepreneurs is by no means guaranteed; those people who could reasonably have been expected to respond might well have been the first wanting to out-migrate to urban areas. Thus, the human factor emerges as the key influence in the ability to exploit opportunities and confront challenges in the changing geography of the European countryside set within its specific institutional and national context.

This takes us further than existing arguments regarding the characteristics of the environment. Whilst factors such as the legitimizaion of entrepreneurial ventures (either at the level of society at large or within a specific social grouping); a supportive ideology; a deeply embedded need for achievement, and, in some cases, a minority (ethnic, religious or otherwise) that experiences status withdrawal are necessary, they are not suffcient to provide fertile ground for new venture creation. To be more precise, in the absence of the factors listed above, rural entrepreneurship is unlikely to flourish. However, entrepreneurship may also fail to flourish in settings where these factors are apparent.

The Role of Local Products

The product's geographic association constitutes a quality characteristic ('authentic', 'healthy' and 'traditional') and brings economic benefits since it allows premium prices. Hence, production of such products is very important for rural peripheral areas. In almost all rural areas there are firms producing 'local products', such as prepared food (jams and marmalades etc.) using 'grandmother's recipes'. The very difficulties that operated for decades as obstacles to the economic modernization of rural peripheral areas (Parrott et al., 2002, p.252) nowadays can be turned to their benefit with the lack of modernization in those areas seen as contributing to the maintenance of 'tradition'. Given that there is a growing public interest in the origin of products, tradition is becoming of major significance even if, in reality, it represents nothing more than a 'setting', in which the visitor might believe. Visitors show no desire to de-construct this myth, however, since it suits them as well.

The expansion of enterprises producing some kind of local product is a very positive influence in the development of a region. It implies the existence of backward and forward linkages of enterprises with the local economy, strengthens many sectors of the economy (such as agriculture, farming, small scale manufacturing, hotels and merchant stores) and promotes pluriactivity such as diversification of farmers into food manufacturing. However, this is not to say that endogenous development is the only developmental track for countryside areas. Such enterprises might have an important role in the development of the region, but they are not adequate on their own. If we consider how important new/innovative ideas, know-how and the ability to sell products in the national and international markets are for the development of an area, then we realize that foreign enterprises might play a crucial role in the development of the countryside.

Enterprises that produce local products and services tend to be much more tied to the local economy. They appear to be more closely associated with very high shares of inputs sourced from within the regions (more than half of firms' total inputs), as well as having a high proportion of employees who live in the vicinity of the firms. The reverse situation occurs with the inputs from abroad; enterprises that produce local products tend to buy lower percentages of their inputs from abroad while a significant percentage of them do not buy inputs from abroad at all.

Almost the opposite happens with the other two types of enterprises, that is those that have 'new' and 'truly innovative' products (Figure 4.1).

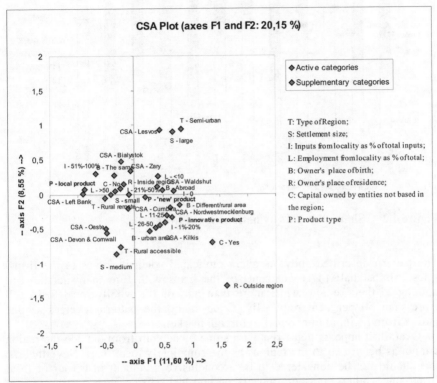

Figure 4.1 Exploration of the characteristics of product types

Local firms source most of their labour from their localities (41.8 per cent of all local firms source all of their labour force from their settlement). In contrast, almost half (47.1 per cent) of all firms with foreign ownership and one third of firms with ownership outside the regions contribute nothing to employment in their localities.

The regional market provides absolutely no inputs to nearly half of the non local firms (both national and foreign). The respective share for local firms is significantly lower, standing at 29.2 per cent, while more than a third source more than 50 per cent of their inputs from the regional market (Figure 4.2). Firms tend to become more outward oriented as we move from local to national to foreign firms. Hence, national firms appear to be those whose inputs mainly originate from the national market, while firms with foreign ownership are apparently far more dependent on foreign inputs.

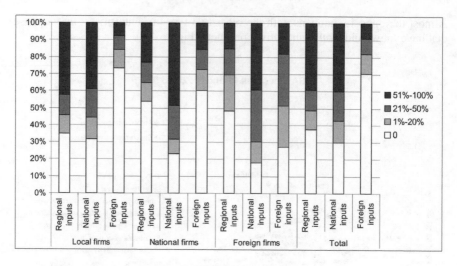

Figure 4.2   Share of inputs by nationality of firm

The pattern described above is again replicated when it comes to the firms' sales. Almost half (47.1 per cent) of the firms with foreign ownership sell nothing to their region, while more than half of the wholly local firms sell more than 50 per cent regionally. Once again, the pattern reverses as one moves from regional to national to foreign markets.

Overall, it appears that firms with some ownership from outside the region are not as beneficial to the regions as the completely local ones. Nevertheless, this should not be considered to be a conclusive argument in favour of local firms since other kinds of impacts of non-local firms such as transfers of technology or know-how (which can potentially be of greater importance than employment creation) have to be taken into consideration.

Non-local firms generally tend to be concentrated in the more accessible locations. In fact, there seems to be a more or less linear relationship between the 'spread' of ownership and the accessibility of the location. Hence, only 17.6 per cent of foreign firms are located in rural remote areas, whilst 55.9 per cent are located in semi-urban areas. In contrast, only 28 per cent of local firms are located in semi-urban locations. A similar type of relationship exists between nationality of ownership and size of community, as foreign firms tend to concentrate in large communities (41.2 per cent).

Entrepreneurs producing local products tend to be much more tied to the community. Most of them appear to have been born and spent their lives in the area and continue to live near the area. Although entrepreneurs producing new and innovative products do not appear to show any preference for living outside the region, still, many of them were born in other areas (both urban and rural). This could be part of the explanation of the relatively low use of local know-how by firms not producing local products. Finally, firm ownership appears to be overwhelmingly local for firms producing local products, while firm ownership by entities residing outside the region (either other parts of the country or abroad) appears to be the most weakly represented category, not affecting any other characteristic.

It must be made clear that many rural peripheral areas are sparsely populated and have a high proportion of elderly people; this makes the successful production of local products an extremely difficult task. The social preconditions for such production are no longer present, since the rural peripheral areas have been at a stand still for long periods, with no action taking place. Local products can contribute to the re-establishment, in completely new terms, of an integrated production system that most likely existed previously in the rural peripheral areas.

The above does not argue in favour of 'endogenous development' theory, which is not always the only track towards development. Neither does it suggest a 'jump into the past', since current socio-economic conditions are very different. It is easy for someone to suggest that 'since at that time there was a certain tradition in the production of that product lets produce it today and sell it as a local product'. It is, however, difficult to continue the production of goods that were produced in past times, even in the same locale, when socio-economic conditions have changed significantly. In Greece, for example certain 'local products' were produced in less developed mountainous areas that were once densely populated and people were expected to work really hard to make ends meet. Nowadays in societies such as those found in Greece, where the desire for easy profit prevails, the search for effortless professional opportunities especially in the service sector (such as rooms, small hotels, restaurants and bars) is the rule, and involvement with manual production occupations is seen as something to be avoided. Hence, even when there is a production of a local, traditional product this is often an illusion, in the sense that it is produced in totally different socio-economic conditions and even using different production methods.

Role of Technology and Knowledge Related Activities

Technology and knowledge constitute key elements in the external environment with the potential to both enable and hinder the entrepreneurial processes in rural areas. In fact, there is a growing belief among some researchers that knowledge is the most important source of local economic transformation (Lundvall, 1992; Herdzina and Blessin, 1996). This is particularly true regarding parts of knowledge involved in untraded interdependencies (uncodified know-how), which cannot be dissociated from their human and social context. Consequently, issues such as the institutional capacity of the area, the capabilities of the political leadership, as well as social rules of conduct and human values, emerge as of equal importance to physical factors in the entrepreneurial process (Doeringer and Terkla, 1990; Putnam, 1993).

Knowledge-based institutions embedded in the traditional milieu of rural areas also play a significant role (OECD, 1992; Morgan, 1997). Indeed, the implementation of technological change is conditioned by the pervasive influence of universities and other R&D providers supporting the interregional and interpersonal transfer of knowledge and technology and reducing regional information deficiencies, thus playing a significant role in the entrepreneurial process (Herdzina and Nolte, 1995). Institutions of this type offer the possibility of gaining new technological knowledge, of taking part in technological change and, in this way, of raising their own innovative and entrepreneurial potential – and thus that of the region's economy.

The Internet offers virtually free access to huge amounts of information. It transcends geographical borders and speeds up the global diffusion of information and, by overcoming distance and isolation, it can revitalize rural communities. Almost 67.6 per cent of the firms in our survey that already use some ICTs feel that ICTs help them to overcome the constraints of being located in a rural area. However, for the benefits to be realised by all the rural areas there needs to be an even distribution of ICTs across regions, which is certainly not the case. The differences between our ten case study areas were impressive, since firms not using ICTs in the German or British regions constituted a very small minority, while almost half of the firms surveyed in the remaining regions did not use any ICT application. The same is also true regarding the types of applications used, with the more technologically advanced applications being more intensely used in the countries with higher adoption rates. Moreover, there are types of information and knowledge exchange that continue to require regular and direct face-to-face contact. Consequently, it is only routinized activities that have become increasingly footloose and relocate from city centres to suburban areas or to urban areas around the globe, while the move towards rural areas is rather limited. Interestingly, the firm's evaluation of the impact of ICTs appears to be negatively correlated with the spread of ICTs. In other words, firms in the German and British regions are much more sceptical about the extent to which ICTs have helped them address the problems associated with their rural location than are the Greek and Portuguese firms. The Polish regions appear to stand out, as they are the ones with the lowest spread of ICTs and the most negative attitudes. Furthermore, the size of the firms is not associated with different evaluations. It is interesting to note that the widespread use of ICTs can also pose a threat to rural areas in the sense that ICTs expose the weaknesses of rural business and make them more vulnerable to outside competition (for example sales through internet auctions).

Conclusion

Rural areas in Europe are very different between as well as within countries. The development constraints that rural peripheral areas of Europe face, may, in great part, be attributed to the limited entrepreneurship apparent in these areas.

The presence of entrepreneurs able to face the problems and exploit the opportunities present in rural peripheral areas should not be taken for granted. Indeed, rural emigration tends to deprive such areas of the most dynamic individuals, who could identify opportunities, and based on their experiences, dynamism and know-how, effectively exploit them. Most recently, rural areas in certain European countries have witnessed a new dynamism, mainly due to a wave of in-migration of relatively affluent formerly urban dwellers who qualitatively affect the features of the rural population as a whole. They often have considerable experience in management, as well as access to networks of information and contacts that are very valuable, and usually non-tradeable resources, for the initiation of business activities.

As discussed earlier, young and educated human capital is crucial for the development of entrepreneurship in European rural peripheral areas to enable them to compete in international markets. However, most European rural peripheral areas still suffer from ageing and depopulation. Hence policies must be developed to secure not only the reduction of out migration but also the instigation of the opposite trend (counter urbanization) that already exists in certain countries (e.g. Britain). A basic prerequisite for that is the provision of a sufficient level of infrastructure (physical and social) in the countryside.

European countries are among the most economically developed in the world. As a consequence, they have to aim for involvement in high value added activities in the international division of labour. This means that European rural peripheral areas have to compete on the basis of quality and value added rather than just price; where less developed countries possess competitive advantages. In this context, investment in human capital (education and training etc.) in rural peripheral areas is essential for expansion. The need for such investments is accentuated by the gradual diminution of the importance of agriculture and the concurrent turn towards more skill intensive activities and pluriactivity.

Notes

1 This chapter is based on the ideas developed in an EU project that I coordinated (Labrianidis et al., 2002). Hence I would like to thank all my partners for their extremely valuable contribution and most of all my fellow co-researchers in the Greek team i.e. Dr Sofia Skordili, Lecturer, Xarokopion University and Dr Thanassis Kalogeressis, Adjunct Lecturer, University of Thessaly and signor researcher in the Regional Development and Planning Research Unit, University of Macedonia.

2 In contrast to aggregative methodologies, such as cluster or factor analysis, where a number of individual regions is aggregated to larger clusters, on the basis of data similarities between them.

3 The data on accessibility was provided by the transport network model of the BBR (former BFLR) (Lutter and Pütz, 1998).

4 That is an unofficial system of political organization based on patronage and 'behind-the-scenes' control within the structure of a representative democracy.

5 That is, the influx of urban migrants into rural areas that often offers an opportunity to revitalize rural economies in terms of demographic, economic and housing consequences (Keeble and Tyler, 1995; Keeble, et al., 1992; Panaiagua, 2002; Townroe and Mallalieu, 1993).

References

Ballas, D., Kalogeressis, T. and Labrianidis, L. (2003), 'A Comparative Study of Typologies for Rural Areas in Europe', *Proceedings of the 43rd European Congress of the Regional Science Association*, Jyväskylä, Finland, 27-30 August.

Baumol, W.J. (1995), 'Formal Entrepreneurship Theory in Economics', in I. Bull, H. Thomas and G. Willard (eds), *Entrepreneurship Perspectives on Theory Building*, Pergamon, New York, pp. 17-33.

Binks, M. and Vale, P. (1991), *Entrepreneurship and Economic Change*, London, McGraw-Hill.

Ceh, B. (2001), 'Regional Innovation Potential in the United States', *Papers in Regional Science, vol. 80*, pp. 297-316.

Cloke, P. (1977), 'An Index of Rurality for England and Wales', *Regional Studies*, vol. 11, pp. 31-46.

Cloke, P. and Edwards, G. (1986), 'Rurality in England and Wales 1981', *Regional Studies*, vol. 20, pp. 286-306.

Clout, H. (1993), 'European Experience of Rural Development', *Strategy Review: Topic Paper 5*, Rural Development Commission.

Cooke, P. and Morgan, K. (1994), 'The Creative Milieu', in M. Dodgson and R. Rothwell (eds), *The Handbook of Industrial Innovation*, Edward Elgar, Aldershot, pp. 25-32.

Cooke, P. and Morgan, K. (2000), *The Associational Economy*, Oxford University Press, Oxford.

Doeringer, P. and Terkla, D. (1990), 'How Intangible Factors Contribute to Economic Development', *World Development*, vol. 18(1), pp. 295-308.

EC (2000), *Migrant Agricultural Workers from non-EU states*, Economic and Social Committee, NAT/051/CES/D/Ho/P/vh.

Ferrão, J. and Lopes, R. (2004), 'Understanding Peripheral Rural Areas as Contexts for Economic Development', in L. Labrianidis (ed.), *The Future of Europe's Rural Periphery*, Ashgate, Aldershot.

Halfacree, K. and Boyle, P. (1998), 'Migration, Rurality and the post-Productivist Countryside', in P. Boyle and K. Halfacree (eds), *Migration into Rural Areas*, J. Wiley & Sons, Chichester.

Herdzina, K. and Blessin, B. (1996), *StrategischeUnternehmensfuehrung als Erfolgsfaktor im Wettbewerb*, Stuttgart.

Herdzina, K. and Nolte, B. (1995), 'Technological Change, Innovation Infrastructure and Technology Transfer Networks', *Industry and Higher Education*, April, pp. 85-94.

Hoggart, K., Buller, H. and Black, R. (1995), *Rural Europe*, Arnold, London.

Ilbery, B. (1998), 'Dimensions of Rural Change', in B. Ilbery (ed.), *The Geography of Rural Change*, Longman, Harlow, pp.1-10.

Kalantaridis, C. (2004), *Understanding Entrepreneurial Behaviour*, Ashgate, London.

Keeble, D. and Tyler, P. (1995), 'Enterprising Behavior and the Urban-Rural Shift', *Urban Studies*, vol. 32, pp. 975-97.

Keeble, D., Tyler, P., Broom, G. and Lewis, J. (1992), *Business Success in the Countryside: the Performance of Rural Enterprise*, PA Cambridge Economic Consultants Ltd, HMSO, London.

King, R. and Rybaczuk, K. (1993), *Southern Europe and the International Division of Labour*, Belhaven, London, pp. 175-206.

Labrianidis, L. (ed.) (2004), *The Future of Europe's Rural Peripheries*, Ashgate, Aldershot.

Labrianidis, L. and Lyberaki, A. (2001), *Albanian Immigrants in Thessaloniki*, Paratiritis, Thessaloniki.

Labrianidis, L., Ferrao, J., Herdzina, K., Kalantaridis, C., Piacescki, B. and Smallbone, D. (2002), *The Future of Europe's Rural Periphery*, financed by European Commission 5th Framework Programme.

Little, J. and Austin, P. (1996), 'Women and the Rural Idyll', *Journal of Rural Studies*, vol. 12(2), pp. 101-111.

Lundvall, B-Å. (1992), 'User-producer Relationships, National Systems of Innovation and Internationalisation', in B-A. Lundvall (ed.), *National Systems of Innovation – Towards a Theory of Innovation and Interactive Learning*, Pinter Publishers, London.

Lutter, H. and Pütz, T. (1998), 'Strategie für einen raum – und umweltverträglichen Personenfernver-kehr', *Informationen zur Raumentwicklung Heft*, vol. 6.

Marsden, T. (1998), 'New Rural Territories', *Journal of Rural Studies*, vol. 14(1), pp. 107-117.

Martinelli, A. (1994), 'Entrepreneurship and Management', in N.J. Smelser and R. Swedberg (eds), *The Handbook of Economic Sociology*, Princeton University Press, Princeton, pp. 476-503.

Morgan, K. (1997), 'The Learning Region', *Regional Studies*, vol. 31(5), pp. 491-503.

OECD (1992), *Technology and the Economy: the Key Relationships*, OECD, Paris.

Panaiagua, A. (2002), 'Counterurbanisation and New Social Class in Rural Spain: the Environmental and Rural Dimension Revised', *Scottish Geography Journal*, vol. 118 (1), pp. 1-18.

Parrott, N., Wilson, N. and Murdoch, J. (2002), 'Spatializing Quality: Regional Protection and Alternative Geography of Food', *European Urban and Regional Studies*, vol. 9(3), pp. 241-261.

Putnam, R. (1993), 'The Prosperous Community: Social Capital and Public Life', *American Prospect*, vol. 13, pp. 35-42.

Rogers, A. (1993), *English Rural Communities*, Rural Development Commission, London.

Saraceno, E. (1994), 'Alternative Readings of Spatial Differentiation', *European Review of Agricultural Economics*, vol. 21, pp. 451-474.

Short, J. (1991), *Imagined Country: Society, Culture and Environment*, Routledge, London.

Townroe, P. and Mallalieu, K. (1993), 'Founding a New Business in the Countryside', in J. Curran and D. Storey (eds), *Small Firms in Urban and Rural Locations*, Routledge, London, pp. 17-53.

Wilken, P.H. (1979), *Entrepreneurship A Comparative and Historical Study*, Amplex, New Jersey.

Williams, R. (1973), *The Country and the City*, Chatto and Windus, London.

Chapter 5

Agri-food Districts:
Theory and Evidence

Cristina Brasili and Roberto Fanfani

The Industrial Districts Approach

There has been renewed interest in the 'industrial district' approach to analysing economic development in the last decades, prompted by the Italian experience. The Italian industrial districts (IDs) are now considered in the national and international literature as one of the main factors in the successful and rapid industrial development of Italy after the Second World War.

The intense and rapid economic and social development of Italy in the post-war period attracted the attention of many researchers and was studied from different perspectives and with different approaches. Traditional dualistic analyses (such as North-South, large-small firms, traditional and modern sectors) were used during the 1950s and 1960s to explain the deep differences within the Italian industrialisation process and how they influenced the country's change.[1]

During the 1970s, the focus of the analysis of development shifted to the decentralisation of activities by the large firms located in North-Western regions, but the role of small and medium sized enterprises (SMEs) became increasingly evident. The decentralisation of parts of productive processes and the production of components outside large firms was regarded as a new strategy, not only to increase productivity but also to promote flexibility in production and in the labour market. At the end of the 1970s, these analyses led to a new geography of Italian development which was influenced by the 'three-Italy' model developed by Bagnasco (1977). He emphasised that the North-West was characterised by concentration of big enterprises, the North-East and the Centre by prevalence of SMEs, while the South was characterised by the greater importance of agriculture and a weak industrial structure.

In the 1980s, the systematic introduction of space and time in the analysis of the economic development of Italy emphasised the presence of different regional patterns of development. The new analysis evidenced the relevance of geographical agglomeration and specialisation of independent SMEs. The pioneering work carried out by Becattini (1987; 1989), and his renewed interest in Marshall's analysis of IDs and external economies of enterprises, stimulated numerous studies (Brusco, 1986 and 1989; Nuti, 1992; Garofoli, 1989). These studies stressed the new role and the different patterns of development of SMEs belonging to the districts compared with that of large enterprises, on one hand, and of isolated SMEs, on the other. Subsequently, the concept of IDs became an important tool for analysing the role of SMEs in the remarkable economic performance of Italy in recent decades.

The complex and diversified process of Italian development at the regional and local level further influenced economic research on IDs, resulting in new definitions and better specification of the main characteristics of the ID concept. Numerous papers focused on the considerable differences existing within IDs and the local system of production: not only the structures and relationships of SMEs, but also the social and historical determinants of these characteristics and the 'life cycle' of IDs (Carminucci and Casucci, 1997). More recently, greater emphasis has been placed on the role of institutions in the development and reshaping of IDs, as well as on the factors influencing the competitiveness of IDs in the national and international market. Furthermore, quantitative analyses have been used in the last decade to evaluate theoretical hypotheses concerning IDs and their performance (Signorini, 1994b and 2000; Bagella and Becchetti, 2000). The analyses of the numerous IDs, of their geographical agglomeration and of regional and local development, have mainly been related to the determinants of endogenous development and so far they have not been closely related to the renewed interest in endogenous growth models. Thus the need arises to overcome these gaps with a view to giving more general support and relevance to regional and local development.

The Theory of IDs and Local Development

The ID approach was rediscovered and adapted by Becattini (1989) in order to improve understanding of recent Italian development. The approach originated from Marshall's (1966) definition of IDs as the aggregation and concentration of many SMEs in one place with the advantages of the division of labour and economies of scale. Marshall's ideas on the spatial concentration of economic activities were regarded as a starting point in the studies of firms' strategies, market structures and industrial competitiveness. Becattini described IDs as a localised thickening of inter-industrial relations with reasonable stability over time. In other words, the Marshallian ID is a socio-economic entity in which there is an active presence of a community of people and a population of enterprises within a limited area. A complex and inextricable network of external economies and diseconomies must exist in order to ensure that a district remains stable over time. These factors are to be understood as external to the enterprise but internal to the region or to the district.[2]

IDs are systems of enterprises and institutions which interface in a specific geographic area to produce specialised and specific types of products. The main characteristics are: 1) close socio-economic relations between firms and families, which evolve jointly and dynamically, with a process of mutual adaptation to changing scenarios; 2) geographical concentration of enterprises with specialised production in a limited area (counties or a few municipalities); concentration and specialisation of production are the key elements in flexibility of production and in the local labour market; and 3) concentration of a network of small and medium-sized independent enterprises, with groups of firms specialised in one stage of the production process and others specialised in specific final products. Inter-firm relations are in many cases based on co-operation and common interests, even if competitiveness plays an important role.

The network relations between enterprises and institutions that characterise IDs are often based on common values shared by families and entrepreneurs, such as the value of work and savings, the propensity to take risk and the exchange of information and technologies. An important role is also played by historical and institutional developments based not only on habits, co-operation and mutual assistance, and community services, but also general services in educational and professional institutions.

The main purpose of ID analysis was to introduce a spatial dimension into the dynamic analysis of Italian development, a factor which was often neglected by traditional economic analysis. Other key elements that the ID approach injected into economic analysis are the relevance of external economies, agglomeration economies and 'industrial atmosphere'. The unique balance between competition and co-operation achieved in IDs, and the division of labour and specialisation within the districts, led to a very successful performance in international markets for several decades (Guerrieri, Iammarino and Pietrobelli, 2001, p. 5).

In Italy, the ID approach was first supported by numerous empirical analyses, which described the regional and local differences between IDs. Analytical efforts to define and describe IDs have been growing over time.[3] The growth of empirical studies brought new insights into many significant aspects related to IDs and local development. In particular, these studies furnished a better understanding of the factors that allow many local economies and SMEs to survive and thrive in an open economy facing national and world competition.

Empirical analyses pointed to considerable differences between the different geographical realities, in terms not only of the type of production specialisation, but also of firms' structures, socio-economic context, relations with national and international markets, productivity and efficiency of production.[4] The predominant geographical location of IDs proved to be the Northern and Central part of Italy, but the most interesting results of these studies was the great importance of exports. In the 65 cases with statistical data, more than half exported over 50 per cent of total production, with an average of about 42 per cent (Sforzi, 1987).

Empirical studies also indicated that Marshall's original definition of IDs is no longer realistic if applied to different productive areas and sectors, such as textiles, clothing, shoemaking or the food industry. Specifically, the structure and role of SMEs change depending on their roles in the networks within the district. This fact led scholars to modify the definition of IDs. A more general term now used in describing the recent Italian experience is 'local system of production' or 'local system of development'.

Different types of models of local development were first proposed by Garofoli (1991) and new contributions were made by Markusen (1996a). They advanced a broader definition of IDs which included several forms of industrial organisation in developed countries and took into account the more successful metropolitan regions of the United States and the impact that larger and multinational firms had on IDs. In particular, they described four types of ID (Marshallian ID; hub and spoke districts; satellite industrial platform, and state anchored ID) according to the main characteristics of the firms, such as size, inter-firm relations and internal versus external orientation (Guerrieri, Iammarino and Pietrobelli, 2001, pp. 17-19).[5]

The changing role of SMEs inside the districts was recently described by Guerrieri, Iammarino and Pietrobelli, (2001), who compared the evolution of SME structures with the emergence of leading enterprises or networks of enterprises. They described three broad modalities of geographical agglomeration of enterprises going from random geographical clustering of firms to IDs and enterprise networks. They also suggested that these are not necessarily sequential stages of development.

The analysis of leading firms and their relations inside and outside the district gained insights from the studies of architecture of smaller firms conducted by Lorenzoni (1990) and Ciciotti (1993). These included different typologies of firm constellations surrounding leading firms (informal, formal and planned constellations) as well as enterprise networks and enterprise groups (Christensen et al., 1990).[6]

In recent decades, the concept of IDs was further developed and applied in a variety of different industrial countries (Pyke, Becattini and Sengenberger, 1990; Garofoli, 1989; Benko and Lipietz, 1992; Schmitz and Musyck, 1994; Markusen, 1996a; Sabel and Zeitlin, 1997; Capello, 1999; Guerrieri, Iammarino and Pietrobelli, 2001) and, in particular, European countries (Crouch et al., 2001). Interesting studies were also focused on developing countries (Rabelotti and Schimtz, 1999; Van Dijk and Rabelotti, 1997; Rabelotti, 1997; Schimtz, 1995; UNCTAD, 1994).

In many respects, the analysis of regional and local development has been receiving increasing attention in connection with the growth in studies of the effect of globalisation. These analyses relied on different concepts and references making it difficult to achieve a systematic comparison of the different experiences of regional and local development in the various countries. The analysis based on IDs (Becattini, 1989; Sabel, 1989; Piore and Sabel, 1984) was accompanied by other approaches, such as 'innovative milieux' (Aydolat, 1986; Maillat, 1995), 'new industrial spaces' (Scott 1988; Scott and Storper, 1992), 'learning regions' (Morgan 1997; Maskell et al., 1998), and 'intelligent regions'. Regional (national) development was also analysed by resorting to the 'industrial cluster' concept (Swann, 1997, Swan et al., 1998), which emphasises geographical proximity and not necessarily specialisation and intra-firm relationships. Industrial clusters were also utilised at the regional level to measure competitiveness, following the suggestion of Porter (1990).[7]

A recent review of the different approaches utilised for regional and local development was carried out by Crouch et al. (2001), who suggested a possible classification of all factors that in different ways influence the success of local economies. The authors clustered these factors into a few groups to allow the different experiences of the regional and local areas in the EU that they investigated to be compared. These were rich external economies (both intangible and tangible), integrated production systems including flexibility, creativity and innovation, and the presence of qualified employees and vocational skills. These groups of factors were considered as the 'local collective competitive goods' that are indispensable for competitiveness and the survival of SMEs in the local system. The production of these collective goods directly involves regional and local institutions. There has been growing interest in the importance of institutions in local development and in the explanation of existing diversities. Crouch et al. (2001) suggested the use of the 'governance approach' to explain the regulation and co-ordination of SMEs and public actors in the system of local and regional development. Local governance takes on a crucial role in making local collective goods available in different forms and quantities and, in many respects, it explains the existing diversities in the path of local development.

As previously noted, the analysis of IDs in recent years has relied on the application of quantitative methods to investigate both the internal and external determinants of ID competitiveness. The main internal factors which may enhance the competitiveness of SMEs belonging to the districts, as previously discussed, may lie in technological and product innovation and its rapid dissemination within IDs; in the level and quality of human resources related to the specific specialisation; in the progressive shift towards intra-firm relationships and common services permitting both vertical and horizontal integration, and in the role played by institutions and local authorities translating into better utilisation of financial resources.

Many studies of the competitive advantage of IDs with particular reference to the analysis of the efficiency and competitiveness of enterprises belonging to the district may be found in Bagella and Becchetti (2000). Quantitative analyses show the positive effect of the 'industrial atmosphere' or of the 'district effect' on enterprise productivity and profitability. The enterprises within IDs also tend to display higher levels of technical efficiency compared with non-district or isolated firms of the same manufacturing sector (Fabiani et al., 2001). This result is, however, not uniform for all the IDs in the different sectors of Italian manufacturing industry.

Interesting results have suggested the positive effect of geographical agglomeration on the relative advantage of imitation in independent R&D efforts, reducing firms' private R&D expenditure. This type of finding resulted, for example, from a study by Bagella and Bechetti (2000) utilising data on the location and R&D expenditure of 4,000 Italian firms. Even if their results are not conclusive for all the sectors and local economies, they exhibit stronger effects in SMEs and in sectors where imitation is an alternative to private investment in R&D (primarily the traditional and state sectors).

The analysis of foreign competitiveness of IDs demonstrates that, at least in the Italian experience, export performance is much stronger in the ID enterprises, especially if they have the same specialisation as the ID where they are located. Bronzini (2000), utilising transition matrices, showed that the most dynamic Italian provinces in terms of exports are those where IDs are more prevalent. Besides, there is evidence that the competitive advantage of IDs in terms of export performance is greater in non-EU markets, where the ID firms have to overcome higher entry barriers (Becchetti and Rossi, 2001). The positive link between geographical agglomeration and export intensity was recently analysed with econometric models by Bagella, Becchetti and Sacchi (2000), who suggested that this is the engine of Italian endogenous growth.

Quantitative analyses of the competitiveness and evolution of the characteristics of IDs are important not only because they offer quantitative measures of district effects, but also because they pinpoint the major weaknesses in numerous studies of local and regional development. In fact, there are many doubts about the possibility of generalising the conclusions drawn by the growing number of analyses carried out in recent years on the outstanding examples of successful local and regional development.

The future advances in quantitative analyses and the growing availability of more disaggregated statistical data at the geographical and sectoral level might give a better understanding of the dynamic evolution of local economies and bring a closer connection to the numerous works on endogenous growth models (Martin and Ottaviano, 1999). The separation of these two fields of research is unfortunate and surprising, since the local and regional development model and the model of endogenous growth both aim to respond to similar questions.

Agri-food Districts in Italy

The rise of IDs in Italy played a crucial role in the rapid process of Italian industrialisation characterised by the presence and persistence of SMEs and by the dissemination of industrialisation in several Northern and Central regions. Until the mid-1980s, the numerous Italian research works carried out on IDs and local systems hardly referred to the agri-food sector. In the late 1980s, the concept of the agri-food system, starting from the seminal works of Davis and Goldberg (1958) and Malassis (1979), stimulated research on the geographical concentration and specialisation of many types of agricultural production and, in particular, of food industries.[8] It was only during the 1990s, however, that several empirical studies showed the presence of agri-food districts and their relevance to the fast and complex changes in Italian agriculture and in the food industry after the second world war (Iacoponi, 1990; Fanfani and Montresor, 1991; Fanfani 1994).

The delay in the development of research on agri-food districts is closely related to the scarcity of research into the role of changes of agriculture in the economic development of Italy. Moreover, there was a delay, especially among agricultural economists, in extending their studies to the growing integration of agricultural production, food processing, retailing and distribution of foodstuffs within the food chain.

In Italy, the value added by the food industry is now reaching and even exceeding that of agriculture and the industry is attracting increasing attention from numerous researchers (Brasili and Fanfani, 2000; Fanfani and Henke, 2001). The increased interest in analysing agri-food districts is also closely connected to the growing importance of food processing industries. There has been a strong tendency towards concentration in the Italian food industry in recent years which has been associated with the creation of some big national groups and with penetration by multinational firms. Nevertheless, SMEs still predominate.

The results of analysing agri-food districts in Italy exhibited two important features. First of all, they have close similarities with other types of IDs, not only in their specialisation and the concentration of production in a limited area, but also in their origin and in the internal organisation of firms. At the same time, they clearly show some of the general limitations of the district methodology.

A specific feature of agri-food districts is their geographical dimension. While IDs are concentrated in a limited area (a few municipalities), the size of agri-food districts varies much more. They may encompass several provinces, as in the case of Parmesan cheese production, or be limited to a part of a province, as in pork processing, or to a few municipalities, as seen in poultry production, and to only one municipality in the case of ham processing in San Daniele (although the meat is supplied from a wider area). Smaller areas are involved in other agri-food districts, such as Vignola's cherries or the flower producing districts (Sanremo, Pescia and Torre del Greco).

The analysis of agri-food districts confirms one of the main strategic weaknesses arising from the use of the ID as an analytical tool. Local systems cannot easily be spread to other areas since the factors responsible for their success cannot readily be transferred (Amin and Robins, 1990). The district implies know-how, skills, traditions and co-operation, institutional involvement in specialised services and infrastructures that cannot be created by using the traditional instruments of regional policy. It is quite possible, however, to devise models of the dynamic processes that are involved in the enhancement of competitiveness, and to create and compare development patterns.

The need to take a local approach to the analysis of the Italian agri-food system was only recently recognised, although there were many previous attempts to disaggregate the complex reality of Italian agriculture at the local level. In the local approach, the analysis starts with the identification of local agricultural systems, of their interrelations with the upstream and downstream stages of agriculture, as well as of the influence of socio-institutional factors on the development of local systems. In the analysis, these interrelations and influences are made progressively endogenous until the 'agri-industrial systems' are defined and characterised (De Rosa, 1996).

Various scholars attempted to extend the interpretation tools of the ID approach by identifying agricultural and agri-food districts. It is worth mentioning that previous studies conducted on agricultural, food or agri-food districts typically could not generalise their results because they referred to special and limited contexts and often took the character of case studies. Among the first studies which tried to introduce the ID concept in the economic analysis of agriculture was the work by Iacoponi (1990), where agriculture still dominates the research, and the study conducted by Fanfani and Montresor (1991), where the concept of 'filière' is extended to the local analysis of the Italian agri-food system.

The studies dealing with specific agri-food districts have been increasingly numerous. Most of them are focused on northern Italy, but some significant analyses also concern Southern Italy. Among the most interesting ones are the studies on the Parmigiano Reggiano system (Bertolini, 1988; Giovannetti 1991) and on the production and processing of pork in the province of Modena (Fanfani, 1994; Mora and Mori, 1995), as well as the analysis of the poultry production system in the provinces of Verona and Forlì. These analyses have been conducted on long-standing and, to some extent, mature agri-food systems. Many other agri-food districts have been described and analysed from the 'red fruits' of Vignola, to the nurseries of Pistoia and neighbouring municipalities and to the vine cuttings of Friuli. An important point of reference for the analysis of local agri-food systems in relation to typical and quality products is the collection of papers presented at the 1997 Parma conferences held in 1997 (Arfini and Mora, 1998).

Long-established and extensively studied agri-food districts showed different origins and different evolution patterns. All of them had a common root, however, namely a strong link with local realities. In fact, the origin of agri-food districts is closely related to the enhancement of the value of local resources and traditions. In many cases, the presence of typical and traditional products represented the basis for the development of art and craft production and preservation activities, which helped overcome problems of seasonality and widen the market. In the case of the local system of production of Parmigiano Reggiano, for instance, compliance with traditional rules of milk and cheese processing was the key to the success of the product both nationally and internationally.

The strong local demand for the typical products of the districts played a critical role in their development, making it possible to achieve scale economies at the initial stage and progressively to diversify the products. The districts which process pork meat for the production of ham and salami (Parma and Reggio Emilia; Modena, and S. Daniele) are cases in point, where a wide range of products is associated with high manufacturing flexibility.

Moreover, the evolution of agri-food districts was favoured by the more general processes of development of Italian agriculture, with gradual concentration and specialisation of production in increasingly narrow areas. Italian farm holdings dropped the practice of producing multiple types of products (typical of self-consumption economies) and became increasingly specialised. Thanks to these trends, the main agricultural products produced in Italy are now concentrated in no more than four or five provinces. The most notable examples are livestock husbandry for milk or meat production, but also the growing of fruit and vegetables (the tomato districts of Piacenza and Parma, on one hand, and of Salerno and Naples, on the other). Furthermore, the link between agriculture and industry in agri-IDs tends to weaken over time and the local processing industry often relies on supplies from outside its own district.

Additionally, local institutions and authorities often play a crucial role in the agri-food districts. However, this role is often overlooked or regarded as negligible not only in the creation and management of general services, but also in the supply of specific services to local enterprises. Their action is instrumental in designing and implementing economic policy programmes and projects targeted at the individual districts. An increasingly significant role in these is played by the local implementation of EU policies. Economic analysis disregarded the role of institutions, not only in terms of the creation and availability of general services (such as education, health and transportation), but also, and above all, from the standpoint of creation of infrastructures and real services for enterprises. Indeed, local authorities play a fundamental role in many consortia and companies providing services to enterprises by facilitating and funding these initiatives.

Investigations of food districts have became increasingly frequent in recent years. Despite the availability of empirical analyses and the rising amount of statistical data, there are still difficulties in singling out the features of and criteria for the definition of food districts. Our efforts were aimed at developing an accurate and reliable methodology for identifying the main districts of the Italian agri-food system. For this purpose, we defined and used six indicators of location, concentration and specialisation (each for local units and employees).[9]

The patchwork distribution of food industry labour and firms is shown in previous studies and by the analyses based on food industry location, concentration and specialisation indicators. These suggest the existence of local production systems and thus the need for conducting more detailed analyses at the local level in order to identify these systems. Indeed, on the basis of the above-mentioned methodology, we identified numerous local systems (and districts) for the main branches of the food industry. For example, the local systems of the dairy industries of the Grana Padano area between the provinces of Milan and Mantova; this area also accommodates large beef and pork slaughter-houses which supply numerous other areas where meat processing is concentrated. Another example is the Parmigiano Reggiano area, which hosts not only establishments for making this cheese, but also major meat (especially pork) production and processing firms. Establishments which produce mozzarella coexist with tomato processing industries in the Southern Italian localities of Caserta and Salerno in Campania. In all these 'local' systems, we observe two key factors, namely the aggregation of municipalities and systems which go beyond provincial or regional borders.

For more than two decades, the importance of local-level analyses has not been paralleled by a policy aimed at acknowledging the positive distinctive features of the local systems of SMEs and, particularly, of local districts. For various reasons, this was a particularly problematic factor for the Italian food industry.[10] Our previous studies show that in both Northern and Southern Italy these local systems are more relevant and may play a more important role, than they have done so far, in the new development policies for Southern Italy.

Efficiency Analysis of Agri-food Districts

Introduction

The quantitative analyses of agri-food districts are far behind those developed recently on IDs. As we have seen in the previous section, the development of quantitative analysis of IDs has taken into account the many determinants of ID competitiveness (technological and product innovation, the level and quality of human resources, the economic performance of the district enterprises, their export performance and competitiveness). In contrast, quantitative analyses of the agri-food districts have, up to now, been limited to some particular aspects, as we will show.

In the past few years, a considerable number of studies, based on balance sheet data showed a clear district effect on the return ratios of firms (Fabiani and Pellegrini, 1998; Fabiani, Pellegrini, Romagnano and Signorini, 2000; Signorini, 1994). These analyses covered the main manufacturing sectors, including food. The latter was no exception, and the rate of return on investment (ROI) and rate of return on equity (ROE) of district firms were sharply higher than those of non-district ones (Fabiani and Pellegrini, 1998).

Building on these findings, the present research estimated a stochastic frontier production function for two sectors, meat and fruit and vegetables, with a view to assessing the district effect. These two sectors were chosen not only because of their importance but also for their substantial diversity. Two districts within each sector were included in the analysis. The food districts included were identified with the methodology described in Brasili et al. (1998).

The data utilised to analyse the meat and fruit and vegetable sectors consisted of a panel of firms derived from the general data bank of manufacturing industries. The firms belonging to the meat and fruit and vegetable sectors were selected from the balance sheets of the food industry (covering more than 3,800 firms) for the years 1996-1999. Further details of the data are given prior to the discussion, in turn, of the analysis of the two sectors.

Efficiency of Firms in Meat Districts

For the meat processing sector, the balance sheets of a panel of 446 meat processing firms (minimum turnover of 1 million euro), which were active in Italy between 1996 and 1999, were studied. Smaller firms decreased in importance between 1996 and 1999 in favour of firms with over 100 employees. In 1999, the number of employees among this panel of firms totalled 24,018, mainly concentrated in the larger firms (15,532 employees).

Table 5.1 Size distribution of panel of firms in the meat sub-sector

	Number of firms				Number of employees			
Employment size	1996	1997	1998	1999	1996	1997	1998	1999
<20	236	231	226	233	2,384	2,393	2,330	2,145
20 – 100	167	172	173	166	6,358	6,496	6,545	6,341
>100	43	43	47	47	14,551	13,957	15,300	15,532
Total	446	446	446	446	23,293	22,846	24,175	24,018

Source: Derived from Cerved data (balance sheets data bank)

Two meat districts were chosen for study. These were the Parma and Reggio Emilia and San Daniele ham producing districts. These districts are economically important within Italy's agri-food industry and epitomise the made-in-Italy brand, increasingly popular both in Italy and abroad (Becattini, 1998). The two districts – although both (mainly) ham production areas – showed strikingly different structural and economic features. The importance of these districts can be briefly described as follows.

The Parma and Reggio Emilia district can be considered as the main system specialising in meat processing (Brasili, 1999). Our previous studies indicated that it included as many as 22 municipalities (15 in the Parma province and 7 in the Reggio one); the district encompassed 516 local units and 4,600 employees. Almost one quarter of the employees were concentrated in the municipality of Langhirano, playing a central role in this local system. Indeed, 65 per cent of all manufacturing employees and as much as 95 per cent of employees in the food industry worked in the meat sector of the municipality of Langhirano. The average size of firms was small in terms of employees (nine per local unit), due to the great proportion of firms exclusively devoted to ham seasoning.

The Parma and Reggio Emilia meat district specialised in pork meat processing. Parma ham was undoubtedly the most valuable local product and is one of the most typical products of Italy's food industry. Its salient feature is that it derives from processing the so-called 'heavy pig', i.e. heads of livestock of 180 kilograms or more. The pigs are raised mainly in the area and, after processing, the ham is seasoned for 12 months or more in the Langhirano firms.

The San Daniele local system, in contrast, covered just the one municipality; where 35 local units and 430 workers were located. This district specialised exclusively on it's typical San Daniele ham seasoning, stocking and marketing; all the raw material came from outside the municipal borders.

The first step in the analysis was to build a balanced panel of firms (446) in the meat sector for the years 1996 to 1999. We classified the firms as follows: non-district firms (306); firms in the Parma and Reggio Emilia district (60); firms in the San Daniele district (10), and firms in other Italian districts (70). Some financial characteristics of the meat firms belonging to these groups are now reviewed in order to determine whether there was a district effect before presenting the analysis of technical efficiency.

The analysis used the most common financial ratios such as ROE, which was calculated as the ratio of the net profit to the company's capital or equity (per cent). Labour cost per employee was also used (in millions of Italian lira per employee) and the innovation ratio, calculated as the ratio of intangible fixed assets to total assets (per cent). The median value of the economic ratios was used because the simple average is more influenced by outliers, which are frequent in the case of balance sheet data.

The Parma and Reggio Emilia and San Daniele meat processing districts generally showed higher returns. In fact, the two districts had a ROI higher than 6 per cent in almost all the years considered (except for the ROI of the Parma and Reggio Emilia district in 1999), while all the other districts and the non-district firms had ROIs lower than 6 per cent (Table 5.2). The ROE never exceeded 3 per cent in non-district firms, whereas in the Parma and Reggio Emilia and San Daniele districts it only fell below 3 per cent once (in 1996 in San Daniele). This confirms the higher return ratios for the firms located in the districts also found in other studies conducted on Italian districts (Signorini, 1994b; Fabiani and Pellegrini, 1998).

Labour productivity was much higher in the Parma and Reggio Emilia and San Daniele district firms (over 30-40 million Italian lira per employee) than in the firms located in the other districts and for the non-district firms. In line with the findings of Signorini (1994b), labour costs were also higher in these district firms because of generally higher salaries; this was true of the Parma and Reggio Emilia district in particular. However, the higher labour costs were more than offset by higher labour productivity. The last variable considered was the debt ratio. This generally turned out to be lower in these districts and they displayed less recourse to external finance.

Table 5.2 Meat sector: balance sheet ratios (median)

R O I (%)	1996	1997	1998	1999
Parma and R .Emilia district	7.0	7.0	6.3	4.4
S. Daniele district	6.7	6.7	7.0	7.0
Other meat districts	5.7	5.3	6.0	4.4
Other meat firms	5.0	4.8	5.5	4.6
Total	5.4	5.1	5.6	4.6
R O E (%)	1996	1997	1998	1999
Parma and R. Emilia district	3.8	6.6	5.5	3.4
S. Daniele district	2.8	3.5	4.5	7.4
Other meat districts	4.2	4.1	3.8	2.6
Other meat firms	2.6	2.8	2.9	2.6
Total	2.9	3.4	3.4	2.8
Labour productivity	**1996**	**1997**	**1998**	**1999**
(millions per employee)				
Parma and R. Emilia district	127.8	138.2	138.9	136.5
S. Daniele district	128.2	122.8	129.3	133.2
Other meat districts	90.4	93.1	95.0	97.8
Other meat firms	87.9	91.3	90.7	97.9
Total	94.6	97.7	97.9	102.5
Labour cost per employee	**1996**	**1997**	**1998**	**1999**
(millions)				
Parma and R. Emilia district	62.7	65.2	56.9	66.9
S. Daniele district	54.6	54.4	50.8	55.4
Other meat districts	55.1	55.3	52.7	55.7
Other meat firms	51.4	53.0	50.1	54.2
Total	53.6	54.6	51.0	55.6
Debt ratio (%)	**1996**	**1997**	**1998**	**1999**
Parma and R. Emilia district	3.7	3.7	3.9	3.9
S. Daniele district	2.6	2.4	2.1	2.1
Other meat districts	5.4	5.3	5.5	5.7
Other meat firms	6.1	6.2	6.0	5.9
Total	5.6	5.5	5.5	5.6

Source: Derived from Cerved data

A stochastic frontier production function was estimated to identify the existence of a district effect on the efficiency of meat processing firms; this involved estimating individual fixed effects relating to meat processing firms belonging to district and non-district firms. A positive district effect was equivalent to a reduction of the technical inefficiency of a given firm. To achieve this goal, a parametric methodology was employed which has already been used in previous research on other sectors of the processing industry (Fabiani et al., 1998; Fabiani and Pellegrini, 1998; Signorini, 1994b).[11]

The above-mentioned stochastic frontier production function was estimated for the 446 firms as follows:

$$\ln(Y_{it}) = \beta_0 + \beta_1 trend + \beta_2 \ln(L_{it}) + \beta_3 \ln(K_{it}) + (v_{it} - u_{it}) \qquad (1)$$

where:

Y_{it} is the value added of the i-th firm at time t;

L_{it} the i-th firm's number of employees at time t;

K_{it} is the value of the net tangible assets of the i-th firm at time t;

v_{it} is a random variable independently and identically distributed according to a normal with null medium and σ_v^2 variance; v_{it} is assumed to be non-correlated with regressors and technical coefficients.

L_{it} The effect due to technical inefficiency u_{it} is specified as follows:

$$u_{it} = \delta_0 + \delta_1 (PR\text{-}REdistr_i) + \delta_2 (SanDanieledistr_i) + \delta_3 (OtherMeatdistrs_i) + \delta_4 (<20empl_i) + \\ \delta_5 (20\text{-}100empl) + \delta_6 (NE_i) + \delta_7 (NW_i) + \delta_8 (Centre_i) + \delta_9 (TecInnInd) + \omega_{it} \qquad (2)$$

where ω_{it} are non-negative random variables measuring technical inefficiency and assumed to be independently distributed along a truncated normal $N(m_{it}, \sigma_u^2)$, and where $m_{it} = z_{it}\delta$ and where z_{it} is the vector of 9 explanatory variables which – in our opinion – may affect the technical efficiency of the firm in equation (2).

The coefficients δ are parameters to be estimated.[12] δ_1, δ_2 and δ_3 are the coefficients of the dummies that refer to district location, while δ_4 and δ_5 are the coefficients relative to the size of the firms. The three dummies δ_6, δ_7 and δ_8 represent the geographical location of the firms in Italy. Finally, δ_9 is the coefficient of the index chosen as a proxy for technical innovation (in particular, it is not an investment in tangible assets).

The main results of the efficiency analysis are given in Table 5.3. The coefficient of the district variable was significant and of the expected sign for firms in the Parma and Reggio Emilia district (about -0.9) with respect to those not included in the meat districts. Moreover, it had the expected sign but a much lower absolute value in the other districts (-0.5 in the San Daniele meat district and -0.2 in the other meat districts).

Size class and geographical location were other distinctive factors in the efficiency of meat industry firms, but in a contrasting way. Inefficiency was higher in small firms, roughly twice as high as in the larger firms. Moreover, belonging to the North-West, North-East and Central geographical areas was a factor decreasing inefficiency compared with belonging to the South of Italy (more than -0.2). Lastly, the coefficient of technological innovation had the expected sign (-0.43), denoting a reduction in inefficiency, but it was not significant.

The results obtained broadly corroborated our previous findings, but two important differences should be emphasised. In the meat sector, the district effect remained strong and significant in Parma and Reggio Emilia, while it was less relevant in the other districts. Size was another factor here – larger firms in the meat sector stood out as being more efficient.

Table 5.3 Stochastic frontier production function and technical efficiency parameters for meat firms (1996-1999)

Variable		Coefficient	Standard error	t-statistic	
Intercept	β_0	4.51	0.08	58.39	**
L: number of employees	β_1	0.02	0.01	2.71	**
K: value of net assets	β_2	0.66	0.01	46.03	**
v: random variable	β_3	0.19	0.01	20.20	**
Intercept	δ_0	-1.29	0.39	-3.30	**
Parma and R .Emilia	δ_1	-0.87	0.16	-5.31	**
S. Daniele district	δ_2	-0.52	0.18	-2.85	**
Other meat districts	δ_3	-0.22	0.08	-2.85	**
<20 employees	δ_4	2.04	0.40	5.08	**
20 – 100 employees	δ_5	1.89	0.40	4.74	**
North-East	δ_6	-0.26	0.06	-4.35	**
North-West	δ_7	-0.28	0.06	-4.46	**
Centre	δ_8	-0.23	0.06	-3.59	**
Technical innovation	δ_9	-0.43	0.45	-0.95	
Ratio of variance	γ	0.42	0.05	8.93	**

Source: Our processing of Cerved data

$$\ln(Y_{it}) = \beta_0 + \beta_1 trend + \beta_2 \ln(L_{it}) + \beta_3 \ln(K_{it}) + (v_{it} - u_{it})$$

$$u_{it} = \delta_0 + \delta_1 (PR\text{-}RE\,distr._t) + \delta_2 (San\,Daniele\,distr._t) + \delta_3 (Other\,Meat\,distrs_i) + \delta_4 (<20empl._i) +$$
$$\delta_5 (20-100empl.) + \delta_6 (NE_i) + \delta_7 (NW_i) + \delta_8 (Centre_i) + \delta_9 (TecInnInd) + \omega_{it}$$

$$\gamma = {\sigma^2}_u \Big/ {(\sigma_u^2 + \sigma_v^2)}$$

* significant for $t_{0.05}$ =1.645
** significant for $t_{0.025}$=1.960

Table 5.4 Median efficiency in the meat firms

	1996	1997	1998	1999
Parma and R. Emilia district.	0.887	0.894	0.885	0.890
S. Daniele district	0.825	0.822	0.815	0.830
Other meat districts	0.783	0.783	0.793	0.783
Other meat firms	0.648	0.649	0.647	0.651

Source: Our processing of Cerved data

The median value of the efficiency in the four years was considered for the groups of firms analysed (Table 5.5). This analysis clearly showed higher values in the district of Parma and Reggio Emilia, but also significant differences (only a few values lower than in the Parma and Reggio Emilia district) in the case of the San Daniele district compared to the other meat districts and other meat firms. The values are fairly steady over the years, but show a small increase in the efficiency of the San Daniele district.

Efficiency of Firms in Fruit and Vegetable Districts

A panel of 227 firms was used over three years (1996 to 1998) in the analysis of the fruit and vegetable industry – see Table 5.5. The firms in the panel increased their employment by 21 per cent between 1996 and 1998, and this increase was concentrated in the largest firms (from 6,206 in 1996 to 8,392 in 1998). The smaller firms with less than 20 employees were numerous (50 per cent of firms) but only accounted for 8 per cent of employees. 62 per cent of employment was accounted for by the large firms.

It was more difficult to analyse the district areas in the fruit and vegetable sector for two main reasons. The first is that a restructuring process which sometimes involved downsizing, took place over the past few years in the Romagna area (Emilia-Romagna region) which is the most important area for fruit and vegetable production. This led to some difficulties in tracking the firms within the panel over several years because some of them closed down and others set up joint ventures. The second reason for some difficulties in this sector is that it had less typical products than found in the meat processing sector and thus, it was less characterised in terms of district location and 'made-in-Italy' production.

Table 5.5 Size distribution of panel of firms in the fruit and vegetable sub-sector

	Number of firms			Number of employees		
Employment size	1996	1997	1998	1996	1997	1998
<20	111	112	113	954	986	1,065
20 – 100	90	91	89	3,997	4,225	4,028
100	26	24	25	6,206	8,155	8,392
Total	227	227	227	11,157	13,366	13,485

Source: Our processing of Cerved data

We attempted to analyse the fruit and vegetable processing sector in the same way as the meat processing one, bearing in mind the two above-mentioned problems. The analysis focused on two district areas, namely the Romagna area (specialised in processing of fruits, e.g. peaches, apricots and pears) and the Salerno area (Campania region, which specialises in vegetables, especially tomatoes).

The fruit and vegetable system of the Emilia-Romagna region is concerned with the preservation and processing of fruit and includes all the provinces but with different degrees of importance. According to the 1991census data, this system consisted of 129 establishments and 8,400 employees, Thus, the average size of firms was fairly large.

The fruit and vegetable system of the Campania region ranks second in Italy. The 1991 census shows there were 254 establishments and 5,390 employees. The most important area corresponds to the provinces of Salerno, Naples and Avellino, and specialises in the preservation of vegetables, especially tomato processing. The firms in this area are smaller on average than in the Romagna area.

Four groups of firms were considered in this study. The two most important areas identified from the census data were the area of the Romagna provinces with high concentration and specialisation in fruit processing (the Romagna district) and the processing and preservation establishments in the provinces of Salerno and Naples (the Salerno district). We considered the other district areas and all the other firms not located in the district municipalities as a whole.

There were only nine firms in the Romagna district and, in 1998, their employment decreased to 723 employees from 1,058 in the year before, revealing signs of crisis. There were 37 firms in the Salerno district and employment declined from 2,289 in1996 to 2,000 by 1998. In the 53 other district firms, there were 2,811 employees in 1998. Employees rose only in the non-district firms, from 5,236 in 1996 to reach 7,728 two years later.

The ROI in the Romagna district was about 5 per cent in both 1997 and in 1998 compared with just over 8 per cent in 1996. Conversely, in Salerno, the ROI had the same trend but with values much lower than in both the Romagna district and the other groups (Table 5.6). The ROE was also much higher in the Romagna district than in all the other groups of firms considered, except in 1997, and there was evidence that the other firms had also experienced some difficulties in 1997.

Turning to labour productivity, Romagna displayed the highest value (about 96 millions per employee). By contrast, the labour cost per employee was almost the same in each group, the difference being roughly 3 millions in each year considered (except in the Romagna district in 1996, where it was much higher).

**Table 5.6 Fruit and vegetable sector districts and firms: balance sheet ratios
(median)**

R O I (%)	1996	1997	1998
Romagna	8.2	4.7	5.5
Salerno	3.5	1.5	2.7
Other F. and V. districts	5.2	4.3	4.6
Other F. and V. firms	4.8	4.2	4.3
Total	4.6	3.9	4.2

R O E (%)	1996	1997	1998
Romagna	6.8	0.3	5.7
Salerno	2.2	1.4	2.8
Other F. and V. districts	4.0	1.8	2.7
Other F. and V firms	6.1	3.3	1.5
Total	4.3	2.5	2.4

Labour productivity (millions lira per employee)	1996	1997	1998
Romagna	103.6	75.2	96.5
Salerno	84.8	86.3	81.5
Other F. and V. districts	81.8	84.0	78.1
Other F. and V. firms	80.3	81.0	80.0
Total	350.5	326.5	336.1

Labour cost per employee (millions lira)	1996	1997	1998
Romagna	75.8	49.0	50.3
Salerno	45.1	47.5	47.0
Other F. and V. districts	50.6	47.5	49.1
Other F. and V. firms	51.3	50.2	50.2
Total	50.4	48.9	49.4

Debt. Ratio (%)	1996	1997	1998
Romagna	2.3	2.8	3.5
Salerno	7.0	7.1	5.9
Other F. and V. districts	5.4	6.0	5.9
Other F. and V. firms	5.3	5.3	5.3
Total	5.4	5.7	5.4

Source: Our processing of Cerved data

The debt ratio had the lowest values in the Romagna district in all the years
considered; it was in the range of 2 or 3 percentage points lower than that of the
other groups and 4 per cent lower than the Salerno district. This first analysis gave

evidence of a district effect for the Romagna district and stronger evidence of a restructuring process in the firms belonging to the fruit and vegetable sector.

In the second stage of the analysis, the district effect was again tested in terms of the effect on technical inefficiency due to location of the firm in a district area. A stochastic frontier production function was estimated using the same methodology as in the meat sector discussed previously. In this case, data for 227 firms in the fruit and vegetable processing industry in the years 1996, 1997 and 1998 were analysed.

The above-mentioned stochastic frontier production function was estimated for these firms. The general equation (1) was utilised and the effect due to technical inefficiency u_{it} was specified as follows:

$$u_{it} = \delta_0 + \delta_1(\text{Romagnadistr}_1) + \delta_2(\text{Salernodistr}_1) + \delta_3(\text{OtherFr.-Veg.distrs}_1) + \delta_4(<20empl_i) + \quad (3)$$
$$\delta_5(20-100empl) + \delta_6(NE_i) + \delta_7(NW_i) + \delta_8(Centre_i) + \delta_9(TecInnInd) + \omega_{it}$$

The features of this equation are the same as equation (1) and were discussed earlier when it was first presented.

Table 5.7 Stochastic frontier production function and technical efficiency parameters for fruit and vegetable processing firms (1996-1998)

Variable		Coefficient	Standard error	t-statistic	
Intercept	β_0	3.73	0.09	40.82	**
L: firm's number of employees	β_1	0.01	0.02	0.44	
K: value of the net assets	β_2	0.59	0.02	40.82	**
v: random variable	β_3	0.30	0.02	24.38	**
Intercept	δ_0	0.57	0.18	3.22	**
Parma and R.Emilia	δ_1	-0.12	0.71	-0.17	
S. Daniele district	δ_2	-0.24	0.15	-1.53	
Other meat districts	δ_3	-0.20	0.14	-1.46	
<20 employees	δ_4	-0.89	0.31	-2.87	**
20 – 100 employees	δ_5	-0.22	0.16	-1.35	
North-East	δ_6	-0.40	0.50	-8.11	**
North-West	δ_7	-0.22	0.70	-3.18	**
Centre	δ_8	-0.77	0.31	-2.48	**
Technical innovation	δ_9	1.21	0.98	1.23	
Ratio of variance	γ	0.60	0.09	6.65	**

Source: Our processing of Cerved data

* significant for $t_{0.05}$ =1.645   ** significant for $t_{0.025}$=1.960

The main results of the efficiency analysis for the fruit and vegetables sector are given in Table 5.7. None of the district variables were significant although they had the expected sign (in terms of inefficiency reduction) with respect to the firms not included in the fruit and vegetable districts. The dummies relating to the size of the firms showed negative coefficients (reduction of inefficiency), but were higher for the smallest firms and significant (-0.9). The dummies relative to geographical location were other distinctive factors. Efficiency was higher in the firms belonging to the Centre (-0.8) and to the North-East (-0.4) and also significant, albeit to a lesser extent, in the North-West (-0.2) of Italy as compared with those belonging to the South of Italy (more than -0.2). Lastly, the technological innovation coefficient proved to be positive, but not in terms of the reduction of inefficiency, and it was not significant.

These results confirmed that there was a very small district effect in the fruit and vegetable sector and this effect was smaller than found in the meat sector. This was also true of Romagna and Salerno, the two most specialised areas of production. However, there were some important favourable features in the Romagna district which showed higher return ratios and sharply higher labour productivity. Moreover, the analysis of the median efficiency in the two districts considered and in the other districts showed that the highest efficiency in the three years was recorded in the local system of the Romagna district, while the lowest was observed in the local system of Salerno, confirming the deep differences inside the fruit and vegetable sector (Table 5.8).

Table 5.8 Median efficiency in the fruit and vegetable firms

	1996	1997	1998
Romagna	0.882	0.880	0.886
Salerno	0.684	0.692	0.699
Others districts	0.820	0.825	0.818
Others firms	0.823	0.822	0.813
Total	0.807	0.800	0.798

Source: Our processing of Cerved data

Conclusion

A debate has taken place for many years about the survival and future evolution of IDs and about how the process of globalisation may undermine the factors that characterise and contribute to the competitiveness and success of local and regional development. The numerous works and approaches utilised in the last decade clearly showed the relevance of studying local and regional development. The differences in the models of local development and the numerous factors that influence the changes in local economies might ensure the capability to adapt to changes in the new international scenario. In fact, in recent years, various local and regional economies have changed their competitive position as a result of the influence of globalisation processes. It is also evident that many local and regional economies have a market orientation which has just become global, whereas their production and innovation systems remain primarily local.

In the analysis of the characteristics and dynamic changes of local and regional economies, the agri-food districts hold a particular and specific position. Wide geographical coverage of the food industry is associated with strong sectoral and geographical agglomeration and specialisation. In fact, we have seen that the analysis of the Italian food industries has no relevance if it is limited to the national level. Likewise, it is not sufficient to consider the different sub-sectors of the food industries at the regional level (NUTS 2 under EU standards). It is necessary to extend the analysis to the provincial (NUTS 3) level in order to take into account the numerous food districts and the local systems of production.

The structural analysis of the food industry in Italy clearly reveals higher concentration and specialisation at the municipal level, emphasising the presence of numerous local systems (agri-food districts). The identification and relevance of local systems and districts has been the focus of many analyses in Italy since the end of the 1970s, whilst only in the 1990s have economic-political measures been taken in favour of IDs. Local systems and districts, which are active in the food industry, are much more numerous than those usually taken into consideration in regional and development studies in Italy.

In general, we have seen that the agri-food districts have the same main characteristics and the same factors of competitiveness as the other districts and local economies. Thus, many of the different approaches and concepts utilised for regional and local development could be applied to them. Nevertheless, the agri-food districts have several distinctive features. One of their specific features is represented by the relations between the food processing industry at the core of these districts and agricultural production and structure. Since there are several different stages of these relationships between local food industries and local agricultural production, with a general tendency towards weakening of these links, the agri-food districts may have more complex typologies, making it more difficult to identify and analyse them.

Other distinctive factors of the agri-food districts are their geographical dimensions, ranging from a very limited area (a single municipality) to several provinces and, often, their geographical concomitance with other IDs or agri-food districts. This fact makes it more difficult to work out criteria for their identification.

The different origin of agri-food districts often determines their production characteristics. Since, in many cases, these districts originated from handicraft tradition and specific local demand, their specialised production is often characterised by typical or high-quality products. In the past, as in IDs generally, these products were niche products for specific and limited markets. Now, these products and markets have tended to expand thanks to the opportunities offered by the greater openness of food markets. Moreover, food demand in developed countries has become increasingly differentiated and specific demand for high-quality and typical food products has grown. The higher demand for quality and typical food products might, as we have stressed, widen the possibility for developing local and regional food districts.

As for the other IDs, there are several studies which apply quantitative analyses to agri-food districts to demonstrate whether or not there are significant district effects for the numerous SMEs belonging to the food districts. These quantitative analyses are not yet as well developed as the ones for the other districts, and, up to now, they have been confined to some particular aspects. Nevertheless, some very interesting results have been obtained from the economic and financial analysis of the balance sheets of a large group of firms in the two sub-sectors in Italy (meat processing and fruit and vegetables) by size classes of enterprises.

The economic and financial analysis was carried out by clustering the panel of firms into different groups according to whether they belonged to specific food districts or not. The analysis shows better results for firms inside the local systems, especially for the meat industry. The economic and financial results are better for the districts. Among the firms belonging to the meat districts, the best results are obtained by the firms in the district of Parma and Reggio Emilia, followed by that of San Daniele and by other meat districts. In the fruit and vegetable sector, the best results are recorded in the district of Romagna, with respect to the district of Salerno and to the enterprises not belonging to districts.

The efficiency of the panel of meat processing firms, estimated with the stochastic frontier production function, validates our previous results in terms of the district effect. There are two important differences. In the meat sector, the district effect remains strong and significant in Parma and Reggio Emilia, while it is less relevant in the other districts. Size is another factor determining efficiency in the meat sector, but only larger firms prove to be more efficient.

As to the fruit and vegetable sector, the district effect is limited especially in comparison with the same analysis conducted for the meat sector. Nevertheless, a low positive district effect is observed in the two most specialised areas of production (Romagna and Salerno). There are, in particular, some important factors in favour of the Romagna district namely higher return ratios and the substantially higher labour productivity.

The quantitative analysis of agri-food districts holds promise and needs to be developed further in order to consider the relevance of the district effect not only on the efficiency of enterprises, but also on the role of innovation, market competitiveness, the role of human capital and local institutions. The development of these analyses might shed more light on the characteristics and dynamic evolution of local and regional development in the agri-food systems of different countries and regions.

Notes

1 Valli (1998) reviews the models utilised to interpret Italy's economic 'miracle' during the 1950s and 1960s.

2 The industrial district offers the advantage of lowering both the transaction and interaction costs between agents, without raising co-ordination costs. At the same time, there is a barrier to entry against outside competitors who do not share information co-

ordination, or face the same barriers to exit from the industrial system when confronted with frequent changes (see, among others, Boyer and Saillard, 1995).

3   Sforzi (1987) found about 60 case studies of local development models; at a later stage, other authors put the figure at around 100. There are now several research centres in Italy which study IDs and the local production systems. Examples include the well known and studied firms of Prato and Biella for textiles, Carpi for knitwear, Arezzo and Valenza for jewellery and Sassuolo for ceramics.

4   Great differences also appear in local systems based on the same type of industry. For example, Prato's textile area is characterised by more than 11,000 firms and 48,000 workers, with a gross output exceeding 5,000 billion lire (2.5 million ECU), of which over 50 per cent is exported. In contrast, the number of firms and workers is much lower in the Biella areas (2,300 and 29,000, respectively), with a higher gross output (over 6,000 billion lire), and much smaller proportion that is exported (30 per cent). IDs are predominantly in the Northern and Central part of the country.

5   Recent advances have analysed the role of foreign investment of multinationals and their complementary and positive links with the development of local industry (Markusen and Venables, 1999; Gorg and Strobl, 2002).

6   Analyses of the role and emergence of leading firms inside IDs have been scarce. In the first and well studied textiles district of Prato (Becattini, 1989, 1987), medium sized firms having leadership in the district were present only in the 1960s and 1970s. These firms belonged to important families or were associated with state intervention.

7   For a review of the different approaches, see Amin (1999). See Fanfani and Lagnevik (1995) for a comparison of Porter's and the industrial district approaches with particular reference to the agri-food system.

8   At first, these studies in Italy were concentrated on vertical integration; only afterwards were they focused on agri-food 'filières' and agri-food districts (Fanfani and Montresor, 1991). For 'filière' analyses, refer to Soufflet (1994) in particular. The impressive change in the geography of Italian agriculture was first described by Rossi-Doria (1969), who initiated research on the 'zonizzazione' of agriculture. Further analyses of geographical transformations of Italian agriculture took into account many other variables, such as demographic changes and general socio-economic variables and, in particular, the role of food industries (Cannata and Forleo, 1998; Boccafogli and Brasili, 1998).

9   For details on these parameters and on their use, see Brasili, Fanfani, Pecci, Montresor (1998); Brasili (1999) and the methodological appendix to this chapter. The recent publication of Industrial Census of 2001 will allow a new analysis.

10 The districts were formally recognised only in 1991, under art. 36 of law no. 317. The implementing decree of law no. 317, establishing the parameters for identifying the districts, was enacted only on 21 April 1993. For the purposes of our analysis, it is worth noting that both law no. 317 and the Ministerial Decree adopted the district identification approach proposed by Sforzi (1987). He drew up a map of 61 Marshallian industrial districts by using 1981 data and his studies officially recognised the value of using highly disaggregated municipal and individual data for economic analyses.

11 For the utilisation of the parametric-type functions, see Fabiani, Pellegrini, Romagnani and Signorini (2000), whose conclusions we share.

12 Simultaneous maximum likelihood estimates for the parameters in equations (1) and (2) were made with Version 4.1 of the FRONTIER programme by Tim Coelli of New England University.

References

Amin, A. (1999), 'An Institutional Perspective on Regional Economic Development', *International Journal of Urban and Regional Research*, Vol. 3(2), pp. 365-378.

Amin, A. and Robins, K. (1990), 'The Re-emergence of Regional Economies? The Mythical Geography of Flexible Accumulation', *Environment and Planning: Society and Space*, Vol. 8 (1), pp. 7-34.

Arfini, F. and Mora, C. (1998), 'Typical and Traditional Products, Rural Effect and Agro-industrial Problems', 52nd Seminar of the European Association of Agricultural Economists, Parma.

Aydolat, P. (ed.) (1986), *Milieux Innovateurs en Europe*, Gremi, Paris.

Bagella, M., Becchetti, L. and Sacchi, S. (2000), 'The Positive Link Between Geographical Agglomeration and Export Intensity: The Engine of Italian Endogenous Growth?', in M. Bagella, and L. Becchetti (eds), *The Competitive Advantage of Industrial Districts*, Physica-Verlag, pp. 95-126.

Bagella, M. and Becchetti, L. (eds) (2000), *The Competitive Advantage of Industrial Districts, Theoretical and Empirical Analysis*, Physica-Verlag, Heidelberg and New York.

Bagnasco, A. (ed.) (1977), *Tre Italie. La Problematica Territoriale dello Sviluppo Italiano*, Il Mulino, Bologna.

Becattini, G. (ed.) (1987), *Mercato e Forze Locali: il Distretto Industriale*, Il Mulino, Bologna.

Becattini, G. (ed.) (1989), *Modelli Locali di Sviluppo*, Il Mulino, Bologna.

Becchetti, L. and Rossi, S. (2001), 'EU and Non EU Export Performance of Italian Firms. Is There an Industrial District Effect?', in M. Bagella and L. Becchetti (eds), *The Competitive Advantage of Italian Districts: Theoretical and Empirical Analysis*, Physica-Verlag, Heidelberg.

Benko, G. and Lipietz, A. (eds) (1992), *Les Régions qui Gagnent. Districts et Réseaux: les Nouveaux Paradigmes de la Géographie Economique*, PUF, Paris.

Bertolini, P. (1988), 'Produzioni DOC e Difesa delle Economie Locali: il Caso del Parmigiano-Reggiano', *La Questione Agraria*, No. 30, pp. 97-122.

Boccafogli, F. and Brasili, C. (1998), 'L'Articolazione Territoriale dello Sviluppo Agricolo in Emilia Romagna', *La Questione Agraria*, No. 70, pp. 67-93.

Boyer, R. and Saillard, Y. (eds) (1995), *Théorie de la Régulation. L'Etat des Savoirs*, La Découverte, Paris.

Brasili, C. (1999), 'L'industria Agroalimentare in Italia: i Sistemi Locali e la Sopravvivenza delle Imprese', Tesi di Dottorato di ricerca *in Economia e Politica Agraria*, Università degli Studi di Siena.

Brasili, C. and Fanfani, R. (2000), 'Localizzazione, Specializzazione e Sopravvivenza nell'Industria Alimentare Italiana', *L'Industria*, No. 21, pp. 51-92.

Brasili, C., Fanfani, R., Montresor, E. and Pecci, F. (1998), The Local Systems of the Food Industry in Italy, 52nd Seminar of the European Association of Agricultural Economists, Parma, 19-21 June 1997.

Bronzini, R. (2000), 'Sistemi Produttivi Locali e Commercio Estero: un'Analisi Territoriale delle Esportazioni Italiane', in L.F. Signorini (ed.), *Lo sviluppo locale. Un'indagine della banca d'Italia*, Donzelli, Roma.

Brusco, S. (1986), 'Small Firms and Industrial Districts: the Experience of Italy', in D. Keeble and E. Wever (eds), *New Firms and Regional Development in Europe*, Croom Helm, London, pp. 184-202.

Brusco, S. (1989), *Piccole Imprese e Distretti Industriali*, Rosenberg and Sellier, Torino.

Cannata, G. and Forleo, M.B. (eds) (1998), *I Sistemi Agricoli Territoriali delle Regioni Italiane*, CNR-RAISA project, Milano.

Capello, R. (1999), 'Spatial Transfer of Knowledge in High-technology Milieux: Learning vs. Collective Learning Processes', *Regional Studies*, Vol. 33(4), London, pp. 353-365.

Christensen, P.R., Eskelinen, H., Forsström, B., Lindmark, L. and Och Vatne, E. (1990), 'Firms in Network: Concepts, Spatial Implications and Policy Implications', in Illeris, S. and Jacobsen, L. (eds) *Networks and Regional Development*, NordREFO Akademisk Forlag, Copenhagen.

Ciciotti, E. (1993), *Competitività e Territorio. L'economia Regionale nei Paesi Industrializzati*, La Nuova Italia Scientifica, Roma.

Crouch, C., Le Galès, P., Trigilia, C. and Voelzkov, H. (2001), *Local Production System in Europe: Rise or Demise?* Oxford University Press, Oxford.

Davis, J.H. and Goldberg, R.A. (1958), *A Concept of Agribusiness*, Harvard University Press, Cambridge, MA.

De Rosa (1996), 'L'approccio territoriale all'analisi del sistema agroalimentare', in F. Arfini and C. Mora (eds), Proceedings of 52nd EAAE Seminar, Parma 19-21 Giugno 1997.

Fabiani, S., Pellegrini, G., Romagnano, E. and Signorini, L. (2000), 'Efficiency and Localisation: The Case of Italian Districts', in M. Bagella and L. Becchetti (eds), *The Competitive Advantage of Industrial Districts*, Physica-Verlag, pp. 45-69.

Fabiani, S. and Pellegrini G. (1998), 'Un'analisi quantitativa delle imprese nei distretti industriali italiani: redditività, produttività e costo del lavoro', in *L'Industria*, No. 4, Il Mulino, Bologna.

Fanfani, R. (1994), 'Agricultural Change and Agri-Food Districts in Italy', in D. Symens and A. Jansen (eds), *Agricultural Restructuring and Rural Change in Europe*, Agricultural University, Wageningen.

Fanfani, R. and Henke, R. (eds) (2001), 'Struttura e Specializzazione Territoriale dell'Industria Alimentare Italiana', *INEA Studi e Ricerche*, ESI Editor, Napoli.

Fanfani, R. and Lagnevik, M. (1995), 'Industrial Districts and Porter Diamonds', Paper presented at *Strategic Discovery*, 15th Annual International Conference of Strategic Management Society, Mexico, August 1995.

Fanfani, R. and Montresor, E. (1991), 'Il Sistema Agro-alimentare: Filiere Multinazionali e la Dimensione Spaziale dello Sviluppo', *La Questione Agraria*, No. 41, pp. 165-202.

Garofoli, G. (1989), 'Industrial Districts: Structures and Transformations', *Economic Notes*, No. 1.

Garofoli, G. (1991), *Modelli locali di sviluppo*, Franco Angeli, Milano.

Giovannetti, E. (1991), 'Efficienza ed Innovazione: il Modello "Fondi-flussi" Applicato ad una Filiera Agro-industriale', in *La Questione Agraria*, No. 43, pp. 73-124.

Goglio, S. and Sforzi, F. (1993), 'Le Differenziazioni Regionali in Italia', *Annali Scientifici dell'Università di Trento*, No. 5-6/92.

Gorg, H. and Strobl, E. (2002), 'Multinational Companies and Indigenous Development: An Empirical Analysis', *European Economic Review*, Vol. 46(7), pp. 1305-1322.

Guerrieri, P., Iammarino, S. and Pietrobelli, C. (eds) (2001), *The Global Challange to Industrial Districts*, Edward Elgar, UK.

Iacoponi, L. (1990), 'Distretto Industriale Marshalliano e Forme di Organizzazione delle Imprese in Agricoltura', *Rivista di Economia Agraria*, No. 4, pp. 711-744.

Lorenzoni, G. (1990), *L'Archiettura di Sviluppo delle Imprese Minori*, Il Mulino ed., Bologna.

Maillat, D. (1995), 'Territorial Dynamic, Innovative Milieus and Regional Policy', *Entrepreneurship & Regional Development*, No. 7, pp. 157-165.

Malassis, L. (1979), *Economie Agroalimentaire*, Cujas, Paris, p. 437.

Markusen, A. (1996a), 'Sticky Place in Slippery Space: a Typology of Industrial District', *Economic Geography*, Vol. 72(3), pp. 293-313.

Markusen, A. (1996b), 'Big Firms, Long Arms, Wide Shoulders: The "Hub and Spoke" Industrial District in The Seattle Region', *Regional Studies*, Vol. 7(30), pp. 651-666.

Markusen, J. and Venables, A. (1999), 'Foreign Direct Investment as a Catalyst for Industrial Development', *European Economic Review*, Vol. 3(43), pp. 335-356.

Marshall, A. (ed.) (1966), *Principles of Economics*, Macmillan, London.

Martin, P. and Ottaviano, G. (1999), 'Growing Location: Industry Location in a Model of Endogenous Growth', *European Economic Review*, Vol. 2(43), pp. 281-302.

Maskell, P., Eskelinen, H., Hannibalsson, I., Malmberg, A. and Vatne, E. (1998), *Competitiveness, Localized Learning and Regional Development: Specialization and Prosperity in Small Open Economies*, Routledge, London.

Mora, C. and Mori, S. (1995), 'Sulle tracce dei distretti agro-industriali: un caso di studio', *La Questione Agraria*, No.59.

Morgan, K. (1997), 'The Learning Regions: Institutions Innovation and Regional Renewal', *Regional Studies*, Vol. 5(31), pp. 491-503.

Nuti, F. (ed.) (1992), *I distretti dell'Industria manifatturiera in Italia*, Franco Angeli, Vol. 1 e Vol. 2, Milano.

Piore, M. and Sabel, C. (eds) (1984), *The Second Industrial Device: Possibilities and Prosperity*, Basic Books, New York.

Porter, M.E. (ed.) (1990), *The Competitive Advantage of Nations*, Macmillan, London.

Pyke, F., Becattini, G. and Sengenberger, W. (eds) (1990), *Industrial Districts and Interfirm Co-operation in Italy,* International Institute for Labour Studies, Geneva.

Rabelotti, R. (ed.) (1997), *External Economies and Co-operation in Industrial Districts: A Comparison of Italy and Mexico*, Macmillan, London.

Rabelotti, R. and Schimtz, H. (1999), 'The Internal Heterogeneity of Industrial Districts in Italy, Brazil and Mexico', *Regional Studies*, Vol. 2(33), pp. 97-108.

Rossi- Doria, M. (1969), *Analisi Zonale dell'Agricoltura Italiana*, INEA, Roma.

Sabel, C. (1989), 'Flexible Specialization and the Re-emergence of Regional Economies', in P. Hirst and J. Zeitlin (eds), *Reversing Industrial Decline*, Berg, New York.

Sabel, C. and Zeitlin, J. (eds) (1997), *Worlds of Possibilities: Flexibility and Mass Production in Western Industrialization*, Cambridge University Press, New York.

Schmitz, H. (1995), 'Collective Efficiency: Growth Path for Small-scale Industry', *Journal of Development Studies*, Vol. 31(4), pp. 529-566.

Schmitz, H. and Musyck, B. (1994), 'Industrial Districts in Europe: Policy Lessons for Developing Countries', *World Development*, Vol. 22(6), pp. 889-910.

Scott, A. (1988), *New Industrial Space: Flexible Production Organization and Regional Development in North America and Western Europe*, Pion, London.

Scott, A. and Storper, M. (1992), 'Regional Development Reconsidered', in H. Ernste and V. Meier (eds), *Regional Development and Contemporary Industrial Response*, London.

Sforzi, F. (1987), 'L'identificazione Spaziale', in G. Becattini (ed.), *Mercato e Forze Locali: Distretto Industriale*, Il Mulino, Bologna.

Signorini, L.S. (1994a), 'The Price of Prato, or Measuring the Industrial District Effect', *Papers in Regional Science*, Vol. 73(4).

Signorini, L.S. (1994b), 'Una Verifica Quantitativa dell'Effetto Distretto', in *Sviluppo Locale*, Vol. 1, pp. 31-70.

Signorini, L.S. (ed.) (2000), *Lo Sviluppo Locale: un'Indagine della Banca d'Italia sui Distretti Industriali*, Donzelli ed., Roma.

Soufflet, J-F. (1994), 'Food Quality Policies and Competition in the Food Chain: Lessons for Farmers', Paper for the 36th Seminar of the European Association of Agricultural Economists at The University of Reading, 19-21 September.

Storper, M. (1989), 'The Transition to Flexible Specialization in the US Film Industry: The Division of Labour, External Economies and the Crossing of Industrial Divides', *Cambridge Journal of Economics*, Vol. 13, pp. 273-305.

Storper, M. and Harrison, B. (1989), 'Flexibility, Hierarchy and Regional Development: the Changing of Industrial Production Systems and their Forms of Governance', International Conference on Industrial Policy: the Regional Experience, Bologna, November.

Svensson, M. (1993), *Structure, Strategy and Competition in the Danish Dairy- and Pork-businesses, School of Economics and Management*, Lund University.

Swann, G. (1997), 'Toward a Model of Clustering in High-technology Industries', in G. Swann, M. Prevezer and D. Stout (eds), *The Dynamics of International Clusters*, Oxford University Press, Oxford.

Swann, G., Prevezer, M. and Stout, D. (eds) (1998), *The Dynamics of International Clusters*, Oxford University Press, Oxford.

UNCTAD (1994), *Technological Dynamism in Industrial Districts: An Alternative Approach to Industrialization in Developing Countries*, United Nations, Geneva.

Valli, V. (ed.) (1998), *Politica Economica*, Carocci, Vol.1, Roma.

Van Dijk, M. and Rebelotti, R. (eds) (1997), *Enterprises, Clusters and Networks in Developing Countries*, Frank Cass, London.

Chapter 6

The Embeddedness of Small Enterprises within the Rural Local Economy of Small and Medium Sized Towns

Eveline S. van Leeuwen and Peter Nijkamp

Introduction

Modern Europe has rural roots. Even nowadays, 80 per cent of Europe consists of rural areas in which just 25 per cent of the population lives. These areas are quite diverse not only geographically and in terms of landscape, but also in terms of the different challenges they face. These challenges range from the restructuring of the agricultural sector, remoteness, poor service provision and depopulation to population influx and pressure on the natural environment, particularly in the rural areas close to urban centres.

It appears that economies in rural areas are characterized by a wide range of economic activities (Terluin, 2001). Although the problems of rural areas are often stressed, the role of rural towns in these areas is noteworthy. Such towns evolved over many years to serve a range of functions – economic, social and administrative – both for their own inhabitants and the surrounding countryside (Courtney and Errington, 2000). These small and medium sized towns (with a population of 5,000-20,000) form an important component in the present national economic structures, especially when taking into account the declining importance of the agricultural sector. They are likely to be very important in the future as urban and rural areas are dependent on each other and as, simultaneously, the direct functional relationships are changing because of new technologies.

Agriculture plays an important role in rural areas. A unique feature of the agricultural sector is its physical link to the soil conditions and therefore its strong relationship with its surroundings. Although the primary sector has become less important in terms of its economic weight and share in employment in most rural areas, agriculture and forestry are still the main land users and they play a key role in the management of the natural resources and in determining the rural landscape and cultural heritage. In spite of its reduced share in overall economic activities, these interdependencies mean that agriculture still has a valuable contribution to make to socio-economic development and to the full realization of the growth potential of rural areas (European Communities, 2003).

Changes within the agri-food sector have had a significant impact on many small and medium sized towns and still form a distinctive component of rural areas. Indeed, they may have an increasingly important role to play in the future diversification of the rural economy and the establishment of multifunctional agriculture. The major challenge currently facing rural areas in Europe is to find and promote appropriate forms of economic development to maintain and improve their social and economic vitality as they adjust to the changing demands placed upon them by society and by the market economy (Courtney and Errington, 2000). Small enterprises can play a key role in this new development context.

This is because the rural economy is generally characterized by small enterprises. For example, almost 90 per cent of employees in the Netherlands work in firms with less than ten people. The percentage is even higher in rural areas as larger offices often are situated in cities or highly urbanized areas. With the relentless decline in employment in agricultural and other traditional rural industries, the identification and encouragement of new sources of jobs for those living in rural communities has become a key priority. It is increasingly believed that most of the new jobs in rural areas are going to come from new and existing small firms, not just from service sectors like tourism but also from some of the lighter manufacturing industries (Tarling et al., 1993). According to North and Smallbone (1996), one of the most important findings from a wealth of the recent research comparing the performance of small businesses in urban and rural locations is that rural firms have shown a superior employment performance to urban firms.

Given the prominent position of rural areas in the economic and geographic landscape of almost all countries, it is interesting to know the extent to which these areas are locally or regionally integrated in terms of linkages between local firms and their surroundings. This chapter focuses on the role of small enterprises in small and medium sized towns located in Dutch rural areas. The analysis distinguishes agricultural firms (referred to hereafter as 'farms') and non-agricultural firms (referred to as 'firms'). There are two reasons for making this distinction. First, there are important differences between the characteristics of firms and farms and, second, it allows spatial linkage characteristics between farms and the firms in nearby towns to be compared. The analysis uses survey information derived from the Marketowns project funded by the European Commission.[1] A large quantity of data about the sales, purchases and employment of firms and farms is available for six different towns in each of five countries, including the Netherlands. With the help of this information, the chapter illustrates the differences in the local embeddedness of small firms and farms.

Rural Areas in the Netherlands

Settlement patterns of small and medium sized towns vary between different parts of Europe. While some of their determinants are universal – such as agglomeration economies – others vary. In the most densely populated countries such as the Netherlands, for example, strong national planning controls have sought to contain economic activity and housing within towns to protect the surrounding countryside. In addition, concern about the social viability of small rural communities in the Netherlands has generated several policy initiatives to protect small villages and hamlets in rural areas. Rural settlements are quite diverse as a result and some of the smallest ones are merely 'dormitory' settlements for bigger towns. In other countries, various settlement patterns are found with some very small settlements still containing a relatively wide range of economic activities (van Leeuwen and Mayfield, 2004).

The Netherlands is a small and very densely populated country with a high degree of urbanization. This greatly affects the significance and use of the countryside. 70 per cent of the Netherlands is made up of agricultural areas (including roads and waterways); 13 per cent is taken up by building development and transport, and 14 per cent consists of woodland and nature areas. Many small and medium sized towns are located in the rural areas. Around 55 per cent of the Dutch population lives outside the 20 main urban agglomerations. Only a limited proportion works in agriculture, and this proportion is expected to decrease further as more citizens choose to live in small towns or in the countryside but not to engage in agriculture. Changes in the primary sector are expected to affect these areas in future. Increasing efficiency is seen as likely to lead to growing unemployment, increased commuting and the exit of young people and these kinds of effects will reduce the quality of life in the local community. Environmental policy and market developments are drastically changing agricultural practices and land-use. Spatial and regional planning will have to offer sufficient scope for the establishment and expansion of agricultural business and different uses of agricultural land if farmers are expected to continue to keep up with social, economic and technological developments.

Nowadays, new economic activities, such as recreation and tourism, are developing in rural areas. The decrease in agricultural activity has led to a decline of service provision in the countryside. The increase in other activities can, however, compensate for this lack of provision. The countryside, with its characteristic peace, space and local identity is becoming increasingly important to urban centres and urban dwellers.

The Data

The data used in this chapter has been derived from the European Union research project 'Marketowns'. The Marketowns project focuses on the role of small and medium towns as growth poles in regional economic development. The flows of goods, services and labour between firms and households in a sample of six small and medium sized rural towns for each of five EU countries were measured for this purpose. The countries reflect the varied conditions of the existing and enlarged EU, viz. France; Poland; Portugal; the Netherlands, and the UK.

Small and medium sized towns in each of the five participating countries have been identified for inclusion in the sample on the basis of three criteria. The first is the type of rural area (namely agricultural, tourist and peri-urban areas) according to the employment level. The second criterion is that no other town with more than 3,000 inhabitants is located in its hinterland (defined as approximately seven kilometres.). Third, the population size of the town is taken into account when small towns and medium towns are distinguished and three of each type are selected for inclusion. Table 6.1 shows the small and medium sized towns in the Netherlands featuring in this study.

Table 6.1 Selected small and medium sized towns in the Netherlands

	Small towns (5-10,000 population)	Medium sized towns (15-20,000 population)
Area where employment in agriculture is above national average	Dalfsen	Schagen
Area where employment in tourism is well above national average	Bolsward	Nunspeet
'Accessible' peri-urban area within daily commuting distance of metropolitan centre	Oudewater	Gemert

Source: Terluin et al. (2003)

Several zones around each town are distinguished to facilitate the measurement of economic linkages of firms and households. The town centre is classified as zone A, the area within a circle of seven kilometres around the town-centre as zone B (the hinterland of the town-centre), the area within seven to 16 kilometres around the town-centre as zone C, and the metropolitan centre (in case of the peri-urban towns) as zone D. The remainder of the province is classified as zone E, the rest of the country as zone F, the rest of the EU as zone G and the rest of the world as zone H. Data have been gathered for each town (zone A) and the immediate surrounding countryside (zone B) from a systematic sample of farming and non-farming households, and farming and non-farming businesses respectively, using postal questionnaires and face-to-face interviews (Terluin et al., 2003).

During the project a total of 18,000 questionnaires were sent out to firms, farms and households in the Netherlands alone, of which 16 per cent were filled in correctly and returned. Table 6.2 shows the usable response for the six Dutch towns.

Table 6.2 Number of usable responses by firms and farms in the six Dutch towns

	Dalfsen	Schagen	Bolsward	Nunspeet	Oudewater	Gemert
Firms	125	136	150	144	126	147
Farms	87	70	64	26	81	87

Source: Terluin et al. (2003)

Embeddedness Indicators (EIs)

Embeddedness emphasizes the importance of social relations in generating trust and discouraging opportunism and also the significance of the linkages that an enterprise may have with a network of enterprises within the region. These include links with local suppliers and customers which are formed by firms in order to help in their activities.

Small and medium sized towns are valuable for future rural development because the concentration of initiatives within these settlements takes advantage of the presence of agglomeration economies and of the existing networks. At the same time, there is the possibility of spreading out the benefits (in terms of both employment and income) from these sub-poles into the surrounding countryside in a way that meets the economic objectives of sustainable rural development.

This spread of benefits into the surrounding countryside is a very interesting phenomenon. Embeddedness indicators (EIs) can be used to measure the linkages existing between small enterprises in small and medium sized towns and the surrounding countryside. These indicators show the proportion of a particular economic activity (input purchases, output sales, employment, etc.) of a particular group of economic entities (e.g., all firms, all households, small enterprises and manufacturing enterprises) allocated to the local economy. For instance, the firms located within town X may derive 25 per cent of their inputs (by value) from other businesses locally (within zone A and B), a further 50 per cent from elsewhere in the country, 5 per cent from elsewhere in the EU and 20 per cent from countries outside the EU. In this case, the local EI for the purchases of this town is 0.25. They may sell only 10 per cent of their outputs to businesses or households in the locality, in which case the local EI for the sales of the town is 0.1. Taken together, and measured for a particular town, these indicators give an immediate measure of the extent to which firms are embedded into their immediate locality or into the national, European or global economy. The indicators derived in this chapter are based on a sample of enterprises and measure the allocation of sales and purchases of the enterprises that responded to the questionnaire.

Table 6.3 The embeddedness indicators and their accompanying zones

Zones	Town	7 km zone	7-16 km zone	City	Rest of province	Rest of country	Rest of EU	Rest of world
	A	B	C	D	E	F	G	H
Local EI	X	X						
Regional EI			X		X			
City EI				X				
National EI						X		
International EI							X	X

Source: Own classification

Five different EIs were explored, as shown in Table 6.3. The local EI has been defined as including the town and the seven kilometre zone around it; the regional EI include the seven-16 kilometre zone around the town as well as the rest of the province. The city EI include the city, if applicable (Gemert and Oudewater); the national EI include the rest of the Netherlands and, finally, the international EI include the rest of the EU and the rest of the world.

Of course, all these EIs are interesting and of importance but as this chapter focuses on the role of small enterprises in small and medium sized towns, the local and regional EIs are especially relevant here. The EIs in the following analysis measure the proportion of purchases, sales and employment of farms and firms allocated to the local and regional economy.

But which values of the different EIs are desirable for the economy of the small and medium sized towns? When a firm or farm buys its inputs on the local market, other (local) actors will have more money to spend. This can lead to new investments or to higher incomes from which local shops and other services in a town can benefit. In turn, this leads to new investments, higher incomes or new jobs. The cumulative effect of this re-circulation of spending is called a 'multiplier effect'. Multipliers are often used in input-output theory. This theory shows that multipliers vary across different sectors of the economy based on the mix of labour and other inputs and the tendency of each sector to buy goods and services from within the region. When sectors import a lot of their inputs from outside the local economy, their spending 'leaks' to the other region and the multiplier effect decreases. Conversely, when sectors sell their products outside the local economy, more money enters the local economy and the multiplier effect increases. This means that desirable effects originate from enterprises that have high local EIs for their purchases and high national or international EIs for their sales. Furthermore, the local economy will benefit from high local employment embeddedness.

Embeddedness of Farms' Purchases and Sales

Unlike firms, farms can be classified into one sector, namely the agricultural sector. Some of the characteristics of farms within this sector are relatively homogeneous with family ownership and a small number of employees being typical, but most of them differ considerably. Therefore the agricultural sector has been disaggregated into five sub-sectors. A data base of 406 farms located in the six towns was used: 242 of the total have between one and three workers including the owner (group 1) and 143 farms have between four and ten workers (group 2). These employment figures represent the number of persons working at the farm and not the full-time equivalents. This affects the size classification of firms, especially in the sub sectors with much seasonal work, such as horticulture.

Table 6.4 shows the EIs of the purchases (P) and sales (S) of farms per sub-sector, related to the size of the farm. The EIs shown in bold indicate the two highest sales and purchase EIs for each sector. The specialist livestock farms, for example, buy most of their input locally and regionally, but sell their products in the region or throughout the rest of the country. In general, most inputs are purchased locally, in the town and its direct hinterland, or in the rest of the region. This holds for almost every sector. At the same time, most of the products are sold on a regional level as well as on a national level. Thus, purchases appear to be more local than sales, which are typically more nationally and internationally oriented.

Table 6.4 Embeddedness of farms' purchases and sales (per cent) by sector and farm size

Sector	Farm size	Local		Region		City		National		International		No. of farms
		P	S	P	S	P	S	P	S	P	S	
Specialist livestock	Group 1	42	23	41	39	6	3	9	28	2	7	80
	Group 2	29	13	32	47	0	3	24	31	16	7	38
	Total	39	19	35	42	1	3	16	29	8	7	118
Mixed livestock	Group 1	47	22	41	36	2	0	10	31	0	10	73
	Group 2	55	39	36	25	1	0	8	22	0	13	45
	Total	49	29	39	34	2	0	11	26	0	11	119
Pig/poultry	Group 1	23	14	42	42	3	2	28	34	5	8	35
	Group 2	30	18	55	39	5	25	6	18	3	0	14
	Total	31	16	44	41	2	13	19	26	4	4	49
Mixed livestock/ arable	Group 1	30	23	48	40	1	1	21	14	0	22	36
	Group 2	29	24	36	25	0	0	8	31	0	1	19
	Total	38	23	52	42	0	0	8	23	2	11	56
Horticulture	Group1	47	13	40	43	0	0	13	9	0	35	7
	Group 2	29	1	52	20	1	0	10	30	8	16	19
	Total	27	3	53	49	0	8	16	33	3	8	45
Total	Group 1	35	20	43	39	3	2	17	29	2	10	242
	Group 2	36	21	46	33	1	6	11	26	5	7	143
	Total	37	18	44	41	1	5	15	29	3	8	406

Source: Own classification

Table 6.4 also shows that the mixed livestock farms and the mixed livestock and arable farms sell more of their products to local and regional buyers whereas horticulture farms have a relatively high share of international sales. In contrast, there are no such striking differences in the behaviour of farms depending on their size although, surprisingly, small farms sell more of their products on the international market. Maybe this is because they sell more products directly and make less use of distributors.

Tables 6.5 and 6.6 respectively show the embeddedness of the purchases and the sales of farms with respect to the small and medium sized towns. Between 60 and 80 farmers responded to the questionnaire in every town except in Nunspeet, where there was a usable response of only 20. It appears that the highest shares of purchases of farms near smaller towns are in the town and its direct hinterland (local). In the medium sized towns, the purchases are more often made somewhere else in the region. Farms near the two agricultural towns (Schagen and Dalfsen) also tend to make most of their purchases in the region. The high share of international purchases of the larger farms in Bolsward is striking. This is due to the concentration of specialist livestock farms in the larger size class (group 2), as shown in Table 6.4

Table 6.5 Embeddedness of farms' purchases (per cent) by farm size and town

Farm size		Local	Region	City	National	International
	Medium towns					
Group 1	Gemert	**55**	32	0	11	2
Group 2		31	**54**	3	11	1
Total		33	**51**	2	13	1
Group 1	Nunspeet	32	**54**	0	14	0
Group 2		**43**	33	0	23	0
Total		34	**49**	0	16	0
Group 1	Schagen	**44**	36	0	21	0
Group 2		35	**49**	0	12	4
Total		41	**42**	0	15	2
	Small towns					
Group 1	Oudewater	**36**	33	6	25	0
Group 2		**45**	44	4	6	0
Total		**38**	36	5	20	0
Group 1	Bolsward	**45**	40	0	15	0
Group 2		37	30	0	16	17
Total		**41**	36	0	16	8
Group 1	Dalfsen	32	**41**	0	18	9
Group 2		38	**42**	0	14	5
Total		35	**42**	0	17	7

Source: Own classification

When looking at the farms' sales related to the kind of town (Table 6.6), it appears that the farms in the agricultural towns sell more products in the rest of the country and the tourist towns (Nunspeet and Bolsward) more in the region. Oudewater stands out because of its high share of international sales. This is mainly due to the sales of mixed livestock farms. There are also significant city EIs in Gemert due to activity in the pigs and poultry sector. When the size of farms is taken into account, it appears that smaller farms have relatively high regional EIs.

Table 6.6 Embeddedness of farms' sales (per cent) by farm size and town

Farm size	Medium towns	Local	Region	City	National	International
Group 1	Gemert	24	**55**	8	13	0
Group 2		19	**43**	17	21	0
Total		14	**51**	16	20	0
Group 1	Nunspeet	12	**73**	0	14	1
Group 2		**54**	40	0	6	0
Total		25	**64**	0	11	0
Group 1	Schagen	22	**33**	0	30	16
Group 2		5	37	0	**46**	11
Total		9	**42**	0	39	11
	Small towns					
Group 1	Oudewater	10	23	4	29	**34**
Group 2		17	24	0	11	**48**
Total		12	23	3	24	**38**
Group 1	Bolsward	22	**45**	0	33	1
Group 2		20	**42**	0	34	4
Total		21	**43**	0	33	2
Group 1	Dalfsen	26	32	0	**40**	2
Group 2		**43**	15	0	42	0
Total		34	24	0	**41**	1

Source: Own classification

Summarizing, purchases of farms are generally more local and sales are more nationally and internationally oriented. The embeddedness of purchases and sales of the different sectors is fairly homogeneous. There is little difference between firms of different sizes. When looking at the six case-study towns, it appears that the shares of the purchases of farms in smaller towns are the highest in the town and its direct hinterland (local). In the medium sized towns, purchases are more often made somewhere else in the region. Furthermore, the two agricultural towns (Schagen and Dalfsen) tend to buy most of their purchases in the region. The local EIs for the sales are generally lower than the indicators for the purchases of the farms.

Embeddedness of Firms' Purchases and Sales

The analysis of the behaviour of firms is based on 533 questionnaires of which most are from relatively small firms. The firms have been disaggregated into eight sectors, many of which belong to the retail or real estate sector. Table 6.7 shows the EIs for firms; the outcomes are much more diverse than those for the farms discussed earlier.

Table 6.7 Embeddedness of firms' purchases and sales (per cent) by sector and firm size

Sector	Farm size	Local		Region		City		National		International		No. of firms
		P	S	P	S	P	S	P	S	P	S	
Manufacturing	Group 1	4	5	37	10	0	0	24	**72**	35	**13**	7
	Group 2	8	24	27	**25**	0	0	42	24	22	**27**	22
	Total	21	4	40	12	0	0	35	**63**	4	**21**	41
Construction	Group 1	23	**44**	47	**43**	3	1	26	11	1	1	34
	Group 2	23	**39**	47	**49**	1	1	23	11	5	0	29
	Total	4	10	21	**45**	1	2	73	**43**	2	0	87
Wholesale and distribution	Group 1	25	13	42	19	4	4	17	**28**	13	**36**	17
	Group 2	4	6	13	8	0	0	41	**48**	41	**38**	20
	Total	6	6	16	17	0	0	41	**44**	37	**33**	44
Retailers	Group 1	14	**66**	23	**26**	0	1	58	7	5	1	45
	Group 2	18	**58**	29	**30**	0	1	42	9	11	2	72
	Total	15	**55**	24	**24**	0	1	56	20	5	1	125
Hotels and restaurants	Group 1	92	**94**	8	**6**	0	0	0	0	0	0	4
	Group2	62	**57**	31	**42**	7	0	0	0	0	0	11
	Total	61	**55**	37	**45**	2	0	0	0	0	0	19
Recreational, cultural and sporting activities	Group 1	72	**43**	13	**39**	1	0	14	18	0	0	17
	Group2	38	**55**	48	21	0	0	13	**23**	1	1	4
	Total	26	25	20	15	0	0	22	**60**	32	0	23
Real estate, renting and business activities	Group 1	7	4	20	**21**	0	1	26	**57**	47	18	82
	Group 2	18	**45**	17	16	2	2	60	**31**	4	6	46
	Total	10	15	21	**22**	2	6	37	**41**	30	15	141
Other services	Group 1	31	**27**	34	20	1	3	32	**50**	2	1	25
	Group 2	29	**68**	23	**14**	0	1	38	13	9	4	16
	Total	21	**39**	34	30	0	0	44	30	1	1	47
Total	Group 1	15	17	28	23	1	1	27	**44**	29	16	231
	Group 2	11	28	21	18	0	1	41	**31**	27	22	222
	Total	11	16	25	28	0	1	52	**42**	11	12	533

Source: Own classification

It appears that, just as for the farms, the region is relatively important for the firms purchases and sales. On the other hand, the national and international embeddedness of firm purchases are relatively high in comparison to those of the farms. Looking at the international indicators, the EIs for firm purchases are higher than the ones for sales, in contrast to the farms. It seems that firm sales and purchases are generally more dispersed over the different zones than those of the farms.

Hotels and restaurants and firms linked to recreational activities are the ones that buy and sell most of their products in the town and its direct vicinity. The smaller hotels and restaurants, in particular, have very high local EIs. Retail enterprises buy most of their merchandise from the rest of the country as well as in the rest of the region, but they sell most of it locally; this is especially true for the smaller firms. The wholesale and distribution sector has high national and international EIs, these firms buy most of their products directly from the producer. When focusing on the smaller (group 1) firms, purchases and, to a lesser extent, sales are more local. In general manufacturing and real estate enterprises are relatively strongly integrated at a national and international level nevertheless the larger firms (with four to ten workers) have higher local EIs than the small firms.

Generally, the smaller firms have higher local and regional EIs for their purchases and lower national indicators than larger firms. The embeddedness of their sales in the rest of the country is relatively high. Group 2 firms sell a larger share of their output locally than regionally.

Table 6.8 Embeddedness of firms' purchases (per cent) by firm size and town

Firm size		Local	Region	City	National	International
	Medium towns					
Group 1	Gemert	19	16	3	18	**44**
Group 2		3	3	1	**66**	27
Total		8	10	1	**56**	25
Group 1	Nunspeet	14	22	0	**55**	9
Group 2		6	14	0	25	**55**
Total		10	29	0	**36**	25
Group 1	Schagen	15	**40**	0	38	7
Group 2		33	**35**	0	26	7
Total		26	**44**	0	24	6
	Small towns					
Group 1	Oudewater	13	29	2	25	**32**
Group 2		13	27	1	**51**	8
Total		6	12	1	**75**	6
Group 1	Bolsward	12	34	0	**40**	13
Group 2		13	31	0	**43**	13
Total		9	34	0	**44**	12
Group 1	Dalfsen	31	23	0	**42**	5
Group 2		7	**42**	0	34	17
Total		22	**48**	0	25	6

Source: Own classification

When looking at the EIs for the six towns, the former conclusion about the relatively strong local and regional embeddedness of the purchases of small firms is confirmed (see Table 6.8). The weak embeddedness of small firms on a national level only applies to the two urban towns, Gemert and Oudewater. But in these towns the international EIs for small firms are extremely high. This is mainly due to the wholesale and real estate enterprises located there. In general, the largest shares of purchases are made in the rest of the country. The international market is important for the medium sized towns, whereas the regional market is most significant for the small towns. Firms in the two agricultural towns, Schagen and Dalfsen, are more strongly integrated with the town and the rest of the region both in terms of purchases and sales.

As Table 6.9 shows, the local sales EIs are much higher than those for purchases. The local sales embeddedness within Bolsward is quite strong. This can be related to the fact that Bolsward is a tourist town with a lot of retail enterprises including hotels and restaurants.

Table 6.9 Embeddedness of firms' sales (per cent) by firm size and town

Firm size	Medium towns	Local	Region	City	National	International
Group 1	Gemert	23	**24**	9	23	22
Group 2		20	11	1	6	**63**
Total		20	16	5	11	**48**
Group 1	Nunspeet	18	31	0	**45**	6
Group 2		18	8	0	**53**	21
Total		20	33	0	**36**	11
Group 1	Schagen	**36**	32	0	24	9
Group 2		**45**	35	0	16	4
Total		**47**	29	0	21	2
	Small towns					
Group 1	Oudewater	8	21	1	**53**	17
Group 2		26	16	4	**48**	6
Total		6	36	2	**47**	10
Group 1	Bolsward	**41**	33	0	19	7
Group 2		**35**	33	0	25	6
Total		23	22	0	47	8
Group 1	Dalfsen	21	19	0	**48**	12
Group 2		**44**	26	0	21	9
Total		16	15	0	**67**	2

Source: Own classification

Again the national EIs are relatively high just as they are for the purchases. Here too, the international embeddedness of sales in Gemert, and to a lesser degree in Nunspeet and Oudewater, is relatively strong. Small firms are more likely to sell their products at a regional and a national level compared to larger firms which are more orientated to local and international markets

Embeddedness of Employment

Purchases and sales are of importance but the employment rate is more important to the community. A relationship clearly exists between the amount of local purchases and the number of jobs but there are a lot of other factors affecting employment. These factors are not discussed in this chapter as it focuses on the embeddedness of the workforce of different kinds of farms and firms.

The employment EIs of the farms are fairly homogeneous, as for sales and purchases. Most of the farm workers live in the town itself or in the seven kilometre hinterland around it – see Table 6.10. From the data behind these figures, it appears that on 61 per cent of all farms most workers (including the owner and his or her family) live in zone B where the farm is located as well. This is especially true for farms with between three and ten workers. The other workers live in the rest of the region; in the case of these farms, they all live in zone C (the seven to 16 kilometre zone around the town). The horticulture sector is relatively more dependent on workers living in this zone.

Table 6.10 Embeddedness of farm employment (per cent) by sector and firm size

Sector	Farm size	Local	Region	City	National	International	No. of workers	No. of farms
Specialist livestock	Group 1	88	12	0	0	0	123	76
	Group 2	87	13	0	0	0	117	37
	Total	88	12	0	0	0	249	113
Mixed livestock	Group 1	91	9	0	0	0	116	65
	Group 2	83	17	0	0	0	109	44
	Total	87	13	0	0	0	271	110
Pigs/poultry	Group 1	78	22	0	0	0	45	29
	Group 2	96	4	0	0	0	53	14
	Total	88	12	0	0	0	106	43
Mixed livestock and arable	Group 1	85	15	0	0	0	54	35
	Group 2	96	4	0	0	0	47	18
	Total	86	14	0	0	0	133	54
Horticulture	Group 1	42	58	0	0	0	12	7
	Group 2	93	7	0	0	0	82	16
	Total	77	23	0	0	0	222	42
Total	Group 1	86	14	0	0	0	373	226
	Group 2	87	13	0	0	0	511	139
	Total	85	15	0	0	0	1061	389

Source: Own classification

The employment EIs of the firms are also quite comparable. Again, most of the workers have their residence in the town and its direct hinterland, this time both in zone A and in zone B. The smaller firms, in particular, have high local EIs but values for group 2 are also higher than the average of all firms. The remainder of the workers live in the rest of the region and some of them in the rest of the country. The larger wholesaling and real estate firms also have fewer workers living in the local area.

Table 6.11   Embeddedness of firm employment (per cent) by sector and firm size

Sector	Firm size	Local	Region	City	National	International	No. of workers	No. of firms
Manufacturing	Group 1	**100**	0	0	0	0	18	12
	Group 2	**65**	34	0	1	0	169	25
	Total	**63**	35	0	2	0	293	50
Construction	Group 1	**94**	6	0	0	0	85	55
	Group 2	**75**	23	0	2	0	248	43
	Total	**65**	31	1	3	0	629	129
Wholesale and distribution	Group 1	**85**	15	0	0	0	41	25
	Group 2	**62**	27	2	8	1	146	23
	Total	**59**	33	1	6	1	311	59
Retailers	Group 1	**79**	19	0	2	0	110	63
	Group 2	**73**	25	0	1	0	503	92
	Total	**74**	25	0	1	0	798	164
Hotels and restaurants	Group 1	**67**	33	0	0	0	6	4
	Group 2	**73**	27	0	0	0	98	14
	Total	**67**	33	0	0	0	181	23
Recreational, cultural and sporting activities	Group 1	**89**	8	3	0	0	36	25
	Group 2	**74**	20	0	6	0	70	10
	Total	**73**	22	1	3	1	143	37
Real estate, renting and business activities	Group 1	**80**	16	1	1	1	196	108
	Group 2	**56**	33	2	10	0	293	53
	Total	**57**	32	2	9	0	706	176
Services	Group 1	**73**	25	0	2	0	55	29
	Group 2	**80**	19	0	1	0	129	26
	Total	**67**	28	0	5	0	323	66
Total	Group 1	**83**	15	1	1	0	550	324
	Group 2	**69**	27	1	4	0	1679	290
	Total	**65**	30	1	4	0	3425	718

Source: Own classification

In general, the local EIs of the firms are lower than the employment indicators of the farms (see Table 6.11). The larger firms have more workers living in the rest of the region and some even live in the rest of the country although the smaller enterprises are embedded in terms of local employment to a comparable extent. The total regional EIs are also of the same size.

Table 6.12 shows the employment EIs for the farms located in the different towns. It appears that the farms in medium sized towns have higher local indicator values. Furthermore this table confirms an earlier observation that the smallest firms have the highest local indicators.

Table 6.12   Embeddedness indicators of employment (per cent) by farm size and town

Farm size	Medium towns	Local	Region	City	National	International
Group 1	Gemert	88	12	0	0	0
Group 2		98	2	0	0	0
Total		93	7	0	0	0
Group1	Nunspeet	97	3	0	0	0
Group 2		76	24	0	0	0
Total		88	12	0	0	0
Group 1	Schagen	85	15	0	0	0
Group 2		81	19	0	0	0
Total		75	25	0	0	0
	Small towns					
Group 1	Oudewater	90	10	0	0	0
Group 2		84	16	0	0	0
Total		87	13	0	0	0
Group 1	Bolsward	86	14	0	0	0
Group 2		75	25	0	0	0
Total		80	20	0	0	0
Group 1	Dalfsen	81	19	0	0	0
Group 2		90	10	0	0	0
Total		87	14	0	0	0

Source: Own classification

Table 6.13 shows the EIs of firms and it appears that the local EIs of the firms are lower than the ones of the farms, but they are still the most important ones. The regional indicators, especially those of the smaller firms are slightly higher than those of the farms. Again, the firms in the medium sized towns have more workers living in the town than the smaller towns. The smallest firms have relatively more local people employed.

Table 6.13 Embeddedness indicators of employment (per cent) by firm size and town

Firm size	Medium towns	Local	Region	City	National	International
Group 1	Gemert	85	11	3	1	0
Group 2		72	24	2	0	2
Total		70	25	3	2	1
Group1	Nunspeet	84	15	0	1	0
Group 2		71	25	0	3	1
Total		69	28	0	2	0
Group 1	Schagen	79	19	0	2	0
Group 2		66	29	0	5	0
Total		68	28	0	4	0
	Small towns					
Group 1	Oudewater	82	18	0	0	0
Group 2		60	30	2	8	0
Total		60	30	2	8	0
Group 1	Bolsward	73	21	0	3	2
Group 2		72	27	0	1	0
Total		64	32	0	3	0
Group 1	Dalfsen	87	13	0	0	0
Group 2		56	38	0	6	0
Total		60	35	0	5	0

Source: Own classification

Differences between Firms and Farms

Now that the proportions of purchase and sales activities of firms and farms allocated to several zones within the economy have been examined, the similarities and differences between the two kinds of enterprises will be considered.

First of all, it appears that the farm EIs are homogeneous when different sectors, different sized firms, or different towns are taken into account. Purchases mostly take place at a local or regional level and sales at a regional or national level. Furthermore, purchases and sales are almost equally distributed among the different spatial zones.

The EIs of the firms are much more diverse. They are not equally distributed among the zones but are more concentrated in certain areas. In general, the regional and national indicators of purchases are relatively high. Sales are more often located in the towns (locally) or in the rest of the country. If the size of the total EIs are taken into account, it is clear that the farms are more locally and regionally embedded and the firms more national and international.

When focusing on the size of the enterprises, it seems that smaller farms sell a relatively high share of their products on the international market compared to larger farms. This is true especially for mixed livestock and arable farms as well as for horticulture farms. Furthermore, the regional EIs for the sales of the small farms are higher in general. This also applies to the small firms, which have high indicators for the rest of the country. While the purchases of small firms are lower on a national level, their inputs are often more local.

The great majority of the workers in both farms and firms live in the locality but the local embeddedness values for firms are lower than those for the farms. The extent of local employment embeddedness of the smaller enterprises is, however, comparable. The total regional EIs for the smaller enterprises are also roughly of the same size. The rest of the firms (excluding group 1) have more workers who live in the rest of the region or sometimes in the rest of the country compared to the farm workers.

Conclusions

Small and medium sized towns form an important component of the economic structure of European countries. Furthermore, the rural economy is generally characterized by small enterprises. Almost 90 per cent of employees in the Netherlands work in firms with less than ten people. It is increasingly believed that most of the new jobs in rural areas are going to come from new and existing small firms, not just from service sectors like tourism but also from some lighter manufacturing industries. Input output theory shows that the kind of sector is important as when firms buy inputs from outside the local economy, their spending 'leaks' to other regions and the multiplier effect they have on the local economy decreases. When firms sell their products outside the local economy, more money enters and the multiplier effect increases. The allocation of purchases and sales by different sectors and types of firms is therefore important to rural development.

The present study has focused on the local embeddedness of sales and purchases of firms and farms as well as on the local embeddedness of their workforces. The extent of embeddedness has been measured by so-called embedddness indicators (EIs) which show the proportion of an economic activity of a group of economic entities allocated to the (local) economy.

Focusing first on purchases, it appears that local EIs of farms are higher than those of firms. Yet there are some exceptions such as the hotels and restaurants, the recreational sector and the real estate sector, which buy most of their inputs locally. On the one hand, as most of the firms obtain their purchases from the rest of the country, it means that their spending leaks out of the local economy. On the other hand, they also sell most of their output on a national and international level, which leads to an inflow of money to the local economy. As the smaller firms have higher local EIs for their purchases, their activities can benefit the local economy more than the larger firms can. Of course, it is important to bear in mind that the figures refer to proportions of spending and not for absolute numbers.

The importance of small enterprises to the local economy and society is also due to their contribution to local employment. Our results show that some employees of both farms and firms live in the region, but most of them live in the central town. Again, the local EIs of the smallest enterprises are the highest.

In summary, the sample of farms studied is more integrated into the local economy than the firms. But more importantly, smaller enterprises, both farms and firms, have a higher local embeddedness than larger enterprises and thus are shown to be of substantial importance to the local economy within the Netherlands.

Note

1 'Marketowns, the role of small and medium sized towns in rural development', is funded under Key Action 5 (Sustainable agriculture, fisheries and forestry, and integrated development of rural areas including mountain areas) of the Work Programme 'Quality of Life and Management of Living Resources'. More details can be found in Terluin et al., 2003.

References

Courtney, P. and Errington, A. (2000), 'The Role of Small Towns in the Local Economy and Some Implications for Development Policy', *Local Economy*, Vol. 15 (4) pp. 280-301.

European Communities (2003), *Factsheet: 'Rural Development in the European Union'*, Office for Official Publications of the European Communities, Luxembourg.

Leeuwen, M. van and Mayfield, L. (2004), 'Local Interdependencies of Small- and Medium-sized Towns in the Netherlands; an Inter-regional SAM Analysis', Paper for AES Annual Conference in London, 2-4 April.

North, D. and Smallbone, D. (1996), 'Small Business Development in Remote Rural Areas: the Example of Mature Manufacturing Firms in Northern England', *Journal of Rural Studies*, Vol. 12 (2), pp. 151-167.

Tarling, R., Rhodes, J., North, J. and Broom, G. (1993), 'The Economy of Rural England', *Rural Development Commission, Strategy Review: Topic Paper 4*, RDC, London.

Terluin, I.J. (2001), *Rural Regions in the EU: Exploring Differences in Economic Development*, R U, Faculteit der Ruimtelijke Wetenschappen, Groningen.

Terluin, I.J., van Leeuwen, M. and Pilkes, J. (2003), *Economic Linkages between Town and Hinterland: a Comparative Analysis of Six Small- and Medium-sized Towns in the Netherlands*, Agricultural Economics Research Institute, LEI, The Hague.

PART III

NEW STRATEGIES IN SMALL BUSINESS DEVELOPMENT

Chapter 7

Organizational Success Factors in Local Agri-food Industries

Gabriella Vindigni, Peter Nijkamp, Giuseppina Carrà and Iuri Peri

Introduction: New Horizons for Innovation and Entrepreneurship

Local industries often face fierce competition within their region, especially where traditional products are concerned. Survival mechanisms may be based on learning principles and organizational networks. The first two parts of this chapter review the most important literature in this field and develop propositions for empirical testing. The later part of the chapter discusses the case of local honey production in Sicily. It first presents the general findings and then the analytical results from using a recently developed artificial intelligence method for nominal (linguistic) information based on decision tree analysis. The new developments in approaches to innovation and entrepreneurship will now be discussed.

The recent interest in innovation has focused attention on the entrepreneur. Entrepreneurship is a creative act leading to a new combination of capital, people and resources. In our modern information age, entrepreneurship normally means an active and guiding involvement in complex network constellations that create value added through changes in business by deploying so-called network externalities. Thus, 'orgware management' (defined as the management of institutional arrangements, as discussed later in the chapter) is a critical source of innovation.

Economic development is the outgrowth of new and creative combinations of economic activity. The dynamics in this process can largely be ascribed to the innovative behaviour of risk-taking entrepreneurs. The interest among economists in studying entrepreneurship has fluctuated over the course of economic history. Illuminating examples can be found in the works of Schumpeter (1934) and Galbraith (1967). An interesting overview can be found, inter alia, in Hébert and Link (1988), who address the motives and economic backgrounds of entrepreneurship. Their fairly comprehensive study distinguishes the German, Chicago and Austrian schools of thought. In general, the entrepreneurial act is pursued by a risk taking, rational person who, in a small-scale business setting, dares to choose new, potentially beneficial directions. Entrepreneurship is based on the inspiring courage of individuals who explore unknown horizons in terms of production or organization; it often finds its origin in small-scale economic activities.

The past two decades have witnessed a renewed interest in the seedbed conditions for small and medium sized enterprises (SMEs) with the recognition that the SME sector has considerable innovative potential (Acs and Audretsch 1990). Many start-ups are small-scale in nature and hence it is no surprise that new entrepreneurship is often found in the SME sector. The current economic conditions also reflect new types of industrial organization among commercial firms (e.g. network constellations) in which entrepreneurship plays a key role. In recent years, particular attention has been paid to the regional and network conditions for the emergence of innovative and competitive entrepreneurship (Foss and Klein, 2002; Nijkamp, 2003; Pineder, 2001). Entrepreneurship can be likened to a sailing voyage under very uncertain and changeable weather conditions and is driven by survival strategies in a competitive and sometimes antagonistic world (see Mehlum et al., 2003; Stough et al., 2002). In such evolutionary economic developments, due attention needs to be given to incubation conditions and to developing the technological processes which drive regional growth.

Recent years have witnessed an avalanche of interest in entrepreneurship, especially in the critical success factors of the modern 'entrepreneurial hero' and regional development implications of emerging entrepreneurship, in particular seedbed areas. Research in this field has focused in particular on fact finding, on theory development and on modelling and has aimed to achieve a better understanding of a complex multi-actor field. Representatives of different disciplines, in particular economics, regional science, industrial organization and behavioural psychology have made contributions. In this context, the critical importance of knowledge and information in our information and communications technology (ICT) driven world is increasingly recognized.

It is thus widely accepted that knowledge is the key to success and that explains why, with the advent of the ICT revolution, so much emphasis is placed on the promises offered by our modern knowledge society (Audretsch and Thurik, 1999; Nijkamp and Stough, 2002). The ICT sector, in combination with drastic changes in industrial organization, will exert profound influences on modern spatial economic systems.

Network-based entrepreneurial activities have the best chance to survive and flourish in this ICT age as the advent of the ICT sector favours network formation. Such constellations based on flexible specialization are usually referred to as 'virtual organizations' or 'virtual enterprises' (Cooke and Morgan, 1993). They refer to organizational networks that have a flexible structure, are governed by trust and innovative spirit and, to the outer world, resemble one unambiguously identifiable and complete organization. The control and command structure is not always very clear and may be flexible as well. According to Hale and Whitlam (1997: 3), 'The virtual organization is the name given to any organization which is continually evolving, redefining and reinventing itself for practical business purposes'. Virtual enterprises may take different forms. Following Noorman (2002), some archetypal examples are:

- *internal virtual organization:* an organization comprising relatively autonomous teams which can be flexibly employed (Campbell, 1997); illustrations can be found in virtual offices and lean offices.
- *stable virtual organization:* an industrial model based on an outsourcing of non-core activities to a relatively small and fixed number of intermediaries.
- *dynamic virtual organization:* large-scale but flexible co-operation between industrial organizations based on ad hoc, opportunistic market motives (Upton and McAfee, 1996).
- *web-enterprise:* an organization centred around a (temporary) network of experts in a given field, sharing knowledge management and information for dedicated purposes.

It is clear that a wide variety of virtual enterprises is emerging, facilitated by developments in the IT sector and, in reality, various mixed forms may be present. The common features are the trend to shorten the product life cycles, to be subject to permanent pressure to innovate, to be information-oriented, to be driven by high quality targets ('zero defects'), to operate in non-hierarchical modes, to be market-oriented through learning-by-using interactions and to take care of the entire value chain (Morgan, 1991).

Knowledge and entrepreneurship are not ubiquitous goods that are freely available everywhere; they clearly have geographical and institutional backgrounds. Recently, there has been an outpouring of studies on the geography of innovation and economic progress (see e.g. Boekema et al., 2000; Gallup et al., 1999; van Oort, 2002). Despite the 'death of distance', physical geography such as access to main transport and communication arteries, is still a major determinant of competitive economic conditions. The recent interest in the new economic geography has clearly pointed out the critical importance of spatial accessibility in regard to the emergence of innovative attitudes and institutional support mechanisms (see Acemoglu et al., 2001; Hall and Jones, 1999). Such institutional ramifications may not only relate to regulatory systems such as property rights or stable political regimes, but also to self-organized modes of cooperation and competition in the private sector. The main research challenge is the identification of promising human capital conditions from a regional–institutional perspective, while taking account of the self-organizing potential of business life in a given area (see Lundvall, 1999; Norton, 2001; Oakey 2002). The concept of a 'learning economy' should be mentioned in this context as well, as this notion indicates that evolution is not a rectilinear development. It is dependent on deliberate choices and cognitive feedback decisions of humans in an uncertain environment, who respond endogenously to new challenges and to creative opportunities offered by social and economic interaction. This new mode of producing and interacting is a major departure from Fordist mass production methods of the past. Learning models are also in perfect harmony with network-based modes of competition and cooperation.

Mass production in large-scale concentrations has been a prominent success factor in the age of industrialization. Labour specialization, later on, capital specialization were a *sine qua non* for a productivity rise that was needed to survive in a competitive economy or to become a winner in a growing market. Mass production, however, also creates a high degree of path dependency, lock-in behaviour and hence inertia in large-scale enterprises, resulting in a lack of flexibility and adaptability to new circumstances. In the course of history, we have learned that mass production is not the only mode of industrial organization but is also accompanied and sometimes even facilitated by SMEs which have often demonstrated a surprising ability to adopt new production possibilities, including distribution and logistics (Marsili, 2001; Suarez-Villa, 1989). The fact that large size is not always the optimal scale of a firm has been thoroughly analysed by You (1995), who offers four explanatory frameworks:

- *technological:* the optimal scale of a firm is determined by economies of scale and scope as well as by the span of control, so that the optimal firm size is the result of scale economies and diseconomies.
- *institutional:* according to the transaction cost theory (see Coase, 1937 and Williamson, 1985), the governance of a complex undertaking with many activities may cause high internal transaction costs, so that it may be more beneficial to resort to the market for specific activities (e.g. non-core activities).
- *organizational:* the type of industrial organization (e.g. monopoly, oligopoly or monopolistic competition) is reflected in the market share of a firm, which is in turn determined by the price, the degree of uniformity of the product and the managerial structure.
- *dynamic:* due to path dependency, lock-in behaviour, cultural environment, age of the firm and other determinants, the past situation of the firm may impact on its future size.

Although the industrial revolution created the seedbed conditions for large scale industries, the importance of a great variety of forms of small scale activities has to be emphasized here. Despite the variety, we observe in almost all cases a decentralized mechanism for governing co-operative relationships. Cooperation becomes volatile, but needs rules and trust. Consequently, the principle of trust has become a popular concept; it is less based on emotion but rather on economic rationality, which may be more transaction-specific (Dasgupta, 1988; Granovetter, 1985; Linders et al., 2004). Consequently, there may be need for more institutional support systems or various forms of institutional embeddedness in order to prevent the destruction of human capital for ad hoc purposes (Hagen and Choe, 1998). This brings us to a major issue public policy question: will non-formal public-private governance mechanisms ensure public interest (e.g. a stable regional development) and enhance private performance (e.g. innovative behaviour)? Availability of resources, developed infrastructure and proper education and training systems, accompanied by close interactions between the business world and the public sector, are critical success factors in this context (see Stough, 2003). Against the background of the previous remark, we will now develop a framework for analysing the role of orgware networks in a regional competitive environment, taking a specific industry (the honey sector in the region of Sicily) as a test case. The main focus will thus be on orgware innovation.

An Analytical Framework for Orgware-oriented Industrial Innovation

In many rural areas, innovation through the adoption of productivity enhancing technologies and new management practices for existing productions operation is an essential key factor for the survival and viability of rural manufacturing. Creation and destruction are critical ingredients for this sector.

Products and machines constitute visible and tangible aspects of innovation, but there are also intangible components that are present in the memories of individuals, in the behaviour of stakeholders and in organizational structures. These intangible components, usually called know-how, are increasingly regarded as the main driving factors for sustainable comparative advantage. Innovation often requires the combination of various new and existing competencies.

A clear exposition of the key components that constitute an innovation can be related to three strongly interrelated territorial dimensions. The first dimension is *hardware*, understood as the infrastructure on which the territory relies, such as the communication and the transport system. The second is *software*, which includes the level of development of intangibles, such as the quality of human resources and the territory's capacity to produce knowledge and information. The final dimension is *orgware*, being the type of economic, social and institutional organization that a territory adopts.

Many different theories seek to explain the influence of knowledge, learning processes and inter-firm cooperation modes in localized innovation systems. The last two decades, in particular, have seen a remarkable rise in popularity of the so-called territorial innovation models, which emphasize the accumulation of tacit knowledge, collective learning and the growth of associative structures as the basis of formal and informal interdependencies. Coordination occurs through trust, reciprocity and long-term strategic agreements, supported by locally embedded structures (Bruijn, 2003).

Transaction cost analyses (Coase, 1937; Williamson, 1985; Langlois and Robertson, 1995), as well as theories based on the competence view (Penrose, 1959; Foss and Knudsen, 1996), have gained dominant positions in the analysis of economic organization and production focusing on firms. Storper (1995) uses the concept of untreated interdependences to refer to conventions, informal rules and habits that coordinate economic actors under conditions of uncertainty. Technological spillovers are mostly coordinated not through market mechanisms, but are 'in the air' as in the Marshallian concept of 'industrial atmosphere'.

The literature on enterprise clusters, industrial districts and dynamics of industrial organization is relevant in this context. In an Italian study of how production is spatially organized, Garofoli (1991) proposed a typology of models of local development that has been quite influential. This classification introduced concepts such as 'local production systems' and 'system areas', and described the rise in the complexity of the local system that may occur, with inter-firm and inter-institution synergies becoming widespread and effective. Markusen (1996) broadens the picture to include several different forms of industrial organization within the definition of an industrial district. She argues that the emergence of 'sticky places' in a 'slippery space' – characterized by dramatically improved communications, and increasingly mobile production factors and enterprises – may be related to numerous variants of industrial districts. Thus she opts for a more extensive interpretation of the idea of an industrial district, which is not confined to the most common and traditional usage (for example, the Marshallian district or its Italian variant). Therefore, the proper definition of a modern industrial district is the following: 'an industrial district is a sizeable and spatially delimited area of trade-oriented economic activity, which has a distinctive economic specialization, be it resource-related, manufacturing, or services' (Park and Markusen, 1995).

Although the various models differ significantly from each other in terms of their conceptualization of innovation, all of them emphasize the importance of knowledge. Some of them focus on the importance of R&D (e.g. Krugman, 1991; Audretsch and Feldman, 1996) while others, more concerned with the use than generation of knowledge, focus on the presence of a skilled/experienced labour force for knowledge spillovers.

Many empirical studies in this set of district theories have adopted a cognitive approach. Firms can be interpreted as a cognitive system, that is a social-productive system in which knowledge, social experiences, mental models and collective beliefs are accumulated in a specific space through time. Firms can be thought of as a 'cognitive lab', where knowledge and information are elaborated in a complex way, and where culture and social values are generated. The local accumulation of tacit knowledge in firms provides the necessary distinctive elements to fuel firm competitiveness.

The application of a psychological metaphor of learning at the level of an organization involves fostering the idea that learning in individuals can be transformed into more general improvements, and that it will led to more success and prosperity for the organization (Rhodes, 1996). Organizational learning is as natural as individual learning, where an organization attempts to adapt and survive in an uncertain world. According to Dogson (1993), just as a psychologist distinguishes different levels of learning, the learning organization can be seen as a move from natural learning, by seeking varied forms of understanding, to other systems including congenital learning, experiential learning, vicarious learning, grafting, searching and noticing.

Huber (1991) contends that learning can occur not only due to knowledge acquisition from outside the organization but also due to the rearrangement of existing knowledge and the revision of the previous knowledge structure. In this context, organizational memory refers to the repository where knowledge is stored for future use. Knowledge management is defined as a process that governs the creation, the dissemination and the leveraging of knowledge in order to fulfil organizational objectives. In this framework, knowledge is the capacity to take effective action and encompasses an organization's intellectual capital (Seemann et al., 2000).

Decision makers store and retrieve not only hard data or information. Skill acquisition, learning, and accumulation of capability over time are the core of knowledge management within an organization (Nonaka, 1994;). The source of information is based on networks because both the organization and its employees are increasingly regarded as a resource of competitive advantage. Knowledge is information that is transformed by the active intervention of organizational participants in such a way that is applicable to specific work functions or situations (Lee and Yang, 2000).

The orgware and learning model posits that networking improves the flow of information. The absorptive capacity of individuals is the ability to recognize and to assimilate, and it incorporates organizational information, either internal or external. The model suggests that absorptive capacity is based on the construct that knowledge can be tacit or explicit. Tacit knowledge is embedded in people, their know-how, skills, practices and experiences, while explicit knowledge is generally held in formal policies, procedures, systems and historical and financial records. Tacit knowledge may be more valuable than explicit knowledge because of its uniqueness.

Pathways to Innovation in Rural Areas: A Regional Case Study

Rural areas have in recent years exhibited dynamic developments. Alongside the process of specialization and concentration of the agri-food sector at the global level, some significant other trends have also emerged.

Recent research suggests that there is an impressive increase in activities that are associated with farm diversification, like agri-tourism, the supply of care facilities, environmental services and so on. This is especially seen in the extension of activities in order to achieve more added value per unit, as in the production of high quality products and regional specialities, on-farm processing and marketing, as well as the creation of alternative supply chains. The innovative behaviour of these enterprises results from their newly created activities and linkages between market and local resources, including the regional environment, local knowledge, personal skills and available assets (Van der Ploeg and Renting, 2000; Marsden et al., 2000). Nowadays we can observe a broad portfolio of local and regional initiatives that all support innovation by firms in the area.

The way in which the enterprises interact with their region may induce the creation of new organizational patterns that offer more opportunities for introducing innovative processes, using external elements in a local style of farming (Iacoponi et al., 1995). Learning-by-experience supports the know-how of the entrepreneurs in mastering the techniques of production and development of the products, adopting new practices through cooperation and close connections with their community.

The improvement of organizational and managerial capabilities through learning constitutes a critical factor in the evolution of the firm. These learning processes are achieved in our case study through the understanding and transfer of past experiences into initiatives that expand the body of knowledge. Furthermore, even though it is non-formalized and unplanned, a system of relationships and exchange of information and experience is developed among the firms which frequently evolves through experimental and imitative behaviour (Becattini, 1987).

The chapter now investigates orgware as a driving force in innovative behaviour based on a field survey among honey producers in Sicily. In particular, it examines how far network use and organizational reform is incorporated in novel behavioural patterns. The survey investigates the entrepreneurs' innovative behaviour and the decisive role that the learning process has in determining the success of the enterprises. The findings underline the importance of the close relationship between learning and entrepreneurial achievement; family background and professional learning are key factors in this process. Other important factors include the specificity of the assets and availability of market opportunities.

The local honey production system is based on small-scale production modes and equipment, a moderate use of machinery and the use of available local resources. On-farm processing and marketing is a distinctive characteristic of this system. Through these activities, individuals or groups of entrepreneurs increase their ability to capture a greater share of the market for their product. The specific physical assets used are characterized by low opportunity costs and the specific human assets involved enable the enterprises to exploit local opportunities and help them to avoid high business risks and threats.

The processing and marketing activities add value to the products and improve their quality as well as the entrepreneurs' bargaining power. Cooperation with other entrepreneurs plays a strategic role in further expansion. In order to see how new activities are integrated into an individual or collective farm strategy of development, it is necessary to understand in more depth how information improves local knowledge and what factors facilitate this improvement.

For the enterprises involved in the production of local or regional goods, innovative behaviour is to a considerable degree a market driven process. New opportunities in quality-oriented marketing strategies are identified by the local producers, which increase their returns through effectively meeting end-user demand. The EU regulation on the designation of labels of origin and on organic food plays an important role in their innovative behaviour, since it has created a new market space and a new source of innovation and symbolic power (Brunori, 2000).

Successful business performance in the following Scillian case study is expressed in terms of sales or sales price increases. It is argued that the enterprise is competitive if it is profitable in terms of market returns, if it supplies products demanded by consumers and if it can flexibly adjust itself to market challenges (Tangermann, 2003). The next section offers a more detailed description of the case study.

The Honey Production System in Sicily

Introductory Remarks

The case study examines a cluster of firms in Monti Iblei, a rural area of Sicily, which specialize in honey production. The local production system is characterized by small-scale owners/producers who have a long tradition in beekeeping and focus on producing niche or high quality and artisan-type products. Although these types of farm-based industries are usually classified as traditional and low tech, they have recently demonstrated a new dynamism. While most of them lack an overall strategy, dynamic, small local farm enterprises that have added value to the agricultural production of the area through innovation were identified in this study.

Most of the firms are small, but some of them have increased their competence level through training and apprenticeship. They have also upgraded their operations in terms of technological capability, and a few are close to the new production frontiers. Firms in these clusters also exhibit the capacity to make adaptations to new technology, to improve quality products and processes and to bring them to the market. A distinct characteristic of this cluster of firms is their cooperation and networking with member firms. Through this process they have became more specialized and more organized.

In the past, these firms simply benefited passively from the externalities spontaneously created through clustering. Recently, in a novel organizational phase, these enterprises engaged actively in the creation of collective efficiencies stemming from a high degree of linkages within and between different actors, in terms of horizontal (coordination) ties, a progressive specialization in the various production phases, frequent exchange of information and regular technical discussions among producers and subcontractors. Tacit knowledge flows were facilitated by this conscious, pro-active set of interactions.

Cooperation between the public and private sector also contributed to meeting the new challenges faced by the firms in this cluster. National and local producer associations played a pivotal role in obtaining public support for establishing technical training facilities, providing a special credit line for providing short-term loans to local manufacturers, facilitating state support, and acting as interlocutor with the local and regional government.

The empirical data for this research stem from in depth personal interviews held in the first part of 2003 among 25 entrepreneurs in the area who have expressed a willingness to be interviewed. Their names were extracted from the information base of the Chamber of Commerce of Siracusa and Ragusa. The work investigated shared characteristics that could identify both the production and organizational systems of honey makers and defined the principal aspects of the innovation process.

General Characteristics

The socio-demographic characteristics of the sample show that beekeeping is a male activity. The majority of interviewees appear to be relatively young and 56 per cent are less than 41 years old. The level of education attained is rather low and generally only up to primary or secondary education, although a few farmers were more highly educated with higher professional training or university education.

Most of the entrepreneurs are active in other areas. Approximately 84 per cent of the entrepreneurs are owners and employ a family work force; moreover, most honey activity is carried out on a part time basis, partly explained by the small-scale activity of the firms. Today, honey production still represents a form of productive diversification of the traditional agricultural enterprise with the aim of increasing returns for the family. Most of the firms (76 per cent) were set up since 1990, and their entry into the industry was favoured by the technological change in the sector.

Entrepreneurial participation in trade associations was investigated in order to analyse their propensity to collaborate with other firms. Only horizontal coordination was found in this study; a majority of the honey producers are members of business associations at the local or national level (64 per cent) or take part in consortia (16 per cent). All producers are involved in the promotion of an initiative for acknowledgment of the PDO (Protected Denomination of Origin) while, at the same time, many of them (76 per cent) have adopted the HACCP system. The organizational structure (96 per cent) of all cases is very simple with a clear concentration of the production, processing and marketing of products in the hands of the holder.

Marketing, Focused Markets and Distribution Channel Logistics

Most of the enterprises (76 per cent) invest in marketing activity. The products are often marketed through direct marketing channels, without recourse to intermediaries. A substantial proportion (42 per cent) of the small-scale honey production is sold by producers directly to consumers; thus they do not have to pay for the services of intermediaries and can maintain closer ties with consumers. The remaining part is sold through retailers (26 per cent) or middlemen (31 per cent). This form of commercialization can be explained, in part, by the fact that many enterprises have continued with the same distribution channels previously used in informal productive activities. Almost all the honey is still sold locally; in a few cases the market is regional, but it is rarely national.

Product and Process Innovation

The probability of innovation is directly related to the motivation to innovate. The principal motives leading the entrepreneurs within the sample to innovate are linked to brand consolidation (16 per cent), labour saving (48 per cent) and increased demand (36 per cent). In this context, it is relevant to note that innovation is an endogenous process and the role played by the public research institutions in fostering innovation is evident in just over half the cases (52 per cent).

One aspect of this analysis concerned product and process innovation. The effects of process innovation are mainly linked to a reduction in costs and an improvement in quality. Quality is a very important variable in competitiveness, especially in the case of typical local products. The adoption of new manufacturing processes is, therefore, of great importance in terms of maintaining these specific characteristics.

At a technical level, there is rapid diffusion of both process innovation, which reduces the costs of production, and product innovation, which satisfies the increasingly complex customer demands requiring a more diverse product set. Innovation in the honey production sector may range from to a change in the packaging to a new quality of honey. For example, 76 per cent of producers have introduced a different packaging, while 64 per cent modified the production characteristics linked to the quality of the product. It is particularly interesting to note that 60 per cent of the producers introduced new equipment and utilized new production technologies. Although honey is appreciated for its intrinsic qualities and its genuineness as a natural product, there is clearly dynamism in the industry in terms of product innovation.

It is noteworthy that typical products possess certain physical characteristics that have been established by tradition and, as previously indicated, they are a result of a convention accepted by manufacturers and consumers; therefore, the application of a new product strategy may make them lose their typical character. In the case of a regulation with formal conditions, this might seriously restrict new product strategies. Small innovations, such as those referred to above, usually do not create important problems.

However, product innovations concerned with the design and introduction of new products call for extensive technological and marketing efforts. It is necessary to launch new products when existing ones are reaching the end of their natural life for various reasons including technical progress, the evolution of consumer tastes, and new products from competitors. A new product technique may comprise a wide range of features, varying from a small change in the product, packaging, or its presentation to putting a totally new product on the market. The percentage of enterprises in the honey sector that have introduced such a product innovation is quite high (78 per cent). Most types of modifications however, are concerned with packaging or incremental innovations. Product innovation is related to the characteristics of a different quality of honey, such us multiflora production modes, as well as a new production of single-flower varieties of honeys (thyme, carob, orange blossom, eucalyptus, and chestnut honey) and other products from the hives such as pollen, royal jelly, propolis, and beeswax. Product innovation also shows up in the introduction of different modes of distribution and packaging to ensure that the utmost care is taken in protecting the valuable properties of the honeys. Diversification of production and the search for new varieties reveal the interest of some enterprises in capturing new consumer segments.

In a traditional agri-food production system, such as found in this case study, the transfer of technical knowledge underlying the traditional family methods of production is mainly based on a transfer between members of the family (84 per cent). At the same time, the process of knowledge acquisition among the sample is also based on learning by doing (64 per cent). Nevertheless, participation in training courses plays an increasingly significant role in the learning processes among owners-entrepreneurs in honey production (72 per cent).

Coordination Forms

The coordination between principal agents, producers, middlemen and consumers also deserves attention. The honey production system is a traditional activity where the relationship between the producers and consumers assumes an intermediate position between a spot market and vertical coordination when it occurs via middlemen. Following Jaffe (1995), contract coordination appears, in most cases, to be the principal institutional arrangement in this intermediate form of relationship between producers and their customers (88 per cent). It is also noteworthy that relationships between producers and consumers are based on trust and most contracts are verbal. These relationships are based on a spot market only in a few cases (12 per cent).

Discussion of Results from a Decision Tree Method

The innovation system in the sample of honey producers exhibits some interesting characteristics and the next step was to identify the influences on the performance of these enterprises. Given the qualitative nature of the data in the survey questionnaire, it is not possible to identify critical success factors by applying standard statistical methods (such as discrete choice models). As mentioned above, qualitative multidimensional techniques that are capable of handling nominal data had to be used. Given the limited sample, conventional multivariate methods like contingency table analysis and log-linear analysis were not suitable either. Our nominal data, however, can properly be treated by a recently developed nonparametric statistical method developed in the artificial intelligence literature, namely classification tree analysis. More details of this decision tree method and the data are given in the appendix.

Decision Tree Results

The empirical experiment presented in this study aims to identify the behavioural patterns of locally based SMEs in the honey sector. The application of decision tree algorithms appears to lead to the identification of very interesting sets of critical success factors (Figure 7.1).

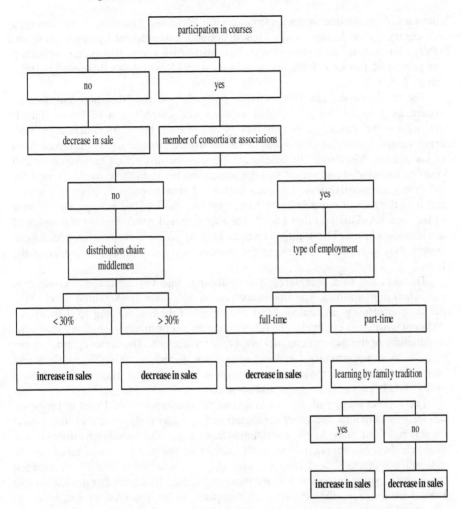

**Figure 7.1   A decision tree representation of the driving forces of
entrepreneurial performance**

The analytical framework developed in this experimental case study sheds light on
the relevance of entrepreneurial participation in training courses in a context where
local know-how accumulates over time, where spatial transfer of creative know-
how among local agents emerges via inter-firm linkages and where there is a
turnover of the labour force within the local environment.

Knowledge and competencies appeared to emerge as the most critical resources
for a firm's competitiveness. Much of the existing literature on innovation in SMEs
has focused on the importance of tacit and codified knowledge as a principal
source of sustainable competitive edge (Polanyi, 1966; Nelson and Winter, 1982;
Spender, 1996). The emphasis on the importance of developing a distinctive core

competence, intangible assets or firm-specific 'dynamic capabilities' has emerged as a central theme in the resource-based strategic management literature (Penrose, 1959). Interest in tacit knowledge has also grown rapidly as an important component of the knowledge used in innovation (Dosi, 1988; Rosemberg, 1982; Pavitt, 1987).

The results of the analysis focus, in particular, on the education and training system as a factor that contributes to the social construction of knowledge. It determines the extent to which this is used as a basis for interaction with organizational structures, the types of labour market and the use of different types of knowledge. Moreover, the case study stresses the distinction between tacit and codified knowledge and shows that the interaction between these modes is vital for the firm's competitiveness. The participation of entrepreneurs in training courses, and thus the role of explicit knowledge, explains most of the entropy endogenous to the data set. This codified knowledge supports and reinforces the dynamics of learning capability. The training courses help to create a responsive educational system that is capable of meeting the competency and skill requirements of the firms.

The decision tree, therefore, appears to split into two branches according to participation in courses. The first branch of the tree takes firms which do not take part in consortia or associations and distinguishes them according to their use of different marketing channels – the direct channel to consumers, which bypasses the middleman, or the indirect channel involving middlemen. The direct channel seems to offer more opportunity for developing sales. It reduces price fluctuations and guarantees the transmission of information through the relationship that is established between the supplier and consumer.

The second branch of the tree refers to the participation of firms in business-oriented associations and other organizational structures, showing that they play a central role and provide an institutional framework and social infrastructure for tacit learning. However, only a small number of the sample firms takes part in national associations, and thus we may question whether a distinction between those participating in national or local organizational structures is relevant. In this branch of the tree, the driving factor appears to be the type of employment, whether full or part time. Here the process of collective learning is attributed to the mobility of the local labour market that leads to the spread of knowledge. Local actors may grasp this cumulative knowledge, which is a source of competitive advantage. A high rate of inter-firm mobility fosters the formation of social networks and skills within the community. It turns out that when such social interaction is absent and these synergies do not exist, the potential competitiveness of the enterprises is not realized.

In accordance with the literature on learning economies, whether knowledge transfer takes place through family tradition represents the major criterion in the the lower branch of the tree. This emphasizes the importance of the tacit component of human knowledge. Although the conceptual distinction between tacit and coded knowledge has been well explored in the literature, they are not separate and discrete in practice. Explicit and tacit knowledge appear to be mutually correlated. Nonaka and Takeuchi (1995) argue that knowledge is generated through the combination and the dynamic interaction of these two modes of knowledge. Similarly, Nelson and Winter (1982) in their evolutionary theory of firms assume that firms provide a special context in which the explicit and tacit modes of knowledge are selected by interaction with the external economic reality and then stored in organizational routines. Thus, over time, firms appear to differ in their capacity to foster the interaction between these two modes of knowledge, and those that can may have superior performance.

Decision Rules

The pattern-class relationship expressed in the tree can also be written as a set of empirical rules in the following way:

Rules:
Rule 1: (7/1, lift 1.4)
    Participation in courses = no
    -> class decrease [0.778]
Rule 2: (18/10, lift 0.8)
    Participation in courses = yes
    -> class decrease [0.450]
Rule 3: (3, lift 2.5)
    Membership of consortia or associations = no
    Middlemen <= 30
    -> class increase [0.800]
Rule 4: (3, lift 2.5)
    Membership of consortia or associations = local and national association
    Type of employment = part-time
    Learning by family tradition = yes
    Participation in courses = yes
    -> class increase [0.800]
Rule 5: (2/1, lift 1.6)
    Membership of consortia or associations = local and national association
    Participation in courses = yes
    -> class increase [0.500]

Each rule consists of a statistic $(n,\ \text{lift}\ x)$ or $(n/m,\ \text{lift}\ x)$ that summarizes the performance of the rule. Specifically, n is the number of training cases covered by the rule, while m, if it appears, shows how many of them do not belong to the class predicted by the rule. The rule's accuracy is estimated by the Laplace ratio $(n-m+1)/(n+2)$. The lift, x, is the result of dividing the rule's estimated accuracy by the relative frequency of the predicted class in the training set.

Two of the most reliable rules in this system of calculation will now be discussed. These two rules demonstrate the way in which the results of the tree analysis are expressed. The first rule states that if the entrepreneurs participate in consortia or associations, if honey production is a part-time activity and if family tradition and training courses play an important role in the learning process, then the firms are competitive in terms of growth in sales. The accuracy of this rule is estimated to be 80 per cent. The second empirical rule refers to the role of the middlemen in the distribution channel and claims that if entrepreneurs do not participate in consortia or other organizational associations but use a direct distribution channel, then the firms are competitive in terms of growth in sales. Again, this rule is estimated to be 80 per cent accurate.

Performance Assessment

In order to explore which class distribution will yield the best classifier, two-performance measures, *classification accuracy* (or error rate) and the *confusion matrix* have been chosen. Classification accuracy is the most common evaluation metric in this type of research and only a low level of error is estimated in the system studied. However, using accuracy as a performance measure assumes that the class distribution is known and, more importantly, that the error costs of incorrectly classified instances are equal. Accuracy is particularly problematic as a performance measure when the data set studied is biased in favour of a majority class (Weiss and Provost, 2001).

An alternative method is to analyse the confusion matrix as it offers better insight into the distribution of classification and misclassification. A confusion matrix contains information about actual and predicted classifications derived from a classification system (Kohavi and Provost, 1998). The performance of such systems is commonly evaluated using the data in the matrix. The following table shows the confusion matrix for a tree classifier related to the honey production data. Both the rows and columns in the matrix have the same headers, but there is a distinction between them. The rows of the table are the classes available for use in the classification process; the columns of the table are the classes chosen during the classification.

Table 7.1 Confusion matrix of the case study classification

Decrease in sales	Increase in sales	Stable sales	Classified as:
14			Decrease in sales
1	7		Increase in sales
2	1		Stable sales

The entries in the confusion matrix represent the number of instances of the row class which have been classified as a member of the corresponding column class. Misclassifications occur when the row and column classes of a cell do not match. If the cell contains no entry, it reflects the absence of any misclassification. The results in this table can be interpreted as follows. Fourteen instances of a pertinent 'decrease in sales' class were correctly classified using the generated rules as members of the class with decreasing sales. Seven instances of the known 'increase in sales' class were correctly classified using the generated rules as members of the 'increase' class. One instance of the 'increase in sales' class was incorrectly classified using the generated rules as a member of the 'decrease' class. No instances of the known 'stable' class were correctly classified using the generated rules as members of the 'stable' class; one instance of the 'stable' class was incorrectly classified using the generated rules as a member of the 'increase' class and two were misplaced into the 'decrease' class.

Concluding Remarks

In modern economies, clusters are often based on networks. This analysis has clearly demonstrated the importance of network organizations and learning mechanisms for innovative behaviour among honey producers and has revealed common elements in their strategies.

In the past, traditional industries that were neither science-based nor knowledge-intensive were thought not to require the kinds of learning and innovation that have propelled growth in high tech industries. The low level of R&D expenditure in such industries gave further support to this belief. The very locus of change in traditional industries, however, makes the level of R&D expenditure a poor indicator of innovation for these sectors. Responses to the intriguing challenge of introducing new products do not easily determine the innovativeness of firms in such industries either. This is because the typical question about the frequency of introducing new products often fails to capture changes in design or materials that significantly modify products but do not result in the creation of an entirely new product.

Where competitive conditions in these industries are changing, sustained sales growth is only possible if firms in these clusters engage in a continuous process of innovation. Under these conditions, the trajectory of a cluster's sales becomes, over time, a useful proxy for innovation. It would be useful to extend the scope of this research to a larger sample, to other regions and to other sectors.

References

Acemoglu, D., Johnson, S. and Robinson, J.A. (2001), 'The Colonial Origins of Comparative Development', *American Economic Review*, Vol. 91 (5), pp. 1369-1401.

Acs, Z.J. and Audretsch, D.B. (1990), *Innovation and Small Firms*, The MIT Press, Cambridge, Mass.

Audretsch, D.B. and Feldman, M. (1996), 'R&D Spillovers and the Geography of Innovation and Production', *American Economic Review*, Vol. 86(3), pp. 630-640.

Audretsch, D.B. and Thurik, A.R. (eds) (1999), *Innovation, Industry Evolution and Employment*, Cambridge University Press, Cambridge, UK.

Becattini, G. (1987), *Mercato e Forze Locali: il Distretto Industriale*, Il Mulino, Bologna.

Boekema, F., Morgan, K., Bakkers, S. and Rutten, R. (eds) (2000), *Knowledge, Innovation and Economic Growth*, Edward Elgar, Cheltenham.

Bruijn, P.J.M. (2003), 'Geographical Innovation System; From Relational to Geometrical Conception of Space', *16th European Advanced Studies Institute in Regional Science*, European Regional Science Association.

Brunori, G. (2000), 'Alternative Trade or Market Fragmentation? Food Circuits and Social Movements', IRSA, *Mundial Congress*, Rio de Janeiro, Brazil.

Campbell, A. (1997), 'Knowledge Management in the Virtual Enterprise', in J. Jackson and J.V.D. van der Wielen (eds), *Proceedings of the Second International Workshop on Telework*, pp. 15-25.

Coase, R.H. (1937), 'The Nature of the Firm', *Economica*, Vol. 4(16), pp. 386-405.

Cooke, P. and Morgan, K. (1993), 'The Network Paradigm: New Departures in Corporate and Regional Development', *Environment and Planning D: Society and Space*, Vol. 11(5), pp. 543-564.

Dasgupta, P. (1988), 'Trust as a Commodity', in D. Gambetta (ed.), *Trust; Making and Breaking Cooperative Relations*, Basil Blackwell, New York, pp. 49-72.

De Fries, R.S. and Chan J.C.W. (2000), 'Multiple criteria for evaluating machine learning algorithms for land cover classification from satellite data', *Remote Sensing of the Environment*, Vol. 74, 503-515.

Dogson, M. (1993), 'Organisational Learning: A Review of Some Literature', *Organization studies*, Vol. 14, 3, pp. 375-394.

Dosi, G. (1988), 'The Nature of the Innovative Process', in G. Dosi, C. Freeman, R. Nelson, G. Silverberg and L. Soete (eds), *Technical Change and Economic Theory*, London, Pinter Publishers.

Foss, N.J. and Klein, P.G. (eds) (2002), *Entrepreneurship and the Firm*, Edward Elgar, Cheltenham.

Foss, N.J. and Knudsen, C. (1996), *Towards a Competence Theory of the Firm*, Routledge, London.

Galbraith, J.K. (1967), *The New Industrial State*, Routledge, London.

Gallup, J.L., Sachs, J.D. and Mellinger, A.D. (1999), 'Geography and Economic Development', *National Bureau of Economic Research Working Paper*, no. 6849, Washington D.C.

Garofoli, G. (1991), *Modelli Locali di Sviluppo*, Franco Angeli, Milano.

Granovetter, M.S. (1985), 'Economic Action and Social Structure, "The Problem of Embeddedness"', *American Journal of Sociology*, no. 91, pp. 481-510.

Hagen, J.M. and Choe, S. (1998), 'Trust in Japanese Interfirm Relations: Institutional Sanctions Matter', *Academy of Management Review*, Vol. 23(3), pp. 589-600.

Hale, R. and Whitlam, P. (1997), *Towards the Virtual Organization*, McGraw-Hill, London.

Hall, R.E. and Jones, C. (1999), 'Why Do Some Countries Produce So Much More Output per Head than Others?', *Quarterly Journal of Economics*, Vol. 10, pp. 463-483.

Hébert, R.F. and Link, A.N. (1988), *The Entrepreneur, Mainstream Views and Radical Critiques*, Praeger, New York.

Huber, G.P. (1991), 'Organizational Learning: the Contributing Processes and the Literatures', *Organizational Science*, Vol. 2(1), pp. 88-115.

Iacoponi, L., Brunori, G. and Rovai, M. (1995), 'Endogenous Development and Agroindustrial District', in G.D. van der Ploeg and G. van Dijk (eds), *Beyond Modernization. The Impact of Endogenous Rural Development*, Assen, Van Gorcum, The Netherlands, pp. 28-69.

Jaffe, S. (1995), 'Transaction Costs, Risk and the Organization of Private Sector Food Commodity Systems', in S. Jaffe and J. Morton (eds), *Marketing Africa's High-Value Foods – Comparative Experiences of an Emergent Private Sector*, Kendall Hunt Publishing Co, Dubuque, pp. 21-62.

Krugman, P. (1991), 'Increasing Returns and Economic Geography', *Journal of Political Economics*, Vol. 99, pp. 483-499.

Langlois, R.N. and Robertson, P.L. (1995), *Firms, Markets and Economic Change. A Dynamic Theory of Business Institutions*, Routledge, London.

Lee, C.C. and Jang, J. (2000), 'Knowledge Value Chain', *Journal of Management Developing*, Vol. 19(2), pp. 783-793.

Linders, G.J., de Groot, H. and Nijkamp, P. (2004), 'Economic Development, Institutions and Trust', *Festschrift in Honour of Jan Lambooy*, Kluwer, Dordrecht.

Lundvall, B.A. (1999), 'Technology Policy in the Learning Economy', in D. Archibugi, J. Howells and J. Michie (eds), *Innovation Policy in a Global Economy*, Cambridge University Press, Cambridge, pp. 19-34.

Markusen, A. (1996), 'Sticky Places in Slippery Space: a Typology of Industrial Districts', *Economic Geography*, Vol. 72(3), pp. 293-313.

Marsden T., Banks J. and Bristow, G. (2000), 'Food Supply Chains Approaches: Exploring their Role in Rural Development', *Sociologia Ruralis*, Vol. 40(4), pp. 424-438.

Marsili, O. (2001), *The Anatomy and Evolution of Industries*, Edward Elgar, Cheltenham.

Mehlum, H., Moene, K. and Torvik, R. (2003), 'Predator or Prey? Parasitic Enterprises in Economic Development', *European Economic Review*, Vol. 47(2), pp. 275-294.

Morgan, K. (1991), 'Competition and Collaboration in Electronics: What are the Prospects for Britain?', *Environment and Planning A*, Vol. 23(10), pp. 1459-1482.

Nelson, R.R. and Winter, S.G. (1982), *An Evolutionary Theory of Economic Change*, Harvard University Press, Cambridge, Mass.

Nijkamp, P. (2003), 'Entrepreneurship in a Modern Network Economy', *Regional Studies*, Vol. 37(4), pp. 395-405.

Nijkamp, P. and Stough, R. (eds) (2002), 'Entrepreneurship and Regional Economic Development', Special Issue, *Annals of Regional Science*, Vol. 36(3).

Nonaka, I. (1994), 'A Dynamic Theory of Organizational Knowledge Creation', *Organization Science*, Vol. 5(1), pp. 14-37

Nonaka, I. and Takeuchi, H. (1995), *The Knowledge-Creating Company*, Oxford University Press, New York.

Noorman, K. (2002), *Flexibele Specialisatie en Virtuele Organisaties*, MA Thesis, Free University, Amsterdam.

Norton, R.D. (2001), *Creating the New Economy*, Edward Elgar, Cheltenham.

Oakey, R. (ed.) (2002), *New Technology-Based Firms in the 1990s*, Paul Chapman, London.

Oort, F. van (2002), *Agglomeration, Economic Growth and Innovation*, Tela Thesis, Rotterdam.

Park S. and Markusen, A. (1995), 'Generalizing New Industrial Districts: A Theoretical Agenda and an Application from a Non-Western Economy', *Environment and Planning A*, Vol. 27(1), pp. 81-104.

Pavitt, K. (1987), 'The Objectives of Technology Policy', *Science and Public Policy*, Vol. 14, pp. 182-188.

Penrose, E. (1959), *The Theory of the Growth of the Firm*, Oxford University Press, Oxford.

Pineder, M. (2001), *Entrepreneurial Competition and Industrial Location*, Edward Elgar, Cheltenham.

Polanyi, M. (1966), *The Tacit Dimension*, Routledge and Kegan Paul, London.

Quinlan J.R. (1986), Vol. 19, Special issue, pp. 45-62.

Rhodes, C. (1996), 'Postmodernism and the Practice of Human Resource Development Organisations', *Australian and New Zealand Journal of Vocational Education Research*, Vol. 4 (2), pp. 79-88.

Rosenberg, N. (1982), *Inside the Black Box: Technology and Economics*, Cambridge University Press, Cambridge.

Schumpeter, J.A. (1934), *The Theory of Economic Development*, Harvard University Press, Cambridge Mass.

Seemann, P., De Long, D., Stukey, S. and Guthrie, E. (2000), 'Building Intangible Assets: A Strategic Framework for Investing in Intellectual Capital', in D. Morey, M. Maybury and B. Thuraisingham (eds), *Knowledge, Management: Classic and Contemporary Works*, MIT Press: Cambridge Mass, pp. 84-98.

Shannon, C.E. (1948), 'A Mathematical Theory of Communication', *Bell System Technical Journal*, Vol. 27, pp. 379-423 and 623-656, July and October. Also see http://cm.bell-labs.com/cm/ms/what/shannonday/shannon1948.pdf.

Spender, J.C. (1996), 'Making Knowledge the Basis of a Dynamic Theory of the Firm', *Strategic Management Journal*, vol. 19 (special issue), pp. 45-62.

Storper, M. (1995), 'The Resurgence of Regional Economics, Ten Years Later: the Region as a Nexus of Untraded Interdependencies', *European Urban and Regional Studies*, Vol. 2(3), pp. 191-221.

Stough, R. (2003), 'Strategic Management of Places and Policy', *Annals of Regional Science*, Vol. 37(2), pp. 179-202.

Stough, R., Kukkarni, R. and Paelinck, J. (2002), 'ICT and Knowledge Challenges for Entrepreneurs in Regional Economic Development', in Z.J. Acs, H.L.F. de Groot and P. Nijkamp (eds), *The Emergence of the Knowledge Economy. A Regional Perspective*, Springer-Verlag, Berlin, pp. 195-214.

Suarez-Villa, L. (1989), *The Evolution of Regional Economies*, Praeger, New York.

Tangermann, S. (2003), 'How Can Policy Contribute to Enhancing Competitiveness of Agriculture', 2nd European Conference on Rural Development, Salzburg, 12-14 November.

Upton, D.M. and McAfee, A. (1996), 'The Real Virtual Factory', *Harvard Business Review*, July-August, pp. 123-133.

Van der Ploeg, J.D. and Renting, H. (2000), 'Impact and Potential: A Comparative Review of European Rural Development Practices', *Sociologia Ruralis*, Vol. 40 (4) pp. 529-543.

Williamson, O. (1985), *The Economic Institutions of Capitalism*, The Free Press, New York.

You, J. (1995), 'Critical Survey: Small Firms in Economic Theory', *Cambridge Journal of Economics*, Vol. 19, pp. 441-462.

Appendix 7.1

The decision-tree method for identifying the hierarchical determinants of firm competitiveness

Learning decision trees with C5/See5

Through classification, it is possible to order the information contained in a multivariate database so as to discover structural relationships between class characteristics and relevant attributes of the phenomena to be classified. The method of decision tree induction, which belongs to the class of multidimensional classification methods (such as neural network analysis, fuzzy set analysis, rough set analysis and decision tree analysis), is widely and increasingly used for classification purposes. This method aims to analyse and predict the membership of a class by the recursive partition of a multi-dimensional data set into more homogeneous subsets (see, for details, Quinlan, 1986). This leads to a hierarchical decision tree structure where instances are classified by sorting them down the tree from the root node to a leaf node.

Each node in the decision tree specifies a test for an attribute of the instance concerned, and each branch descending from the node corresponds to one of the possible values for this attribute. An instance is classified by starting at the root node of the decision tree, testing the attribute specified by this node and moving to the next node down the tree branch that corresponds to the value of the attribute. This process is then repeated at the node on this branch and so forth, until a leaf node is reached.

In a decision tree algorithm, the critical step method is used to assess splits at each internal node of the tree. Often the information theory approach, which examines entropy in relation to the information contained in a probability distribution, is employed (see Shannon, 1948). The aim is then to select the attribute that is most useful for classifying instances, based on the so-called information gain (which is a measure for the goodness-of-separation for a given attribute in a data set according to their classification; for details, see DeFries and Chan, 2000). Entropy is then used as a measure of the reduction of disorder when ordering a set of variables in a data set with respect to different classes. By interpreting information gain as a measure of the expected reduction in entropy, we can – by considering the next node down – define a measure of the effectiveness of an attribute in classifying the data, caused by positioning the instances according to this attribute. The process of selecting a new attribute and positioning the cases is then repeated for each non-terminal descendent node, this time using only the data associated with the node concerned. Attributes that have been incorporated higher in the tree are excluded, so that any given attribute can appear at most once along any path in the tree.

Formally, the information gain of an attribute is computed by means of the corresponding entropy expression. Given a training data set T, composed of observations belonging to one of k classes {C1, C2 ... Ck}, the amount of information required to identify the class for an observation in T is :

$$Info(T) = -\sum_{j=1}^{k} \frac{freq(C_j, T)}{|T|} * \log_2 \left(\frac{freq(C_j, T)}{|T|} \right)$$

where freq(Cj , T) is equal to the number in of cases in T belonging to class Cj, and |T| is the total number of observations in T. It is the average amount of information required to define the class of a sample from the set T. In terms of information theory, it is called entropy of the set T. The same estimate, after separation of the set T with X, is provided by the following expression:

$$Info_X(T) = \sum_{i=1}^{n} \frac{|T_i|}{|T|} * Info(T_i)$$

Then, the following formula is the criterion of the attribute choice:

$$Gain(X) = Info(T) - Info_X(T)$$

This criterion is calculated for all the attributes and the one that maximizes the expression is then selected. This attribute is the test used in the current tree node, and will be used for further tree derivation.

Chapter 8

The Implementation of Information and Communication Technologies in SMEs

Martine Boutary and M-Christine Monnoyer

Introduction

This research aims to investigate the underutilization of information and communication technologies (ICTs) among small and medium-sized firms (SMEs) and the problems relating to their adoption by the actors concerned. Two particularly pertinent points have been highlighted in the economics, sociological and managerial literatures (see, for example, Bergeron and Raymond, 1996; Baile, 1995; Vallès and Carrasco, 1997; Gadille and D'Iribarne, 2000; Benghozi et al., 2000; Jouet, 2000): first, the extremely diverse forms of introduction – although this is not a recent phenomenon – and, second, that the powerful tools offered by these technologies tend to be underutilized as they have only 'local' applications. It is a challenge for both researchers and the public bodies involved to try to understand the diversity of situations and the apparently paradoxical position regarding ICTs from an economics perspective. The former, in their effort to understand the organizations, tend to seek out meaningful variables – be they strategic, organizational or environmental – which are linked to adoption and usage. The latter – because of the regional visibility of these firms as actors, investors and employers – are obliged to consider the nature of the barriers and/or incentives for adoption by SMEs to assist in their role of encouraging such firms to integrate ICTs into their businesses.

A multidisciplinary team of six researchers carried out this research investigating the usage of ICTs by SMEs between December 1999 and December 2000. The project used a qualitative methodology to analyse 21 SMEs. The firms within the sample had a degree of similarity but were not homogeneous in all respects. Their common traits were small size (on average 30 people), financial independence, a movement from thinking about adoption to the actual use of ICTs and that they were all located in two French departments – the Tarn and the Haute Garonne – for practical purposes.[1] However, the firms did not belong to the same sector of activity. Five sectors were represented: agri-food production, clothing and accessories, construction, computers and telecommunications, and medical equipment with different levels of ICT installation and integration. Forty-two interviews were carried out with top managers and those in charge of computer services. Where possible, the hierarchical structure of the business was taken into account. Three interview guides, chosen according to the position of the respondent, were used to collect data (see Appendix). The first focussed on getting general information about the business and its operation; the second dealt with the installation of ICTs (such as who buys, decides, trains, and maintains) and the consequences of introducing ICTs; and the last concerned the use of ICTs (roles and functions). Analysis of the data provided themes which were examined by the various researchers within the multidisciplinary team according to their personal competence; each person constructed different interpretation grids around a common topic.

The use of a multidisciplinary approach and qualitative analysis appeared to be most appropriate for this research. The aim was to gain an in depth understanding of situations that had already been described elsewhere. The idea that SMEs were simply too weighed down by financial or material constraints to adopt and integrate these new technologies was not accepted at the outset. The aim of the observations made in this research was to 'appreciate the problem' (Girin 1981) and, in order to achieve this, to pool information from the widest variety of actors possible. The diversity of experience and backgrounds within the team increased the potential understanding of the situation by increasing the angles of approach taken to the same phenomenon. Gombault (2000) calls this a 'beam of theories', that is to say different frames of reference are used conjointly to give a much clearer understanding of the organizational reality.

The constraints influencing the very nature of any multidisciplinary work (Mayère, 2001) were a source of enrichment for the research team, as much for the number of variables evoked as for the quality of the themes studied. The interviews were conducted by pairs of researchers and the complete transcript of the interviews was made available to each researcher, thus permitting personal work on common material. In this way, each researcher was able to analyse the interview data in their own way, from the standpoint characterizing their discipline, and this allowed what the rest of the team might have just accepted as 'the normal state of affairs' (Guattari, 1992 in Mayère 2001)) to be brought into question.

The aim of this chapter is to present this composite picture. To start with, the conclusions of the first stage of the research are briefly reviewed. The second part builds on this and proposes a new typology of modes of managing ICTs in SMEs.

The General Context for SMEs: A Proximity Network Search

The objective of this research was to observe SMEs in all their distinctiveness. The approach taken in the study was firmly anchored in the work of Torres (2000), which defines the particular characteristic of these firms as being involved in a great variety of searches for proximity in their whole management (information but also decision making or coordination). The policies in relation to the integration and adoption of ICTs seem especially sensitive to this particular management characteristic and its influence can be felt as much in initial decision making as in how the tools are eventually used. Generally speaking, the SME's top management networks with acquaintances and professional contacts to obtain the information necessary to make management decisions for their enterprise (Julien, 1998; Mattei Pasture, 1993; Fallery, 1983). The introduction of ICTs is no exception to this rule but, if the overall benefits of ICTS are clearly perceived, the same cannot be said for the panoply of tools available and their possible uses. To change this state of affairs, there is an almost systematic recourse to the network of acquaintances – be they in relational or in geographical proximity. This work, however, underlines a paradoxical aspect of such behaviour; disappointment is frequent, particularly regarding the limited impact of the technology installed. Despite this, there is little evidence of the merits of using the usual informal system to aid decision-making being questioned as a result – perhaps because management has found this type of networking to be extremely useful and effective in other circumstances.

In the case of ICTs, the resources of the existing network are insufficient, and interlocutors tend to have only a partial appreciation of the situation. The very nature of the information provided is unsuitable. It focuses mainly on the technical qualities and potential of the tools while ignoring the necessity of choosing a system in keeping with the strategic needs of the firm (Raymond et al., 1998) which, in any case, are often ill-defined. As a result, a 'mirage' effect surrounds ICTs in that the satisfaction of being able to develop its close external relationships especially with users, one of the competitive advantages of an SME, by an ITC-facilitated contact masks the difficulty of implementing a more significant reconfiguration of the business (Venkatraman, 1995). Despite their strong technical potential, the actual use of the tools, once introduced, may be limited to those in the firm directly concerned with their introduction or to those showing a particular personal interest. Such a phenomenon leads to only partial configuration and function in existing – though independent and isolated – operational activities. In these cases, only a chance meeting of the actors may create links that give the impression that the adoption process is making headway. This tends to happen on only an extremely random and unstructured basis. If proximity in all its forms facilitates information exchange, in no way does this offer an efficient mechanism for creating a strategic vision and translating this into effective ICT use.

Towards a Typology

Looking further than the simple context within which the sample firms were working, certain very diverse movements could be identified as far as ICTs are concerned. In the beginning, the observations led to the establishment of four typologies. Two of them focus on the ICT adoption process employed by the actors and the other two focus on the functions assigned to ICTs and on the business process. Each will be discussed in turn.

Looking first at the adoption process, a key variable appears to be the characteristic of the top manager and his or her personal involvement. The influence of a manager's personality on strategic choices in SMEs has been widely discussed in the previous literature (see, for example, Marchesnay and Julien, 1987; Roux, 1991; Saporta, 1986) while the influence of the manager's environment emerges from the analysis of proximity (Torres, 2000). As Harrison et al. (1997) pointed out, the criteria applied in the decision to invest in ICTs are not the same as those used in deciding on whether to make other investments within SMEs. These observations led to the identification of four types of behaviour in this research based on the degree of manager proactivity (modest or high) and their attitude towards these technologies (initiator or follower).

The four behavioural types are as follows. The 'curious' were the managers with a personal interest in ICTs. With the help of small teams, and without modifying the firm in any way, this type of manager gradually introduces a small number of tools for a few well-defined functions. The 'follower' tends to be influenced to accept the introduction of ICTs by a close contact such as a client, supplier, partner or other member of his network, but then relies mainly on individual interest and the personal initiatives of employees to develop their use. The 'enterprising' are those managers with an interest in ICTs who have ideas and develop projects around ICTs although finding that it is not always easy to engage others in this task. Finally, the 'strategist' is interested in ICTs and seeks to use it to redefine the firm's strategic positioning, products, and organization. He sets up or suggests a multiplicity of applications and is keen to develop these with a long-term perspective.

This first typology suggests that the behaviour of a manager and his team, who are confronted with the organizational and strategic changes that ICTs may bring, should be analysed to decipher the possible ICT development scenarios in such a context. As the second typology shows, however, the nature of manager behaviour, even if it is proactive and instigative, will not guarantee the efficacy of the tools adopted.

The way in which change is integrated in the organization is very important. The work of Mintzberg and Wesley (1992) brought together strategic vision and modes of development. These were used as reference bases for constructing and defining scenarios of behaviour in businesses confronted with change. Three scenarios have been created which associate strategic vision (culture, strategy and need) with modes of development (training, scheduling, and general project strategy). The three scenarios are as follows. First, are the 'go-getters'. In such SMEs, there is the combination of particular projects affecting the company's intrinsic characteristics (transformation) and scheduling, illustrating the existence of general project strategy. In this scenario, the inducing factors are often both exogenous and endogenous; the change agents behave as prospectors and as experimenters. Second, there are the 'strollers' in which each change brings about adaptive action, in most cases hesitantly. As a consequence, the behaviour of the decision makers appears to be 'analytic' (they want to control everything before deciding, even if sometimes they forget to decide), if not defensive. Finally, there are the 'hikers', representing an intermediate situation in which a change – not yet significant enough to be designated as a transformation – is nevertheless planned. Voluntarism and the co-operative and consensual behaviour of the actors seem to be important factors in helping organizations to progress in their perceptions towards change. The above typology shows that it is possible for an organization to pass from inductive learning to scheduling its actions. The prerequisite is consensus among the actors, co-operative attitudes towards the changes underway, and the involvement of all those concerned.

Having focused on the actors themselves, the research next looked at how ICTs were used and the functions that the sample SMEs assigned to them. These functions were multiple and sometimes unevenly distributed within the business. Initially, a grid categorizing the function of information was used to classify them (Vacher 2001); subsequently, a grid analysing the stakes associated with the commercial use of ICTs was employed.

Introducing new information technologies implies using them in an existing operational framework and they need to be integrated in such a way as to fulfil the firm's diverse needs which are linked to the socio-economic context or strategic position of the firm. Following Vacher (1997), four information functions were identified, namely to 'produce', 'show', 'socialize', and 'reassure'. The relative weight of each activity in the research sample was identified through the comments of the actors and from the different ways that ICTs were organized. In this way, five types of behaviour were identified among the sample firms which will be defined next.

'One-eyed' behaviour corresponds to the activation of one function only (not always the same function in each firm). The common point in the cases studied which were in this category resides in the imbalance between the firm's strategy – when it is expressed – and actual ICT use. Firms showing 'hyper-active' behaviour are those where it is regarded as more important to do than to share with others what is being done. Two functions are activated, namely 'produce' and 'socialize'. Firms with 'under-pressure' behaviour activate two information functions – 'produce' and 'show'. They adopt a lively mode of behaviour, reacting quickly, but the social approach in the long term is extremely weak. 'Distressed' behaviour corresponds to 'produce' and 'reassure' which are apparently contradictory functions. There is neither any social dialogue, nor any will to share what is being done. Feverish behaviour is visible, though not necessarily efficacious. Finally, there is 'jack of all trades' behaviour, which means that the firm activates three or four functions. Strong coherence exists between the functions assigned to ICTs, the firm's strategy and the use of other management tools and information systems. No computer specialist is present in four of the six organizations where this type of behaviour was observed, although they were the largest among the organizations studied.

ICTs stimulate firms but do not form an independent pole in the organization. The information functions grid (technology and collective management: produce, show, socialize and reassure) enabled the differences in the importance of the role given to information and its management to be highlighted. As any development of SME commercial activity generates IT needs, attention was focused on the degree of ICT adoption by the commercial managers of these firms.

The diversity of the applications initiated supposes an understanding – this time on a commercial level – of the expected and actual effects, as well as the underlying objectives. Levy (2000) distinguished three distinct potential commercial advantages associated with ICTs: the automation of commercial functions, improvement of the commercial proposition, and substitution of a tangible offer with a digital offer. By using the approach of Saporta (1986) which identifies innovation, reinforcement and redeployment strategies among small businesses, the strategic stakes potentially involved in the implementation of these commercial advantages could be detailed concurrently in this research.

After analysis, three groups of businesses were identified – those to which ICTs bring no distinctive commercial advantage, and two others for which ICTs represent sources of value generation either because of greater differentiation in the market place or because of resulting cost reductions. There are firms in which these two phenomena appear simultaneously. These two observations led the researchers to question the respective roles in the choice of ICT tools of strategic reflection and of learning through adoption.

The Search for a Business Model

This study does not cast doubt on either the strategic character of information or its place as a competitive element for the firms. Similarly, it does not call into question the economic and social importance of SMEs and the resulting interest that public bodies show in trying to orient policies that actively support such firms in adopting and using ICTs. Rather, the study discards the idea that SMEs behave identically in matters of ICTs – in relation to their uses as much as to their adoption. The second part of the chapter aims to give a composite picture which will allow some of the firms reading this to position themselves and help both firms and researchers to understand the multiplicity of variables involved in ICT adoption and use in each and every case. Hopefully, this work will also allow public bodies to adjust their support measures by using more appropriate types of segmentation not solely based on the size of the firm or the amount of capital invested in ICT introduction.

To finalize this study and to be as accurate as possible in crosschecking the data (Hlady-Rispal, 2002; Gombault, 2000), the websites of the firms concerned (where available) were observed and the level of coherence between the intentions expressed and actual projects carried out were evaluated. By comparing the previous analyses with the characteristics of the existing websites, four situations were distinguished.

In the first, the website was coherent with the firm's objectives. The actors were planning ICT adoption or were engaged in an inductive adoption process; the management tended to be pro-active though they had not always initiated the process. The relationship and interaction with clients seemed to be one of the key objectives of the site, in which the actors saw the potential for developing their competitive advantage. As a result, they increased the potential for extra-market information and introduced virtual meeting places (such as forums and clubs).

Firms in the second situation had only a partially developed site but the strategic behaviour of the actors and the business expansion process augured change. Although planned, caution surrounded the introduction of ICTs. The idea of being on the web effectively seduced the 'go-getting' management but its development was not a priority, and it was not considered to be an essential way of improving client relations in the short term. In more thriving organizations however, the site retained its importance.

In the third type of situation which could be distinguished among the sample firms, the website was well designed and sophisticated but the results were hardly satisfying in management terms. There was dissonance between the ambitions of initiating managers and those of the 'strategists' – thanks to their knowledge of business and ICTs. The idea of a site as a 'competitive weapon' on the one hand and, on the other hand, the under-utilization of the ICT functions and poor results in practice (for example in terms of turnover generated by the site) disappointed the actors and those working with them.

In the final case, the website was static, its visibility and usefulness were limited, and expansion projects were almost non existent. Firms in this situation had chosen to create a site to reassure themselves, but did not integrate such a system into their development programme. Uses were extremely limited and totally dependent on the individual's choice to either pursue or abandon them.

Website analysis was thus a transition between a collection of individual observations focussed on a group of firms and an analysis by business of the different typologies proposed. This comparison highlights the point that ICT integration and adoption strategies should not be judged solely on the tools developed. Certain results appear surprising, or disappointing, or even inexplicable if the amount of investment is simply compared to returns in terms of turnover generated. Because the company as the unit of analysis was analysed from many very different angles in this research, and its specificity as a small business taken into consideration, it emerged that there is no incoherence between choices concerning the websites and the strategic choices of the businesses. If we consider that performance is based on coherence, we cannot be completely disappointed by this kind of choice. The observations in this study, as in those of others previously, confirmed that setting up ICTs in SMEs brings about organizational changes as varied as the applications they introduce. The strategic character of some applications led on to an analysis of decision-making and strategic action. As Lauriol (1998:72) said, 'the strategic decision is represented either as a product resulting from the process dedicated to its formulation, or as a dimension which allows organizational action to take shape and constitute the strategy of the organization'. The debate concerning ICTs revolves round two types of modality. The first is related to the tools and to the kind of tinkering necessary to integrate them correctly into management activity; the second is associated with the visionary ambitions of actors more or less prepared to make their visions a reality. Following this, the respective roles of each of these modes of operation were examined in order to study small business behaviour vis-à-vis ICTs and to derive recommendations for management. The duality referred to above may seem surprising, particularly as one might suppose that SMEs are less subject to a choice between organization and strategy than other firms because of their management style, in which proximity has a strong influence. Organization and strategy go hand in hand in SMEs – or almost. In such structures, strategic action is an emergent rather than planned process. Marchesnay and Julien (1997) believe that the lightness of their structure offers an explanation of this. Using a sociocognitive approach, Lauriol (1998) shows that strategies often form in real time as the social dimensions, (such as human resources, skills) affecting the action contribute to the production of knowledge which retrospectively influences strategic decisions.

This research enabled two major categories of firm to be identified in keeping with the above – some SMEs modify their organization first and then, to different degrees, change their strategy; others have a strategic vision and only adapt their organization afterwards. The chapter now endeavours to draw inferences from the above findings.[2]

Organization Before ICT Strategy

The first category – where organization precedes strategy – was illustrated in this research by two types of firm, the 'follower' and the 'go-getter'. The example of Batirenov was characteristic of the first category. Considered a 'follower', as 'under-pressure', highly influenced by active links with its proximity network (professional and social), this firm had not formalized its strategy and showed strongly reactive behaviour. As a result, it had accrued an awareness of business opportunities (both on a regional and on an international level) and an ability, even ingenuity, in developing its ICT use. Its 'stroller' classification, however, characterized an inductive approach to ICTs; factors affecting ICT introduction were exogenous, and the firm progressively adapted to the environment and its constraints at its own pace, without the assistance of specialized ICT personnel. This was possible thanks to the contributions of strong functional and relational proximity connections (as also in the case of Arvin) or because of pressure from a powerful client (the Infotec case).

Several firms (Arvin, Infotec and Renaldia) were in this 'follower and stroller' category; ICT usage was organized reactively and in a more or less sophisticated manner. Their way of working seemed to be modulated by the existence and strength of their proximity network and by the functions that they attributed to ICTs. Infotec was dominated by a powerful client, did not possess a proximity network providing a multiplicity of points of view and developed few opportunities on a commercial or on an ICT application level; it was therefore classified as 'distressed'. Nonetheless, it could be directly interested in the tools, their technical possibilities and technical knowledge concerning ICTs in general, and would rapidly ask for support for ICT financing or training. It is easy to see that offering financial aid to help firms like Infotec to develop tools would lead only to modest changes.

In the case of Renaldia, there was a computer engineer or analyst in charge of ICT policy. The firm's network had many dimensions – professional, socio-professional, and social – and outside agencies were used to help in the introduction of particularly important software (SAP for example, which is one of the best known data processing software packages).[3] In spite of all this, deployment was limited. The firm seemed far too weak in its assertion of strategic objectives to optimize ICT development. The 'stroller', motivated by exogenous factors, willingly calls on its network for reassurance, even if those solicited intervene only on the 'tools' aspect of ICT integration. Improvements in organization, the preferred type, are not sufficient in themselves to propel the structure into a strategic leap towards a business centred on ICTs.

A last 'follower' case deserves attention, namely Terrinos which was classified as 'follower' and 'hiker'. Followers have a project approach and this firm seemed to be at the beginnings of strategy formalization; this appeared to be a very positive element for the future deployment of ICTs, and made real configurations a possibility, thanks to the quality of the firm's relational network. The environment had its constraints (super/hypermarket trade) and this may explain the extremely limited range of its applications.

In an 'enterprising' structure, organization is again a dominant activity. There are multiple projects and ICT applications may be diversified. In spite of this marked project approach, the place of ICTs is not yet strategic. Management is handled in real time and is dependent on situations as they arise and on individual enthusiasm. Its context is a strong functional proximity network that nevertheless gives most weight to the short term in assessing ICTs. The 'enterprising' advanced more or less quickly, ('hiker' versus 'stroller'), and seemed easily influenced by their environment. Their sites were not yet operating (in the case of the 'stroller') or they were lodged on someone else's site (in the case of the 'hiker' or the 'go-getter'). It might be expected that the firms in this category would have adopted the 'jack of all trades' behaviour mode, but this was not so. Weakness in the relational network of some (Kadal) and the absence of a previously established strategic vision may partially explain this finding.

Modifying the organization through the introduction or training of new personnel specialized in ICTs and investing in new tools may create disappointment in a context of insufficiently defined strategic plans which is linked to insufficient deployment of technological potential. Networks and tools, even if their efficacy can be improved over time, will not bring about a true revolution in the businesses concerned or any profound transformation in its processes; they will remain at the evolutionist phase described by Venkatraman (1995).

It hardly seems opportune, then, to provide these SMEs with new sources of outside assistance to develop the networks to which they belong, or even to provide exclusively ICT oriented training immediately. Their weakness lies in the lack of strategic vision which prevents ICTs being fully deployed. It would be preferable to encourage these firms to develop a more formalized strategic approach, which in turn will induce a more complete adoption of tools and fuller exploitation of their potential uses.

Strategy and Tools

This second category of firm, unlike the previous one, brought 'ICT visionaries' together. Here, strategic ambition was a priority and organization was more or less complete, as was seen from the websites of these businesses (which were either non-existent or schematic for the 'curious' but consistently available and of a high quality for the 'strategists'). Depending on the business environment, the relational context of the manager and the incentives to introduce ICTs, the applications were more or less diversified. These firms were categorized in the research as 'one-eyed', 'distressed', or 'hyper-active'. The higher level of education of the manager appeared, in several cases, a not insignificant element in this capacity to 'imagine the firm of the future' in the long term and in a global fashion – even where this was not related to the sector of activity of the business. For example, the manager of the textile firm, Chouet ('curious', 'go-getter', 'hyper-active'), had a PhD in chemistry. The visionary character of ICT strategy was clear although the firm's ambitions had yet to be achieved. In this example, the change drivers emanated from the firm, and more particularly from top management, which operated as a prospector; it was active and dynamic – almost excessively 'hyper-active' – and mobilized a sizeable relational network and there was a 'go-getter' project-oriented approach. The firm's efforts were handicapped by the difficulties of integrating information collected from different sources and by lack of time and adequate tools.

The same 'curious' profile may also be a 'stroller' (Akugui) or 'hiker' (Medoux); bulimia as regards information seems less evident, but the situation is very similar in terms of its lack of human and material resources. The strategic profile seems predominant. In the same way, these 'curious' businesses showed themselves able to mobilize either a sizeable relational network (Chouet) or a more modest one (Akugui). In the first case, this network may – if it is sufficiently diversified – offset certain weaknesses by providing the business with new knowledge (with all the reservations mentioned earlier concerning the nature of the information transmitted and the mode of transmission used). In the second case, a major contact with the local supplier was not sufficient to fulfil the needs of the firm.   In these cases, it would be useful to mobilize a larger network or to concentrate on building up strengths through recruitment, training or investment support.

The 'strategists' (e-cave, Copevin and Montrinfo) had the means for developing the place of ICTs in their firms. These firms were the most advanced in terms of ICT purchase and adoption. Organization was not the prime concern; it followed and reflected the firms' long-term strategic development decisions. The process of change was underway in a more or less visible way in the 'stroller' and the 'hiker', even if it was not particularly efficient or profitable.

These cases point to another type of question: the relevance of effects on SME performance. Investments in ICTs are often expensive and adoption can weigh heavily on the company's financial results. The two most 'revolutionary' cases in terms of ICT integration (Vétimin and e-cave) were also the two where the adoption of ICTs was not adding to profit in the short term. To withstand this difficulty, Vétimin had chosen to develop new activities (in terms of production and selling) around ICTs but kept the largest part of its turnover in more traditional activities unaffected. The lack of profitability then only affected activities which had been organized using ICTs, which was helpful to the firm, especially in its relationships with the banks. This is rather paradoxical considering that these tools, by the contribution they make to performance, are vital to keep the firm competitive in the longer term. E-cave decided to throw itself whole-heartedly into the exercise but had to mobilize new funds from external sources to continue operating, thus forgoing its financial independence.

As time goes on and even the most surprising innovations become familiar, the same is true for these technologies. In the case of the 'followers', it appeared that those which advanced rapidly (mainly the 'go-getters') sometimes advanced too rapidly and lost the ability take a step back and re-evaluate strategic planning. In the case of Vétimin ('strategist'), the considerable involvement of an outside IT consultancy combined with economic pressure and the obligation to get results may lead in time to the initial strategic project being suffocated. It would be useful if banks, indeed organizations specialized in financing SMEs or ICTs as well, began thinking more seriously about this question, increasing the likelihood of long-term support.

Conclusion

The objective of this research was not to conclude with a fashionable SME model. Instead, the pooled findings highlighted the importance of segmenting these firms and their needs before any support policy is set up. The work also established that such a policy would only be willingly accepted if it responded to a correctly identified, perceived need. It appeared that firms with particular profiles are more likely to succeed than others because by nature they are more evolutionary. The results can be summarized in Figure 8.1 which places the sample firms according to two variables – the extent of ICT adoption (horizontal axis) and the strength of strategic vision about ICTs (vertical axis).

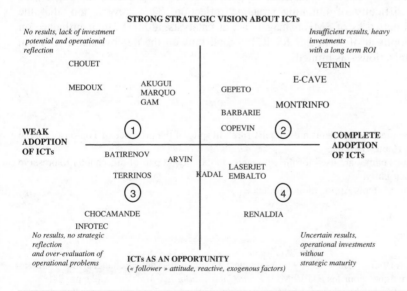

Figure 8.1   ICTs: strategies and levels of implementation

The firms not mentioned in the text are shown as examples of relative positioning in the figure. Firms placed above the horizontal axis, in spite of different levels of results, are similar because they preferred to think about strategy before thinking of ICTs. It seems necessary to provide support to help them to become operational (through the presentation of tools and of their potential applications, support for investment and accompanying support for change aimed at both users and managers). Such support could allow the development of projects still not yet realized (quadrant one of the figure) or better appropriation of tools already acquired by the firms (quadrant two). We think it is important, in this case, to avoid any other investment decision, in order to move to global competitiveness.

Firms with limited strategic consideration of ICTs lie below the horizontal axis. Those in quadrant three of the figure have already begun to introduce some tools. If these firms do think about strategy, they will probably move toward more important improvements. Essentially they need strategic support to ensure that the tools adopted by most employees serve a well defined objective. Firms in quadrant four seem to be in a risky position, being involved in an important investment process, without any long term vision. Financial risk is heavy, return on investment is quite uncertain, and it is difficult to make recommendations at this stage about appropriate support.

In conclusion, researchers as well as public organizations, private consultants and firms need to construct complex grids that take into account not only the attitude and needs of the firm regarding ICTs, but also its evolution. Without denying the importance of material support, these results re-affirm the importance and the difficulty of initiating strategic reflection. They reveal, too, that the relational networks of SME managers act as catalysts, although their influence on the development of strategies for ICTs – and thus on the deployment of ICTs in new organizations – is limited.

Notes

1 Both of these departments are globally rural, in spite of the presence of Toulouse, a large city in Haute Garonne.
2 Fictitious names are used for the companies in the second part of this chapter to preserve confidentiality.
3 SAP or Systems Applications Products.

References

Baile, S. (1995), 'Bénéfices et Avantages Compétitifs des Echanges de Données Informatiques pour les PME/PMI ', *Revue Internationale PME*, Vol. 8 (2), pp. 7-48.
Benghozi, P.J., Flichy, P. and d'Iribarne, A. (2000), 'Le Développement des NTIC dans les Entreprises Françaises', Réseaux No. 104, pp. 33-57.
Bergeron, F. and Raymond, L. (1996), 'EDI dans la PME et la Grande Entreprise: Similitudes et Différences', *Revue Internationale PME*, Vol 9 (1), pp. 41-60.

Fallery, B. (1983), 'Un Système d'information pour les PME', *Revue Française de Gestion*, No. 43, November/December.

Gadille, M. and d'Iribarne, A. (2000), 'La Diffusion d'Internet dans les PME', *Réseaux*, No. 104, pp. 61-91.

Girin, J. (1981), 'Quel Paradigme pour la Recherche en Gestion?', *Economies et Sociétés*, Vol. 12 (10, 11, 12), October/November, pp. 1871-1889.

Gombault, A. (2000), 'La Construction de l'Identité Organisationnelle: Etude Exploratoire du Musée du Louvre', Thèse pour le Doctorat de Sciences de Gestion, Université de Bordeaux IV.

Harrison, D., Mykytyn, P. and Riemenschneider, C. (1997), 'Executive Decisions about Adoption of Information Technology in Small Business: Theory and Empirical Tests', *Information Science Research*, Vol. 9 (2), June, pp. 171-195.

Hlady Rispal, M. (2002), *La Méthode des Cas*, De Boeck Université, Bruxelles.

Jouet, J. (2000), 'Retour Critique sur les Usages', *Réseaux*, Vol. 100, pp. 490-521.

Julien, P-A. (1998), 'Stratégie et Contrôle de l'information dans les PME. Pour un Elargissement du Concept d'entreprise afin de mieux Appréhender la Stratégie des PME, Dyamiques', *Management International*, Montréal.

Lauriol, J. (1998), 'Une Nouvelle Approche de la Décision Stratégique', *Revue Française de Gestion*, Vol. 121, pp. 65-79.

Lévy, J. (2000), 'Impacts et Enjeux de la Révolution Numérique sur la Politique d'offre des Entreprises', *Revue Française de Marketing*, pp.13-28.

Marchesnay, M. and Julien, P-A. (1987), *La petite entreprise, Principes d'économie et de gestion*, Ed. Vuibert, Paris.

Mattei Pasture (de), F. (1993), *L'information, Elément Immatériel à Gérer et à Maîtriser par la PME*, Working Paper, Université de Mons Hainaut, Belgique.

Mayère, A. (2001), *Mutations Organisationnelles et Evolutions des Systèmes et Activités d'information et Communication*, HDR, Université Paul Sabatier Toulouse.

Mintzberg, H. and Westley, F. (1992), 'Cycles of Organizational Change', *Strategic Management Journal*, Vol. 13, pp. 39-59.

Raymond, L., Bergeron, F., Leclerc, C. and Gladu, M. (1998), *Impact de la Congruence des TI sur la Performance des PME: une Etude Empirique*, Actes du 6eme Congres Européen sur les Systemes d'Information, Aix en Provence.

Roux, E. (1991), *Les Facteurs Explicatifs de la Décision d'exporter en PMI: Rôle de l'attitude du Dirigeant Envers le Risque*, Thèse d'Etat, IAE Aix en Provence.

Saporta, B. (1986), *Stratégies pour la P.M.E.*, Montchrestien, Paris.

Torres, O. (2000), *Du Rôle et de l'importance de la Proximité dans la Spécificité de Gestion des PME*, Actes du Congrès International Francophone sur la PME, Lille, 25-27 Octobre.

Vacher, B. (1997), 'La Gestion de l'information en Entreprise', *Enquête sur l'oubli, l'étourderie, la Ruse et le Bricolage Organisé*, ADBS Editions, Paris.

Vacher, B. (2001), *Les Fonctions des TIC: ce qu'en disent les PME*, Actes du Congrès de l'AIM, Nantes, June, pp. 337-346.

Vallès, R.S. and Carrasco, L.V. (1997), 'Les PME peuvent elles Obtenir des Avantages et Bénéfices à partir de l'utilisation d'EDI?', *Gestion 2000*, Juillet, pp.185-202.

Venkatraman, N. (1995), 'Reconfigurations d'Entreprises Provoquées par les Technologies de l'information', in M. Scott Morton (1995), *L'Entreprise Compétitive du Futur*, Ed. d'organisation, pp. 151-195.

Appendix 8.1 Interview guides

1.   Knowledge of the firm and business

     a.   Activity
     b.   History of the firm and of people interviewed (age, education, life place, professional life)
     c.   Statistics (employees, turnover, export turnover, distributing channels)
     d.   Competitive advantage
     e.   Vision of the future (development project)
     f.   Use of networks to take decisions: professional, family or friends, geographical

2.   Installation of ICTs

     a.   Needs of the firm concerning ICTs
     b.   External proposals
     c.   Environmental constraints
     d.   Competitors
     e.   Decision to buy
     f.   Attitude of the manager
     g.   Attitude of employees
     h.   Public support
     i.   Other support
     j.   Financial support
     k.   Maintenance of tools
     l.   Impact for the firm

3.   Use of ICTs

     a.   Use of computers
     b.   Technical network
     c.   Web site
     d.   Uses of web site
     e.   Internet connections
     f.   Use of electronic mail
     g.   Changes in usage over time
     h.   Evolution of strategy in the firm
     i.   Organizational change
     j.   Social change
     k.   Evolution of relationship with distributors
     l.   Business on line

Chapter 9

Break-Out Strategies of Ethnic Entrepreneurs

Tüzin Baycan Levent, Enno Masurel and Peter Nijkamp

Introduction

A significant shift in the orientation of ethnic groups towards self-employment has been observed in recent years. This movement is generally referred to as ethnic entrepreneurship (see, for example, van Delft et al., 2000; Masurel et al., 2002; Min, 1987; Waldinger et al., 1990; Ward and Jenkins, 1984) and is distinguished from 'normal' entrepreneurship through its orientation towards ethnic products, ethnic markets and customers or indigenous ethnic business strategies (see Choenni, 1997). Gradually, as their market area has expanded to provide a much broader coverage of urban demand, ethnic entrepreneurs have become an indigenous and significant part of the local economy (see Greenwood, 1994).

From the perspective of 'break-out strategies', an exclusive focus on a limited market can pose a serious threat to the future of many ethnic minority firms. These firms normally start with a focus on clients from their own ethnic group, with traditional products, services and communication channels. They are often established in areas where many fellow countrymen live. After a while, ethnic entrepreneurs may seek to expand their market domain by offering products and services for a broader group of clients, outside their own ethnic group. Some succeed in this goal and thus bring their firms into the next development stage. Some are unsuccessful in this strategy and are left to the commercial constraints of selling to their own group. A number of entrepreneurs deliberately choose to stay in this market niche.

The aim of this chapter is to investigate the trends in break-out strategies of ethnic entrepreneurs by addressing the three important aspects of such strategies, viz. capital sources, composition of clients and composition of employees. It uses data obtained through several case studies. The next section describes ethnic characteristics in entrepreneurship, while addressing business motivation, labour and capital conditions and customer relationships, and discusses the difficulties in break-out strategies stemming from these characteristics. The empirical results from the individual cases follow and the trends in break-out strategies are then examined on the basis of a comparative evaluation of the case evidence. The final section concludes with a discussion of the results and gives recommendations for further research.

Ethnic Characteristics in Entrepreneurship and Break-Out Strategies

A break-out strategy in ethnic entrepreneurship can be defined as a strategy to get away from the situation in which factors such as capital, clients and employees are dominated by the ethnic group to which the entrepreneur belongs. The critical aspects of break-out strategies refer to the special relationships between ethnic entrepreneurs and their ethnic niches in terms of business motivation, labour and capital conditions and customer relationships. Each of these will be discussed in turn.

The business motivation for ethnic entrepreneurship is to be found largely in the challenges imposed by their less favoured position. Social exclusion, discrimination, high levels of unemployment and cultural factors push an increasing number of immigrants towards entrepreneurship. They usually set up their business in those sectors where informal production would give them a competitive advantage. Social networks amongst the community and the family play a major role in the operation of ethnic enterprises (Deakins, 1999; Johnson, 2000; Kloosterman et al., 1998; Ram, 1994; Wilson and Portes, 1980). From the perspective of break-out strategies, it can be said that the traditional business strategies may give the impression of a safe haven, but do not create promising opportunities for economic expansion by the firms concerned. Niches outside traditional sectors might be expected to offer potential opportunities but the older generation of migrants tends to be more oriented towards traditional sectors serving the needs of their own ethnic groups. The younger generation is more open, often has more experience with non-ethnic situations, and tends to look for new opportunities outside the traditional markets.

Turning now to labour and capital conditions, social networks make up one of the critical, ethnic-related attributes and structures that may give a potential comparative advantage in undertaking a new economic activity (Delft et al., 2000). These social networks are multi-faceted. They provide flexible and efficient possibilities for the recruitment of personnel and the acquisition of capital. In general, ethnic businesses rely heavily on labour from the co-ethnic group and, more specifically, the family. Capital can be more easily borrowed in an informal way. In addition, there is mutual trust within the network of ethnic people allowing an informal way of doing business and exchanging information. The success of ethnic minority business firms can therefore be explained by the existence of social resources such as rotating credits, a protected market and a labour source, among other things (Deakins et al., 1997; Lee et al., 1997). The use of networks can also create a major bridge into mainstream business development. Through their networks of relatives, co-nationals or co-ethnics, new firms have a privileged and flexible access to information, capital and labour (Basu, 1998; Kloosterman et al., 1998).

Looking at customer relationships in the context of kinship relationships and social bonds, it seems plausible that there are special connections between ethnic minority business firms and their co-ethnic customers. Several studies refer to an intra-cluster ethnic loyalty, while highly intensive communication behaviour within the ethnic community offers potential competitive advantages for ethnic firms (Donthu and Cherian, 1994; Dyer and Ross, 2000). Socio-cultural bonds therefore appear to create a more than average loyalty between the ethnic firm and its clients and result in specific customer relationships. Although marketing to their own ethnic group offers the entrepreneurs certain advantages in terms of customer loyalty, it seems that this focus also makes them vulnerable and withholds opportunities for expansion. So there is a paradox concerning the ethnic minority entrepreneur and his ethnic group. Reliance on it can be seen as both a strength and a weakness but, in the end, it seems to be a life-threatening weakness for many ethnic firms.

The above mentioned critical aspects of break-out strategies are evidence of a multi-faceted phenomenon. This phenomenon incorporates a focus on the supply of capital, labour and information as well as the market and marketing strategies (for marketing strategies, see Masurel et al., 2004). In order to implement a break-out strategy, the marketing mix should be reconsidered as well. Common elements in this marketing mix are products (or services or assortment); people (employees and entrepreneurs); place (e.g. outlet); promotion (or communication), and prices (especially the price level). Changes in products, people, place, promotion and prices should be envisaged in order to develop a break-out strategy.

Trends in Break-Out Strategies: A Comparative Evaluation

Introduction to the Case Research

This chapter offers evidence of the break-out strategies adopted by ethnic entrepreneurs deriving from several empirical case studies. These case studies were conducted between 1999 and 2002 among different ethnic groups, including Turkish, Indian/Pakistani and Moroccan male and female entrepreneurs in Amsterdam. The findings from these case studies are evaluated to highlight break-out strategies of both ethnic male and female entrepreneurs. The evaluation of the findings addresses goals and strategies, in particular, as well as examining the composition of the clients and employees of ethnic entrepreneurs. Other important factors, such as motivation and driving forces and performance, are also addressed.

The first case was conducted among three different ethnic groups including Turkish, Indian/Pakistani and Moroccan male entrepreneurs; the second was conducted among Turkish female entrepreneurs and the third was conducted among Turkish male entrepreneurs in Amsterdam. First, these three case studies are described in turn. A comparative analysis of the three case studies from the perspective of break-out strategies is then presented by addressing the three important aspects discussed earlier, namely capital, clients and employees.

Empirical Results

Case Study One: Turkish, Indian/Pakistani and Moroccan Male Entrepreneurs in Amsterdam

This case study (Masurel et al., 2002) focused on differences in starting and continuing a business between three different ethnic groups, including Turkish, Indian/Pakistani and Moroccan male entrepreneurs in Amsterdam and addresses the critical success conditions for their survival and performance. The empirical data for this research is based on in-depth personal interviews held in the second part of 1999 among 40 ethnic entrepreneurs in Amsterdam. The sample contains 14 Turkish, 15 Indian/Pakistani, and 11 Moroccan entrepreneurs who had expressed a willingness to participate in a personal interview.

Tables 9.1 and 9.2 show the most important personal characteristics of these entrepreneurs and their enterprises (for further information, see Masurel et al., 2002). The most important personal characteristic to emerge was the bi-polar distribution in terms of educational level, with a majority having a low level of education. 17.5 per cent were unemployed prior to starting the business and 20 per cent cited unemployment as the reason for becoming an entrepreneur. However, the main motive for becoming an entrepreneur is to be one's own boss.

Table 9.1 Personal characteristics of Turkish, Indian/Pakistani and Moroccan entrepreneurs (% of sample)

Characteristic		%
Age	31-40	42.5
Marital status	Married	67.5
Education level	Primary and secondary school	52.0
	Higher vocational and university	35.0
Language ability	Fluent or good	50.0
Position before starting	Employed	55.0
	Entrepreneur	25.0
	Unemployed	17.5
Reasons for becoming an entrepreneur	To be own boss	70.0
	Unemployment	20.0

Source: Adapted from Masurel et al. (2002)

Table 9.2 shows that the majority of the enterprises belong to the retail and service sectors and that they were reasonably successful in terms of development of sales and profit in the previous year.

Table 9.2 Features of Turkish, Indian/Pakistani and Moroccan enterprises (% of sample)

Feature		%
Activity	Manufacturing-wholesale	25.0
	Retail	30.0
	Service	45.0
Starting situation	Newly started	42.5
Development of sales	Increase	47.5
	Same	27.5
Profit in the previous year	Positive	87.5
	Same	7.5

Source: Adapted from Masurel et al. (2002)

Despite the many common characteristics of ethnic entrepreneurs, the findings of this study show that there is a great variation in motives, attitudes and behaviour between different ethnic groups. Indian/Pakistani people appear to have a relatively high share in ethnic business life, whereas Moroccans play only a minor role and Turkish people occupy an intermediate position.

Case Study Two: Turkish Female Entrepreneurs in Amsterdam

The second case study (Baycan-Levent et al., 2002 and 2003) examines the phenomenon of ethnic female entrepreneurship by investigating Turkish female entrepreneurs in Amsterdam. The focus of the research is on the ethnic female profile and the dual character of ethnic female entrepreneurs, i.e. the combined characteristics or indicators of ethnic entrepreneurship and female entrepreneurship. This case study research is based on in-depth personal interviews, held in the first part of 2002 among 34 Turkish female entrepreneurs in Amsterdam.

Tables 9.3 and 9.4 give the most important personal characteristics of these Turkish entrepreneurs and the features of their enterprises (for further information, see Baycan-Levent et al., 2002 and 2003). As Table 9.3 shows, the majority of these respondents have lived in the Netherlands for more than 20 years, and have received education in the Netherlands; three quarters were qualified to the middle vocational level. All were either employed or acting as entrepreneurs previously and the main motive for becoming an entrepreneur was to be their own boss.

Table 9.3 Personal characteristics of Turkish female entrepreneurs (% of sample)

Characteristic		%
Age	31-40	61.76
Marital status	Married	73.53
Education level	Middle vocational	73.53
Language ability	Fluent or good	82.35
Arrival year	1971-1980	47.05
Position before starting	Employed	70.59
	Entrepreneur	20.59
Reasons for becoming an entrepreneur	To be own boss	70.59

Source: Adapted from Baycan-Levent et al. (2002)

Female entrepreneurship has become more important in Turkish immigrant groups in the last decade and Table 9.4 shows that more than 90 per cent of the Turkish female enterprises started after 1990. These enterprises are generally small, belong to the service sector, and demonstrate considerable success in terms of development of sales and profit in the year prior to the study.

Table 9.4 Features of enterprises owned by Turkish females (% of sample)

Feature		%
Activity	Driver school	35.29
	Hairdresser	14.71
	Fashion shop	17.65
	Human resource management	11.77
Foundation year	After 1990	91.18
Starting situation	Newly started	73.53
Proprietorship	Sole proprietorship	88.24
Number of employees	No employees	50.00
	1-5 employees	41.18
Development of sales	Increase	44.12
	Same	23.53
Profit in previous year	Positive	61.76
	Same	14.71

Source: Adapted from Baycan-Levent et al. (2002)

The findings of this research on Turkish female entrepreneurs show a special female profile in terms of the duality (ethnic and female) in their characteristics. Turkish female entrepreneurs are special female entrepreneurs, particularly in terms of personal and business characteristics, driving forces and motivations. The most prominent characteristics of Turkish female entrepreneurs are very similar to non-ethnic female characteristics in general and they are closer to the species of female entrepreneurs than to that of ethnic entrepreneurs. The personal characteristics of Turkish female entrepreneurs and the features of Turkish female enterprises are very similar to the characteristics of non-ethnic female entrepreneurs and non-ethnic female enterprises in most countries.

Case Study Three: Turkish Male Entrepreneurs in Amsterdam

The third case study (Masurel et al., 2003) seeks to analyse the differences between first and second generation ethnic minority entrepreneurs in terms of entrepreneurial motivation. The empirical research is based on in-depth personal interviews held in the second part of 2001 among 40 Turkish entrepreneurs in the hospitality sector in three Dutch cities: the majority (28) was in Amsterdam, eight were in Alkmaar and four in Zaandam. There is only one female entrepreneur in the sample so, like the first case, the third case study reflects the attitudes and behaviour of male entrepreneurs.

Tables 9.5 and 9.6 show the most important personal characteristics of entrepreneurs and the features of the enterprises (for further information, see Masurel et al., 2003). As this case study research focuses on generation differences, the age of the entrepreneurs is one of the most striking characteristics in Table 9.5. More than half of the entrepreneurs were less than 25 years old. A lower educational level of the large majority also appears to characterise these entrepreneurs. While just over three-quarters of the sample has had previous experience as an employee or entrepreneur, the main motivation to become an entrepreneur is to be one's own boss.

Table 9.5 Personal characteristics of Turkish entrepreneurs (% of sample)

Characteristic		%
Age	Under 25 years old	57.5
Education level	Primary and secondary school	95.0
	Higher vocational and university	5.0
Position before starting	Employed	50.0
	Entrepreneur	27.5
	Unemployed	10.0
	School	12.5
Reasons for becoming an entrepreneur	To be own boss	80.0
	Unemployment	10.0

Source: Adapted from Masurel et al. (2003)

As Table 9.6 shows, this case study was conducted in the hospitality sector and, due to the characteristics of this sector, the size of the enterprises in terms of the number of employees is rather small; 80 per cent of the enterprises only have between one and five employees. Approximately one third of the enterprises were newly started and more than one third were owned by other shareholders.

Table 9.6 Features of enterprises owned by Turkish males (% of sample)

Feature		%
Activities	Hospitality	100.0
Starting situation	Newly started	30.0
Proprietorship	Shareholder	37.5
Number of employees	1-5 employees	80.0
	6-20 employees	20.0

Source: Adapted from Masurel et al. (2003)

The findings of this case study show a number of differences between the first generation and second generation, particularly in terms of motivation. The younger generation appeared more open and looked for new opportunities outside the traditional markets.

The results of these three studies highlight the common trends in motivation. In all three, the respondents' main motive for becoming an entrepreneur was to be their own boss (70-80 per cent of responses). However, when the background of the entrepreneurs is examined, it is clear this motive can be shaped by negative reasons such as lack of education, language problems, lack of job alternatives or unemployment. These negative reasons, or push effects, seem especially important in the decisions of male entrepreneurs to become entrepreneurs in the first and third case studies. In contrast, the desire of female entrepreneurs in the second case to be their own boss seems to be determined by positive reasons, or pull effects, such as education level and experience.

A Comparison of Trends in Break-Out Strategies

The characteristics of ethnic entrepreneurs and the ethnic enterprises in the three cases above show many similarities. However, an overall evaluation of these studies also draws attention to the differences, especially between male and female entrepreneurs, first and second generations and different ethnic groups. In this section, the results of the three cases are compared from the perspective of break-out strategies by addressing the three important aspects identified earlier in the literature review, namely capital, clients and employees. As discussed previously, when a break-out strategy is defined as a strategy to get away from the situation in which the entrepreneur's own ethnic groups dominate, considerations about capital, clients and employees gain importance due to the ethnic dependency generally observed in these factors and market conditions. A comparison of the trends in these may help us to identify how far ethnic entrepreneurs are from dependence on their ethnic groups or their ethnic niches in the market.

Table 9.7 gives the comparative results from the three cases in terms of ethnic entrepreneurs' capital sources, composition of employees and composition of clients. This comparison draws attention to two general trends: first, a rather high dependency on ethnic networks in terms of capital and labour sources, and second, the transformation process in providing services from ethnic towards non-ethnic groups.

The results, taken together, show that more than half of the entrepreneurs combine their own capital with capital from family and friends. Female entrepreneurs show a relatively balanced combination of capital sources. They tend to use their own capital rather than the capital obtained from family and friends. This is in contrast to male entrepreneurs, who tend to be heavily dependent on family capital. This financial support from family or friends can reach up to 75 per cent for Turkish male entrepreneurs active in the hospitality sector. The tendency to hire employees from the entrepreneur's own ethnic group mirrors the ethnic dependency apparent in the acquisition of capital. The majority of the employees in all three cases are from the entrepreneur's own ethnic group. When employees of mixed race, including the entrepreneur's own ethnic group, are categorised as within the same group, this share can reach 60 per cent.

The ethnic dependency observed in the acquisition of capital and the composition of employees is not reflected in the composition of clients. A break or a transformation in the composition of clients can be observed in the case studies, with the majority of the clients being drawn from other groups. The share of non-ethnic clients is almost 80 per cent for ethnic male enterprises. These enterprises are clearly in a further stage of change in terms of orientation towards clients from ethnic towards non-ethnic origin. However, this fact can partly be explained by the choice of economic activities. In the first case considered, the respondents were in the manufacturing, wholesale and retail sectors, not just services, and this means that they are naturally more open to all clients without regard to ethnicity. In case one and case two, the majority of the service sector is made up of hotels and restaurants, and these sectors are also far from being ethnic services; on the contrary, they are open to all clients. This non-ethnic orientation seems less strong for ethnic female enterprises. Although the share of non-ethnic clients is more than 50 per cent, the higher ethnic dependency observed in the ethnic female enterprises may be explained by the stronger niche strategy adopted by female entrepreneurs. This might also result from the later entrance of female entrepreneurs to the market. As they are in the early stages of their economic activities, it is natural that they might be more dependent on their own ethnic groups, not only in terms of capital and labour sources but also in terms of clients. This general trend in terms of composition of clients in all three case studies demonstrates a stage of change in orientation towards non-ethnic groups.

Table 9.7 A comparison of break-out strategies of different ethnic minority entrepreneurs

Features	Case study one: Turkish, Indian/ Pakistani, Moroccan male entrepreneurs	Case study two: Turkish female entrepreneurs	Case study three: Turkish male entrepreneurs
Year of the research	1999	2002	2001
Sample	40	34	40
Focus of the research	Motivation and driving force	Ethnic female entrepreneurship	Generation differences in motivation
Aspects of break-out strategies	%	%	%
Capital sources			
Own capital	22.50	44.12	72.50
Family or friends	55.00	41.18	75.00
*Composition of employees**			
Employees from own ethnic group	57.50	61.16	48.70
Employees from other groups	2.50	38.84	12.80
Mixed	7.50		38.50
Composition of clients			
Clients from own ethnic group	21.00	44.00	26.00
Clients from other groups	79.00	56.00	74.00

* Composition of employees is based on the number of employees for case study two and the number of firms for case study one and case study three.

Ethnic entrepreneurs have clearly become service providers not only for their own ethnic group, but also for the other groups in the market. However, this trend is strongly dependent on the sector and it is too early to call this a real transformation process in some sectors. For example, the driving school sector constitutes more than one third of the sample enterprises in the second case study (see Table 9.4) and the clients of this sector are all from their own ethnic group. In contrast, the majority of the clients of hairdressers or fashion shops in the same sample are from other groups. It seems that these entrepreneurs tend to benefit from their ethnic niche, but they do not limit themselves to this small group and they also orient themselves to other groups to a greater of lesser extent depending on the sub sector of activity. The chosen orientation results not from ethnic reasons, but from economic reasons. If an own ethnic orientation provides more opportunities, they orient themselves to their own group but if the entrepreneurs see a greater potential in the other groups, they are oriented to these groups.

Besides these two general trends showing a high degree of dependency on ethnic networks and a transformation process in providing services, the specific results of the case studies show other interesting trends. As this comparative study is based on three differently formulated case studies and different data sets, it considers the common and comparable data in all case studies from the perspective of break-out strategies. However, factors such as goals and strategies of ethnic entrepreneurs or orientation to non-traditional markets are also very important to understand the break-out strategies of ethnic entrepreneurs. The first case study has focused on motivations and performance and, for this reason, does not contain any information about entrepreneurial goals and strategies. The second case study examines the goals and strategies of ethnic female entrepreneurs while the third case study evaluates generational differences and the orientation to non-traditional markets.

It is often argued in the literature that ethnic entrepreneurs (and also female entrepreneurs) tend to pursue a niche strategy and to pursue continuity rather than growth. In addition, they usually adopt a defensive and specialised strategy (Brush, 1992; Carter et al., 1997; Cliff, 1998; Cromie and Birley, 1991; Verheul et al., 2001). However, the results of the second case study show that this hypothesis is not supported for Turkish female entrepreneurs. As can be seen in Figure 9.1, most of the Turkish female entrepreneurs indicated that they wanted to grow their businesses. Only eight entrepreneurs did not want any change and all the others wanted growth. Approximately 24 per cent of the entrepreneurs wanted to increase their number of employees, 15 per cent wanted a bigger shop, 15 per cent wanted a second shop and 9 per cent wanted to open new shops in different cities. 15 per cent wanted to expand their interest fields and 9 per cent wanted to increase the number and diversity of their products. These figures show that Turkish female entrepreneurs are quite convinced about their success and the niches they have found in the urban economy and this self-confidence encourages them to increase the size of their enterprises. This desire for growth can also be explained by the smaller size and early stage in the life cycle of the business, as well as the type of activity (services).

From the perspective of break-out strategies, these findings can be evaluated according to two distinct objectives: first, to grow the business in terms of size and the number employed and, second, to expand into other related activities. The first objective refers to the quantitative dimension of break-out strategies that were defined by entrepreneurs as a bigger shop, a second shop or shops in other cities; an increase in the number of employees is seen as a necessary condition for all these moves. The second type of objective refers to the qualitative aspect of these strategies such as the related side-activities, product diversification, participation in training and so on. Some entrepreneurs mentioned during the interviews that they wanted to expand their business, for example, from being a hairdresser to having a beauty salon or by introducing shoes and other accessories into the existing fashion shop. However, some entrepreneurs indicated that their enterprises were already running different activities at the same time, such as finance, insurance and tourism.

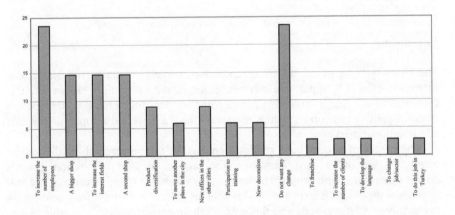

Figure 9.1   Goals, plans and strategies of Turkish female entrepreneurs

Source: Baycan-Levent et al. (2003)

This fact can be explained on the one hand, by the existence of a great many potential clients within an ethnic niche. On the other hand, this could also be a break-out strategy to open the business to other markets and clients from other nationalities. An overall evaluation of the goals and strategies of Turkish female entrepreneurs shows the existence of very complex and interrelated break-out strategies. In the first stage, these strategies are based on economic reasons, such as clients' potential, and are constructed to increase the size of business and the number of employees. In the second stage, the focus moves from a quantitative to a qualitative basis focusing on expanding the business with other related activities and diversification of the products. However, this process and the priorities of the entrepreneurs change according to their sector of operation and the needs of this sector.

The results of the second case draw attention to the different motivation of the second generation entrepreneurs that could also be very important in break-out strategies. According to the results of this study, first generation ethnic minority entrepreneurs tend to have relatively negative 'push' motivations, whereas second generation entrepreneurs have quite positive motivations pulling them towards entrepreneurship. This difference in motivation may also lead to some differences in orientation towards non-traditional markets. The younger generation is observed to be more open and to look for new opportunities outside the traditional markets. This new orientation can also help to break-out from ethnic dependency or to escape from an ethnic enclave.

These case studies therefore highlight the transformation process that has begun to emerge from the perspective of break-out strategies in both an orientation towards non-ethnic groups and non-traditional markets. However, a high dependency on ethnic networks is still evident.

Conclusions

The characteristics of ethnic entrepreneurship, namely ethnic niches and ethnic networks, offer a comparative advantage for ethnic enterprises. However, this comparative advantage may also create some barriers for break-out strategies in terms of gaining new opportunities to expand the business and to open to new and non-traditional markets.

The results of several case studies compared in this research show that ethnic enterprises are in an early transformation process in their orientation towards clients from non-ethnic origin. The results also show that these enterprises are still dependent on ethnic labour and capital sources. There is still a strong orientation towards own ethnic groups and this makes ethnic entrepreneurs vulnerable. Some crucial changes are necessary to overcome this vulnerability and to achieve success in break-out strategies. These include more formal business planning, a different marketing mix and an orientation towards outside information sources.

This picture of ethnic dependency draws attention to the trust within the ethnic networks. A focus on trust in future research may allow more detailed insight into ethnic dependency. The results of the case studies draw attention to another transformation process in terms of the different motivation and orientation to non-traditional sectors of the young generation entrepreneurs. Future research could usefully pay more attention to this younger group.

References

Basu, A. (1998), 'An Exploration of Entrepreneurial Activity among Asian Small Businesses in Britain', *Small Business Economics*, Vol. 10(4), pp. 313-326.

Baycan-Levent, T., Masurel, E. and Nijkamp, P. (2002), 'Entrepreneurial Process and Performance: A Study on Turkish Female Entrepreneurs in Amsterdam', Paper presented at the 42nd European Regional Science Association Congress, August 27-31, 2002, Dortmund, Germany.

Baycan-Levent, T., Masurel, E. and Nijkamp, P. (2003), 'Diversity in Entrepreneurship: Ethnic and Female Roles in Urban Economic Life', *International Journal of Social Economics*, Vol. 30(11), pp. 1131-1161.

Brush, C.G. (1992), 'Research on Women Business Owners: Past Trends, a New Perspective and Future Directions', *Entrepreneurship Theory and Practice*, Vol. 17(4), pp. 5-30.

Carter, N.M., Williams, M. and Reynolds, P.D. (1997), 'Discontinuance Among New Firms in Retail: The Influence of Initial Resources, Strategy, and Gender', *Journal of Business Venturing*, Vol. 12(2), pp. 125-145.

Choenni, A. (1997), *Veelsoortig Assortiment*, Het Spinhuis, Amsterdam.

Cliff, J.E. (1998), 'Does One Size Fit All? Exploring the Relationships Between Attitudes Towards Growth, Gender, and Business Size', *Journal of Business Venturing*, Vol. 13(6), pp. 523-542.

Cromie, S. and Birley, S. (1991), 'Networking by Female Business Owners in Northern Ireland', *Journal of Business Venturing*, Vol. 7(3), pp. 237-251.

Deakins, D. (1999), *Entrepreneurship and Small Firms*, Second Edition, McGraw-Hill, London.

Deakins, D., Majunder, M. and Paddison, A. (1997), 'Developing Success Strategies for Ethnic Minorities in Business: Evidence from Scotland', *New Community*, Vol. 23(3), pp. 325-342.

Delft, H. van, Gorter, C. and Nijkamp, P. (2000), 'In Search of Ethnic Entrepreneurship Opportunities in the City', *Environment & Planning C*, Vol. 18(4), pp. 429-451.

Donthu, N. and Cherian, J. (1994), 'Impact of Strength of Ethnic Identification on Hispanic Shopping Behaviour', *Journal of Retailing*, Vol. 70(4), pp. 383-393.

Dyer, L.M., and Ross, C.A. (2000), 'Ethnic Enterprises and their Clientele', *Journal of Small Business Management*, Vol. 38(2) pp. 48-66.

Greenwood, M.J. (1994), 'Potential Channels of Immigrant Influence on the Economy of the Receiving Country', *Papers in Regional Science*, Vol. 73(3), pp. 211-240.

Johnson, P.J. (2000), 'Ethnic Differences in Self-Employment among Southeast Asian Refugees in Canada', *Journal of Small Business Management*, October, Vol. 38(4), pp. 757-793.

Kloosterman, R.C., Leun, J. van der, and Rath, J. (1998), 'Across the Border; Economic Opportunities, Social Capital and Informal Businesses Activities of Immigrants', *Journal of Ethnic Migration Studies*, Vol. 24(2), pp. 367-376.

Lee, Y., Cameron, T., Schaeffer, P. and Schmidt, C.G. (1997), 'Ethnic Minority Small Business: A Comparative Analysis of Restaurants in Denver', *Urban Geography*, Vol. 18(7), pp. 591-621.

Masurel, E., Nijkamp, P., Tastan, M. and Vindigni, G. (2002), 'Motivation and Performance Conditions for Ethnic Entrepreneurship', *Growth and Change*, Vol. 33(2), pp. 238-260.

Masurel, E., Yuzer, M. and Holleman, J. (2003), 'Ethnic Minority Entrepreneurs: The Generation Effect, An Analysis of Motivational Differences Between First and Second Generations', *International Workshop on 'Modern Entrepreneurship, Regional Development and Policy: Dynamic and Evolutionary Perspectives'*, 23-24 May 2003, Amsterdam, The Netherlands.

Masurel, E., Nijkamp, P. and Vindigni, G. (2004), 'Breeding Places for Ethnic Entrepreneurs: A Comparative Marketing Approach', *Entrepreneurship and Regional Development*, Vol. 16(1), pp. 77-86.

Min, P.G. (1987), 'Factors Contributing to Ethnic Business: A Comprehensive Synthesis', *International Journal of Comparative Sociology*, Vol. 28(3/4), pp. 173-193.

Ram, M. (1994), 'Unravelling Social Networks in Ethnic Minority Firms', *International Small Business Journal*, April-June, Vol. 12(3), pp. 42-59.

Verheul, I., Risseuw, P. and Bartelse, G. (2001), 'Gender Differences in Strategy and Human Resource Management', *Rotterdam Institute for Business Economic Studies*.

Waldinger, R., Aldrich, H. and Ward, W. (eds) (1990), *Ethnic Entrepreneurs*, Sage Publishers, Newbury Park, Ca.

Ward, R. and Jenkins, R. (eds) (1984), *Ethnic Communities in Business*, Cambridge University Press, Cambridge.

Wilson, K.L. and Portes, A. (1980), 'Immigrant Enclaves: an Analysis of the Labour Market Experiences of Cubans in Miami', *American Journal of Sociology*, Vol. 86(2), pp. 295-319.

Chapter 10

Rural Entrepreneurship: An Innovation and Marketing Perspective

Anabela Dinis

Introduction

Entrepreneurship is now seen by most politicians as well as by academics as an important ingredient in rural development. Rural areas are, however, often characterized by low densities in demographic, institutional, relational and economic terms. Entrepreneurship is particularly difficult in such circumstances. Nevertheless, examples can be found of innovative entrepreneurship in such areas all over the world, including in rural areas of Portugal. This chapter intends to highlight the characteristics of the new global and information economy and the opportunity that this represents for rural areas and their small firms using two conceptually related instruments, namely innovation and marketing. It argues that, at the organizational level, niche marketing strategies are the most appropriate for rural firms as they allow them to innovate and take advantage of the opportunities opened up by the new economy. This is illustrated by reference to some Portuguese examples. Finally, some policy conclusions are drawn.

The Rural Context and the Role of Entrepreneurship

Entrepreneurship can be understood as the process of creation of new firms and/or the development of small firms. The term 'development' in this context is usually connected with the development of new products and new processes of production (Nijkamp, 2003; Wortman 1990) as well as new markets (Wortman, 1990). Thus, entrepreneurship is by definition an innovation related concept.

Three interwoven elements are fundamental to entrepreneurial processes (and thus also to innovation) namely the individual; the organization, and the environment. Where rural entrepreneurship is concerned, the environment is, at least partially, defined by a set of common characteristics. So in order to understand rural entrepreneurship, we must first understand the meaning of the term 'rural' and then how this specific context affects and is affected by entrepreneurship.

Definition of Rural

Defining the term 'rural' is not an easy task since it has been used in different contexts – from developed countries in Europe or the United States to the more undeveloped countries in Africa or Asia – and in each of these contexts, rural areas present very different characteristics. Furthermore, rural also means different things to different people. To some it refers to landscapes with natural beauty whilst to others it means agriculture and/or ancient traditions. According to Diniz and Gerry (2002) these everyday definitions represent three definitional groupings that have dominated different areas of knowledge, namely behavioural, functional and ecological categories.

The behavioural definition has its origins in sociology and assumes that there is a distinction between rural and urban behaviours due to different population densities. This perspective relates rural to traditional and conservative values and practices. Nevertheless, in an era of rapid evolution in information and communications technology and of increasing migration movements, this distinction is blurred, since small rural communities are no longer isolated from global trends.

The functional definition, drawn from economics, is based on the economic and occupational characteristics of those areas which are traditionally associated with agriculture and/or the exploitation of other natural resources (forestry, cattle raising, mining, fishery and hunting). Nowadays, however, there is an increasing trend to pluriactivity among rural populations. Indeed, agricultural activities are losing their importance in favour of industrial activities in some cases, such as in some rural industrial districts. This functional definition can therefore be problematic when used to distinguish urban from rural.

The ecological definition highlights the characteristics of the natural environment and its relationship with human beings. Its first version placed greater emphasis on the natural component of rural areas, seen as small communities surrounded by large areas of open landscape where human activity was viewed as detrimental. In its most recent versions, it incorporates the cultural and social environment as well, and emphasizes the sustainable exploitation of natural, cultural and national resources as the crucial characteristic of rural areas and their development.

The evolution of these three definitional categories suggests that one single definition is not sufficient. In fact, the European Commission clearly states that rural areas 'are complex economic, natural and cultural locations, which cannot be characterized by one-dimensional criteria such as population density, agriculture or natural resources (European Commission, 1999: 23). It also makes clear that 'with regard to the paths taken in development and prospects for development they differ greatly from each other' (idem: 24). This means that while some rural territories have successfully assimilated structural changes and achieved a considerable level of economic development, others remain behind and have become increasingly peripheral in economic terms. So rural areas are currently characterized by diversity, not only in terms of their cultural, social and political inheritance, but also in terms of their future. Of course, the areas with structural problems of adjustment are those which most need the attention of public authorities and governments.

The European Commission (1988) report on the future of the rural world recognized three different types of rural areas with different problems to solve. First, there are the rural areas that lie just beyond the boundaries of large cities and face problems related to the pressure of modern development, including excessive development and conflicts over the different potential use of land. Second, there are rural areas that face social and economic decline. A decline in agriculture not compensated by new rurally based industries means that young people, in particular, have moved elsewhere in search of jobs. The effect of young people leaving these regions leads to continuing economic decline and a further reduction in the quality of life. Finally, there are the more distant and less favoured rural areas, usually consisting of mountainous zones and also certain islands, which constitute a more extreme example of the second case. Rural decline, depopulation and the abandonment of land are already significant in these areas and there is very little prospect for economic diversification.

Arzeni et al. (2002) identify four different types of rural area in Europe and highlight the varied requirements for rural development policies according their specific characteristics. According to these authors, rural areas near to urban centres have to deal with their integration with metropolitan areas in facing issues related to residential provision for city-dwellers, local demand and the production of traditional or new products and services. Rural areas that act as natural, historical and leisure resorts are concerned with tourist development and the sustainable exploitation of their resources. In areas where the agricultural sector is dominant, there is a need to certify and add value to the local and typical produce in order to compete in agricultural markets. In addition, remote and distant territories need to be integrated by policy makers and to have the right incentives to stop migration. Although this classification suggested by Arzeni et al. includes four types, there is a close relationship with the threefold classification discussed earlier. Rural areas that are natural, historical and leisure resorts can be included in the second type mentioned in the previous classification alongside agricultural areas.

This chapter is particularly concerned with peripheral rural regions (i.e., regions that fall into the two last two types within the European Commission classification, and to the three last types defined by Arzeni et al., 2002) because they reflect the reality of most Portuguese rural areas. In fact, Portugal has a dualist economy in which the relatively well developed large urban centres, such as Lisbon and Oporto, are located on the coast and the underdeveloped, low density areas are located inland. The term 'low density' is used by Magalhães et al. (2001) and refers not only to demographic features but also to other characteristics. These may be institutional (a small number of entities with responsibilities and competencies for development at local level); relational (a small number and variety of people and institutions with which to interact); occupational (few employment opportunities which are usually concentrated in agriculture) and economic characteristics (small scale local production and few opportunities for increasing turnover).

The rural areas represent more than 80 per cent of the geographical area of Portugal but less than one third of the Portuguese population, a proportion that is reducing over time with the continuing trend towards the concentration of population in the larger urban centres. A United Nations (2001) study suggests that by 2015, more than 45 per cent of the national population will live around Lisbon and 24 per cent will be in the metropolitan area of Oporto. Comparing the Portuguese case to the same projection in other European countries (see Figure 10.1), it is clear that Portugal represents an extreme case of concentration in large urban areas and the consequent abandonment of other parts of the country. This means that if the same path of development is maintained, there is no prospect of a movement to convergence or cohesion in the country. Under these circumstances, rural development and the mechanisms that can promote it are crucial in the overall development of Portugal.

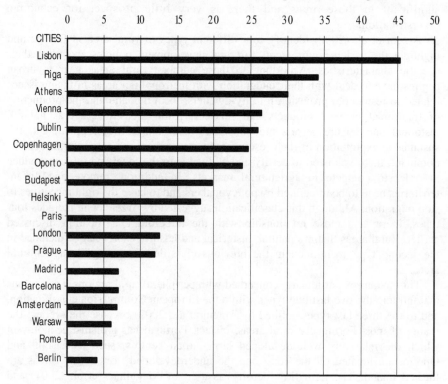

Figure 10.1 Population living in European cities in 2015 (% of total population of each country)

Source: United Nations (2001)

Entrepreneurship and Rural Development: A Mutual Relationship

According to the European Commission (1999: 24), 'The key to the sustainable development of rural regions lies in the development of an independent perspective and the discovery of indigenous potential...' These words reflect the view that currently rules rural development. Endogenous theories of development emerged at the end of the 1970s as result of disillusionment with traditional exogenous models based on neoclassical or Keynesian theories. The policies of encouraging urban poles of development did not result in convergence as had been expected. On the contrary, they increased the differences between regions in several cases (Benko, 1999). Furthermore, it was clear that in a climate of economic crisis, growth can not be spread because growth does not exist. So another model of development was needed.

The empirical observation by some Italian sociologists (Bagnasco, 1977) and economists (Becattini, 1979, 1989; Garofoli, 1983) of local phenomena that appeared to be outside the traditional development model in the so called 'Third Italy' drew attention to an alternative method of rural development. These phenomena, usually called 'industrial districts', represent 'a new articulation of the industrial system which is a product of the emergence of local initiative in the territories in development and not as result of firms' inter-regional mobility' (Garofoli, 1983: 1279). This line of research was developed in several countries and later crossed with theories of innovation resulting in new terms like 'innovative milieux' (Aydalot, 1986; Maillat, 1998) and 'learning regions' (Florida, 1995). But all the territories studied shared some common characteristics, namely close relationships between SMEs in the local productive system; flexible production; local initiatives (endogenous entrepreneurship); different ways of accessing and treating information, and entrepreneurial patterns of learning and innovation.

These empirical findings reinforce the concept of endogenous development (Friedman and Weaver, 1979) or development from below (Stöhr and Taylor, 1981). In this approach, the fundamental issue in regional development is no longer the capacity of the region to attract new enterprises but its internal capacity to generate the conditions for transformation of its own productive structures. Contrary to the previous exogenous paradigm, the endogenous paradigm considers the rational and sustainable exploitation of local resources to be of crucial importance. But if the region is to benefit from the economic exploitation of its own resources, agents belonging to the territory must be responsible. SMEs resulting from local initiatives should therefore be seen as the main agents of local/regional economic development. With successful local initiatives, the living standards of local populations become sustainable. However, in a context of growing globalization and rapid change, the survival of both regions and firms depends on their ability to achieve competitive advantages in the global economy and to conquer new markets. This idea is currently the basis of European rural development models. The Cork Declaration (Declaration, 1996: 1) explicitly recognized that rural development should be based on strategies which 'promote, in all possible ways, local capacity building for sustainable development in rural areas, and, in particular, private and community-based initiatives which are well-integrated into global markets'.

Studies of local systems of production, including industrial districts, innovative milieux and learning regions (e.g. Becattini, 1979; Garofoli, 1983; Aydalot, 1986; Florida, 1995) also make clear that local initiatives depend on territorial development or, to put it another way, the existence of a supportive environment. These studies highlight the concept of social capital as a source of innovation, and social innovation as a part of that supportive environment. They also emphasize the importance of social and spatial proximity which generates external economies of agglomeration (Chevassus-Lozza and Galliano, 2003). These external economies include economies of specialization, which derive from the division of work, economies of work which occur through the formation and accumulation of specific and tacit knowledge, and economies of diffusion resulting from easier communication and the more effective circulation of information (Bottazzi and Peri, 2003). These characteristics together result in a stronger capacity to innovate and to compete in a global economy. This line of research makes clear that the territory is the place where, besides allocating generic resources, specific assets can be generated from localized learning and coordination between firms.

So firms and entrepreneurs are embedded (Granovetter, 1985, 1993) in a territory in a dynamic and relational way. The firm contributes towards the local industrial/entrepreneurial context and, in turn, the context is a fundamental element of support for its existence and good performance. However, this mutual relationship can represent a problem for backward rural regions where this type of positive relational dynamic does not exist. In these more peripheral regions, firms are scarce and, because they are scarce, neither an entrepreneurial spirit nor a supportive environment exists. The emergence and success of new firms is, therefore, a very rare phenomenon. At this point, two related questions must be addressed. How can this vicious circle be broken? And how can firms in rural and peripheral regions manage to be successful even within an unfavourable local environment?

Marketing and Innovation: A Partnership Towards Firms' Success in Rural

Factors Affecting Small Firms' Innovation and Success in Rural Areas

Theories about entrepreneurship and small firms usually consider three factors as affecting the success of small firms, first, the entrepreneur, second, resources and strategic choice, and, finally, the environment. These same factors help to understand success or failure in rural contexts (Niittykangas, 1996; Diniz and Gerry, 2002). Since success is a function of competitive advantage which, in turn, results from the capability to promote innovation, these factors can also be seen as affecting innovation (see Figure 10.2). The characteristics of the environment have been discussed earlier so the features of the two factors in rural and peripheral areas will now be discussed:

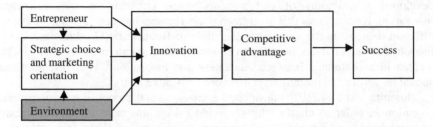

Figure 10.2   Factors affecting innovation and success of small firms

The Entrepreneur as a Promoter of Innovation

The view of innovation as based on individual effort can be traced to Schumpeter (1912, 1934), who emphasized the role of the entrepreneur as a promoter of innovations that creatively disrupt the existing order in the market place. The entrepreneur's motivation to innovate is the search for increased profits. Innovation as a source of differentiation or exclusivity can create a monopolistic structure in the market, allowing superior returns until imitative competitors cause these returns to fall to an equilibrium level. Of course, this equilibrium is constantly changed by the introduction of more innovations that create a dynamic market and economic growth. Innovation is based on the creative thinking of the entrepreneur and, in this sense, the entrepreneur is at the centre of the process of innovation and economic progress.

Reflections on the Schumpeterian notion of the entrepreneur generated debate about the concept of an entrepreneur. This dominated the field of entrepreneurship theory for a long time and led to research into entrepreneurial traits which aimed to identify specific characteristics of the entrepreneur (Carland et al., 1988; Hoy, 1987; Wislow and Solomon, 1989; Green et al., 1996). These characteristics are usually associated with demographic features (e.g. age and sex), attitudes (e.g. risk propensity), and values and motivations (e.g. the need for independence, locus of control). A small but growing body of research deriving from this work assumed that entrepreneurs have specific, characteristics but these must be found in their cognitive structures (e.g. Baron, 1998; Buttner and Gryskiewicz, 1993; Palich and Bagby, 1995; Busenitz and Lau, 1996; Levenhagen and Thomas, 1993; Huuskonen, 1993). This approach explores individual perceptions and the factors affecting the subjective realities that drive behaviours and attitudes, specifically the decision to start and develop an entrepreneurial project.

The discussion of entrepreneurial characteristics (both the trait and cognitive approaches) originated basically from two different conceptions of the entrepreneur. For some, an entrepreneur is simply the owner of a business, while others argue that this is not necessarily true since not all business owners show the creative thinking, linked to innovation, which characterizes entrepreneurs. Later work shows that a definition drawn on dichotomy between the existence and non-existence of creative thinking attempts too sharp a distinction. Manimala (1996) developed a taxonomy of entrepreneurs based on their orientation toward innovation. He concludes that all entrepreneurs (business owners) are innovative to different degrees. In the same way, the study of Buttner and Gryskiewicz (1993) identified different styles of problem resolution among entrepreneurs that can be located in a continuum between adaptation and innovation.[1] Thus, the question should be why are some entrepreneurs more innovative than others?

Busenitz and Lau (1996) developed a cross-cultural model of entrepreneurial cognition in order to clarify why some individuals are more inclined to create ventures inside and outside their home country than others. They concluded that factors such as social context (social capital) ethnic or cultural values and individual variables have a relevant impact on the nature of individual cognition and can be a source of competitive advantage.

Innovation, Marketing, Strategic Choice and Competitiveness

Defining the entrepreneur as a creative destructor and constructor of a new order (Johannisson, 1992) means that the entrepreneur is the person who creates new ways of fulfilling needs not currently satisfied or creates more efficient ways to satisfy them. In this sense, innovation goes beyond technological innovation. According to Porter (1980), it includes improvements in technology and better ways of doing things in all aspects of business. In other words, it is everything that increases the effectiveness and efficiency of resources and the ability to satisfy market needs. This idea is compatible with Schumpeter's (1912, 1934) view of innovation that includes five types of innovation, namely modifications to existing products as well as the development of new products, market sourcing, organizational innovation and process innovation. In the same vein, North and Smallbone (2000) identified and measured five dimensions of innovative behaviour, namely product and service innovation, market development, marketing methods, process technology and innovation in the use of computers and information technology in administration.

According to these enlarged perspectives, innovation refers not only to productive processes and/or products, but also to organizational processes and marketing approaches. The European Commission recently referred to the several types of innovation in the following way: 'In addition to the term *technological innovation*, covering innovation derived from research, further classifications may be identified. *Organizational innovation* reflects the recognition that new ways of organizing work in areas such as workforce management...distribution, finance, manufacturing, etc. can have a positive influence on competitiveness. This term may also include *business model innovation*. *Presentation innovation* is beginning to be used as a comprehensive term to cover innovation in areas such as design and marketing.' (European Commission, 2003: 6-7). The last type of innovation – the last to be recognized by intellectuals and politicians but not the least – includes concerns about design, presentation, image, segmentation and all the concepts related to the marketing approach. As the European Commission stresses, 'the most important economic contribution does not necessarily come from the "early [technological] adopter" but from the "fast follower" who adopts the innovative design that captures the international market' (European Commission, 2003: 7).

In this sense, the success of any innovation and hence the competitiveness of firms and regions depends on having a marketing orientation with the ability to adjust to, or better still, to anticipate market tendencies. This is also a basic argument within strategic management theory (Dobni and Luffman, 2003) which stresses the need for alignment between internal capabilities and the external demands of the environment (e.g. Ansoff, 1965; Andrews, 1971; Porter, 1980; Waterman, Peters and Philips, 1980). Both tangible and intangible resources are combined through organizational routines creating organizational capabilities (Barney, 1991; Oliver, 1997). If these capabilities are valuable to the consumer, difficult to replicate, acquire or appropriate by other parties in the long run, they form the bases of sustainable competitive advantage and superior economic performance. Strategic management theory suggests both internal and external analyses in order to understand which resources and capabilities will allow the firm to achieve a sustainable competitive advantage (Andrews, 1971; Porter, 1980). The selection and accumulation of resources and capabilities is an internal decision, made by business owners/entrepreneurs in the case of small firms, in light of their perception of the environment. Strategic choice is seen as a rational choice, guided by efficiency, effectiveness and profit motivations, and results in decisions about the business idea – a combination of markets, product line and a way of doing business.

This strategic thinking can also be applied to rural areas. North and Smallbone (2000) conclude from a comparison of rural and urban locations that there is no clear indication that location in a remote rural environment has an adverse effect on the overall ability of SMEs to innovate. To survive in remote rural areas, SMEs need to be adaptable and this can result in them being more innovative in some respects than firms elsewhere. This happens mainly as regards new products and marketing developments. In other respects, their location appears to be a barrier to innovation, as in use of computers and new information technologies (Premkumar and Roberts, 1999).

Thus, it is necessary to develop marketing and strategic knowledge, as well as technological expertise, in the process of innovation in order to increase competitiveness. The analysis of market trends and their implications is fundamental to appropriate strategic choice.

Information and Knowledge Economy: the Opportunity for Rural Entrepreneurship

The global economy is currently undergoing a transformation in which the industrial economy is giving way to the information economy. In this new era, information, exchange of data and communication are of vital importance for economic development. This transformation was caused by the rapid advances in technology in the last decades and is impacting both demand and supply conditions. This revolution represents an opportunity for rural entrepreneurs to integrate into the global economy and for rural and peripheral areas to change their status from being at the economic periphery.

Technological advances and the growing urbanization resulting from industrialization in developed countries in general, including Portugal, have induced a transformation in life style. This transformation can be seen in several domains (Dinis, 2000; Magalhães et al., 2001). Higher levels of family income mean that more can now be spent on goods and services other than necessities. The development of an information society, with the expansion of new information technologies, brings a more transparent market and reduces information asymmetries, as well as ensuring easier and faster access to the desired products. Increased levels of literacy, training and information result in a more selective and demanding consumer and in different interests and motivations, including those relating to the acquisition and development of knowledge about different cultures and traditions. People have more free time as a result of reduced working hours, longer holiday periods, shorter working lives (partly because of longer periods of study) and increases in life expectancy. In contrast to this general tendency, there are some segments of the population where time is scarce during their working life, representing a 'time poor and money rich' paradox. Accessibility has increased due to a generalized reduction in transportation costs and better mobility conditions. The prevalence of an urban lifestyle results in an appreciation of what is genuine and different and a desire for uniqueness. Finally, there is a more generalized concern about and appreciation of scarce natural resources. All the trends in demand mentioned above are not homogeneous. However, they do affect a significant part of the population and, for that reason, result in meaningful segments of the market.

Technological advances also affect productive systems and the conditions of market supply. They mean that production processes and transportation may require less capital outlay. They also allow sharp increases in the quality and flexibility of output. Furthermore, information and knowledge, the bases of the emerging economy, are not location specific and can be easily created and used in remote sites at relatively low cost (Mackenzie, 1992). For instance, as Pancucci (1995) notes, a simple computer connected to the Internet allows access to a university research library or to other centres of research and information.

At the same time, knowledge and information also demand more creativity, not only because imitation will be more rapid but also because the consumer is more informed, selective and demanding. In this context, firms and their products will only be successful if they are able to identify and quickly respond to the changing needs of the 'new' consumer. As a result, it is necessary to have more detailed and more continuous information and knowledge about consumers. In addition, mass production, the dominant force within the economy since the industrial revolution, is progressively being superseded by speciality production directed to the specific needs of each consumer or client.

This means that the new economic paradigm is also in a new organizational paradigm. Individuals and small firms with access to information and knowledge and the ability to use them creatively and innovatively will be able to outdo cumbersome corporations as the dominant producers of wealth and holders of power (Toffler, 1990). This new model of organization is reflected in what Piore and Sabel (1984) called 'flexible specialization', which is characterized by industrial districts and other local productive systems (e.g. Kalantaridis, 1997). Thus the key elements of successful economic reorganization within the new economy include not only access to necessary resources and technology but are also contingent upon a set of relationships which are based at the local and regional level. This represents a new opportunity for firms in rural and peripheral areas.

Niche Marketing Strategies for Rural Products

Competitiveness, as we have seen, relates to the strategic choice made by the entrepreneur. The strategic choice is a result of analysing the external conditions of demand and the resources available to the firm. The previous section focused on the external conditions impacting rural firms; the resources available in the rural world that can form the bases of a firm's competitive advantage will now be discussed.

Craft production and traditional products, with all the uniqueness, genuineness and respect for nature that they represent, are valuable products for some global market segments. Also the informal, traditional life style and the contact with nature that characterize rural regions put them in a unique position to respond to growing concerns about the quality of life in general, and about health, safety, personal development and leisure in particular. In general, the analysis of social trends shows that there are rural resources that are highly valued by a growing part of the society, a part with more purchasing power and free time, but also with more awareness and knowledge about natural and cultural heritage. This led Ray (1998) to suggest the need to commoditize local culture and give a new value to 'place' through its cultural identity. North and Smallbone (2000) found evidence that some sectors (mainly food and tourism) benefit from being in a rural environment by being able to introduce products based on traditional, rural craft skills to the market.

This means that some activities and products that usually constitute an invisible part of the fabric of rural areas can offer business opportunities. Examples include a gastronomic speciality with a recipe passed down in the family, home made bread, embroidery and home produced fabrics made in free time between agricultural and domestic work, as well as the casual work done by a more skilful neighbour. Products like these are specific to the rural world, and thus difficult or impossible to imitate. They represent the uniqueness of each region and for that reason they are a source of competitive advantage for rural firms and must be at the centre of their strategy. If correctly directed to the market segment that values them through an appropriate niche marketing strategy, they can bring in far more revenue and provide more employment than producing products widely available elsewhere ever would. Those who adopt niche marketing strategies tend to cater to segments that large competitors overlook or ignore and avoid direct confrontation with large companies by specializing along market, customer, product or other marketing mix lines (Porter, 1980; Kotler 2000). Firms who follow a niche marketing strategy understand the needs of their clients so well that they can charge a premium price.

Several authors have highlighted the viability of such a strategy for rural products. For instance, Dimara et al. (2003) argue that the creation of niche markets for food and drink products can promote the sustainable development of peripheral, rural regions. Locality becomes increasingly important in the process of adding value to traditional or conventional agricultural products. Taken together, locality and quality can structure a specific image for agricultural products. This image is the key feature in creating niche markets. Using a social ecology theory (a social construction approach) the authors propose an explanation of the factors underlying the creation of niche markets which is applied to the study of organic cultivation. They conclude that organic cultivation gives farmers the opportunity to develop a specific image for their product based on quality assurance. In that sense, organic cultivation provides a high profile image, consisting of a more risky choice but with potentially higher anticipated benefits. Other authors using Porter's typology (Brester and McNew, 2002; Ariyawardana, 2003) examine how some firms have found ways to add value to farm products and compete in regional, national and global markets. In these studies, niche marketing appears as one viable strategy. Tregear (2003) analyses the market orientation among craftsmen and craftswomen. She concludes that as well as perceiving themselves as prioritizing non-commercial, lifestyle goals, adherence to craft principles positively contributes to marketing advantage and commercial success in the specialist niche in which these participants operate.

Thus resources that are specific to the rural world, allied to the identified trends in demand, open up a large market of speciality or niche products for rural firms. According to Kotler (2000: 419) speciality products, are 'goods or services with unique characteristics or brand identification for which a significant group of buyers is willing to make a special purchase effort.[2] Lane and Yoshinaga (1994) identified a set of potential niche products and services rural firms might provide, classifying them according to whether they relate to natural resources, tradition and cultural heritage or environment and amenity resources, as shown in Table 10.1.

Niche marketing strategies imply the need for niche marketing techniques based on, first, the identification of groups of consumers willing to spend more on products that better satisfy their specific needs and second, innovation to attract the desired, high quality consumers. Innovation is a multidimensional concept as discussed earlier. The European Commission has emphasized, 'the search for new, untapped, market space is another driving force [of innovation]. This may rely on technological innovation, or on reconfiguring existing products and services so as to present a radical change that will be perceived by customers as offering more or better value ("value innovation")' (European Commission, 2003: 6). Rural firms will achieve increased competitiveness with the incorporation of new technologies but design, presentation and image innovations may be even more important. Organizational innovation is also fundamental. Some characteristics of the rural society such as family and community ties are the basis of the new model of production known as 'flexible specialization.' As Piore and Sabel note, 'Among the ironies of the resurgence of craft production is that its deployment of modern technology depends on its reinvigoration of affiliations that are associated with the preindustral past' (Piore and Sabel, 1984: 275).

Table 10.1 Matrix of niche goods and services in rural areas

		Resources		
		Natural resources	Tradition and cultural heritage	Environment and amenity resources
Niche	Goods	**Goods produced using rural natural resources including value-added and processed agricultural, sea, river, forestry and mineral products** High quality vegetables and fruits Traditionally made cheese Organic production Medical plants Local pickles Dried flowers Fish paste and dried fish Mineral waters Dried fruits	**Goods produced and marketed using historical cultural skills and traditions** Crafts such as ceramic & pottery Jewellery Embroidery Rugs Wooden toys and bowls Traditional costumes Flax knits	**Goods produced in areas because of their high-quality natural environment** Attractive environments, good climate, clean air which may attract research centres and high-technology enterprises Goods produced using local energy or scarce resources such as pure or mineral water
	Services	**Services specifically requiring rural natural resources including specialized forms of tourism and recreation** Toolmakers, porters and guides for hunting, fishing, camping and skiing Hotels and inns Restaurants serving local specialities Holiday farms Ecological museums Natural parks	**Services based on rural heritage and traditions** Historical monuments Traditional architectures Local museums Local festival and folk dances Restaurants serving traditional cuisine	**Services making much of the rural environment and amenities as a marketable commodity** Holiday villages and rest or retirement homes Health and fitness centres with accommodation

Source: Lane and Yoshinaga (1994: 16).

In sum, the new rules of the economic game provide an opportunity for rural and peripheral areas and their firms to achieve a better position on the chess board of the global economy. They give added significance to a set of characteristics of the rural world, transforming them into valuable assets on which rural firms can base their strategy and achieve global competitiveness.

Rural Entrepreneurship in Peripheral Areas: Some Successful Examples from Portugal

This section presents some successful cases of entrepreneurship in Portuguese rural and peripheral areas. The cases all relate to the introduction of traditional and heritage resources in the global market.

Martinlongo and Cachopo are two neighbouring rural localities located in the extreme south-east of Portugal. Together they have around 1600 inhabitants. Their main economic activities are agriculture, cattle raising and some commerce associated with leather, cork and olives. The first embroidery course was developed in 1985 at the request of the local authorities and with the support of the General Direction for adult education and of IM (Swedish Individual Support). In 1986, a set of firms was created as the second phase of this project aimed at the professionalization of the trainees. The three firms, 'Flor de Agulha' (in Martinlongo), 'Linha Serrana' (also in Martinlongo) and 'A Lançadeira' (in Cachopo), work in close relationship in different but complementary areas. Linha Serrana produces two annual collections of exclusive designs influenced by traditional, rural, bourgeois costumes of the region. They use hand made fabric produced by Lançadeira and embroideries made by Flor de Agulha. Flor de Agulha also embroiders material made by Lançadeira for use in home decoration. This partnership has been quite successful not only because it created jobs but also because the produce attracts high prices in both national and international markets.

Another similar, successful example is in Montemuro, located in North West Portugal which is one of the most peripheral areas in the country. Subsistence agriculture and cattle raising are traditionally the main economic activities in this area. A firm called 'Capuchinhas de Montemuro' was set up in 1986 as a result of the efforts of the Institute for Cultural Affairs. As in the previous case, women were the main participants in the new venture. Again thanks to a set of training courses, some women were organized to work together in the production of fashion and home textile products strongly influenced in their design by tradition. Natural and traditional materials such as flax and wool were used, materials on which women have traditionally worked in their homes, putting into practice what they have learnt from their mothers and grandmothers. This firm was the first to emerge but, as a result of the energy created, the cooperative 'Combate ao Frio' was set up nearby some time later. Using wool and traditional techniques and designs, the ten women that form the cooperative have reactivated the production of knitted gloves, socks and round caps used in the region. Later, they also began to develop a line of other knitted garments as well as woven coats, waistcoats, skirts and curtains. In the manual weave and knit of their grandmothers, they reproduced the fabric which their ancestors had used to protect themselves from the mountain cold. But the story does not finish there. Another organization, working in collaboration with the previous ones, was later started by women in the same region. A decisive factor in both cases was the initiative taken by a Swedish fashion designer, supported by IM, who helped these women to create their own models and promote exports to their own country. The products described have the national and international urban market as their main destination and are mostly sold in speciality shops.

The final example is from Manteigas, a small village in a mountainous region in the centre of Portugal. In the middle of the 1990s, João Clara, a young man born in Manteigas but living in Lisbon since his youth, decided to return to his origins.

The decision was triggered by the death of his father, who was a traditional weaver in Manteigas. His father produced a coarse wool fabric and blankets traditionally used by the shepherds of that region. Partly because of his emotional ties with the activity of his father, but mainly because he saw a potentially good business if redirected towards an urban market, Clara left Lisbon and returned to develop his father's business. Thanks to his local ties, he could easily learn more about traditional weaving from the older people who still knew the traditional techniques. He was also able to organize a production network with local women at home making this type of fabric either on their own weaver's loom or ones he lent them. By outsourcing the work in similar fashion to the entrepreneur of the pre-industrial age, he did not need to provide workshop space.

Thanks to his personal abilities and commitment, Clara was able progressively to develop new products and move towards the urban centres as his main markets. His fabric was, and still is, largely used by 'Capuchinhas' and 'Combate ao Frio' but meanwhile he developed new applications for the same product, including home décor, specially aimed at tourism enterprises. In 1998, he also began to produce clothes and started his own rural tourism business. By 1999, he had enlarged his line of products to include clothes and accessories made with knitted wool. These products are now available in several places in Portugal, Spain, France, Italy and the Nordic countries. Undoubtedly this internationalization is partly accounted for by Clara's own international mobility. Benefitting on occasion from some public support, he participated in several international craft fairs and personally contacted potential clients. Furthermore, Clara is quite aware of the needs of his potential clients, referring to 'natural, ecologic, design and presentation' as the main needs met by his products.

These cases suggest the applicability of the niche marketing strategy that demands innovation to attract the desired high quality consumers. Innovation is present in several dimensions. Product innovation results from the association of traditional techniques with innovative designs (e.g. clothes of Linha Serrana and Capuchinhas de Montemuro) and in the development of new applications for traditional products (e.g. handmade fabric for home decoration in the cases of Lançadeira and João Clara). Market developments include the specific approach to urban markets (in all cases) and also to new types of customers (e.g. tourism enterprises like hotels, in the case of João Clara). Innovation in marketing methods is also present in all cases and includes changes in perception and the promotion of the image of rural products. This was achieved through their careful presentation, high price and selected channels of distribution. There is also evidence of organizational innovation. The new institutional arrangements were based not only on local economic, social and cultural linkages (in all the cases presented), but also on regional; national/international linkages with other firms (in the João Clara case) and socio-cultural institutions (in the cases located in Martinlongo, Cachopo and Montemuro). Niche marketing strategies imply the identification and detailed knowledge of the desired target market. In the cases presented, the target was clearly the national and/or international urban population. This met all the conditions necessary to be defined as a worthwhile market for niche products.

Conclusions and Policy Considerations

The theoretical frameworks and examples considered in this chapter make it clear that the integration of local and regional economies into the global economy is both a challenge for local actors and an opportunity for small and underdeveloped regions to survive and grow. However, competitiveness and the conquest of new markets in the global economy depend on the firms' capacity to innovate. Innovation includes not only the use of new technologies in products and/or processes but also organizational and marketing innovation.

The new trends in demand, as well as the new flexible specialization in production, represent new hopes for rural and peripheral areas condemned by the traditional industrial model of mass production to the maintenance of their peripheral status. However, enthusiasm for the new opportunities should not allow us to forget that there are a number of liabilities that these regions still face. These include the lack of critical mass to support development of specialized services such as health care, transportation and technological support on site, as well as the lack of electronic infrastructures and people with the necessary competencies to operate them and manage the information (MacKenzie, 1992). Furthermore, the vision of these regions as peripheral, resulting from their long standing secondary position in the context of the industrial society, can constitute an important psychological obstacle to inhabitants becoming entrepreneurs and can also make it difficult to attract financial and human capital.

So rural areas face threats and opportunities, as well as possessing weaknesses and strengths. How these weaknesses will be overcome and these strengths reinforced depends on the strategy of both firms and the regions as a whole. And strategy, as we have seen, is ultimately a question of choices made by individuals and by local and national governments and institutions (see Figure 10.3).

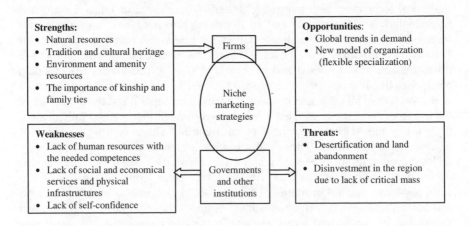

Figure 10.3 SWOT analysis of rural and peripheral areas

This chapter has mainly focused on rural firms and how they can take advantage of the opportunities of the emerging economic paradigm, following niche marketing strategies based on the specific resources of rural areas. However, some consideration must also be given to the role of governments and other institutions as these are the other fundamental actors in the promotion of rural entrepreneurship. It is their responsibility to find ways to overcome the weaknesses of rural and peripheral areas and to mitigate the threats.

For many years, public policy was directed to the construction of a material infrastructure that could support entrepreneurial initiatives and to the promotion of entrepreneurship through various types of aid such as financial incentives, tax reliefs and direct subsidies for chosen firms or industries. Portuguese economic policy is no exception. In Portugal, however, SME policy is defined and financially endowed by national and supra-national government. It follows a national logic with few or no local considerations. The problem with this type of policy is that it does not consider the huge differences between localities as, for example, in access to information. In central urban areas, information flows quite rapidly and effectively through the social system, allowing economic agents to access the available support and be aware of opportunities; in more peripheral areas information hardly circulates. Because business firms and services to firms are few in those regions, information about available support and business opportunities is scarce or difficult to obtain (Haskins and Gibb, 1987; Good, 1996; Dinis, 1998).

The success of some rural economies based on small firms that emerged naturally shows the importance of networks and the need among small firms for an information and business network that supplements the advantages they may derive from being small, namely their flexibility and ability to respond quickly. It seems clear that, as Pyke and Sengenberger (1990: 4) state, 'the key problem for small firms appears not to be that of being small, but of being isolated'. This was also illustrated by the examples presented.

Thus, governmental and other institutional support should be directed not, or not mainly, at the individual entrepreneur but at the creation of network structures which promote the organizational context of entrepreneurship and reduce the impact of borders (Dinis, 2002). In terms of development, this means that if a small village or a rural region is to be revitalized through the creation of small businesses, the construction of local and wider networks must also occur. Interventions with this aim need to have a strong territorial orientation.

Governmental intervention can contribute through direct financial support but, more importantly, should jointly with local agents promote information about financial support available to SMEs and also about the basic steps in establishing and running a firm. This process of information diffusion will certainly speed up if some pivotal individuals or institutions summarize, simplify and make information accessible to those establishing new businesses in peripheral areas. At the same time, it is important to invest in technical and professional training and so increase the ability to use the information.

Last but not least, and connected with the previous considerations, territorial marketing strategies are also crucial. The aim of economic authorities must be to help firms progressively to integrate into market niches that transcend the limits of the local territory. Thus, promoting the external image of the rural territory is critical, since it represents an important vehicle to connect rural resources to the market. Furthermore, it is a way to attract some segments of the population both with competences to run business and support services, or simply to generate critical mass. But the use of marketing tools demands a strategic vision about the territory and the segments of market that it intends to tap. The construction of that strategic vision is also the collective responsibility of the local and national authorities as well as of all the socio-economic agents in the territory. This type of intervention should achieve two complementary objectives, both making territories more competitive and creating conditions encouraging active segments of the population to remain. In short, it will break the all too common vicious circle within which 'because there is no local entrepreneurship, local development is not achieved; because there is no local development, local entrepreneurship is not achieved'.

Acknowledgment

I would like to acknowledge the valuable comments and suggestions of the reviewers.

Notes

1   Assuming the idea of a continuum between adoption and innovation leads to the notion of innovativeness as the degree to which an individual is earlier in adopting new ideas than the other members in his system (Rogers and Shoemaker, 1971: 27; Hyvärinen, 1997: 159). If we consider the system as the rural and peripheral community, it can be argued that any business owner in this system is an innovator (thus an entrepreneur) no matter what product s/he produces, process he applies or organization he runs, since any firm represents a high degree of innovativeness in that context.

2   It is important to note that the willingness to pay an extra amount is fundamental to defining niche products as marketable products. For instance, Weeden (2002) analyses ethical tourism as a niche marketing opportunity. She concludes that it would be wrong to suppose that the decision to purchase an ethical holiday also includes the intention by the consumer to pay a premium price. In fact, while consumers may feel some sympathy with ethical issues, this does not necessarily mean they will pay higher prices for products that claim to contain some ethical elements. From a marketing perspective, this can indicate the importance of also associating personal benefit with rural products in order to convince potential consumers to pay a higher price.

References

Andrews, K. (1971), *The Concept of Corporate Strategy*, Richard D. Irwin, Homewood, Illinois.

Ansoff, I.H. (1965), *Corporate Strategy: An Analytical Approach to Business Policy to Growth and Expansion*, MacGraw-Hill, New York.

Ariyawardana, A. (2003), 'Sources of Competitive Advantage and Firm Performance: The Case of Sri Lankan Value-Added Tea Producers', *Asia Pacific Journal of Management*, March, Vol. 20(1), pp. 73-90.

Arzeni, A., Esposti, R. and Sotte, F. (2002), *European Policy Experiences with Rural Development*, Associazione 'Alessandro Bartola', European Association of Agricultural Economists, Wissenschaftsverlag Vauk Kiel KG.

Aydalot, P. (1986), *Milieu Innovateur en Europe*, GREMI, Paris.

Bagnasco, A. (1977), *Tre Itale. La problemática Territoriale dello Sviluppo Italiano*, Il Molino, Bologna.

Barney, J. (1991), 'Firm Resources and Sustained Competitive Advantage', *Journal of Management*, 17(1), pp. 99-120.

Baron, R.A. (1998), 'Cognitive Mechanisms in Entrepreneurship: Why and When Entrepreneurs Think Differently than Other People', *Journal of Business Venturing*, Vol. 13, pp. 275-294.

Becattini, G. (1979), 'Dall'settore industriale al distretto industriale. Alcune considerazioni sull'unita d'indagine dell'economia industriale', *Rivista de Economia e Politica Industriale*, Vol. 5(1) pp. 7-21.

Becattini, G. (1989), 'Les districts industrielles en Italie', in M. Maruani (Dir.), *La Flexibilité en Italie*, Syros-Alternates, Paris, pp. 261-268.

Benko, G. (1999), *A Ciência Regional*, Celta, Oeiras.

Bottazzi, L. and Peri, G. (2003), 'Innovation and Spillovers in Regions: Evidence from European Patent Data', *European Economic Review*, Vol. 47, pp. 687-710.

Brester, G. and McNew, K. (2002), 'Value-added Agriculture', *Montana Business Quarterly*, Vol. 40(2), pp. 12-17.

Busenitz, L.W and Lau, C-M. (1996), 'A Cross-cultural Cognitive Model of New Venture Creation', *Entrepreneurship Theory and Practice*, Vol. 20(4), pp. 25-39.

Buttner, E.H. and Gryskiewicz, N. (1993). 'Entrepreneurs' Problem-solving Styles: an Empirical Study using the Kirton Adaptation/innovation Theory', *Journal of Small Business Management*, Vol. 31(1), pp. 22-29.

Carland J.W., Hoy, F. and Carland, J.A. (1988), '"Who is the Entrepreneur?" Is the Question Worth Asking', *American Journal of Small Business*, Spring, pp. 33-39.

Chevassus-Lozza, E. and Galliano, D. (2003), 'Local Spillovers, Firm Organization and Export Behavior: Evidence from the French Food Industry', *Regional Studies*, Vol. 37(2), pp. 147-158.

Declaration of the Participants (1996) 'The Cork Declaration – A Living Countryside', *European Conference on Rural Development – Rural Europe: Future Perspectives*, Cork, Ireland, 7-9 November, http://europa.eu.int/comm/agriculture/rur/cork_en.htm.

Dimara, E., Petrou, A. and Skuras, D. (2003), 'The Socio-economics of Niche Market Creation – A Social Ecology Paradigm for the Adoption of Organic Cultivation in Greece', *International Journal of Social Economics*, Vol. 30(3), pp. 219-235.

Dinis, A. (1998) 'Apoio Institucional às Pequenas e Médias Empresas, O Caso da Beira Interior', *Seminário da Beira Interior: Actualidade e perspectivas de Desenvolvimento*, Covilhã, UBI, Outubro.

Dinis, A. (2000), 'Futuro e Tradição: um Novo Paradigma de Competitividade para as Regiões Rurais e Menos Desenvolvidas', *Perspectivas de Desenvolvimento para as Regiões Marítimas*, Colecção APDR, pp. 545-556.

Dinis, A. (2002), 'Rural Entrepreneurship: Individual or Collective Phenomena', *Portuguese Journal of Management Studies*, Vol. VII(2), Special Issue, pp. 111-126.

Diniz, F. and Gerry, C. (2002), 'A Problemática do Desenvolvimento Rural', *Compêndio de Economia Regional*, APDR, pp. 535-570.

Dobni, C.B. and Luffman, G. (2003), 'Determining the Scope and Impact of Market Orientation Profiles on Strategy Implementation and Performance', *Strategic Management Journal*, Vol. 24(6), pp. 577-585.

European Commission (1988), *The Future of Rural World*, Communication from the Commission to the Council and European Parliament PSTA/PO/1007, Brussels.

European Commission (1999), *ESDP – European Spatial Development Perspective: Towards Balanced and Sustainable Development of the Territory of the European Union*, May.

European Commission (2003), *Innovation Policy: Updating the Union's Approach in the Context of the Lisbon Strategy,* Communication from the Commission to the Council, the European Parliament, the European Economic and Social Committee and the Committee of the Regions, COM (2003) 112 final, Brussels, 11 March.

Florida, R. (1995), 'Toward the Learning Region', *Futures*, Vol. 25 (5), pp. 537-536.

Friedman, J. and Weaver, C. (1979), *Territory and Function*, E. Arnold, London.

Garofoli, G. (1983), 'Le Aree-sistema in Italia', *Politica ed Economia*, XIV(11), pp. 17-34.

Good, W. (1996), 'Support Systems for Small Business, Their Levels of Awareness and Perceived Importance', *Journal of Small Business and Entrepreneurship*, Vol. 13(4), Winter, pp. 34-49.

Granovetter, M. (1985), 'Economic Action and Social Structure: the Problem of Embeddedness', *American Journal of Sociology*, Vol. 9 (3), pp. 481-510.

Granovetter, M. (1993), 'The Nature of Economic relationships', in R. Swedberg (ed.), *Explorations in Economic Sociology*, Russel Sage Foundation.

Green, R., David, J. and Dent, M. (1996), 'The Russian Entrepreneur: a Study of Psychological Characteristics', *International Journal of Entrepreneurial Behaviour and Research*, Vol. 2(1), pp. 49-58.

Haskins, G. and Gibb, A. (1987), 'Support for Small Business Development in Europe', in K. O'Neill, R. Bhambri, T. Faulkner and T. Cannon (Eds), *Small Business Development: Some Current Issues*, Gower, Avebury, Hampshire, pp.45-68.

Hoy, F.S (1987), 'Who are the Rural Entrepreneurs?', in B.W. Honadale (Ed.), *Proceedings of the National Rural Entrepreneurship Symposium*, Knoxville, TN.

Huuskonen, V. (1993), 'The Process of Becoming an Entrepreneur: a Theoretical Framework of Factors Influencing Entrepreneurs' Start-up Decisions', in H. Klandt (Ed.), *Entrepreneurship and Business Development*, Avebury, Aldershot, pp. 43-53.

Hyvärinen, L. (1997), 'Innovativeness and its Indicators in Small and Medium-sized Industrial Enterprises', in L. Davies and A. Gibb (Eds), *Recent Research in Entrepreneurship*, Avebury, Aldershot, pp. 154-179.

Johannisson, B. (1992), 'Entrepreneurship – The Management of Ambiguity', in T. Polesie and I-L. Johansson (Eds), *Responsibility and Accounting – the Organizational Regulation of Boundary Conditions*, Studentlitteratur, Lund, pp. 155-179.

Kalantaridis, C. (1997), 'Between the Community and the World Market: Garment Entrepreneurs in Rural Greece', *Entrepreneurship and Regional Development*, Vol. 9, pp. 25-44.

Kotler, P. (2000), *Administração de Marketing*, Prentice Hall, São Paulo, 10th Edition.

Lane, B. and Yoshinaga, K. (1994), 'Niche Markets for the Rural World', *The OECD Observer*, Vol. 190, October/November, pp. 14-18.

Levenhagen, M. and Thomas, H. (1993), 'Entrepreneurs' Competitive Definitions: Evidence from computer-software start-ups', in H. Klandt (Ed.), *Entrepreneurship and Business Development*, Avebury, Aldershot, pp. 67-83.

Mackenzie, L.R. (1992), 'Fostering Entrepreneurship as a Rural Economic Development Strategy', *Economic Development Review*, Fall, pp. 38-44.

Magalhães, A., Oliveira das Neves, A. and Relvas, S. (2001), 'Competitividade das Áreas Rurais: uma Abordagem na Perspectiva de Marketing', *1º Congresso de Estudos Rurais*, UTAD, Vila Real, 16-18 September.

Maillat, D. (1998), 'Innovative Milieus and New Generations of Regional Policies', *Entrepreneurship and Regional Development*, Vol. 10, pp. 1-16.

Manimala, M.J. (1996), 'Beyond Innovators and Imitators: A Taxonomy of Entrepreneurs', *Creative and Innovation Management*, Vol. 5(3), pp. 179-189.

Niittykangas, H. (1996), 'Enterprise Development in Different Rural Areas of Finland', *Entrepreneurship and Regional Development*, Vol. 8, pp. 245-261.

Nijkamp, P. (2003), 'Entrepreneurship in a Modern Network Economy', *Regional Studies*, Vol. 37(4), pp. 395-405.

North, D. and Smallbone, D. (2000), 'The Innovativeness and Growth of Rural SMEs during the 1990s', *Regional Studies*, Vol. 34(2), pp. 145-157.

Oliver, C. (1997), 'Sustainable Competitive Advantage: Combining Institutional and Resource-Based Views', *Strategic Management Journal*, Vol. 18 (October), pp. 697-713.

Palich, L.E. and Bagby, D.R. (1995), 'Using Cognitive Theory to Explain Entrepreneurial Risk-taking: Challenging Conventional Wisdom', *Journal of Business Venturing*, Vol. 10(6), pp. 425-439.

Pancucci, D. (1995), 'Remote Control', *Management Today*, April, pp. 78-80.

Piore, M.J. and Sabel, C.F. (1984), *The Second Industrial Divide: Possibilities for Prosperity*, Basic Books, New York.

Porter, M.E. (1980), *Competitive Strategy: Techniques for Analyzing Industries and Competitors*, The Free Press, New York.

Premkumar, G. and Roberts, M. (1999), 'Adoption of New Information Technologies in Rural Small Businesses', *OMEGA, The International Journal of Management Science*, Vol. 27 (4), pp. 467-484.

Pyke, F. and Sengenberger, W. (1990), 'Introduction', in F. Pyke, G. Becattini and W. Sengenberger (Eds), *Industrial Districts and Inter-Firm Co-operation in Italy*, International Institute for Labour Studies, Genova, pp. 1-9.

Ray, C. (1998), 'Culture, Intellectual Property and Territorial Rural Development', *Sociologia Ruralis*, Vol. 38, pp. 1-19.

Rogers, E. and Shoemaker, F. (1971), *Communication of Innovations. A Cross-Cultural Approach*, The Free Press, New York, 2nd Edition.

Schumpeter, J.A. (1912, 1934), *The Theory of Economic Development*, Oxford University Press, Oxford. Reprint of 1934 edition.

Stöhr, W. and Taylor, D. (1981), *Development from Above or Below?*, Wiley, Chichester.

Toffler, A. (1990), *Power Shift: Knowledge, Wealth, Violence at the Edge of the 21st Century*, Bantam Books, New York.

Tregear, A. (2003), 'Market Orientation and the Craft Person', *European Journal of Marketing,* Vol. 37(11/12), pp.1621-1635.

United Nations (2001), 'World Urbanization Prospects: The 2001 Revision', *Population Studies.*

Waterman, R. Jr., Peters, T. and Phillips, J.R. (1980), 'Structure Is Not Organisation', *Business Horizons*, Vol. 23(3) June, pp. 14-26.

Weeden, C. (2002), 'Ethical Tourism: An Opportunity for Competitive Advantage?' *Journal of Vacation Marketing*, March, Vol. 8(2), pp. 141-153.

Wislow, E.K. and Solomon, G.T. (1989), 'Further Development of Descriptive Profile of Entrepreneurs', *Journal of Creative Behaviour*, Vol. 23(3), pp.149-161.

Wortman, M.S. (1990), 'Rural Entrepreneurship Research: An Integration into the Entrepreneurship Field', *Agribusiness*, Vol. 6(4), pp. 329-344.

PART IV

CASE STUDIES

The Adoption of Information and Communication Technologies among Smaller Food Firms in Rural Areas of Greece

Elena Georgoudaki, Efthalia Dimara and Dimitris Skuras

Introduction

Information and communication technologies (ICTs) have now become strategic technologies that permit transactions almost globally and among all sectors of the economy. Major policies relating to their diffusion have been planned and launched by the EU and by national states in the last two decades. Such policies aim at accessing new, distant markets and increasing competitiveness. Regionally implemented policies have focused both on creating infrastructure and networks and on assisting innovative actions towards developing technology applications (LEADER, 2000). Despite this, the adoption rates of ICTs remain low and the results of these policies are disappointing compared with expectations. Even in cases where tailored measures have been applied, such measures often failed to interpret the conditions and needs of the target regions and enterprises correctly so that enterprises, for example, have ended up with communication technologies that are of no use to them.

The integration of new technologies in the modern economy has a double-edged effect on rural areas. Rural areas can be easily penetrated by exogenous businesses that bring 'imported' goods and services with them. Yet with the use of ICTs, rural companies can overcome geographical restrictions and develop an export orientation. Grimes (2000) conjectured that the introduction of ICTs would increase the 'centralization' effect as regards the extent to which core operations were assigned to regional units. Rural areas would retain only low value added activities by exploiting their competitive advantage with respect to cheap labour and a specialized labour force. In contrast, decentralization has been proposed as a possible scenario, as uniform infrastructure and technological tools would be available in rural areas and would aid spatial expansion and the outsourcing of business activities. In practice, decentralized activities proved to be related to standardization, simplicity of operations, mass production and routine functions. In addition, such activities were usually located in areas near urban centres and not in remote locations (LEADER, 2000).

In order to implement regional policies successfully, factors such as the organizational, institutional and socio-cultural environment of the specific region, as well as of the rural enterprises, should be taken into consideration. Storper (1997) has integrated these factors into a model of the economic process and has transformed them into 'conventions'. Conventions in these terms are the mainly implicit rules governing actions and methods of coordination, which have been generated over time and become routinized. These conventions compose the bases of what Storper terms 'frameworks of economic action', which are further divided into four possible 'worlds of production'.

The aim of the present chapter is to identify the reasons for ICT adoption among rural small and medium sized enterprises (SMEs). The approach avoids considering firms as uniform economic agents. Instead, ICT adoption is examined among differentiated clusters of rural SMEs. One aspect that differentiates the behaviour of firms considerably is their product offering. Storper (1997) offers a thorough classification of firms' behaviour according to the type of output produced. This classification provides a robust theoretical framework for examining differences in the extent to which firms have adopted ICTs and the different adoption rates of particular ICTs.

The next section contains the literature review. This is followed by the results of the empirical research concerning the installation and implementation of new technologies. The study was carried out among producers drawn from enterprises located in four Greek NUTS III regions. Their strategies are analysed by categorizing the firms studied into three out of Storper's four worlds of production and by tracing the reasons for different levels of ICT adoption and for the adoption of different technologies. Next, the factors that encourage or inhibit the implementation of information and communication technologies in business practices are presented. The final section contains the main conclusions, a discussion of the policy implications and some suggestions regarding strategies for policy makers.

Literature Review and Hypotheses

It is commonly believed that ICTs offer a new means of revitalizing rural economies that have been in severe economic decline for a long time and have experienced outward urban migration. According to OECD (2001), the main benefits of modern computer-mediated technologies which diminish the impacts of distance and time are increased access to information and the opportunity provided to rural and remote enterprises to serve new markets. The perception of such benefits led to the term 'the information revolution'. The term was first used in the 1990s to describe the widespread changes in societies, institutions and economies due to, or aided by, ICTs (Winden, 2001).

ICTs are taken to encompass technologies and tools such as computers, digital networks and other types of software that process and transmit data. ICT adoption can be defined as the use of ICTs in proprietary networks. Both the adoption of new technologies within networks and the use of ICTs by individuals are studied in this chapter.

Three types of digital networks may be found in the business sector. First, intra-company networks are used to enhance internal management, reduce organizational costs, and improve quality control and firm logistics. Second, extra-company or trans-firm networks coordinate business functions, transmit and process data and documentation so facilitating business relationships among different firms, e.g. between suppliers, distributors, agents and customers. Third, there are inter-company networks which are expanded trans-company networks using both proprietary and public telecommunication infrastructures to conduct businesses with partners which are not initially defined (OECD, 1992).

ICT adoption is most developed in business functions such as management, accounting and stock control. The current tendency is to integrate various applications and solutions. Enterprise Resource Planning systems (ERP) were developed for large food manufacturers and potentially can cover the entire value chain of activities under a unified technological platform. Standardized applications are usually installed in medium sized enterprises but often fail to be tailored to the firm's specific needs. An exception is the case of firms employing personnel who are specialized in new technologies. Employees with a fair knowledge of information systems are keen to adjust standardized applications to the firm's functions and to develop the most useful digital instruments for the needs of company.

Several variables affecting the adoption of new technologies are mentioned in the literature. These include relative advantage, cost-effectiveness, complexity, observability, compatibility, reliability, application, communality and radicalness (Premkumar et al., 1999; Eastin, 2002; Dearing et al., 1994). These variables have been studied mostly from the viewpoint of innovation. Innovation is an idea, a way of action or an object that is perceived as new by the adopter (Premkumar et al., 1999) while 'adoption refers to the decision of any individual or organization to make use of an innovation' (Frambach and Schillewaert, 2002: 163). Adoption is characterized by the awareness stage, where information is gathered for the innovation, the persuasion stage, and the implementation and confirmation stage (Premkumar et al., 1999). There has also been considerable research on attitude theory and the theory of reasoned action to offer insights into the adoption process. The emphasis here is on the perceived benefits offered by the new technologies (Frambach and Schillewaert, 2002; Legris et al., 2003; Riemenschneider et al., 2003).

The three types of management that predominate in small enterprises can affect the decision to adopt new technology. These are entrepreneurial management, which generates innovative actions, owner-management, which emphasizes survival and tends to have less interest in new practices and, finally, professional management where directors are more cautious and reluctant to take on risky ideas (Swamidass, 2003). From the viewpoint of economics, adoption is influenced by variables such as compatibility with existing technology, acquisition costs and employees' skills that may restrain entrepreneurs from upgrading the technology (McDade et al., 2002). Entrepreneurs' opportunistic motivations, e.g. for cost reduction, seem to predominate in the adoption of Internet functions (Sadowski et al. 2002). This is related to the degree of perceived relative advantage (Eastin, 2002; Rogers, 1995). Sadowski et al. (2002) suggest that strategic decisions to implement Internet services stem from the wish to improve the firm's long-term market position within its immediate business environment.

There are three aspects of the strategic use of the Internet. The first aspect refers to communication with partners, competitors and customers. In this case managers' need to establish new communication channels with business partners is found to be of great importance in overcoming the initial resistance from the employees to new ways of carrying out their business (Premkumar et al. 1999). The second aspect is related to the degree of competition in the business environment, which affects the pressure on entrepreneurs to seek better production methods, products of better quality and investments that will secure or gain competitive advantage for the firm based on either product differentiation or lower costs. Currently, advanced manufacturing technologies smooth the choice between these two competition strategies by providing profitable variety/low cost combinations (Efstathiades et al., 2002). The third aspect is external support and incentives that influence the use of new communication technologies. The provision of information on these instruments increases awareness and that, in turn, increases adoption levels. Regional agents therefore aim to create awareness and provide training to the local workforce on new technologies. Technological upgrading of a region is believed to aid the improvement of regional economy, attract investment and to motivate young inhabitants preventing their migration to urban centres (OECD, 2001).

Advanced information technologies may provide tools enabling new long-term strategies and increase the flexibility of business decisions (Spanos et al., 2002). This may create a new cycle of innovative activities. According to Efstathiades et al. (2002), the need to upgrade production technology may be realized after the shift of management goals allowed by advanced technology. ICTs also assist management to control units located in remote or distant areas. Information systems provide quick access to data and allow the performance of dispersed outlets to be easily monitored, so helping to secure quality, consistency and uniformity among different units (Hammer and Mangurian, 1987). Companies which already use ICTs are potential adopters of management systems related to strategic planning, finance and human resource management (Spanos et al., 2002).

Firms that are internationally or non-locally oriented or have developed financial and technological collaborations with distant and/or foreign companies have a greater tendency towards implementing communication technologies (Lal, 2002; Mitchell and Clark, 1999). According to Mitchell and Clark, companies that interact with small partners and produce locally distributed, low value-added products are frequently low adopters. In addition, the localization of firms and the development of clusters of firm that belong to the same sector seem to have limited impact on technology adoption. The same applies to the presence of universities in a region (McGranahan 2002; Harrison et al., 1996; Gale, 1997).

The reasons for non-adoption may be found in the early stages of the adoption process (Frambach and Schillewaert, 2002). These include inadequate knowledge or lack of understanding of the potential benefits derived from the applications and functions of ICTs, which precede the awareness stage (Chapman et al., 2000). In addition, the lack of the economic and financial resources needed to implement new technologies may result in the postponement of functional upgrading. In this case, the adoption process usually stops immediately after the persuasion stage. For SMEs, this is an important factor as they frequently have limited resources and cannot afford to invest in ICTs (Sadowski et al., 2002). Also, some entrepreneurs believe that there is no need for such technologies within their businesses, in which case the persuasion stage is not successfully completed.

The obstacles to adopting ICTs among rural SMEs seem to be more cultural than financial (OECD, 2001). Current technologies used by SMEs tend to have isolated forms or are separated in 'islands', e.g. accounting software, logistics and production technologies. The use of ICTs, however, demands different business structures and direct communication between the different departments of the firm. In addition, most businesses in rural areas are usually family-owned and use traditional managerial practices that are carried over from one generation to the other (OECD, 2001). New technologies, though, penetrate local communities allowing non-local enterprises to have access to their markets. Entrepreneurs may realize that traditional management should be altered but still remain reluctant to use ICTs.

The persistent use of inferior technological tools because of network externalities when better technologies exist is called 'excess inertia' or 'lock-in' in the economics literature. Businesses might not install or upgrade their ICTs because their clients or suppliers are not equipped with compatible technologies. In this case, the benefits from moving to a higher technological level are below the adoption risk, which is usually related to jeopardizing the business' current network through expanding the use of ICTs (McDade et al., 2002).

New networks have emerged in the food sector, enhancing the globalization of food provision and leading to an increase in standardized production processes. New technologies allowed the mass production of uniform products, which were often considered as unnatural and of low quality by consumers. In parallel, some local producers kept their traditional production methods and secured specific qualities of local products. Still, many rural producers have moved towards standardization of production techniques, which resulted in a decreasing number of farmers in rural areas and a loss of rural identity, bio-diversity and landscapes (Verhaegen et al., 2001). There are currently two main trends in food consumption; first, the provision of greater variety of products and second, the growing emphasis on the health, nutritional and environmental attributes of food products. As a result, new technologies need to aim for differentiation in production and for food safety.

The technology systems that may be adopted by a business are affected by the nature of its products. Taking the example of food products, some are transformed from commodity to differentiated branded foods while others are simply packaged and offered for consumption (Salin, 1998). Food products may be categorized into functional products, which are staple goods that have predictable demand, and innovative products, which are differentiated, come in many varieties and usually have short life cycles (Salin, 1998). New technologies may be installed in order to automate order processing for functional products, for example via EDI, and to schedule warehouse, delivery and control systems and enable quality assurance in production. As regards innovative food products, the focus is on systems that link orders to sales and provide just-in-time production in order to limit stocks and reduce the cost of products perishing in the warehouses (Salin, 1998).

Storper (1997) has identified four 'worlds of production', which he distinguished according to the characteristics of products within them. According to Storper, standardized products are those produced with widely diffused methods and where competition is based on price discounts. Specialized products are produced with specific technology, know-how and inputs and the production method is regionally restricted, so they compete through their quality attributes. Generic products are widely distributed and have well known attributes. Dedicated products are customized commodities distributed to particular market segments.

Storper (1997) identifies four different 'worlds of production' based on these different products types. The *industrial world* is the world of standardized, generic products, where mass production techniques are used and where codifiable knowledge is involved. This is in contrast to uncodifiable knowledge, which is completely intangible or 'tacit' and is disseminated through personal communication channels (Mole et al., 2001; Steinmueller, 2000). Conventions in the industrial world are related to commercialism, efficiency and branding. The *market world* is consumer driven and is associated with standardized dedicated production. Some products are made according to standardization conventions with each production run dedicated to the demands of a specific client. When consumers perceive products as standardized, they will not be loyal or committed to any particular producer. The lack of loyalty and commitment by buyers means that producers will be in close competition with one another (Storper and Salais, 1997). The *interpersonal world* is the world of specialized dedicated products for which there is no formal process of knowledge development and conventions refer to health, ecology and trust. 'In the interpersonal world, individuals know each other and their histories, both individual and collective, are constituted as tradition' (Storper and Salais, 1997:36). The firms in this world display considerable internal flexibility, producing a changing variety of products based on specialized know-how and technology. In the *world of intellectual resources,* specialized generic products are produced whose generic qualities are developed by specialized knowledge.

Turning now to the influence of the external environment, Preissl (1995) examined the impact of the business setting and the intensity of competition on the creation of incentives and, consequently, on the impulse to use new technologies (Sadowski et al., 2002). Competitive pressure can lead to an adoption decision especially in highly competitive sectors, where innovation becomes the key to keeping or improving market position (Frambach and Schillewaert, 2002; Premkumar et al., 1999). Premkumar et al. (1999) suggest that competition will affect the adoption decision for two reasons. First, it prevents customers from turning to competitors who already have innovative technologies and, second, it acts as a strategic tool to maintain or improve their market position. According to Lancioni et al. (2003), the Internet has encouraged a shift from single firm competition to competitive supply chain networks.

Kreps (1990) defined networks as groups of organizational actors participating in a general pattern of interaction. Networking as a business strategy presupposes building on social communication, informal relationships and continual training and education (Nijkamp, 2003). In order to interact and transact with partners, communication tools are necessary and ICTs can improve the relationships qualitatively and quantitatively (Nouwens and Bowman, 1995). Networks are also carriers of social structures as individuals and organizations communicate within their frames (Redmond, 2004). Interaction within informal and formal networks may accelerate or inhibit the diffusion of a new technology. The speed of diffusion is also related to the degree of information shared between the partners in the network (Frambach and Schillewaert, 2002). Businesses active in networks which are mainly based on digital collaboration usually focus on their core competencies and outsource other activities to partners (Romano et al., 2001). Furthermore, Premkumar et al. (1999) found that horizontal networks are ahead of vertical ones as far as technology upgrading is concerned.

Parent companies, franchises or larger partners may develop their technological systems to subsidize smaller partners (Premkumar et al., 1999). The emphasis here is on the creation of steady long-term relationships with customers as value added activities. Relations with customers may be improved through the use of ICTs (Pires and Aisbett, 2003). There are also cases where business customers or suppliers may demand the use of a specific type of ICT, such as EDI, as a prerequisite for doing business. This could turn into a long-term partnership in the form of vertical and/or horizontal networks between companies that use compatible ICTs (Kinsey, 2000).

Integrated quality assurance in the food sector is facilitated by the functions offered by new technologies and, by ensuring the production of high quality products and by coordinating and upgrading production processes, can increase profitability in the entire supply chain (Ziggers and Trienekens, 1999). In order to achieve such integration, standardized technologies and product identification need to be developed and implemented (Simchi-Levi et al., 2000). Standardization allows transactions among different partners' systems and the common translation of data which feeds into supply chain decisions. For example, information obtained from retail points of sale may be shared with suppliers and manufacturers and production and delivery linked to demand.

According to McGranahan (2002), a positive external climate may facilitate and promote the exchange of knowledge and technology dissemination among firms active in different industries but located in the same area. Mole et al. (2001) point to the existence of an innovative milieu, in the supply chain and in the area in which the firm is located, as helping to create and accelerate the expansion of innovative practices and products such as communication technologies. The generation of tacit knowledge and the creation of innovative practices may also be the outcome of interactions among local network partners and the local labour force, which is the carrier of tacit knowledge in an area (Kourliouros, 2001; Mole et al., 2001).

The hypotheses of the present chapter are based on the different conventions and strategies that firms, divided into worlds of production, have developed and also on the way in which the conventions and strategies affect the decision to adopt ICTs. It should be expected that firms in the 'industrial world' seek computer-mediated technologies to reduce production costs, standardize products and access information about new markets. In contrast, firms operating in the 'market world' have more incentive to install ICTs that will improve the quality of their products, facilitate their communication with customers and assist in the search for information related to customers' needs and preferences. Finally, firms in the 'interpersonal world' will be more interested in technologies that increase their brand awareness, particularly those that are export-oriented. They will also wish to ensure the quality of their products and improve their internal performance. Variables such as the entrepreneur's educational level, the size of the firm, its partnerships and export activities are assumed to influence the adoption of ICTs among the firms studied.

Case Study and Data

The adoption and intensity of use of ICTs was studied among food producers in lagging rural areas of Greece within the framework of a European Union funded project (SUPPLIERS – QLK5 – CT – 2000 – 0841). The sample consists of 98 SMEs located in the prefectures of Achaia, Ilia, Arcadia and Argolida, all NUTS III areas. Data collection took place through semi-structured interviews during the first three months of 2002 following a pre-test study. The firms were selected from the registers of food producers provided by the relevant local chambers of trade and industry. The small size of the targeted population in the aforementioned areas allowed preliminary contacts with the firms so that the sample chosen for study contained only those firms agreeing to participate in the survey. Only a small proportion of firms refused to participate (less than 20%) and these had no particular characteristics distinguishing them from the respondents that might bias the results. The firms sampled are involved in the production of fresh and processed citrus fruits, apples, fresh and pickled vegetables, fruit juices, currants, wine, liqueur, feta cheese and candied fruits.

The 'worlds of production' framework as set out by Storper and Salais (1997) was used to categorize the firms which were found to fit within three out of the four worlds. Each is discussed in turn below.

Industrial World

As already mentioned, the industrial world includes products that are standardized and generic. Standardized products are those generated from widely diffused production methods and generic ones are those with well known attributes distributed to the general market. Products are considered as generic when producers perceive their customers as forming one uniform group without diversified needs. Similarly, consumers in this world choose among products which are perceived to be of similar quality; they consider therefore producers as roughly equivalent and price guides their purchase decision.

Thirty-six of the sample were classified to the industrial world. These include firms producing fresh and processed citrus fruits; apples, fresh vegetables and fruit juices are included (Figure 11.1). These firms produce products with standardized (codified) quality, using dedicated but rather inflexible technology focused on economies of scale. They compete on the basis of price (commercial convention) since these products are believed by customers to be little different in quality, and cater to importers, manufacturers and end-consumers. Among the products selected, only fruit juices seem to differ much in quality. They were still included in this world since the firms exporting fruit juices compete on price rather than on quality. Firms in the industrial world take into account general trends in consumption to expand their markets, i.e. healthier nutrition is met with sugar-free and preservative-free juices. Nevertheless, their profit margins remain low due to the fact that they belong to long supply chains and the importers, wholesalers and retailers tend to have greater bargaining power than the producers and manufacturers.

Market World

As discussed, the market world consists of standardized and dedicated products. In the sample, 17 firms producing currants and pickled vegetables fell into this group.

The competition in supplying these products is centred on price together with rapidity of response.

Producers in this type of world have to deal with uncertainty as regards quantities and prices so they usually use written agreements with clients and seek long-standing business relationships. They also try to focus on the quality attributes of their products as a way of differentiating themselves from other producers. Furthermore, producers differentiate their products in order to serve specific market segments. For example, currants are distributed both to supermarkets and to food industries with the producers using different packages and offering different packaging conditions in terms of desirable product humidity. Uncertainty is the main factor that inhibits full process standardization.

The producers know the customers for both currants and pickled vegetables and these customers influence the production methods used. In the case of currants, the main clients are British importers who regularly visit the factories located in Northwest Peloponnese and check whether conditions, usually related to hygiene, are adhered to during the production and packaging process. Producers of pickled vegetables travel to the USA and North-European countries with the aim of promoting their products and signing agreements with customers. They have to comply with the production standards imposed in different countries if they wish to export their products.

Interpersonal World

Firms belonging to the interpersonal world face great uncertainty as knowledge and preferences for their products cannot be expressed in terms of codified norms (Storper and Salais, 1997). Individuals have to develop a common language to communicate with consumers, attract new clients, create long-term loyalty relationships and acquire specialized skills. However, all these attributes remain within a closed community, usually found in specific geographical regions. Forty-five (45) of the sampled firms were classified into this category, amongst them wine, liqueur, candied fruits and feta cheese producers (Figure 11.1). These firms emphasise local relationships and the local promotion of their products and use specialized local inputs, for example. grapes grown in specific denominated locations or milk produced in an area known for its climate and environmental conditions. Interpersonal relationships are the basis of this world and they are related to tradition (domestic convention). Products and producers are not anonymous, as in the previous two worlds.

WORLDS OF PRODUCTION

	INDUSTRIAL WORLD	MARKET WORLD	
STANDARDIZED PRODUCTS	Fresh and processed citrus fruits, apples, fruit juices, fresh vegetables Medium adoption of ICTs Cost leadership strategy Relationships with suppliers and customers based on trust	Currants and pickled vegetables High adoption of ICTs Focus strategy Contractual agreements with suppliers and customers	ECONOMIES OF SCALE
SPECIALIZED PRODUCTS	INTELLECTUAL WORLD	INTERPERSONAL WORLD Wine, liqueur, feta cheese, candied fruits Little adoption of ICTs Differentiation strategy Relationships with suppliers & customers based on trust and locality	ECONOMIES OF VARIETY

GENERIC PRODUCTS   DEDICATED PRODUCTS

Figure 11.1   Worlds of production

The New European Rurality

Table 11.1 Business characteristics in the three worlds of production

Business characteristics	Worlds of production			
	Industrial	Market	Interpersonal	Total
Family owned business (%)	19.4	11.8	57.8	35.7
Legal form: Ltd (%)	41.7	35.3	15.6	28.6
Established by the current owner (%)	75.0	58.8	60.0	65.3
Inherited (%)	19.4	29.4	31.1	26.5
Maintain mainly written contracts with suppliers (%)	22.2	65.0	11.1	24.5
Maintain mainly written contracts with customers (%)	22.2	65.0	11.1	24.5
Products retain firm's label down the supply chain (%)	83.3	23.5	78.0	70.4
More than 80% of the firm's suppliers are stable (%)	80.0	70.6	82.2	78.6
More than 80% of the firm's suppliers are local (%)	66.7	59.0	69.0	66.3
Serving customers located in the rest of the country or abroad(%)	66.7	82.4	22.2	49.0
Having more than one outlet (%)	41.7	23.5	37.8	36.7
Size (mean number of employees)	14.3	30.2	4.3	12.5
Mean turnover (million Euros)	5.6	4.4	0.9	3.8
Firms with growth of sales above sector's growth (%)	58.3	47.0	48.9	63.8
Managers with 3rd level education (%)	45.8	53.3	37.2	42.7
Distance of firm from nearest urban centre (km)	17.6	10.5	24.9	19.7
Mean number of years PCs have been installed in the business	8.0	8.6	3.0	5.8
Sample size (N)	36	17	45	98

Firms in the industrial world exhibit the highest turnover, operate as limited liability companies, more than half of them are family owned and occupy usually full-time personnel. Firms in the interpersonal world show the smallest average number of employees, an indication of the predominance of small size of firms in this world. A large proportion of the products from firms in the industrial and interpersonal worlds keep their firms brand name when forwarded downstream. On the contrary, only a small percentage of the products in the market world keep their firms' brand-name traceable in the wholesale and retail markets, since most of these products are used as intermediate inputs in the food industry or are repacked by the wholesalers.

The majority of firms in the market world use written agreements with suppliers while only a small percentage of firms in the industrial and in interpersonal worlds have contractual relationships with the providers of their inputs. As far as the customers are concerned, the overwhelming majority of the agreements are written for firms in the market world while only 30 per cent and 13 per cent of the firms in the industrial and interpersonal worlds respectively follow the same convention. Firms in the market world seek to reduce the uncertainty of transactions when transacting with partners through contractual agreements while firms in the interpersonal world firms base their business transactions on trust and the friendly relationships developed with their partners in their supply chain. Nearly the same groups of suppliers provide the greatest proportion of the raw material in all three worlds indicating a very steady network with suppliers. In addition, the majority of the suppliers are located in the same geographic area, especially as concerns firms in the interpersonal world. This indicates the close relationship that firms, in the three worlds and particularly in interpersonal, have with local firms. However, most customers in the market world are from outside the geographic area where the business is located.

Adoption of ICTs

Three different levels of ICT adoption are distinguished among the sample firms. The lowest level includes firms using only mobile phones, the fax and PCs for general office use. The medium level includes firms using professional software for office use, e.g. accounting software, technologies for automation and control in production together with e-mail and the Internet. The highest level consists of firms that operate their own website, intranet and extranet facilities, EDI systems and advanced professional software. Table 11.2 shows the distribution of the firms sampled according to these three levels of adoption of ICTs.

Table 11.2   Adoption of ICTs (% of sample)

Adoption level:	Industrial world	Market world	Interpersonal world
Low	16.7	11.8	44.4
Medium	52.8	41.2	40.0
High	30.6	47.1	15.6
Sample size (N)	36	17	45

Just over half the firms belonging to the industrial world have a medium level of ICT adoption, which includes technologies for administrative functions and production automation. According to Storper (1997), firms in this world invest in technologies for production purposes in order to benefit from economies of scale. In the market world, there is great dependence on customers' selection decisions, so these firms tend to invest more on technologies related to communication, i.e. e-mail, a web-site, and EDI, in order to strengthen relationships with clients, access new clients and increase their rapidity of response. There is a small degree of technological automation since workers have to check the quality of each input, vegetable or currant, before any processing takes place. Finally, firms in the interpersonal world have lower adoption level as they are more locally oriented, use traditional production methods and have relatively small levels of production and so have no need to install automation technologies. Moreover, the variety of products and the standardization and automation of production tend to be negatively correlated (Storper, 1997). These firms use new technologies in order to secure production quality and comply with globally recognized standards, such as the ISO series and HACCP. Managers of such firms believe in promoting their business by word of mouth and they create personal stable relationships with their partners.

Business Characteristics of Adopters

Table 11.3 depicts the basic characteristics of firms and entrepreneurs/managers according to the identified worlds of production. The vast majority of the firms with a high adoption level have higher growth rates than the respective average growth rate in the sector. In addition, the higher the level of ICT adoption, the higher is the percentage of customers maintaining steady relationships with the firm. As Pires and Aisbett (2002) state, relations with customers are improved with the use of ICTs. The number of firms that operate from more than one place of business is positively correlated with the level of adoption of new technologies. This could be related to the fact that businesses with more than one outlet are usually the larger enterprises. According to Mitchell and Clark (1999) they have greater potential to invest in advanced technologies as their business functions are more dispersed. As a result, the scope for using ICTs is broader and they are also more able to afford the installation and maintenance costs of computer-mediated information and communication systems. The latter may also facilitate the monitoring of dispersed outlets to ensure quality consistency and uniformity among the different units (Hammer and Mangurian, 1987).

Table 11.3   Business characteristics of adopters (%)

Business Characteristics	Adoption level (%)			
	Low	Medium	High	Total
Firms with growth of sales above				
sector's growth	29.6	52.2	77.0	52.0
Steady relations with customers	88.9	90.9	100.0	92.9
Firms with own outlets	14.8	34.0	65.4	36.7
Managers with degree	16.0	50.0	63.6	42.7
Sample size (N)	27	44	26	97

Note: one missing observation as regards relations with customers

The entrepreneur's or manager's level of education is positively related to the adoption level. As Lal (2002) concluded, the higher the educational level of the entrepreneur, the more intense is the use of ICTs.

Reasons for Using ICTs

Table 11.4 depicts the main reasons for the current level of use of ICTs by the sample firms. Production automation and control, information gathering, management and internal performance are the main reasons for which most industrial enterprises have installed information and communication systems. Storper (1997) suggests that industrial firms should benefit from production technologies through improved capacity and costs minimization. Automation in production is usually related to capital intensive production of standardized products and scale economies. Enhanced control mechanisms in production assure the quality of the firm's output. The installation of HACCP systems in industrial and marketing businesses is an example of a quality control application. Technological upgrading is also related to innovation in production and the transformation of new generic outputs into standardized products which according to Storper (1997) constitute an innovation in the industrial world. Some of the sample firms process and trade organic products in innovative, environmental friendly packages.

Moreover, the search for information may lead to information asymmetries. Those who obtain information are more likely to introduce novelties and improvements in production. In the industrial world, however, the advantage derived from an innovation is 'always fragile' (Storper, 1997) as it can be quickly imitated by competitors. Industrial enterprises are also interested in obtaining information related to rivals' activities, as they trade products that are perceived as homogenous by the clients. This is also related to the fact that these businesses have the higher percentage use of ICTs in order to identify and enter new markets.

   The need for information is also the main reason for installing ICTs in the market world. The producers of dedicated products have to deal with the risk of not satisfying the customers' preferences. They are therefore interested in obtaining information that will help them to improve their products' characteristics. Thus, market world enterprises ranked using the Internet for gathering information more highly as a reason for adoption than did other types of firms. In addition, customers' demands for new technologies led almost half of the market enterprises to adopt communication systems such as e-mail and EDI. The improvement of internal performance and the recognition of the benefits that new technologies yield are two more important reasons for adopting ICTs. In this kind of world, firms seek economies of variety. Transactions with public services are now taking place through the Internet among almost half of the businesses in the industrial and market world. These usually concern official certifications and electronic payment of taxes and state insurance.

Table 11.4 Reasons for using ICTs (%)

	Worlds of production			
Reasons for using ICTs	Industrial	Market	Interpersonal	Total
Promotion	50.0	47.0	44.4	46.9
Production automation	52.8	23.5	42.2	42.9
Production control	50.0	35.3	48.9	46.9
Transactions with public services	47.2	47.0	17.8	33.7
E-sales	2.8	17.6	4.4	6.1
Information about competitors	47.2	47.0	28.9	38.8
General business information	55.4	64.7	35.5	50.0
New markets	36.1	23.5	17.8	25.5
Information about customers	36.1	47.1	6.7	24.5
Performance enhancement	67.0	53.0	51.1	57.1
External incentives	8.3	11.8	17.9	13.3
Information on wider competitive environment	11.1	6.0	20.0	14.3
Information management	55.6	5.9	11.1	26.5
ICTs potential	8.3	47.0	20.0	20.4
Sample size	36	17	45	98

   Businesses in the interpersonal world regarded performance enhancement and production automation and control as the most important reasons explaining ICT adoption. ICTs can be used as strategic tools that considerably increase economic performance (OECD, 1992). Operational performance related to product quality and market share (Hoffer, 1987; Kaplan, 1983) can also be improved through the use of ICTs. The latter improve both the static efficiency, i.e. better allocation of given resources to given economic activities, and the dynamic efficiency, i.e. the generation and introduction of technological, product and organizational innovation, of enterprises (Antonelli, 1992). Information gathering, the activities of competitors, external incentives and entry to new markets are some further reasons for installing computer-mediated technologies. Information related to customers' preferences and gaps in the market may influence the development of specialized attributes in the firm's products.

Moreover, competitive pressure may lead to adoption especially in highly competitive sectors, where innovation becomes the key for keeping or improving one's market position (Frambach and Schillewaert, 2002; Premkumar et al., 1999). Premkumar et al. (1999) suggest that competition will affect the adoption decision for two reasons, either as a tool to prevent customers from turning to competitors or as a strategic tool that sustains or improves market position. External incentives increase awareness concerning the use of new technologies and reduce the costs incurred during the installation phase. Information and communication technologies provide the ability to create and actively shape markets and niches and to overcome geographic restrictions (Hammer and Mangurian, 1987).

Most enterprises consider the use of ICTs as important for their business performance and for their relations with clients. Nearly 30 per cent of the market world firms perceive the new technologies as a very important part of their enterprises. The latter believe that they would lose an important part of their market and internal efficiency without ICTs and might even have to close down. On average, companies in the industrial and market worlds have had PCs for longer (more than eight years) than firms in the interpersonal world (around three years).

Impacts of Adoption

According to Storper and Salais (1997), technological adoption is usually related to increasing returns. Still, only the minority of the firms studied perceived that the use of ICTs actually increased its turnover. Market firms adopt new technologies in order to improve their relationships with clients. Few, though, have noticed an increase in the number of customers after the entrance of ICTs and even fewer benefited in their business transactions with distant markets. The installation of new technologies is believed to lead to cost reduction in production rather than in administration and to impact the products' quality, especially in interpersonal firms. An increase of specialized personnel was noticed by the market firms, which, together with industrial businesses, also benefited from the improved access to information.

Table 11.5 below depicts the firms' perceptions concerning the impacts of adopting ICTs. The majority of entrepreneurs are aware of the new technologies that can be applied in their businesses but lack the necessary capital and specialized personnel to install them. This is more obvious in the market world firms. Here the businesses that produce and trade currants and pickled vegetables are willing to upgrade their technologies and procedures as they are almost totally dependent on markets in UK and in the USA. The financial constraint, though, is the main reason for postponing technological improvements in their businesses. The industrial and interpersonal entrepreneurs, in contrast, do not perceive any benefits from the use of ICTs. In the literature, the lack of top management support is mentioned as an important obstacle to diffusion (Leroux, et al., 2001, Premkumar et al., 1999). Besides that, firms have to conform to the requirements of their customers and suppliers (Mitchell et al., 1999). Hence, there is no pressure to use ICTs when partners are small and low value-added products are made for local areas. The situation described above is often encountered in firms in the sample in the interpersonal and industrial worlds. In addition, many rural enterprises are trapped in a vicious cycle, where lack of a cheap communication infrastructure and services reduces the demand for computer-mediated technologies, which in turn restricts potential future investment for infrastructure and service provision (Premkumar et al., 1999).

Another impediment to the adoption of ICTs is the employees' reluctance to change business processes. As Rogers (1995) has noted, adoption is delayed when innovation is not compatible with the current practices and there is a need for training and learning. In order to accept ICTs, their functions have to be compatible with the existing values, past experiences and the needs of workers (Eastin, 2002). Besides, in addition to the installation and maintenance costs, the enterprise will have to bear the costs of training employees during their working hours. Hence businesses recognize the necessity of employing multi-skilled personnel (Spanos et al., 2002). In general, the demand for educated employees influences and is influenced by the adoption level of new technologies (Chun, 2003). Almost half of the enterprises in the industrial and the market worlds have personnel specialized in computer applications while the proportion is only one in five enterprises in the interpersonal world. More than half of the enterprises in the market and industrial worlds offer training opportunities while only one third do so in the interpersonal world. Training inefficiencies are another impediment, as training courses provided by local agencies are not usually well organized and most ICTs users are self-trained. This results in ICTs underperforming as firms fail to exploit their full potential (Mitchell et al., 1999).

Table 11.5 Effects of adopting ICTs (%)

Effects of adoption (% of firms)	Worlds of production			
	Industrial	Market	Interpersonal	Total
Increased turnover	22.2	35.3	22.2	24.5
Increased number of customers	38.9	35.3	33.3	35.7
Increased market reach	52.8	29.4	31.1	38.8
Administrative costs reduction	19.4	35.3	17.8	21.4
Production costs reduction	41.7	47.0	46.7	44.9
Improved quality of products	38.9	35.3	44.4	40.8
Hiring specialized personnel	13.9	47.0	11.1	18.4
Improved business information	72.2	52.9	26.7	47.9
Sample size	36	17	45	98

In agriculture, the activities involved in the purchase of inputs, the sale of products, and the arrangement of transportation are traditionally conducted face-to-face and not through digital forms of communication (Leroux et al., 2001). The small percentage of written contracts, especially in the industrial and interpersonal worlds, is indicative of the significance of trust and personal relationships in business contacts. In addition, Porter (2001) mentions the lack of physical connectedness as a limiting factor for Internet transactions. In the cases of feta cheese, candied fruits and liqueur, the firms use traditional production methods to a great extent and have short supply chains, usually within the area where they are located, distributing their products mainly in the local market. Networks of enterprises that could boost the use of ICTs are not yet adequately developed. Only wine producers have formed an official network, called 'The trails of the Peloponnese' that aims to promote the regional wine and link wine businesses with tourism. Their products are also available through digital distribution networks and some wineries participate in e-marketplaces.

The lack of cyber laws and of perceived safety in digital transactions slows down the development of e-commerce in food enterprises. Moreover, both the perishability of food products and the difficulty of maintaining a standard quality in each output impede the diffusion of e-commerce practices.

Discussion

The factors influencing rural SMEs to adopt ICTs were examined in this chapter. The approach was developed using a theoretical framework derived from Storper and Salais (1997) that depicts economic activity in the so-called 'worlds of production'. Different factors, according to the world in which each firm operates, influence decisions related to the adoption level and the type of ICTs employed. It appeared that the main reasons forcing enterprises towards a high level of adoption are external, usually related to customers' requirements for quality standards, food safety and taste preferences, and the need to confront price competition with low cost policies. Mitchell and Clark (1999) have also pointed out that the requirements of customers were likely to be the most influential factor leading to the formation of a two-tiered economy in rural areas as regards the adoption of ICTs.

Both exogenously and endogenously oriented policies have been implemented to increase the adoption and diffusion of ICTs in rural areas. The former refers to creating infrastructure to attract the operations and investments of external businesses in order to increase regional employment rates and knowledge spillovers to rural firms. The endogenous development model is mostly supported by EU policy makers (Grimes, 2000) and concerns the development of ICT applications within the region with respect to the economic, socio-cultural and political dimensions of the area (Moulaert and Sekia, 2003). According to Grimes (2000), endogenous models present more difficulties, as they have to tailor business practices regarding ICTs to the regional and business culture, otherwise risking a disappointing performance using computer-mediated tools.

Selective policies should be adopted and political measures and incentives should be developed with respect to regional conditions and rural firms' needs. Policies should alter their focus from being exclusively technology orientated (e.g. the installation of the Internet and creation of an e-mail address) to becoming business orientated (taking into account not only the need to communicate with distant customers but also to upgrade stock control systems and secure quality). Tailor-made applications could also be developed with the aid of local agents and institutions, thus assisting local entrepreneurs to extract the highest benefit from using ICTs. Instead of requiring businesses to adjust their functions to predetermined ICTs applications, the latter should fit within the businesses operations and contribute to the improvement of their procedures. Local authorities, agents and business associations should take an active role in the formation of diffusion policies for ICTs in their region.

Moreover, awareness programs and training courses should be monitored periodically and evaluated in relation to their expected results. Subsidies should be selectively distributed, according to some predetermined quantitative and qualitative criteria, such as the potential of the firm, current performance, market share and export orientation. Favourable policies should be focused on specific sectors and products that, for example, are related to local or national images and have the potential for market expansion. In this way, they could serve individual firm's needs more efficiently. Networking among rural SMEs should be a prerequisite to providing ICTs for business communication and not the other way round. ICTs cannot form business networks but only assist in their development (Gibbs and Tanner, 1996). To serve this purpose, local agents, business associations and chambers of commerce could promote the formation of local networks by various means (e.g. by developing a project for market expansion, such as the creation of an e-marketplace for local firms). Tax and regulatory instruments such as tax breaks for firms investing in new technologies, training or accelerated depreciation for investment in ICTs should be used to encourage their adoption (OECD, 1992).

References

Antonelli, C. (1992), 'The Economic Theory of Information Networks', in C. Antonelli (ed.), *The Economics of Information Networks*, Elsevier Science Publishers B.V., Amsterdam.

Chapman, P., James-Moore, M., Szczygiel, M. and Thompson, D. (2000), 'Building Internet Capabilities in SMEs', *Logistics Information Management*, Vol. 13(6), pp. 353-360.

Chun, H. (2003), 'Information Technology and the Demand for Educated Workers: Disentangling the Impacts of Adoption versus Use', *The Review of Economics and Statistics*, Vol. 85(1), pp. 1-8.

Cuadrado-Roura, J.R. and Garcia-Tabuenca, A. (2004), 'ICT Policies for SMEs and Regional Disparities. The Spanish Case', *Entrepreneurship and Regional Development*, Vol. 16(2), pp. 55-75.

Dearing, J. and Meyer, G. (1994), 'An Exploitation Tool for Predicting Adoption Decisions', *Science Communications*, Vol. 16(1), pp. 43-57.

Eastin, M.S. (2002), 'Diffusion of E-commerce: an Analysis of the Adoption of Four E-commerce Activities, *Telematics and Informatics*, Vol. 19(3), pp. 251-267.

Efstathiades, A., Tasou, S. and Antoniou, A. (2002), 'Strategic Planning, Transfer and Implementation of Advanced Manufacturing Technologies (AMT). Development of an Integrated Process Plan', *Technovation*, Vol. 22(4), pp. 201-212.

Frambach, R.T. and Schiellewaert, N. (2002), 'Organizational Innovation Adoption: A Multi-level Framework of Determinants and Opportunities for Future Research', *Journal of Business Research*, Vol. 55(2), pp. 163-176.

Gale, H.F. (1997), *Is There a Rural-Urban Technology Gap: Results of the ERS Rural Manufacturing Survey*, Washington DC: U.S. Department of Agriculture ERS AIB, pp. 736-801.

Gibbs, D. and Tanner, K. (1996), 'Information and Communication Technologies and Local Economic Development Policies: The British Case', *Regional Studies*, Vol. 31(8), pp. 765-774.

Grimes, S. (2000), 'Rural Areas in the Information Society: Diminishing Distance or Increasing Learning Capacity?', *Journal of Rural Studies*, Vol. 16(1), pp. 13-21.

Hammer, M. and Mangurian, G.E. (1987), 'The Changing Values of Communication Technology', *Sloan Management Review*, Vol. 28(2), pp. 65-71.

Harrison, B., Kelley, M. and Gant, J. (1996), 'Innovative Firm Behavior and Local Milieu: Exploring the Intersection of Agglomeration, Firm Effects, Industrial Organization, and Technological Change', *Economic Geography*, Vol. 72(3), pp. 233-258.

Hoffer, C.W. and Sandberg, W.R. (1987), 'Improving New Venture Performance: Some Guidelines for Success', *American Journal of Small Business*, Vol. 12 (Summer), pp. 11-25.

Kaplan, R.S. (1983), 'Measuring Manufacturing Performance: A New Challenge for Managerial Accounting Research', *The Accounting Review*, Vol. 58(October), pp. 686-705.

Kinsey, J. (2000), 'A Faster, Leaner, Supply Chain: New Uses of Information Technology', *American Journal of Agricultural Economics*, Vol. 82(5), pp. 1123-1129.

Kourliouros, I.A. (2001), 'Routes of Space Theories, Economic Geography of Production and Development', *Critical Geographic Concept*, Ellinika Grammata, Athens (in Greek).

Kreps, G.L. (1990), *Organizational Communication, Theory and Practice*, Longman, White Plains, New York.

Lal, K. (2002), 'E-business and Manufacturing Sector: a Study of Small and Medium-sized Enterprises in India', *Research Policy*, Vol. 31(7) pp.1199-1211.

Lancioni, R.A., Smith, M.F. and Jensen Schau, H. (2003), 'Strategic Internet Application Trends in Supply Chain Management', *Industrial Marketing Management*, Vol. 32(3), pp. 211-217.

LEADER European Observatory (2000), 'Information Technologies and Rural Development', *Observatory Dossier* No.4.

Legris, P., Ingham, J. and Collerette, P. (2003), 'Why Do People Use Information Technology? A Critical Review of the Technology Acceptance Model', *Information and Management*, Vol. 40(3), pp. 191-204.

Leroux, N., Wortman Jr, M.S. and Mathias, E.D. (2001), 'Dominant Factors Impacting the Development of Business-to-business (B2B) E-commerce in Agriculture', *International Food and Agribusiness Management Review*, Vol. 4(2), pp. 205-218.

McDade, S.R., Oliva, T.A. and Pirsch, J.A. (2002), 'The Organizational Adoption of High-technology Products "for Use". Effects of Size, Preferences, and Radicalness of Impact', *Industrial Marketing Management*, Vol. 31(5), pp. 441-456.

McGranahan, D.A. (2002), 'Local Context and Advanced Technology Use by Small, Independent Manufacturers in Rural Areas', *American Journal of Agricultural Economics*, Vol. 84(5), pp.1237-1245.

Mitchell, S. and Clark, D. (1999), 'Business Adoption of Information and Communication Technologies in the Two-tier Rural Company: Some Evidence from the South Midlands', *Journal of Rural Studies*, Vol. 15(4), pp. 447-455.

Mole, K. and Worrall, L. (2001), 'Innovation, Business Performance and Regional Competitiveness in the West Midlands: Evidence from the West Midlands Business Survey', *European Business Review*, Vol. 13(6), pp. 353-364.

Moulaert, F. and Sekia, F. (2003), 'Territorial Innovation Models: A Critical Survey', *Regional Studies*, Vol. 37(3), pp. 289-302.

Nijkamp, P. (2003), 'Entrepreneurship in a Modern Network Economy', *Regional Studies*, Vol. 37(4), pp. 395-405.

Nouwens, J. and Bowman, H. (1995), 'Living Apart Together in Electronic Commerce: The Use of Information and Communication Technology to Create Network Organizations', *Journal of Computer-Mediated Communication*, Vol. 1(3), http://www.ascusc.org/jcmc/

Organization for Economic Co-operation and Development (1992), Information Computer Communications Policy 30, *Information Networks and New Technologies: Opportunities and Policy Implications for the 1990s*, OECD, Paris.

Organization for Economic Co-operation and Development (2001), *Information and Communication Technologies and Rural Development*, Territorial Economy, OECD, Paris.

Pires, G.D. and Aisbett, J. (2003), 'The Relationship Between Technology Adoption and Strategy in Business-to-business Markets. The Case of E-commerce', *Industrial Marketing Management*, Vol. 32(4), pp. 291-300.

Porter, M. (2001), 'Strategy and the Internet', *Harvard Business Review*, March, pp. 61-78.

Preissl, B. (1995), 'Strategic Use of Communication Technology – Diffusion Process in Networks and Environments', *Information Economics and Policy*, Vol. 7(1), pp. 75-99.

Premkumar, G. and Roberts, M. (1999), 'Adoption of New Information Technologies in Rural Small Businesses', *OMEGA, The International Journal of Management Science*, Vol. 27(4), pp. 467-484.

Redmond, W.H. (2004), 'Interconnectivity in Diffusion of Innovations and Market Competition', *Journal of Business Research*, Vol. 57(11), pp. 1295-1302.

Riemenschneider, C.K., Harrison, D.A. and Mykytyn, P.P. (2003), 'Understanding IT Adoption Decisions in Small Business: Integrating Current Theories', *Information & Management*, Vol. 40(4), pp. 269-285.

Rogers, E. (1995), *The Diffusion of Innovation*, 4th edition, Free Press, New York.

Romano, A., Passiante, G. and Elia, V. (2001), 'New Sources of Clustering in the Digital Economy', *Journal of Small Business and Enterprise Development*, Vol. 8(1), pp. 19-27.

Sadowski, B., Maitland, C. and van Dongen, J. (2002), 'Strategic Use of the Internet by Small and Medium-sized Companies: an Exploratory Study', *Information Economics and Policy*, Vol. 14(1), pp. 75-93.

Salin, V. (1998), 'Information Technology in Agri-Food Supply Chains', *International Food and Agribusiness Management Review*, Vol. 1(3), pp. 329-334.

Simchi-Levi, D., Kaminski, P. and Simchi-Levi, E. (2000), *Designing and Managing the Supply Chain, Concepts, Strategies, and Case Studies*, Irwin/McGraw-Hill, IL.

Spanos, Y.E., Prastacos, G.P. and Polymenakou, A. (2002), 'The Relationship Between Information and Communication Technologies Adoption and Management', *Information & Management*, Vol. 39(8), pp. 659-675.

Steinmueller, E.W. (2000), *Will New Information and Communication Technologies Improve 'Codification' of Knowledge?*, Oxford University Press, Oxford.

Storper, M. (1997), *The Regional World, Territorial Development in a Global Economy*, The Guilford Press, New York and London.

Storper, M. and Salais, R. (1997), *Worlds of Production – the Action Framework of the Economy*, Harvard University Press, Cambridge, Massachusetts and London.

Swamidaas, P.M. (2003), 'Modeling the Adoption Rates of Manufacturing Technology Innovations by Small US Manufacturers: a Longitudinal Investigation', *Research Policy*, Vol. 32(3), pp. 351-366.

Verhaegen, I. and Van Huylenbroek, G. (2001), 'Costs and Benefits for Farmers Participating in Innovative Marketing Channels for Quality Food Products', *Journal of Rural Studies*, Vol. 17(4), pp. 443-456.

Winden, W.V. (2001), 'The End of Social Exclusion? On Information Technology Policy as a Key to Social Inclusion in Large European Cities', *Regional Studies*, Vol. 35(9), pp. 861-877.

Ziggers, G.W. and Trienekens, J. (1999), 'Quality Assurance in Food and Agribusiness Supply Chains: Developing Successful Partnerships', *International Journal of Production Economics*, Vol. 60-61(April), pp. 271-279.

Chapter 12

The Allocation of Public Support to Small Food Firms in Belgium, Ireland and the UK

Tessa Avermaete, Jacques Viaene and Eleanor J. Morgan

in co-operation with
Eamonn Pitts, Nick Crawford, Denise Mahon and Xavier Gellynck

Introduction

Small firms are considered as engines of growth and job creation and are therefore seen as crucial for economic welfare (Grunert et al., 1997; Kotey and Meredith, 1997; McDonagh and Commins, 1999). However, small firms have some specific disadvantages in competing with larger firms. In response, governments have developed various support measures in favour of SMEs (Behrens-Ramberg, 1985; Drabenstott and Morris, 1989; Riding and Haines, 2001). In particular, SME programmes have been developed to support innovation, which is a key factor in competitiveness (Baardseth et al., 1999; Martin and Scott, 2000). Empirical findings show that not all public support measures for smaller firms have been successful; some support measures have encouraged competitiveness whereas other measures have failed to reach their objectives (Hÿvonen and Kola, 1998; Morck and Yeung, 2001; van Beers and de Moor, 2001).

The current chapter investigates the drivers of public support. The aim is to analyse the impact of innovativeness, firm performance, information searching capabilities and aims of the business on obtaining public support and the extent to which these characteristics determine participation in innovation oriented support programmes. The research focuses on small food manufacturing firms (hereafter 'small food firms') which make a particularly important contribution to employment in rural areas, and are considered to have a potentially significant role in safeguarding cultural diversity in the EU (McDonagh and Commins, 1999; Noronha Vaz and Nicolas 2000).

The chapter is structured as follows. The conceptual framework is developed in the next section and the hypotheses are formulated. The following section provides details of a survey that was carried out among 177 small food firms in the EU to obtain the necessary data. The analyses are then presented and the results discussed. The final section contains the conclusion and formulates the managerial and policy implications of the research.

Conceptual Framework

Evaluations of public programmes have focused on the impact of public support. In the short run, however, any relationship between public support and the firm's characteristics is mainly due to the fact that some firms are more likely to apply for public support successfully than others. This tendency holds especially true for public programmes supporting R&D, as research generally suffers from long lags between actual investment and final output (Barnes, 1999).

The allocation of public support across firms is an issue that has recently gained attention among researchers and policy makers (Blanes and Busom, 2003; Wallsten 2000). Empirical findings, particularly on the distribution of public support to SMEs in European manufacturing industry, suggest that a complex array of factors influence a firm's decision to participate in public support programmes (Colombo and Grilli, 2003; Romano et al., 2000). The most important drivers of public support include entrepreneurial characteristics, firm size, business goals and innovation behaviour.

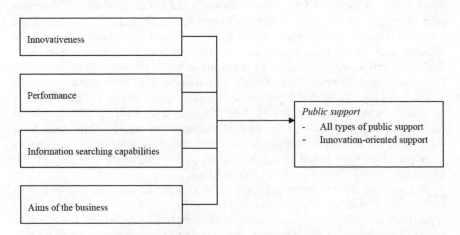

Figure 12.1   Conceptual framework for analysing the allocation of public support to small food firms

The conceptual framework used to analyse the allocation of public support to small food firms is visualised in Figure 12.1. The framework consists of one dependent variable and four independent variables. The dependent variable reflects whether the firm has received public support, in general, and innovation-oriented support in particular. The four independent factors within the framework are (1) innovativeness; (2) performance; (3) information searching capabilities, and (4) the aims of the business.

Over past decades, governments have developed measures to enhance the competitiveness of SMEs, as such firms are thought to play a crucial role in economic growth (McDonagh and Commins 1999). Various types of support programmes exist including financial aid of the traditional kind, such as tax incentives and aid with premises, as well as training and consultancy services to entrepreneurs, assistance for co-operation between SMEs, creation of networks, support for investment and R&D support (European Commission, 1999). The focus on innovation oriented support stems from the fact that innovation is a key factor in competitiveness (Grunert et al., 1997). The European Commission, as well as regional and national governments, has launched support programmes to enhance innovation across SMEs. The programmes comprise direct R&D support, support for investment, enhancement of inter-firm co-operation and the establishment of networks between firms and research institutes (for example, see Baardseth et al. 1999; Diederen et al., 2000; Reid, 1998). Four hypotheses were formulated in accordance with the conceptual framework.

Hypothesis one: innovative firms are more likely to obtain public support than non-innovative firms. Innovative firms will search more intensively for public support than firms that do not plan innovations. This holds particularly true for innovation oriented support programmes, such as support for research activities. Experience from previous innovation programmes helps innovative firms to estimate the costs and benefits of projects and manage the administration involved with participating in public support programmes.

The allocation of public support across innovative and non-innovative firms has recently been explored in the literature. Generally, it is expected that innovative firms will apply more often for public support than their non-innovative counterparts. This view is reflected in the results of Freel (1999), who conducted a survey among 238 manufacturing SMEs and found that 24 per cent of the non-innovative firms applied for public sector grants as compared to 32 per cent of the innovative firms. A possible explanation for this tendency is found in Romijn and Albaladejo (2002). Focusing on innovation grants to small high tech firms, the authors came to the conclusion that these grants are generally more relevant to the needs of innovative firms. The authors also argue that innovative firms have experience in writing research proposals and are therefore more likely to apply for innovation grants successfully. In the case of large firms and multinationals, however, innovation programmes tend to attract less innovative firms whereas large scale innovators seek other sources of external funding (Morck and Yeung, 2001).

Recent studies have investigated the distribution of R&D support. This empirical work suggests that firms with experience in R&D are more likely to obtain R&D support (Blanes and Busom, 2003; Wallsten, 2000). According to Blanes and Busom (2003), firms performing R&D are more likely to apply for a R&D subsidy because it allows them to expand their R&D capacities without having to incur set-up costs.

Hypothesis two: small and medium-sized firms are more likely than very small firms to obtain public support. It is expected that SMEs will have advantages over very small firms in obtaining public support. Despite the numerous programmes that have been developed to strengthen the competitiveness of small firms, very small firms still face many obstacles and constraints in managing the administration required to participate in public support programmes (Keizer et al., 2002; Major and Cordey-Hayes, 2000; Romijn and Albaladejo, 2002). Cost-benefit analyses of loan guarantee programmes show that in very small firms, debts associated with applications for public support often exceed the benefits gained (Barnes, 1999; Riding and Haines, 2001). The difficulties that very small firms have in obtaining public support are mainly due to the organisation and lack of resources of these firms. According to Major and Cordey-Hayes (2000), those working in very small firms have multiple roles and there is a lack of organisational slack which makes dealing with people outside the company much more difficult.

Apart from the lack of personnel, the ability to obtain external funding depends on the firm's financial performance. Firms with a relatively low annual turnover have been found to be averse to sources of capital beyond traditional commercial banking arrangements, such as state funds (Romano et al., 2000; Van Auken, 2001). In addition, the conditions of public support programmes may be a burden for firms with low turnover. Public support for investment, for example, generally requires co-financing by the firm. The risks associated with involvement in such public programmes may be too high for firms with limited financial capacities.

The importance of firm size and financial performance for public support is illustrated by Baardseth et al. (1999) who evaluated the Norwegian Advisory and Network Programme to increase technology transfer to food SMEs. The food enterprises that are suited to participation in this project are 'well-established firms that have enough resources to take part in the network, with both time and money to run a project in the enterprise'.

Hypothesis three: the firm's chances of obtaining public support are related to its information searching capabilities. The intention to apply for public support is driven by the information searching capabilities of the firm. Two aspects are of key importance. First, firms need to be aware of public support programmes. Awareness describes the process by which an organisation scans for and discovers what information is available (Major and Cordey-Hayes, 2000). Intermediaries, such as trade organisations and business networks, play a valuable role in informing small firms of relevant programmes and in helping them to apply for support successfully. Intermediaries are also important in bridging the gap between firms and governments and may also help governments to design more appropriate support measures. Second, successful application for public support requires considerable and persistent efforts by people who are experienced in dealing with the often complex subsidy regulations (Keizer et al., 2002). Experience in subsidy regulations and a good management team tend to determine a firm's chances of obtaining external funding, in general, and public support in particular (Freel, 1999; Frenkel, 2003; Grunert et al., 1997; Orser et al., 2000). The entrepreneur traditionally plays a key role in the management of small firms (Cowling, 2003; Kotey and Meredith, 1997). In this context, successful application for public support also depends upon entrepreneurial characteristics. According to Kotey and Meredith (1997), the effectiveness of assistance programmes among small firms depends on a thorough understanding of owner-managers and how they operate. The age and the level of education of the entrepreneur have been found to be very important for the firm's decision making about its capital structure (Diederen et al., 2000; Romano et al., 2000).

Hypothesis four: the likelihood of obtaining public support is related to the aims of the business. Firms that are about to leave the industry have less interest in searching for public funding as compared to firms with long term strategic aims. This hypothesis is closely related to the first, in the sense that innovativeness is an important aspect of the firm's strategic behaviour. But whereas hypothesis one stresses the firm's actual strategy, hypothesis four focuses on the firm's objectives. Although it is an unexplored area in the literature, the relationship between business goals and success in obtaining public support can be derived from current policies towards business in the EU. At the beginning of the 21st century, governments emphasised competitiveness and innovation and, consequently, support programmes address the needs of firms that appear to have the potential to remain competitive in the future and are willing to introduce changes (Wallsten, 2000).

Survey

The data necessary to test the hypotheses was obtained from a survey conducted among small food firms within the framework of the EU funded Innovaloc project. Data were collected in six European regions: Hereford and Worcester as well as Devon and Cornwall in the United Kingdom, South West and Northwest Border in the Republic of Ireland and West Flanders and Hainault in Belgium (Noronha et al. 2001). The target population included small food manufacturing firms with three to 50 employees. Based on information from national institutes of statistics, regional and local authorities and commercial bodies, about 691 firms were identified fulfilling the research criteria. Quota sampling was used to select the firms with the aim of studying 30 firms in each region. In the UK, there was a high response rate with only five firms refusing to co-operate. In contrast, more firms in the Irish and Belgian regions refused to participate in the survey, mainly because of time pressures. The final response rate comprised 177 small food firms, representing more than one fourth of the target population. A pilot survey was carried out in May 2001 and the final survey was conducted from July to December 2001. The survey was based on in-depth face-to-face interviews with the top manager or owner of the firms. Each interview lasted between one and one and a half hours.

Several variables were selected for each of the five blocks of the conceptual framework. The description of each of the variables is provided in the appendix. Three variables were used to account for public support. A first variable measured whether the firm had received any kind of public support. The two other public support variables dealt with innovation-oriented measures, namely R&D support and support for investment. Four variables measured the firm's innovativeness: product and process innovation, intensity of organisational innovation, R&D activities and patenting behaviour. Empirical research has shown that product innovation is crucial for the majority of the small food firms (Avermaete et al., 2003) so a distinction was made between firms that introduced both product and process innovation and all other firms. Annual turnover and employment were used to measure the firm's performance. Information searching capabilities were captured in four variables: age of the entrepreneur, educational level of the entrepreneur, percentage of qualified staff and involvement in networks. Finally, three aspects of the firm's objectives were selected: exit or survival, enlargement of the range of products and developing export markets.

Logistic regressions using SPSS for windows were carried out to measure the impact of the independent variables on obtaining public support. In a first phase, a logistic regression on public support in general was developed. In a second phase, the analysis was repeated for the specific case of R&D support and support for investment. Missing values, particularly on the firm's annual turnover, meant that the regression was based on 148 firms instead of the total sample of 177 firms.

Results and Discussion

Table 12.1 compares the characteristics of firms that received public support with the characteristics of firms that did not have public support. The results show that the majority of the firms received public support. The type of support that the firms received varied widely, with support for investment and support for training personnel being the most frequent. Despite the lack of personnel in small firms, it appeared that most firms managed to apply for support successfully.

Focusing on the innovation oriented support measures, the figures show that 95 respondents received support for investment whereas only 22 firms benefited from support for R&D activities. The low figures for R&D support are mainly due to the fact that the firms only have small scale R&D activities and that public research programmes tend to be too broad for the research needs of these firms. In line with previous results, several of the respondents were sceptical as to the usefulness of collaboration with research institutes or public innovation centres (Baardseth et al., 1999; Diederen et al., 2000).

Some overall conclusions about the characteristics of firms that received public support and innovation-oriented support can be drawn from Table 12.1. A higher proportion of supported firms introduced product and process innovation as compared to the other firms. Further, the firms that received support had, on average, a lower annual turnover as compared to non-supported firms. With respect to the firm's capabilities, the figures indicate that firms benefiting from support were run by younger entrepreneurs and had a relatively higher number of qualified staff. Finally, the figures suggest that firms that aimed to develop export markets were more likely to rely on public support as compared to firms that did not want to exploit export markets in the future.

Table 12.1   Characteristics of firms that have obtained public support (N=177)

	Public support		R&D support		Support for investment	
	No	Yes	No	Yes	No	Yes
Innovativeness						
Product and process innovation	40 %	61 %	52 %	86 %	50 %	62 %
Organisational innovation	1.35	1.93	1.80	1.77	1.74	1.85
R&D activities	60 %	71 %	65 %	91 %	68 %	68 %
Patents obtained	5 %	9 %	6 %	23 %	9 %	7 %
Firm's performance						
Turnover	3.32	3.10	3.17	2.99	3.29	3.04
Firm size	15.78	18.04	17.64	16.73	17.93	17.18
Information-searching capabilities						
Age of entrepreneur	4.50	4.06	4.23	3.64	4.33	4.01
Degree of entrepreneur	75 %	62 %	70 %	62 %	66 %	64 %
% Qualified staff	25 %	29 %	27 %	40 %	26 %	30 %
Involvement in networks	72 %	85 %	83 %	82 %	83 %	82 %
Aims of the business						
Exit or survival	25 %	23 %	24 %	22 %	23 %	23 %
Enlarge product range	55 %	52 %	55 %	51 %	50 %	73 %
Exploit export markets	20 %	38 %	26 %	41 %	30 %	59 %
Number of firms	40	137	155	22	82	95

The results of the logistic regression to identify the characteristics of firms that received public support are provided in Table 12.2. The chi-square value of the model is highly significant, which implies that the hypothesis that all effects of the independent variables are zero can be rejected. The R square measure shows that the model performs with acceptable values.

The relationship between the existence of innovation and obtaining public support is highly significant. The results are in accordance with the hypothesis that innovative firms are able to apply for and obtain external financing more easily, including access to public support programmes. Innovative firms generally have more experience with public support programmes and are more aware of the type of projects for which public support is available. The regression coefficients of organisational innovation, R&D activities and patenting are small and not significantly related to obtaining public support.

The t-values indicate further highly significant differences in performance between supported and non-supported firms. Supported firms had a lower annual turnover and were larger as compared to firms that had not received public support. The two factors illustrate an apparent paradox. On the one hand, firms with a low annual turnover have more difficulties in getting bank loans compared to firms with a higher turnover. It can therefore be assumed that the latter group relies more heavily on other sources of external funding, such as bank loans and private investors. On the other hand, a firm needs to have enough personnel successfully to apply for public support. Very small firms, in which the workforce fulfils several functions, lack the time to seek sources of public support and to manage the application requirements.

Table 12.2   Logistic regression on the allocation of public support to small firms (N=148)

	Coefficient	T – value
Constant	8.695	13.025***
Innovativeness		
Product and process innovation	1.643	7.066***
Organisational innovation	-0.878	0.604
R&D activities	-0.193	0.110
Patents obtained	0.026	0.001
Firm's performance		
Turnover	-2.116	10.278***
Firm Size	0.099	8.458***
Information-searching capabilities		
Age of entrepreneur	-0.921	11.275***
Degree of entrepreneur	-0.309	0.293
% Qualified staff	1.080	0.542
Involved in networks / organisations	1.225	3.744*
Aims of the business		
Exit or survival	-0.433	0.555
Enlarge product range	-0.347	0.442
Exploit export markets	1.519	4.848**
Chi Square	40.353***	
- 2 Log likelihood	108.869	
Nagelkerke R²	0.376	
N	148.0	

* Significant at 10 % level, ** Significant at 5 % level, *** Significant at 1 % level

With respect to the firm's capabilities, Table 12.2 shows that supported firms were run by younger entrepreneurs than non-supported firms. Young entrepreneurs, who are more likely to have long-run perspectives concerning the business, are more likely to explore the possibilities of external funding as compared to older entrepreneurs who are about to leave the business. Moreover, younger entrepreneurs are more able to find relevant support programmes. Firms run by an entrepreneur with a university degree or firms that have a relatively higher number of qualified staff are no more likely to apply for public support than other firms. Involvement in networks, in contrast, is positively and significantly related to obtaining public support.

Finally, there is a significant difference between the two groups of firms in their intention to exploit export markets. The interest in developing export markets is positively related to obtaining public support. This tendency can also be seen in Table 12.1, which shows that about 38 per cent of the firms receiving support had plans to develop export markets whereas only 20 per cent of the non-supported firms wanted to exploit export markets in the future.

Table 12.3 details the results of the logistic regressions for R&D support and support for investments respectively. The chi square value for both regressions is highly significant. Some of the drivers of public support, in general, remain important determinants of these two types of public support. However, there seem to be measure dependent characteristics that do not contribute to achieving public support generally although they are related to a specific type of support.

Table 12.3   Logistic regression on the allocation of innovation-oriented support to small food firms (N=148)

	R&D support		Support for investment	
	Coefficient	T – value	Coefficient	T – value
Constant	-2.761	1.174	5.481	10.666***
Innovativeness				
Product and process innovation	2.033	5.717**	1.049	5.964**
Organisational innovation	-2.679	4.352**	-1.329	2.716*
R&D activities	1.027	1.159	-0.043	0.010
Patents obtained	1.360	1.937	-0.679	0.812
Firm's performance				
Turnover	0.094	0.020	-1.222	6.901***
Firm size	0.006	0.024	0.046	4.058**
Information-searching capabilities				
Age of entrepreneur	-1.016	6.678***	-0.554	8.414***
Degree of entrepreneur	-0.448	0.372	-0.184	0.193
% Qualified staff	3.085	3.647*	0.549	0.277
Involved in networks / organisations	0.225	0.054	-0.241	0.225
Aims of the business				
Exit or survival	0.877	0.691	-0.401	0.706
Enlarge product range	2.232	6.873***	-0.252	0.423
Exploit export markets	2.497	8.421***	1.081	5.608**
Chi Square	41.969***		30.487***	
- 2 Log likelihood	67.594		172.490	
Nagelkerke R²	0.472		0.249	
N	148		148	

* Significant at 10 % level, ** Significant at 5 % level, *** Significant at 1 % level

Firms that introduced product and process innovation are significantly more likely to obtain R&D support and support for investment. This tendency is very clear for R&D supported firms. Among the 22 R&D supported firms, 19 claimed they introduced product and process innovation. The results are in line with the previous empirical studies which have found that innovation support programmes are most relevant to firms that have experience in innovation (Romijn and Albaladejo, 2002). Further, the results imply that firms who carry out intensive organisational changes are less likely to obtain R&D support and support for investment. This result points towards the role of organisation in applying for public support; small firms that face major changes in their organisation lack the time and personnel to manage the demands of public support programmes. An important issue arises from the figures on R&D expenditures in relation to R&D support. In contrast with previous empirical work, firms with R&D activities are not found more likely to obtain R&D support as compared to other firms (Romijn and Albaladejo, 2002). Apparently, R&D support programmes for small food firms also attract firms without R&D activities. This may be because several of the existing R&D programmes aim to increase the link between research institutes and firms rather than supporting internal R&D activities (Baardseth et al., 1999). In this way, the risks and set-up costs of R&D activities associated with public R&D programmes are limited and firms that have no R&D facilities are encouraged to participate.

Moving to the impact of the firm's performance, the results indicate that firm size and annual turnover are not related to obtaining R&D support. However, employment is positively related to obtaining support for investment whereas annual turnover shows a negative relationship. This outcome is similar to the results of the logistic regression on obtaining public support (see Table 12.2).

The age of the entrepreneur is significantly associated with the receipt of R&D support and support for investment. Young entrepreneurs are more likely to receive the two types of innovation-oriented support than older entrepreneurs. The motivation and the awareness of young entrepreneurs can be suggested as the most important explanations of why younger entrepreneurs apply more often for public support than their older colleagues. Further, the results point towards the role of a qualified workforce in receiving R&D support. Firms with a higher proportion of qualified staff are more likely to obtain R&D support as compared to other firms. Almost 40 per cent of the workforce can be classified as qualified among firms that received R&D support compared with only 27 per cent for firms that have not received R&D support. This reflects the role of qualified managerial and scientific staff in obtaining R&D support. A good management team is often required to find relevant public support measures and deal with the administration of such support programmes; a strong scientific staff increases the chances of producing a research proposal that meets the requirements of policy makers.

Finally, the role of the firm's objectives in receiving innovation-oriented support is highlighted. Firms that aim to exploit export markets are more likely to obtain both R&D support and support for investment. Firms that aim to enlarge the range of products are found to obtain R&D support more often, which suggests that innovation-oriented programmes not only attract innovative firms but also those firms that are willing to innovate.

Conclusions

The aim of this research was to investigate the extent to which the characteristics of the firm contribute to obtaining public support, in general, and to accessing innovation-oriented support in particular. The research was based on a survey which provided information on the characteristics of 177 small food firms in three EU countries. Hypotheses were put forward concerning the likelihood of obtaining public support based on four variables, namely innovativeness; firm performance; information searching capabilities, and finally, the aims of the business.

The research confirms that the four factors selected are relevant indicators for the likelihood that the firm will have obtained public support. A focus on R&D support and support for investment shows that these support measures attract a very specific group of firms.

Four main conclusions can be drawn. First, the investigation indicated that innovativeness in the form of product and process innovation is related to obtaining public support, in general, and innovation oriented support in particular. Firms that are introducing changes in their organisation, in contrast, are less likely to obtain innovation oriented support. Second, the firm's performance is associated with whether a firm receives public support including support for investment. Firms with a lower turnover and larger firms were most likely to obtain support. Nevertheless, the performance of the firm was not related to obtaining R&D support. Third, younger entrepreneurs were most likely to obtain public support. This also held true for innovation-oriented support. Involvement in networks appeared to contribute to receiving public assistance while the proportion of qualified staff was positively associated with obtaining support for R&D. Fourth, the objectives of the firm have a significant influence on obtaining support. This tendency was particularly pronounced in the case of R&D support where both the aim of enlarging the range of products and of exploiting export markets were found to be significant.

The managerial and policy implications of the research are twofold. From the manager's point of view, the results imply that dynamic firms are most likely to find appropriate public support. Small food firms should be aware that governments have developed programmes to support business activities that lead to sustainable growth. As innovation is considered a key factor in competitiveness, support programmes tend to focus on innovators and potential innovators. Managers of small food firms whose strategic behaviour is innovation oriented are most likely to find and obtain relevant support programmes.

Policy makers, for their part, should be aware of the distribution of public support across firms. The finding that support programmes not only attract innovative firms but also those firms that are willing to innovate is encouraging. Governments seem to have succeeded in lowering the managerial burden of public support programmes allowing small firms to profit from innovation oriented policy measures. However, whereas small firms rely heavily on support for investment, only a small percentage of small food firms participate in R&D support programmes. In order to increase the competitiveness of the entire sector in the long run, government needs to increase the awareness and the relevance of R&D

support programmes (Barnes, 1999). For this purpose, governments can either directly address the firms that are not performing R&D activities or make use of intermediary organisations, such as trade associations and other business bodies.

A final note concerns possible future research. The study reported here focused on the incidence of public support obtained by small firms. However, it would also be interesting to explore the type of support that the firms received from public agencies in more detail. In addition, the impact of public support programmes on the firm's performance is also worth studying and would require information covering a longer period to be collected. Both areas of research should help governments to design more effective support programmes.

Acknowledgements

This research was undertaken with support from the European Union's fifth framework programme: project Innovaloc N° HPSE-CT-1999-00024. The content of the chapter is the responsibility of the first three authors. Eamonn Pitts and Denise Mahon provided the Irish data and Nick Crawford assisted with the questionnaire design and collection of the UK data.

References

Avermaete, T., Viaene, J., Morgan, E.J. and Crawford, N. (2003), 'Determinants of Innovation in Small Food Firms', *European Journal of Innovation Management*, Vol. 6(1), pp. 8-17.

Baardseth, P., Dalen, G.A. and Tandberg, A. (1999), 'Innovation/technology Transfer to Food SMEs', *Trends in Food Science and Technology*, Vol. 10, pp. 234-238.

Barnes, A.P. (1999), 'Commercial R&D Linkage with Public Agro-food Institutions', *Food Policy*, Vol. 24, pp. 349-355.

Behrens-Ramberg, W. (1985), *Steuerliche Anreize bei Innovativen investitionen Kleiner und Mittlerer Industrieunternehmen unter vergleichender Berücksichttigung Nichtsteurlicher Hilfen*, Poeschel, Stuttgard.

Blanes, J.V. and Busom, I. (2003), 'Participation in R&D Subsidy Programs, Who Gets the Money? The Case of Spanish Manufacturing Firms', *WZB Economic Seminar Series*, 16 June 2003, Berlin.

Colombo, M.G. and Grilli, L. (2003), *Italian Public Support to NTBFs, An Empirical Investigation*, University of Pavia and CIRET Politecnico di Milano, Italy.

Cowling, M. (2003), 'Productivity and Corporate Governance in Smaller Firms', *Small Business Economics*, Vol. 20(4), pp. 335-344.

Diederen, P., van Meijl, H. and Wolters, A. (2000), *Eureka! Innovatieprocessen en Innovatiebeleid in de Land- en Yuinbouw*, LEI, Den Haag.

Drabenstott, M. and Morris, C. (1989), 'New Sources of Financing for Rural Development', *American Journal of Agricultural Economics*, Vol. 71(5), pp. 1315-1323.

European Commission (1999), *Sixth Periodic Report on the Social and Economic Situation and Development of the Regions of the European Union*, Regional Policy and Cohesion, Brussels.

Freel, M.S. (1999), 'The Financing of Small Firm Product Innovation within the UK', *Technovation*, Vol. 19, pp. 707-719.

Frenkel (2003), 'Barriers and Limitations in the Development of Industrial Innovation in the Region', *European Planning Studies*, Vol. 11(2), pp. 115-137.

Grunert, K.G., Harmsen, H., Meulenberg, M., Kuiper, E., Ottowitz, T., Declerck, F., Traill, B. and Göransson (1997), 'A Framework for Analysing Innovation in the Food Sector', in B. Traill and K.G. Grunert (eds), *Product and Process Innovation in the Food Sector*, Blackie Academic & Professional, London, pp. 1-37.

Hyvönen, S. and Kola, J. (1998), 'New Policies, New Opportunities, New Threats: the Finnish Food Industry in the EU', in B. Traill and E. Pitts (eds), *Competitiveness in the Food Industry*, Blackie Academic & Professional, Chapman & Hall, London, pp. 253-287.

Keizer, J.A., Dijkstra, L. and Halman, J.I.M. (2002), 'Explaining Innovative Efforts of SMEs. An Exploratory Survey among SMEs in the Mechanical and Electrical Engineering Sector in the Netherlands', *Technovation*, Vol. 22, pp. 1-13.

Kotey, B. and Meredith, G.G. (1997), 'Relationships among Owner/Manager Personal Values, Business Strategies, and Enterprise Performance', *Journal of Small Business Management*, Vol. 35(2), pp. 37-64.

Major, E.J. and Cordey-Hayes, M. (2000), 'Engaging the Business Network to Give SMEs the Benefit of Foresight', *Technovation*, Vol. 20, pp. 589-602.

Martin, S. and Scott, J.T. (2000), 'The Nature of Innovation Market Failure and the Design of Public Support for Private Innovation', *Research Policy*, Vol. 29, pp. 437-447.

McDonagh, P. and Commins, P. (1999), *Globalisation and Rural Development, Demographic Revitalisation, Entrepreneurs and Small Business Formation in the West of Ireland*, Ashgate Publishing Company, Aldershot.

Morck, R. and Yeung, B. (2001), 'The Economic Determinants of Innovation', *Industry Canada Research Publication Program. Paper No 25*, New York University, New York.

Noronha Vaz, M.T. and Nicolas, F. (2000), 'Innovation in Small Firms and Dynamics of Local Development', *ISEG Workshop*, Lisbon, January 24-25.

Noronha Vaz, M.T., Cesario, M. and Avermaete, T. (2001), 'Territorial Systems in the Rural Areas of the European Union', *Confidential Report D2 to the European Commission, Contract N°HPSE-CT-1999-00024*.

Orser, B.J., Hogart-Scott, S. and Riding, A.L. (2000), 'Performance, Firm Size, and Management Problem Solving', *Journal of Small Business Management*, Vol. 38(4), pp. 42-58.

Reid, C. (1998), 'Managing Innovation in the British Herring Fishery: the Role of the Herring Industry Board 1945-1977', *Marine Policy*, Vol. 22(4-5), pp. 281-295.

Riding, A.L. and Haines, G. (2001), 'Loan Guarantees: Costs of Defaults and Benefits to Small Firms', *Journal of Business Venturing*, Vol. 16, pp. 595-612.

Romano, C.A., Tanewski, G.A. and Smyrnios, K.X. (2000), 'Capital Structure Decision Making: a Model for Family Business', *Journal of Business Venturing*, Vol. 16, pp. 285-310.

Romijn, H. and Albaladejo, M. (2002), 'Determinants of Innovation Capability in Small Electronics and Software Firms in Southeast England', *Research Policy*, Vol. 31(7), pp. 1053-1067.

Van Auken, H.E. (2001), 'Financing Small Technology-based Companies: The Relationship between Familiarity with Capital and Ability to Price and Negotiate Investment', *Journal of Small Business Management*, Vol. 39(3), pp. 240-258.

Van Beers, C. and de Moor, A. (2001), *Public Subsidies and Policy Failures*, Edward Elgar Publishers, Cheltenham.

Wallsten, S.J. (2000), 'The Effects of Government-industry R&D Programs on Private R&D: The Case of the Small Business Innovation Research Program', *RAND Journal of Economics*, Vol. 31(1), pp. 82-100.

Appendix 12.1 Description of the variables used in the logistic regressions

Variable	*Description*

Public support

Public support	Firms that have received any kind of public support over the past five years code 1, otherwise 2
R&D support	Firms that have received public support for R&D activities over the past five years code 1, otherwise 2
Support for investment	Firms that have received public support for investment over the past five years code 1, otherwise 2

Innovativeness

Product and process innovation	Firms that introduced both product and process innovation over the past 5 years code 1, otherwise 2
Organisational innovation	Number of domains in which major organisational changes were carried out over the past 5 years. Distinction is made between 7 domains: management, marketing structure, financial structure, production, R&D, logistics, other functional areas. The score is divided by 7 so that the variable ranges between 0 and 1.
R&D activities	Firms that have R&D activities code 1, otherwise 2
Patents obtained	Firms that have obtained patents code 1, otherwise 2

Firm's performance

Turnover	Log of the firm's annual turnover
Firm size	Number of firms that work in the firm

Information searching capabilities

Age of entrepreneur	Age of the entrepreneur: 2 = 20-29 years old, 3= 30-39 years old, etc.
Degree of entrepreneur	Entrepreneurs with a university degree (bachelor or master) code 1, otherwise 2.
% Qualified staff	Qualified staff as percentage of total workforce
Involvement in networks	Firms involved in networks or organisations code 1, otherwise 2

Aims of the business

Exit or survival	Firms with survival or sale the business as main aim code 1, otherwise 2
Enlarge product range	Firms in which the main aim is to enlarge the range of products code 1, otherwise 2
Exploit export markets	Firms in which the main aim is to develop export markets code 1, otherwise 2

Chapter 13

A Medium Term Economic Outlook for Cyclical Markets: A Case Study of Mexican Pig Farms

Myriam Sagarnaga Villegas, Rene Ochoa Ochoa, José Salas González, Edmundo Haro and Guillermina García Figueroa

Introduction

It is widely known that the pig market displays cyclical behaviour. Prices follow a pattern called the pig (or 'hog') cycle, which was first noted in the United States during the 1930s. Data from the mid nineteenth century to the present indicate that the pig cycle, measured from peak to peak or low to low, lasts an average of four years (Spenser, 1978; Piccinini and Loseby, 2001).

The Mexican market has shown cyclical behaviour since its borders were opened to the international market and the cyclical behaviour of the American market, in particular, is transmitted to the Mexican market through imports. At the National Congress of Hog Producers, it was concluded that 'In the face of increased imports of pork, hogs and their by-products, the price of domestic pork has been mainly influenced by the prices of the United States market with regards not only to live animals, but also to primary cuts that have little value in the original market due to a lesser appreciation of the consumer' (Cerdos Tecnología Internacional, 2002: 17).

An earlier economic outlook for Mexican pig farms by Sagarnaga et al. (1999) found that 'Price predictions for the domestic price of pork demonstrate a cyclical behaviour with a tendency towards growth. The period of 1995-2004 holds two cycles. In the first cycle, the price of pork reached its highest level in 1997 and ended in 1998, when the nominal price reached its observed minimum. The second price cycle reached its maximum level in 2001 and the minimum in 2003.' Sagarnaga et al. (1999: 38) concluded, 'If the utilized predictions adequately reflect the reality of hog production in Mexico, it is possible to say that in 1998 Mexican hog production will face the most critical conditions of the present market cycle. A better economic situation than the existing is expected for the farms during the period of 2000-2002 only to later face a new depression during 2003.' Those predictions proved to be very accurate. Prices have shown a tendency to decrease from their peak in 2001. The average price for early 2003 was 15 per cent lower than in 2002.

Fluctuations in price can be very damaging to producers, depending on their production costs. According to the Secretaria de Agricultura, Ganadería, Desarrollo Rural, Pesca y Alimentación (SAGARPA-CEA, 2003), the average production cost per kilo of live pigs in 2002 in high technology farms was $10.97 Mexican pesos, while intermediate technology farms had unit production costs of $15.51 Mexican pesos. This means that falling prices cause serious problems for some pork producers, particularly those with less technologically based farms.

Objectives and Methodology

The main goal of this chapter is to evaluate pig farms' competitiveness in the Mexican state of Guanajuato, one of the main pork producing states in Mexico. A secondary objective is to analyse the impact of certain technical and economic strategies on the competitiveness of those farms. This chapter illustrates how the chosen methodology can be used to assess the outlook for future performance in a particular sector, which is of interest from a European policy perspective.

The sensitivity of the Mexican swine sector to the domestic and foreign economic environment makes the analyses of the future financial viability of pig production difficult if traditional methods are used. The application of simulation techniques, however, allows the economic and financial performance of pig production under different scenarios to be assessed *ex ante* with relative ease.

The whole farm simulation model, FLIPSIM, is used in this analysis to model the financial performance of pig operations. FLIPSIM is an excellent tool for analysing the economics of farms operations where indicators of future economic performance are needed in advance to assess the effects of adoption of a specific technology or the effects at the farm level of applying changes in government policy to a country's agriculture sector.

The representative farm panel process has been successfully utilized in analysing the farm level impacts of agriculture policies (Richardson and Nixon, 2000). Simulation techniques used in conjunction with data from a panel of representative farms have proved widely successful in farm level analyses. Simulation modelling techniques using representative farms have been applied in the study of agriculture and ranching in the USA, for example, and in determining the financial and economic viability of livestock and dairy farms in Mexico (Ochoa et al., 1998). By applying these techniques to pig production in Mexico, it should be possible to give the producers, as well as legislators and public policy makers, the necessary information for decision making. This would have direct benefits for the country, commercial producers and their partners and for consumers in general.

This work includes data for six Mexican pig panels. These pig panels were selected to allow analysis of the main Mexican productive systems. Panellists were chosen with the support of the Unión Ganadera Regional de Porcicultores de

Guanajuato (UGRPG), which is the main pig producer association of the Mexican state of Guanajuato. At least five representative pig producers participated in each panel. The panels generated information about three representative integrated farms (small, medium, and large scale, LEON60, IRA300 and IRA1200 respectively), two grower farms (small and large scale, CORT300 and CORT400 respectively) and one breeding farm (small scale JARAL50), located in Guanajuato.

For the purpose of this study, the farms were listed according to their location and scale. Thus JARAL50 is a farm with 50 sows located in the Municipality of Jaral. The same scheme was followed in coding the remaining farms. The complete cycle integrated farms analysed were LEON60, IRA300, and ANA1200. JARAL50 is a breeding farm specializing in selling young pigs to be raised on other farms. CORT300 and CORT4000 buy young pigs and wean them to market weight.

Information generated by the panel was used to represent the current situation of pig farms in 2002 and to project their competitiveness for the planning horizon 2003-2009. Projections of economic viability were made applying price projections (pork and sorghum) and macroeconomic indicators (inflation and exchange rate) from the Food and Agricultural Policy Research Institute (FAPRI). The following economic indicators were estimated in order to project the competitiveness of pig farms – production costs, net cash income, the ratio of cost to income, the rate of return on investments, the return on capital, adjusted net income, capital net worth and the annual change in net capital.

Predictions

The predictions initially present an unfavourable panorama for pig production since the accumulated increase of GDP is estimated to be 48.18 per cent in the period 2002-2009 and the exchange rate is expected to appreciate by 32.8 per cent, while the pig prices increase only 9 per cent over the same period (Table 13.1). This indicates that farms' production costs will grow at a faster rate than income, diminishing farm profits.

Table 13.1   Projected annual increase in Mexican GDP (%), projected annual exchange rate appreciation (%) and pig price projections (Mexican pesos per kilogram)

	2002	2003	2004	2005	2006	2007	2008	2009
GDP	8.1	6.4	6.4	6.0	5.8	5.8	5.8	5.8
Exchange rate	5.7	5	4.2	3.6	3.6	3.6	3.6	3.6
Pig price projections*	10.00	9.56	10.2	10.73	11.21	11.03	10.96	10.92

* Barrow and Gilts national base, 51-52% lean equivalent

Source: Predictions derived from FAPRI data

Predictions for the domestic price of pork show a cyclical tendency, although less marked than in the US market (Figure 13.1). It is anticipated that 2003 will be the most critical period of the cycle with prices starting to recover in 2004. The growth trend is maintained throughout the planning period but this might be due to the tendency of the exchange rate to appreciate so such results must be viewed with caution.

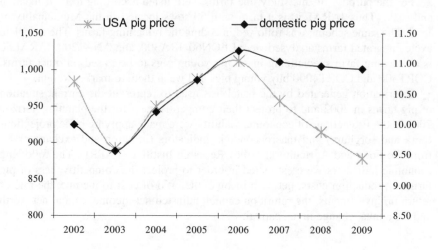

Figure 13.1 Pig price predictions (Mexican pesos and US dollars)

Source: Predictions derived from FAPRI data

The sale price of pork provided by the panels fluctuated between $10.3 Mexican pesos and $11.00 (Table 13.2). The price of sorghum used in the analysis fluctuated between $1.50 and $2.2 per kilogram. The cyclical behaviour of pig prices and growing sorghum prices confirm the expectation that profits will diminish.

Table 13.2   Sorghum price, pig sale price and production cost from the producer panels (Mexican pesos per kilogram), 2002

	LEON60	IRA300	ANA1200	JARAL50	CORT300	COTR4000
Sorghum	1.55	1.20	2.00	1.50	1.70	2.20
Pig production cost	11.71	11.47	8.91	17.04	8.23	10.58
Pig sale price	10.30	10.30	10.50	31.70	10.50	11.00

Source: Own data processing from the producer panels

Results

Farm LEON60

This panel represents a complete cycle farm with 60 sows on only one site. It produces low quality (standard) pigs that are sold to middlemen for the local market. It is dependent on the market for its supply of agricultural feedstuffs which are mixed by hand at the farm. Technology is limited and six days of labour are required per sow per year. In 2002, investment per sow was $15,000.00; 265 tons of feed were consumed a year or 258 kilogram per fattened pig. Total annual production of the farm was 762 pigs, 14 pigs per sow per year. This farm presents lower levels of efficiency than the national average. The annual feed conversion rate of the farm was 3.66 kilogram of feed per kilogram of meat produced. The farm does not receive technical assistance.

Results indicate that this farm is not competitive. The cost of production per fattened pig was $1,067.00 in 2002 and the production cost per kilogram was $11.71 (Table 13.2). Net cash income was negative in the base year. Losses increased throughout the planning period. The average ratio of cost to income is 133 per cent. The farm shows a constant loss of capital, beginning with the base year and worsening towards the end of the planning period. Rates of return on investments and capital are negative. Adjusted net income indicates that this farm should increase its income by 67 per cent or decrease its costs by 41 per cent if there is to be no change in net capital throughout the planning period, taking into account inflation in land prices.

The problems of competitiveness would be solved with a simple technological change that permitted a larger number of fattened pigs to be brought to market. This could be accomplished in various ways, but technical assistance would be very important as a means of introducing appropriate technical changes.

Farm IRA300

This is a semi-technical, complete cycle farm located in the Municipality of Irapuato, Guanajuato. It has 300 sows at only one site. The farm also produces agricultural products, although it does not meet its own total demand for grains and has to resort to the local market. The grains are mixed on the farm with other ingredients to make feed for the pigs. The farm sells its pigs to intermediaries that supply half to the regional market and the other half to Mexico City. Investment per sow was $7,333.00 in 2002; 12.17 days of work were required per sow per year; 1,413 tons of feed were consumed per year which is equivalent to 250 kilograms per pig. The total annual production of the farms was 4,383 pigs, 17.6 pigs to market per sow a year. The annual feed conversion rate of the farm was 3.39 kilograms of feed per kilogram of meat. The main problem of farm IRA300 was a high mortality rate. This farm only received technical assistance which was offered free from the distributors of veterinary products.

Analysis revealed that this farm was not competitive in the base year with a $11.47 production cost per kilogram of live pig. The farm's lack of competitiveness was despite the surpluses it generated through other agricultural activities.

Farm ANA1200

The farm handles 1200 sows that are completely confined to two sites. It has its own feed plant, artificial insemination laboratory and waste water treatment plant. It has no other agricultural activities so it buys all the sorghum it requires. It sells all the pigs, which are of the highest quality (supreme), to regional brokers.

Investment per sow was $9,167, feed consumption was 6,972 tons per year equivalent to 337 kilograms per pig. Total annual production of the farm was 20,652 pigs or 19.55 pigs per sow per year, which is above the national average. The annual feed conversion rate of the farm was 3.31. This farm received specialized technical assistance from USA experts.

In 2002, the production cost per pig was $909.25, generating a profit of $235.60 per pig. Cost per kilogram is estimated at $8.91, the lowest observed for the farms carrying out the complete cycle (Table 13.2). Net cash income was estimated to be positive until 2006 but after 2007, the farm will make losses. The ratio of average costs to income is 99 per cent and the average capitalization index for the period is 0.66. The average ratio of interest on assets and capital is negative. The average of the ratio of financial costs to total costs is lower than one per cent for the period analysed. Projections of net adjusted income shows that it is necessary for this farm to increase its income by 19 per cent or to reduce its expenditures by 16 per cent to keep net capital unchanged.

Farm JARAL50

This farm is traditional and produces fattening pigs. It has no other agricultural activities so all the feed required must be bought. The pigs are sold directly to local fattening farms. In 2002, investment per sow was $12,000.00, labour requirements were 7.3 days and the feed consumed was 50.316 tons, equivalent to 1006 kilograms per sow. The farm produced 868 pigs amounting to about 18 pigs per sow a year sent to market, which is above the national average. The annual feed conversion rate was 5.8. The analysis of this information reflects a total cost per sow of $2,958.50 and a total income of $5,503.20. Each sow, therefore, produced a net cash income or profit of $2,544.70. The production cost per kilogram of fattening pig was $17.04 (Table 13.2) and the sale price was $31.70, thereby generating a profit of $14.66 per kilogram of pig sold. This farm does not receive technical assistance. Producers are willing to adopt new technologies, but they are not willing to pay for them.

The predictions indicated that this farm will be competitive throughout the planning period but the degree of competitiveness will decrease over the period studied. The average ratio of cost to income is 69 for the period 2002-2009. Real net capital gain and the rate of return on assets are negative on average, although positive in some years. The average rate of return on capital during the period is 7 per cent. The projections of adjusted net income show that the farm should increase its income by 7 per cent or lower its costs by 8 per cent on average so as not to face further problems.

Farm CORT300

This farm specializes in fattening pigs and has installations capable of fattening 300 pigs in three groups each year. The pigs produced are of the highest quality and are sold at the farm to regional brokers. Commercial feed is used based on sorghum and concentrates that are mixed at the farm. In 2002, investment per pig on the farm was $2,550.00 pesos. 3.65 days of work a year were required per pig fattened and feed consumption was 68.7 tons a year or 231 kilograms per fattened pig. The total annual production of the farm was 295 pigs. The annual feed conversion rate of the farm was 2.38. In 2002, the total cost per fattened pig was $806.06, which was sold for $1,073.41, giving the producer a profit of $267.36 per pig sold. The production cost per kilogram is $8.23 (Table 13.2). This farm does not receive technical assistance.

The predictions indicated that this farm will be competitive until 2008,[1] after which it will not be profitable. Real net capital of the business is decreasing; the capitalization index increases during the main part of the planning period, although it decreases towards the end.

Farm CORT4000

This farm which specializes in fattening pigs is located in the Municipality of Cortazar, Guanajuato. Its installations have the capacity to fatten 4,000 pigs in three groups a year. The fattened pigs are of the highest quality and are sold at the farm to intermediaries who take them to Mexico City or to other states. The feed is mixed at the farm, which has no other agricultural activities. In 2002, the farm's investment was $1,250.00 per fattened pig; 0.37 days of work were required for each pig sold a year; feed consumption was 3,820 tons per year which is equivalent to 260 kilograms per fattened pig. Total annual production of the farm was 14,250 pigs and the annual feed conversion rate of the farm was 2.68. This farm does not pay for technical assistance.

This farm has problems as regards its competitiveness starting from the base year. The reported price of sorghum was the highest of all farms at $2.20 per kilogram, even higher than that reported by the smaller farms that bought a smaller volume of the product. If the price reported by the smallest fattening farm is used instead, the farm is competitive for the base year with a total cost per fattened pig of $1,058.32, giving a profit of $118.68 per pig with a sale price of $1,177.00. Production cost per kilogram of live pig was $10.58 (Table 13.2).

Predictions show that, despite these adjustments, this farm still has difficulties as regards its competitiveness soon after the base year. Net cash income is positive until 2005 and later becomes negative. The ratio of average costs to income ratio is

104. The average rate of return on assets and capital over the period is negative. The capitalization index is positive during the main part of the period analysed, but it becomes negative towards the end.

Support for Technology Adoption in Mexico

There is no a well defined government policy toward innovation and technological change in Mexico. The Mexican government has created the Grupos Ganaderos de Validación y Transferencia de Tecnología (GGAVATT) in order to encourage technology adoption among small scale producers. These are groups of eight to ten small producers led by a veterinarian who demonstrates the new technologies and encourages their adoption. The salary cost of this specialist is split equally between the government and the producers. There is no equivalent policy oriented towards medium to large scale producers.

Small scale producers, including pig producers, are the focus of this programme in Guanajuato state. Preliminary results indicate that pig producers which participate in GGAVATTS, are adopting new technologies. The results suggest that the government should invest more resources in this kind of programme, since it has the potential to increase the technological level of the farms and to help solve some of their problems regarding competitiveness.

Conclusions

Pig producers in Mexico faced problems of competitiveness under the market conditions and technical management that prevailed during this study. During the base year (2002), a majority of the farms were profitable, with the exception of farms LEON60 and IRA300. Losses in LEON60 and IRA300 were solved by certain technological adjustments but most of the farms do not receive technical assistance. Some of them receive some technical support from the distributors of veterinary products but this is conditional on purchasing such products. Only the large scale integrated farms pay for specialized technical assistance; the smaller scale farmers are aware of the importance of technical assistance but they are not willing to pay for it.

If the predictions in this study are accurate, the competitiveness of the farms will worsen throughout the planning period and some of them will be loss making within a few years. Most of the farms have the necessary income to meet direct production costs and most of fixed costs. Nevertheless, income is sufficient neither to permit the replacement of the means of production at the end of their productive life nor to generate the resources necessary to meet the producers' cost of living.

Failure to replace the means of production will have repercussions in the short term because outdated production plants increase production costs and lead to a further deterioration in the competitiveness of pig production. The inability of producers to support a standard of living meeting their needs and expectations will have repercussions in that the majority of the producers will have to seek additional activities or leave the industry, become unemployed and possibly migrate.

The adoption of new technologies could contribute towards solving the economic problems faced by some farms which could, in reality, be alleviated by making relatively small changes in technical management. Although there is no well designed government policy to encourage the diffusion of technology in Mexican agriculture, some small pig producers are adopting new technologies thanks to GGAVATT, a small programme oriented to the livestock sector. The results of this study suggest that it would be worthwhile for the Mexican government to invest more resources in encouraging the adoption and technological change process among small pig farmers.

Note

1   Note that the FAPRI forecasts indicate that the maximum price for pork will be reached in 2004.

References

Cerdos Tecnología Internacional (2002), 'Conclusiones del Encuentro Nacional de Porcicultura', Editorial Internacional *Cerdos. Tecnología Internacional*. Vol. 5(60), October, pp. 17.

Gallardo, J.N. and Galarza J.M. (2003), 'Situación Actual y Perspectiva de la Producción de Carne de Porcino en México 2003', SAGARPA-CEA.

Ochoa, R.F., Anderson, D., Outlaw, J., Richardson, J., Knutson, R., Schwart, R. and Miller, J. (1998), 'Granjas Lecheras Representativas en México. Panorama Económico 1998. Documento de Trabajo AFPC 98-10', Agricultural and Food Policy Center, Department of Agricultural Economics, Texas A&M University.

Piccinini, A. and Loseby, M. (2001), *Agricultural Policies in Europe and the USA, Farmers Between Subsidies and the Market*, Palgrave, Great Britain.

Richardson, J.W. and Nixon, C.J. (2000), 'Description of FLIPSIM V: A General Firm Model Policy Simulation Model', *Agricultural and Food Policy Center Bulletin B1528*, Department of Agricultural Economics, Texas A&M University.

Sagarnaga, MV., Rene O., José Ma. S., Anderson, D., Richardson, J.W. and Ronald K. (1999), 'Granjas Porcinas Representativas en México. Panorama Económico 1995-2004', Reporte de investigación, *AFPC Research Report 99-16*, Enero. Agricultural and Food Policy Center, Department of Agricultural Economics, Texas A&M University.

Spenser, S. (1978), *Economía Contemporánea*, Ed. Reverte S.A. Spain.

Chapter 14

Adopting Innovations in Agriculture: An Exploratory Analysis Using Discrete Choice Models

Shlomo Bekhor, Daniel Shefer and Mordechai Cohen

Introduction

This chapter is concerned with the development of an agricultural product and the spatial diffusion of innovations as an important element in the economic development of a rural region. Specifically, the chapter considers the development of greenhouse tomatoes and their spatial diffusion in the North Western region of the Negev in Israel. Two aspects of innovation diffusion will be dealt with: first, the selection of a specific tomato variety and, second, the choice of a fertilization technique.

Many researchers have dealt with questions relating to the spatial diffusion of innovations in manufacturing industries and its relationship to regional development. Most of the recent studies have focused on the industrial sector, although in the past studies were concerned with the agricultural sector. Examples of such past studies can be found in Mansfield (1968), Yeats (1974), and Rogers (1983). These researchers studied the process of generating innovations, their spatial diffusion, and the consequent economic and social impacts. Discrete choice models have been used in many such studies carried out in the industrial sector: Frenkel et al. (2003) is a recent example. There are several studies in the agricultural sector which have used discrete choice models: see, for example, Feder and Umali (1993), Feder et al. (1985) and more recently, Marra et al. (2003). However, in the specific context of modelling innovation of an agricultural product, such as greenhouse tomato, there is less evidence in the literature. This study aims to apply the process observed in the manufacturing sector to sophisticated, advanced farming practices.

The mathematical models used to describe diffusion processes assume that new products do not change throughout the adoption period. However, many studies have showed on-going product improvements, together with new-product generation, competition, and changes in the production processes in the adoption period. Examples can be found in Metcalf (1981), Kamien and Schwartz (1982), and Davelaar (1991).

In addition, geographical aspects have long been recognized as important factors in the spatial diffusion of innovations, as can be seen in the studies of Hagestrand (1967) and Meir (1981). One of the seminal papers demonstrating the importance of distance to information source for adoption decisions was by Lindner et al. (1982).

In the agricultural sector, environment plays an important role, as one would expect. In most countries, agricultural production is split among many small producing units which are generally spread over a large area and, therefore, located far from urban centres and the services associated with them. For this reason, the contribution of Research and Development (R&D) centres situated close to agricultural farms may be quite significant, but also detrimental, as found in several studies; see, for example, Griliches (1957), Evenson and Kislev (1975), and Arndt et al. (1977).

The main objective of the present chapter is to identify the factors affecting farmers' decisions to adopt innovations and the factors inducing the process of knowledge-diffusion in rural regions. The approach adopted is the use of discrete choice models, based on random utility theory.

This study concentrates on the North Western region of the Negev in Israel, a relatively new region where the government has encouraged farmers to grow export-oriented products. The greenhouse tomato was selected to be a suitable crop for that purpose. Concomitantly, it was decided to establish an agricultural R&D centre in the region for the purpose of augmenting the farmers' ability to cope with the tough competition involved in exporting tomatoes, particularly to Europe and North America.

The chapter is divided into four sections. The first section deals with the theoretical background, followed by the research methodology and data sources. Empirical results of disaggregate logit models are presented in the subsequent section. Summary and conclusions form the last part of the chapter.

Theoretical Background

The models derived in this chapter are based on the perceived attractiveness of each of the available alternatives. These alternatives are defined as the different tomato varieties. The available alternatives are expressed as weighted sums of attributes; the attributes can be classified as regional, local, or personal. The measure of attractiveness of an alternative is referred to as its 'utility'. The basic theory used in the derivation of the models is the discrete choice-random utility theory which is briefly summarized here. For a more comprehensive review, see Ben-Akiva and Lerman (1985).

Each farmer is assumed to perceive the utility associated with each variety of tomato available, and to choose the one with the greatest perceived utility. The utility U_{in} of alternative i for individual n can be broken down into two terms: a deterministic term V_{in}, which is associated with the measured attributes of the alternative, and a random error ε_{in}, representing the difference between the measurable utility and the true utility of the alternative for individual n. The random error accounts for factors that affect the utility of an alternative not included in V_{in}, as well as for other factors that are fundamentally unobservable.

The probability that individual n will choose alternative i from the set of available alternatives J_n is equal to:

$$P_n(i) = P(U_{in} \geq U_{jn}, \forall j \in J_n) = P(V_{in} + \varepsilon_{in} \geq V_{jn} + \varepsilon_{jn}, \forall j) \tag{1}$$

Rearranging the terms yields:

$$P_n(i) = P(\varepsilon_{jn} - \varepsilon_{in} \geq V_{in} - V_{jn}, \forall j \in J_n) \tag{2}$$

Thus the probability that a particular alternative will be chosen depends on the joint distribution of the differences between the error terms.

Several different models have been developed according to the distribution assumed for the error terms, the most common being the probit model and the logit model. The probit model is obtained by assuming that the random terms in the equations above are normally distributed. The logit model is obtained by assuming that the random terms are independent and identically distributed according to a negative double exponential (also known as Weibull or Gumbel distribution). The functional form of the multinomial logit model is as follows:

$$P_n(i) = \frac{\exp(V_{in})}{\sum_{j \in J_n} \exp(V_{jn})} \tag{3}$$

Probit and logit models are well known. The probit model does not have a closed functional form, and for this reason the estimation procedure becomes more complicated. The logit model has a simple functional form, and the parameter estimation is relatively straightforward. Another interesting point stems from the distribution properties of each model. One the one hand, the sum of normally distributed variables is also normally distributed, but the maximum of normally distributed variables can only be estimated by approximation. On the other hand, the maximum of Gumbel distributed variables is also Gumbel distributed. It is possible to interpret this property as follows: since the error terms account for unobservable attributes, the modeller (who estimates the parameters with a set of observable attributes) tries to maximize the difference between the random components, instead of simply summing them up.

The multinomial logit model is suitable for alternatives that can be unambiguously defined. When the alternatives have similarities or when the decision process is made in a conditional way (which is often the case), the simple logit model is not suitable. For example, if the aim is to model the choice of growing a specific tomato variety, the multinomial logit may suffice. However, if one wishes to model the choice of growing a tomato variety conditional on a specific fertilization technique, the multinomial logit model cannot take into account this hierarchy of the decision-making process. The nested logit model, which is more general than the multinomial, can take this feature into account.

The nested logit model was developed by assuming that the error terms are not independently distributed; i.e., the alternatives are correlated. The model is based on the assumption that the alternatives from the choice set can be divided into mutually exclusive, collectively exhaustive groups (nests) m in such a way that the error term is represented as the sum of the group-related ε_m and alternative-specific ε_i components, with the group-related component expressing the similarity between the alternatives. The analytical form of the nested logit model is presented as follows:

$$P(i) = \frac{\exp\left(V_i + (\mu - 1)\ln\sum_{k \in J_m}\exp(V_k)\right)}{\sum_{j \in J}\exp\left(V_j + (\mu - 1)\ln\sum_{k \in J_m}\exp(V_k)\right)} \tag{4}$$

Where μ is a scale parameter representing the nesting coefficient. To be consistent with random utility theory, this parameter should lie between 0 and 1. When μ is equal to 1, the model collapses to the multinomial logit model.

The next section presents the explanatory variables used in the different models and the estimation results of the parameters in the different models.

Methodology and Data Sources

The research was intentionally performed in a region where the diffusion of new technologies can be traced and observed. The North West region of the Negev (Southern Israel) was selected for this study because of the high concentration of agricultural settlements in this region. In addition, the government established a regional R&D agricultural centre there that provides services and incentives to the farmers to grow new varieties and employ new fertilization techniques. The greenhouse tomato was initially developed in this region, which saw the development and testing of new varieties. Successful new technologies tested were later imitated by other rural regions in Israel.

The present research used data gathered from two main sources. The first source was aggregate data on agricultural settlements in the region, such as socio-economic indicators. The second was a survey conducted among 151 farmers from 21 different agricultural settlements in the region. This survey collected data at the individual level, which formed the basis for the empirical models tested in this study. A detailed description of the methodology and data sources can be found in Cohen (1997).

To model the adoption of innovations, two variables in the sample that may represent this effect were selected: the tomato variety chosen to cultivate and the use of a new fertilization technique. At the time of the research, the tomato varieties were classified into three main categories namely the old variety (corresponding to tomato number 121); the common variety (corresponding to tomato number 144), and new varieties (corresponding to tomato number 175 and up).

The fertilization technique was classified into two categories: a new technique based on Combo Bees inside the greenhouse, and old techniques that represent several other techniques, such as hormones, mechanical bees, and ventilation. Table 14.1 presents the distribution of tomato varieties and fertilization techniques in the sample.

Table 14.1   Distribution of tomato varieties and fertilization techniques in the sample

Tomato variety	Fertilization technique		Total
	New	Old	
Old (121)	22	32	54
Common (144)	47	39	86
New (175 and up)	6	5	11
Total	75	76	151

As expected, the common variety forms the majority of the sample. Only 11 farmers chose to grow a new tomato variety. With respect to fertilization technique, however, the sample is balanced as 50 per cent of the farmers had already introduced the use of the new technique. This may be explained by the fact that the implementation of the new technique was subsidized from the R&D centre.

Model Estimation

Discrete choice models were used to estimate the parameters that influence the choice between alternative tomato varieties and fertilization techniques. Specifically, the Multinomial Logit (MNL) and the Nested Logit (NL) models were used in the estimations.

The MNL and NL models are commonly used in such disciplines as transportation (choice among transport modes, for example), and market research (choice among beverages, for example). In these disciplines, practitioners have a good deal of information on the main variables that can influence the model. This is not the case in the current study. For this reason, much effort was placed on an investigation of the relevant variables that may affect the choice of new technologies. In order not to disqualify any variable that might be significant, several trials were performed, each of them combining many of the possible variables collected in the survey. The chapter presents the results of the selected models used in the analysis, which captured the main variables that significantly influenced the choice among alternative technologies.

It is possible to represent the multinomial logit and the nested logit in a tree diagram as depicted in Figure 14.1.

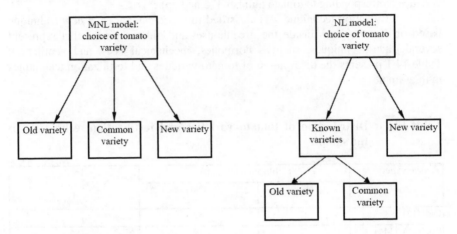

Figure 14.1 Tree diagram of MNL and NL models

Figure 14.1 illustrates a hypothetical choice among three tomato varieties (old, common and new), which could be modelled in two different ways. The MNL model assumes that each alternative is distinct and therefore each is on the same level. In the NL model, the old and common varieties are assumed to have a certain amount of correlation (termed 'known' varieties), and then are grouped in a common nest.

The present study deals with two possible alternative sets: (1) the different tomato varieties and (2) the different fertilization techniques. The estimation results for each of three different models are presented below. The first model is related to the choice of tomato varieties, the second to the choice of fertilization techniques, and the third is a mix of fertilization techniques and tomato varieties. Note that several sets of variables were tested for each model and only the models with the best fit are shown.

Results

Model One

The first model tested was the MNL model that estimated the choice among different tomato varieties. The varieties were grouped into three categories related to tomato varieties cultivated in 1995. The first category corresponds to old varieties (type 121 and previous types); the second to the most common variety (type 144); and the third to new tomato varieties (type 175 and subsequent types). Table 14.2 summarizes the estimation results for model one.

Table 14.2 Estimation results for model one – choice among tomato varieties

Variable	Alternative	Coefficient	T-value
Constant	1	1.511	1.7 *
Constant	2	4.289	5.5 **
Export percentage	1 and 2	0.083	1.8 *
Greenhouse- area ratio: farmer / total settlement	2 and 3	11.370	1.6 *
Dummy variable: propensity to innovation	3	2.757	3.3 **
Dummy variable: use of new fertilization technique	1	– 0.709	-1.6 *
Settlement age (years)	1	0.070	3.9 **
Distance to R&D centre (km)	2	– 0.069	-4.4 **

* Significant at 0.1 level
** Significant at 0.05 level
Total number of observations: 148
Log-likelihood (null model): -162.59
Log-likelihood (constants only): -128.51
Log-likelihood (final model): -95.88
Rho-bar squared w.r.t. null model: 0.41
Rho-bar squared w.r.t. constants: 0.25

The second column of the table indicates the relationship between the coefficient estimates and the utility of each alternative. Since the probability calculation is based on the difference among alternatives, the constant of an alternative is set to zero (in this case, alternative 3). The same applies to dummy variables. In general, it is common practice to relate a dummy variable to a specific alternative in order to allow for easy interpretation. The t value of 1.6 and above indicates that it is possible to reject the null hypothesis that the coefficient is equal to zero at a 90 per cent confidence level.

The following conclusions can be drawn from the estimation results. The positive coefficient of the export percentage means that export-oriented farmers prefer to grow old and common varieties which have proven results. The ratio of a farmer's greenhouse area to the total settlement area coefficient indicates that farmers with a high ratio will be more likely to try new varieties.

The dummy variables exhibit expected signs. The first dummy variable, related to the use of new technologies, is negative, meaning that the utility of alternative 1 (old varieties) decreases when the farmer use new technologies. The second dummy variable, related to the propensity to innovate, is positive, meaning that the utility of alternative 3 (new varieties) increases.

The sign of the settlement age coefficient, related to the first alternative, indicates that the older the settlement, the higher is the propensity to use old varieties. Less intuitive is the sign of the distance to the R&D centre, which may be explained as follows. The most common variety was developed and stimulated by the R&D centre some years ago and therefore settlements close to the R&D centre were the first to be exposed to this variety.

Model Two

The second model tested relates to the choice of fertilization technique. Note that technique was a dummy variable in the first model. This model represents an alternative way of modelling innovation, in which the fertilization technique is the choice, and the tomato variety is an explanatory variable. This dichotomy (independent versus dependent variable) may also occur in other disciplines. For example, a possible explanatory variable in modelling choice among transport modes is auto ownership. Alternatively, to model auto ownership, the transport mode may serve as an explanatory variable.

The second model has two alternatives. The first alternative consists of existing fertilization techniques, such as hormones, mechanical bees, and ventilation. The second alternative is a new fertilization technique, based on Combo Bees inside the greenhouse. Table 14.3 presents the estimation results.

Table 14.3   Estimation results for model two – choice among fertilization techniques

Variable	Alternative	Coefficient	T-value
Constant	1	4.464	2.6 **
Settlement age (years)	2	0.037	2.7 **
Greenhouse area ratio: farmer / total settlement	2	9.918	2.0 *
Dummy variable: consult R&D centre	2	0.759	1.8 *
Dummy variable: grow new tomato varieties	2	0.029	1.9 *

* Significant at 0.1 level
** Significant at 0.05 level
Total observations: 150
Log-likelihood (null model):   -103.07
Log-likelihood (constants only):   -103.97
Log-likelihood (final model):   -94.04
Rho-bar squared w.r.t. null model: 0.10
Rho-bar squared w.r.t. constants: 0.10

The overall measures of fit (final likelihood and rho-bar squared) obtained in this model are inferior to the measures obtained in model one. In both models, the greenhouse area coefficient has the same order of magnitude and sign. However, contrary to the first model, the settlement age influences the use of new fertilization techniques positively. This means that the relative strength of the farmer in the settlement influences the use of new fertilization techniques positively.

The dummy variables exhibit expected signs. Note that both variables are related to alternative 2 (new fertilization techniques). The first dummy variable indicates that if the farmer consults the R&D centre, it increases the probability of using new fertilization techniques. The second dummy variable indicates that if the farmer cultivates new tomato varieties, it also increases the probability of using new fertilization techniques. However, the constant value is relatively high compared to the dummy variables, indicating that these variables do not influence the choice probability in this model as much as in model one.

The overall conclusion from these two models is that farmers are more sensitive to choice among tomato varieties than choice among fertilization techniques. Nevertheless, variables that account for the adoption of an innovation are significant in both models.

Model Three

The third model combines features from models one and two. The first two models were estimated using simple MNL models. The third model indicates that the choice of fertilization technique is conditional on the choice of tomato variety. Since it is the purpose of the study to model the adoption of innovations in agriculture, the hypothesis is that the choice of a new fertilization technique follows the choice of the new (innovative) tomato variety.

In order to model the choice of tomato variety and fertilization technique, the NL model was used. The structure of the NL model may vary, and generally the modeller's judgment plays a significant role. Again, using an example from transportation, the choice among car, bus and train may be modelled as a nesting structure between car and transit, with the transit nest including the choice between bus and train. However, if the train alternative represents a high-speed train, the model would be differently represented; the nesting structure could then be 'attractive' modes, which would include car and train in the same nest.

It should be noted that the nesting structure could be formed in different ways, each of them resulting in a different model. In the case of fertilization techniques and tomato varieties, several nesting structures were tested. The model that gave the best fit was estimated with the nesting structure presented in Figure 14.2.

Note that the 'common' tomato variety alternative in the tree diagram of model three appears as two independent alternatives. This is due to the similarity of fertilization techniques among farmers who cultivate the most common variety. The decision process in this case is as follows: the top nest indicates the choice among fertilization techniques and the choice of tomato variety is conditioned on the choice of technique. At most, we can construct six alternatives in this way. The correlation between old fertilization techniques and new tomato varieties, however, is very low, as is the correlation between new fertilization techniques and old tomato varieties. For this reason, the final model contains four alternatives.

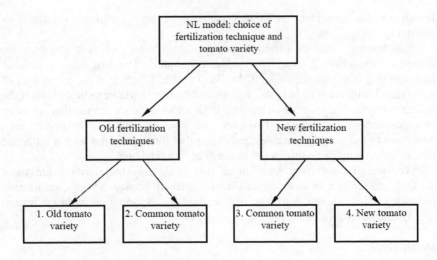

Figure 14.2   Tree diagram of model three

Table 14.4   Estimation results for model three – choice among fertilization techniques and tomato varieties

Variable	Alternative	Coefficient	T-value
Export percentage	1	0.016	2.2 **
Settlement age (years)	1	0.042	3.8 **
Greenhouse area ratio: farmer / total settlement	2,3,4	18.800	2.9 **
Distance to R&D centre (km)	3,4	- 0.048	-1.6 *
Dummy variable: awareness of R&D centre	3	1.558	2.4 **
Dummy variable: visit R&D centre	3,4	1.413	1.8 *
Dummy variable: propensity to innovate	4	2.095	3.0 **
Ratio investment in greenhouse / greenhouse area (NIS / square meter)	4	- 0.727	– 3.6 **
Logsum coefficient	All	0.610	1.7 *

* Significant at 0.1 level
** Significant at 0.05 level
Total observations: 148
Log-likelihood (null model): -205.17
Log-likelihood (constants only): -197.72
Log-likelihood (final model): -172.38
Rho-bar squared w.r.t. null model: 0.16
Rho-bar squared w.r.t. constants: 0.13

The results presented in Table 14.4 do not include alternative-specific constants, which were not significantly different from zero. However, this third model has additional dummy variables to those in models one and two, and every dummy variable in the model reduces the significance of the constant.

All the variables in Table 14.4 show the expected signs, apart from that of the ratio of investment in a greenhouse divided by the greenhouse area. It was anticipated that this variable would be positive, indicating that greater investments would impact the selection of new varieties. This is partly explained by the time lag between the investment and the actual production, which cannot be captured by the static structure of discrete choice models used in this study.

Summary and Conclusions

This chapter has presented a new approach to modelling the adoption of innovations in the agricultural sector. The approach is based on discrete choice analysis, in which the chosen sets are selected among different tomato varieties and fertilization techniques. In both sets, new techniques and varieties represent an alternative in the choice process.

The results of applying the disaggregated Logit Model indicate that regional, local and individual attributes all have a bearing on the farmers' decision-making process regarding the choice of tomato varieties. Among the variables found to be significant to the growers were the percentage exported, the farmer's use of advanced techniques, the age of the settlement, the farmer's relative share of greenhouses area in the settlement, the distance from the regional R&D centre, the inclination to adopt innovations, the farmer's age, and the investment in greenhouses relative to the total area allocated to them in the settlement.

Regarding the decision processes involving choice among various alternative fertilization techniques, it was found that the most significant factors were the following: the age of the settlement, the farmer's tendency to consult R&D personnel, the growing of new varieties, a farmer's relative greenhouse area in the settlement, the frequency of visits to the regional R&D centre, and the extent of investments in greenhouses.

The chapter also presented results for a combined model of the adoption of alternative choices of fertilization technique and tomato variety. The advantage of this third model over the two simpler ones is that two innovation processes are included in a joint structure, whereas the simpler models can take into account only a single innovation process. The fact that more than one innovation process may be modelled raises interesting questions, such as the precedence of selecting one innovation process over another. The results presented in this chapter indicate that the choice of tomato variety is conditioned by the choice of fertilization technique.

The application of disaggregate choice models depends on the quality of data available. The present study collected extensive data on individual farmers which enabled model specification and estimation. More research is needed to compare the applicability of such models to other issues concerning agricultural crops.

References

Arndt, T.M., Dalrymple, D.G. and Ruttan, V.W. (1977), *Resource Allocation and Productivity in National and International Agriculture Research*, University of Minnesota Press, Minneapolis.

Ben Akiva, M. and Lerman, S.R. (1985), *Discrete Choice Analysis: Theory and Application to Travel Demand*, MIT Press, Cambridge, MA.

Cohen (Kedmon) M. (1997), *Spatial Diffusion of Innovations in Agriculture and Regional Development: The Case of Greenhouse Tomatoes in Israel*, Ph.D. dissertation, Technion, Haifa.

Davelaar, E.J. (1991), *Regional Economic Analysis of Innovation and Incubation*, Ashgate Publishing, Aldershot, UK.

Evenson, R.E. and Kislev, Y. (1975), *Agricultural Research and Productivity*, Yale University Press, New Haven.

Feder, G. and Umali, D.L. (1993), 'The Adoption of Agricultural Innovations: A Review', *Technological Forecasting and Social Change*, Vol. 43, pp. 215-239.

Feder, G., Just, R.E. and Zilberman, D. (1985), 'Adoption of Agricultural Innovations in Developing Countries: A Survey', *Economic Development and Cultural Change*, Vol. 33, pp. 255-297.

Frenkel, A., Shefer, D. and Stephen, R. (2003), 'Public Policy, Locational Choice and the Innovation Capability of High-Tech Firms: A Comparison between Israel and Ireland', *Papers in Regional Science*, Vol. 82, pp. 203-221.

Griliches, Z. (1957), 'Hybrid Corn: An Exploration in the Economics of Technological Change', *Econometrica*, Vol. 25(4), pp. 501-522.

Hagestrand, T. (1967), *Innovation Diffusion as a Spatial Process* (Translated by A. Pred), The University of Chicago Press, Chicago.

Kamien, M.I. and Schwartz, N.L. (1982), *Market Structure and Innovation*, Cambridge University Press, Cambridge.

Lindner, R. K., Pardey P.G. and Jarrett, F.G. (1982), 'Distance to Information Source and the Time Lag to Early Adoption of Trace Element Fertilizers', *Australian Journal of Agricultural Economics*, 26, 98-113.

Mansfield, E. (1968), *The Economics of Technological Change*, Norton, New York.

Marra, M., Pannell, D.J. and Abadi Ghadim, A. (2003), 'The Economics of Risk, Uncertainty and Learning in the Adoption of New Agricultural Technologies: Where are We on the Learning Curve?', *Agricultural Systems*, Vol. 75(2/3), pp. 215-234.

Meir, A. (1981), 'Innovation Diffusion and Regional Economic Development: The Spatial Diffusion of Automobiles in Ohio', *Regional Studies*, Vol. 15, pp. 111-122.

Metcalf, J.S. (1981), 'Impulses and Diffusion in the Study of Technical Change', *Futures*, Vol. 13 (5), pp. 347-359.

Rogers, M.E. (1983), *Diffusion of Innovations*, The Free Press, New York.

Yeats, M. (1974), *An Introduction to Quantitative Analysis in Human Geography*, McGraw-Hill, New York.

Chapter 15

Assisting Small and Medium Sized Enterprises: Technological Innovation Policies in Rural Areas

Federica Cisilino

Introduction

Innovation is a difficult concept to define and it is still more difficult to track in the agri-food sector, characterized as it is by small and medium sized firms (SMEs). The ability to innovate, however, is one of the most important factors in competitiveness. It requires a continual series of actions and decisions concerning the adoption of new technologies and new commercial policies as well as adapting methods and job procedures, maintaining lean structures, identifying and dealing with areas of weakness and finding new solutions in order to face the challenges posed by increasing competition and continual market evolution.

In this scenario, SMEs have some widely recognized advantages, among which the main ones can be summarized as flexibility in adapting to new market/consumer requirements; the possibility of taking decisions quickly; few barriers between management and operations, and their smaller internal bureaucracy. These 'people embodied' or behavioural advantages, however, exist alongside 'resource embodied' disadvantages which are evident, for example, in the lack of financial resources; lack of staff; lack of training and qualifications among the work force and management, as well as greater barriers to information and also the need to concentrate on reaching profitability in the short run. These lead to difficulties in meeting the innovation challenges and mean that appropriate government support, in particular to aid the transfer of knowledge to small firms, can be vital to competitiveness.

Rural development depends greatly on the ability of SMEs to stay competitive and this leads to the question of whether local rural policies are suitable to support them. The aim of this chapter is to analyse the relationship between the development of SMEs through technological innovation and some specific public policies designed to address this issue in a rural context. It seeks to shed some light on whether regional policies respond to SMEs' needs as far as competition and innovation are concerned. The chapter refers to an Italian rural region, Friuli-Venezia Giulia.

The first part of the chapter presents a brief overview of the main regional tools to stimulate innovation among SMEs, with particular attention to the Interreg Italy/Slovenia Programme and the Rural Development Programme (RDP). The second part aims to assess the importance of public policies to support R&D through the development of an interaction decision model. An empirical analysis is presented to highlight the strategic role of the government in supporting R&D investments. The empirical work is based on information about rural policies together with enterprise data about some of the main technological innovation and production characteristics of SMEs in Friuli-Venezia Giulia that is derived from the FADN regional databank.

The Context of the Study

Friuli-Venezia Giulia – A Small Border Region

Friuli-Venezia Giulia is the region at the extreme north-east of Italy. It stretches from the Alps to the Adriatic Sea. The region borders Austria to the north, Slovenia to the east, the Adriatic Sea to the south, and Veneto, another Italian region, to the west. Trieste is the administrative Center of Friuli-Venezia Giulia, whose provinces include Gorizia, Pordenone and Udine. The region ranks seventeenth in size (7,855 square km) and fifteenth in population (1,184,000).

The mountainous part of Friuli-Venezia Giulia constitutes little more than half of the territory; the higher part is not very fertile and is little cultivated. The *Carso* area is almost without any type of crop. The lowland, in contrast, is very fertile. The region does not have a particularly high gross domestic product according to official statistics (ISTAT, various issues). The main crops are maize, rye, sugar beet, tobacco and fruit. The most common type of cultivation is in vineyards, which are found throughout the lowlands and in the hills. Many of the wines produced are exported all over the world. There is intensive breeding of beef and dairy cattle as well as pigs, where the products are of high quality.

The Italian-Slovenian Border Area: Interreg III A PHARE CBC Programme

Italy and Slovenia have both a land and coastline border. The maritime border between Italy and Slovenia is on the Upper Adriatic, in the gulf that includes Venice, Trieste and Koper. Altogether, the Italian-Slovenian border touches 24 Italian municipalities and 13 Slovenian ones and covers an area of about 200 kilometres. It includes, on the Italian side, the following areas (classified as NUTS III): Udine, Gorizia, Trieste (Friuli-Venezia, Giulia region) and Venice (Veneto region). On the Slovenian side, the NUTS III areas are Obalno-kraška and Goriška region and the municipality of Kranjska Gora, as shown in Table 15.1.

Table 15.1   Main characteristics of the Italian-Slovenian cross-border region (Phare CBC, Interreg IIIA)

NUTS III Areas	Area (sq. km.)	Population (31.12.98)	Density (inhab./sq. km.)
Trieste	211	248,998	1,176
Gorizia	466	137,909	296
Udine	4,893	518,630	106
Venice	2,460	815,009	331
Total: Italy/Interreg IIIA region	8,031	1,720,546	170
Obalno-kraška	1,044	102,565	98
Goriška	2,325	119,967	52
Total: Slovenia/Phare CBC region	3,369	222,532	66

Source: ISTAT, Statistical Office of the Slovenian Republic

This border represents a much less important internal border since Slovenia's accession to the EU in May 2004, with different issues and problems. In fact, with the gradual integration of Eastern European countries into the EU, the position of this area in the EU will become more central, with the focus on the new and increasingly important East-West communication axes.

Taking the Italian provinces of the border area as a whole, 50 per cent of all companies, including the primary, secondary and tertiary sectors, are in the province of Venice. Eighty per cent of companies in the secondary sector are in the provinces of Venice and Udine. The service sector shows a more balanced distribution. Figure 15.1 shows the percentage of companies in each of the cross-border Italian provinces operating in the different broad sectors of activity. The service sector is by far the most important in Trieste. The other provinces show a more balanced distribution among the various sectors of activity, though the service sector predominates in each case.

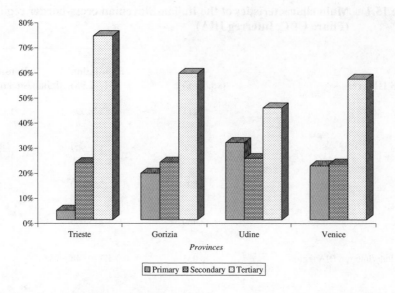

Figure 15.1   Distribution of companies in the Interreg IIIA Italy/Slovenia provinces by sector (1998)

Source: ISTAT

The Primary Sector in the Italian and Slovenian Cross-border Area

There are approximately 34,000 people working in agriculture in the Italian cross-border area, accounting for 4.9 per cent of the total working population compared with the national average of 6.7 per cent. The sector's added value is mainly derived from meat and milk production, the growing of cereals (maize, wheat and barley), wine, apples and kiwi fruits and industrial cultivation (soy beans and sugar beet). Wine stands out as a particularly important product and it contributes significantly, both in terms of quality and quantity, to the area's exports which show positive annual balances. The export orientation has increased over the years and the value of products exported has constantly risen since the mid 1980s.

In the agricultural sector, the declining number of small enterprises is counterbalanced by a constant consolidation of family run, medium sized businesses, which are managed directly by farmers. An analysis of the structure of agricultural production in the Italian area shows that the distribution of the agricultural companies basically reflects the distribution of the agricultural surface area in the Italian provinces. Fifty-five per cent of the surface area and 51 per cent of companies are in the province of Udine; 42 per cent of the surface area and 34 per cent of companies are in the province of Venice; and 1 per cent of the surface area and 4 per cent of companies are in the province of Gorizia. Trieste plays a very marginal role, with 0.1 per cent of the agricultural surface area and three per cent of the companies.

The agricultural sector is characterized by the fragmentation of land (companies with less than five hectares of land on average account for more than 70 per cent of the total, with the maximum of 83 per cent in the province of Venice). The agricultural entrepreneurs are an ageing group, with associated difficulties of generation change and entry of new entrepreneurs. There is an increase in part-time activities in other sectors amongst those involved in farming, especially in tourism and industry, as a means of supplementing farming income.

There are three areas in the Goriška region where agriculture is economically significant, namely the Upper Vipava Valley, the Lower Vipava Valley and Brda. The main agricultural products of the Upper Vipava Valley are wine, fruit, milk, dairy products and cattle. Wine growing is the most important of these activities. The Vipava wine growing area has some 1,700 hectares of vineyards. A fundamental role in supporting and developing agricultural production in the area are an agricultural co-operative, active in vine growing and dairy products. The main agricultural products of the Lower Vipava Valley are wine, fruit and vegetables. The main producer, (the leader) in this area is an enterprise that has created a proper trade mark (Fruits of Gorica, Vegetables of Gorica). The area of Brda is a traditional wine producing and fruit growing area. The leading wine producer is an agricultural co-operative serving 724 farmers. Many successful, independent wine producers have also emerged during the last ten years. There are 1,900 hectares of vineyards in this area, of which the co-operative is responsible for 1,400 hectares. The wine growing boom over the last decades has destroyed fruit growing, which was another traditional agricultural activity in the area. Revitalization of the ancient tradition of olive growing is underway and fruit growing needs to be revitalized.

Barriers to Innovation, EU Funding and Regional Support

There are both internal and external barriers that can prevent the development of innovation in SMEs. The internal factors that contribute to constraining R&D activity are well known and include a lack of information and competence; a lack of internal communication; financial inertia; labour force obstacles, and attention being given to the existing business instead of innovation, together with strong individualism. There are also numerous external barriers preventing the development of R&D, despite policies designed to assist. These include difficulties in acquiring know how, information and financial support.

In this chapter, attention is focused on the external barriers. The conventional legislative approaches to R&D are shown to be inadequate in many cases and, in others, even counter-productive. In general, one of the main problems is that policy does not distinguish between activity sectors and the size of the beneficiary enterprises. This occurs both in terms of seeing the different problems faced by firms in innovating and in developing and implementing suitable solutions.

Information and know-how are often supplied by centres of research or information points, both public and private, which are not well co-ordinated. Many of these centres offer technical assistance for the development of innovation projects or for searching out partners, but the majority of SMEs do not respond to the opportunities available to them. In addition, investment by SMEs in research or in technological innovations is hindered by the lack of funds. Enterprises aim to limit their expenditure on new systems or machinery during recessionary periods, so economic cycles have a marked impact on technological innovation processes.

Some EU co-funded projects are currently in progress between Friuli-Venezia Giulia region and Slovenia. The majority of them (83) are under Interreg III Italy/Slovenia, which is one of the border co-operation programmes of the EU.[1] These EU programmes are tools to support and encourage co-operation between regions located inside and outside the EU to promote a harmonious, balanced and long-lasting development of the Community. They were introduced to help avoid national borders hindering the balanced development and integration of the European territory .

Table 15.2 describes the objectives, priorities and measures which characterize the Interreg Italy/Slovenia. Measure 2.3.3, which relates to 'modernization and innovation of the enterprises of the primary sector in the cross-border area', is the most relevant for this study. This action aims at strengthening, from a sustainable and cross-border point of view, the economic potential of the eligible area, in order to improve the competitiveness of the local systems relative to international markets. It focuses on SMEs and the resources of the primary sector. This action has a number of aims. These include the encouragement of innovative production techniques and management methodologies; the development of integrated production and common products and the development, supply and use of common services; the development of collaboration by assisting in the search for partners; the transfer of know-how, of product and/or process innovations and common services to enterprises in the primary sector; the development of reproducible and transferable pilot projects and best practices, as well as helping to show the need to consider the environment and ensure sustainable development and effects on employment. Other aspects within its scope include the encouragement of the joint use of cross-border infrastructures by the primary sector; the maintenance and increase in sustainable activities and practices; the enhancement of information provided to the consumer; contributions to improvements in marketing and the penetration of markets external to the programme and, finally, assistance to help improve product quality and food safety.

The contributions to projects developed under the Interreg Italy/Slovenia programme so far total about 102 million euro and the forecast total cost of the projects is more than 127 million euro (Department of Agriculture, Friuli-Venezia Giulia region). In the Italian case, 46 per cent of the funds are sourced from the EU and 54 per cent are provided nationally. The latter are funded by the Italian government (60 per cent) and by the region (40 per cent). The projects are of four kinds. First, there are projects that are synergistically connected with other publicly financed projects. Second, there are projects that are synergistically implemented in both regions. Third, some projects share a common planning stage. Finally, some projects involve a significant sharing of know-how on relevant issues in different subject areas. The Interreg IIIA Italy/Slovenia Programme recently opened again for the submission of projects under some of its provisions.

Table 15.2 Interreg IIIA Italy/Slovenia general structure

Objectives	Priorities	Measures
Sustainable development of the territory	Sustainable development of the cross-border territory	1.1 Protection, preservation and development of the environment and the territory 1.2 Development and strengthening of cross-border organizations, infrastructures and networks
Overcoming of barriers and peripheral situation	*Economic co-operation*	2.1 Improvement in competitiveness and co-operation 2.2 Cross-border co-operation in tourism *2.3 Cross-border co-operation in the primary sector* 2.3.1 Development of typical and quality products and of fish and forest products of the cross-border area 2.3.2 Up-grading and creation of infrastructures for the primary sector in the cross-border area *2.3.3 Modernization and innovation of the enterprises of the primary sector in the cross-border area* 2.3.4 Cross-border rural tourism
Development of human resources	Human resources, cooperation and systems' harmonization	3.1 Human resources' vocational training and retraining and innovative initiatives on the labour market 3.2 Cooperation in culture, communication and research and between institutions for the systems harmonization
Strengthening of cross-border co-operation	Special support for regions bordering candidate countries	4.1 Special support for regions bordering candidate countries
Cross-border co-ordination	Support to co-operation	5.1 Technical assistance 5.2 Evaluation, information, publicity and co-operation

Source: Interreg IIIA Italy/Slovenia

The European Union legal interventions in favour of the Rural Development are contained in the regulation Reg. CE 1257/99 (1999), recently modified by Reg. CE 445/02 (2002) and Reg. CE 1783/03 (2003). This brings together all the legislation previously presented under different programmes. The most innovative and important element of this package of reforms is the 'horizontality character' assumed by rural development. Rural development is defined here as the second pillar of the Common Agricultural Policy, and guarantees the application of the related measures to all areas classified as objective one and five b areas. This means that there is now a single programme to develop rural areas and two systems of programmes and financing are in place: those dealing with the objective one areas and those applying to areas not classified as objective one, such as Friuli-Venezia-Giulia. Those areas, which are not eligible for structural funds, have the option of presenting a single Rural Development Plan (RDP).

Table 15.3 shows the different measures and their application in Friuli-Venezia Giulia. The measures are divided into three axes: the environmental axis (A), the competitiveness axis (C) and the development of rural territories and agricultural producers (S).

Table 15.3   Measures and eligible areas of the Friuli-Venezia Giulia Rural Development Plan

FVG – RDP Measures	Axes	Eligible areas
a) Investments in agricultural firms	C	All the region
b) Settling young farmers	C	All the region
c) Education	C	All the region
e) Disadvantaged areas	A	Disadvantage areas (dir. CEE n,273/1975)
f) Agri-environment measures	A	Specified areas
g) Improvement of agricultural products, processing and trading	C	All the region
h) Afforestation of agricultural lands	A	All the regional agricultural lands, with the exception of 'mountain communities', or those with hydrogeological bounds, permanent meadows, humid areas, pasturelands etc.
i) Other forest measures	A	Specified areas
m) Trading of quality agricultural products	S	m1a, all the region. m,1b disadvantaged areas (dir. CEE n, 273/1975)
s) Incentives for tourist and craft activities in disadvantaged areas	S	Disadvantaged areas (dir. CEE n,273/1975)

Source: Regional Rural Development Plan

Table 15.4 shows the distribution of public funds in Italy as a whole and in Friuli-Venezia Giulia originating from national, regional and EU sources for each measure within the RDP. Looking at the situation in Fruili-Venezia Giulia, about 72 per cent of public funds and about 77 per cent of FEOGA funds are directed towards the environmental axis (A). The competitiveness axis (C) receives about 20 per cent of public funds and about 18 per cent of FEOGA funds. Less than 10 per cent of the total amount of support is concerned with the development of rural territories and agricultural products. The table shows that there are some differences between the national and the regional distribution of funds. A higher percentage of resources are directed to measures b, m, s, e, h, and i in Friuli-Venezia Giulia than in Italy as a whole.

Table 15.4   Financial resources (m. euro) by RDP measure in Italy and in Friuli-Venezia Giulia[2]

Type of measure	Italy				Fruili-Venezia Giulia			
	Public expenditure		FEOGA		Public expenditure		FEOGA	
	m. euro	%	m. euro	%	m. euro	%	m. euro	%
A	1,037.95	15.55	337.63	11.62	14.05	6.60	4.22	4.23
B	365.07	5.47	176.48	6.07	18.67	8.77	9.34	9.36
C	50.57	0.76	25.24	0.87	1.04	0.49	0.52	0.52
G	501.59	7.52	183.28	6.31	9.98	4.69	3.74	3.76
Total axis C	**1,955.18**	**29.29**	**722.63**	**24.87**	**43.74**	**20.55**	**17.81**	**17.87**
E	366.32	5.49	168.22	5.79	20.34	9.55	10.17	10.20
F	2,367.17	35.47	1,183.58	40.73	77.81	36.56	38.91	39.02
H	431.38	6.46	216.54	7.45	26.05	12.24	13.03	13.06
I	335.43	5.03	140.87	4.85	30.54	14.35	15.07	15.12
Total axis A	**3,500.30**	**52.45**	**1,709.21**	**58.82**	**154.74**	**72.69**	**77.17**	**77.40**
M	71.79	1.08	27.25	0.94	5.38	2.53	2.02	2.02
S	63.57	0.95	22.24	0.77	9.00	4.23	2,70	2.71
Total axis S	**135.36**	**2.03**	**49.49**	**1.71**	**14.38**	**6.76**	**4.72**	**4.73**
Total 10 measures	5,590.84	83.77	2,481.33	85.39	212.86	100.00	99.70	100.00
Total 22 measures	6,673.39	100.00	2,905.87	100.00				

Source: Derived from Friuli-Venezia Giulia RDP (2000)

This chapter focuses on measure 'a' – investments in agricultural firms. As Table 15.4 shows, this kind of support ranks sixth in Friuli-Venezia Giulia in terms both of public expenditure and FEOGA, which suggests that the government does not emphasize its role in supporting rural development. FADN data are used to highlight the importance of public policies to support SMEs' R&D and to analyse their impact on the productive system. The FADN regional sample allows some of the main technological innovation characteristics of Friuli-Venezia Giulia SMEs to be examined.

FADN Database and the Regional Sample

FADN (Farm Accountancy Data Network) is an important source of microeconomic data about the European agricultural sector.[3] It consists of structural and economic data for a large sample of farms and includes an average of about 18,000 Italian farms each year, representing 31 per cent of the total European sample. The Italian FADN sample includes those farms that are regarded as 'commercial'. A commercial farm is defined as a farm that is large enough to provide a main activity for the farmer and a level of income sufficient to support his or her family. In order to be classified as commercial, a farm must exceed a minimum economic size. The EU universe of farms is a set of farms of at least one hectare, while the Italian data set establishes a limit in terms of European size units or ESU. The value of one ESU is based on a fixed level of gross profit from production activities expressed in the standard European currency (EUR/ECU).[4]

The Friuli-Venezia Giulia sample consists of about 700 farms from the total regional population of some 24,000 farms (ISTAT, 2000), selected using a stratified sampling method based on the firm's geographical location, its technical and economic orientation and its economic characteristics or size.[5] Both size and the technical and economic orientation are based on the standard gross margin of production activities. The regional database for 2001 was used for this analysis. In order to allow further analysis, two sub-sample of farms were distinguished, namely the innovative farms (leaders) and non-innovative farms (followers).

SMEs' Innovation and Competitiveness

The distinction between leaders and followers within the sample of FADN farms in 2001 was made by reference to nine variables within the FADN database. The following variables were considered: the number of farms by sector of production (TEO); the agricultural surface area (UAS); the economic size of farm (ESU); new investments; the number of agricultural machines/tractors; the number of machine cultivators; expenditure on cultivation; breeding expenses, and expenditure on mechanization (see Table 15.5).

Forty sectors of production are distinguished in the FADN database and these have been grouped into ten more aggregated levels of activity in Table 15.5. This table shows the number of farms in Friuli-Venezia Giulia in each sector and their division into different groups according to their technological and economic orientation (TEO). Farms belonging to TEO group 7, 5, 10, 1 are the most innovative and form 41.3 per cent of the total sample with cattle rearing (mainly dairy herds) forming nearly 20 per cent of the total. The rest, representing 58.7 per cent of the sample, are taken as being non-innovative. The largest number of farms is engaged in viticulture (28.2 per cent of the total) but this category is not included in the innovative group. The innovative farms cluster has a higher ESU on average than the sample as a whole. The same is observed for the UAS, with the exception of the viticulture group. These results confirm that larger economic size is associated with innovation.

It appears that, in 2001, SMEs rearing hens, pigs and poultry have been the most innovative, having the highest values of new investments and mechanical expenses and coming second in terms of the average number of agri-machines. SMEs producing meat and dairy cattle were the second most innovative group. SMEs in the viticulture sector were less innovative than expected but this is already one of the most advanced sectors in the region from a technological point of view. The viticulture sector is one of the most important and dynamic fields of the regional agriculture. It has been supported in the past and currently is healthy in terms of production, turnover and exports. It is notable that much of the financial support to agricultural farms under the RDP financial resources (measure a) is directed to the viticulture sector. It must be remembered in interpreting these results, however, that they are based on only one year of data.

Table 15.5   FADN farms by technological and economic orientation (TEO) and innovation proxy variables (2001) – average values

		Farms				new	mach.	moto	Expenditure (euro)		
TEO	Activity Area	No.	%	UAS (ha.)	ESU	invesmt. (euro)	tractor (no.)	cultiv (no.)	cultiv.	breeding	mech.
7	hens, pigs, birds	11	1.7	221.42	6	142,325	3.1	0.5	14,501	290,759	13,610
5	cattle (dairy and meat)	129	19.5	4155.00	6	94,364	3.4	0.5	17,514	62,262	12,215
10	mixed growing and breeding	62	9.4	2,100.65	6	75,929	3.1	0.5	23,799	45,999	12,074
1	Seeds	72	10.9	2,518.84	5	54,986	3.0	0.5	32,232	4,319	11,949
6	mixed goat, and cattle grazing	9	1.4	792.64	4	54,231	1.7	0.7	9,252	7,104	5,592
4	fruit and other permanent growing	44	6.6	715.37	6	48,754	2.7	0.3	31,656	6,073	8,748
3	viticulture	187	28.2	2,501.94	5	46,899	2.6	0.4	15,627	120	8,408
8	mixed growing	114	17.2	2,390.8	5	29,280	2.5	0.6	21,471	4,183	7,959
9	mixed breeding	22	3.3	612.76	6	28,732	4.0	0.5	23,095	34,194	10,492
2	flower growing	13	2.0	75.9	5	27,551	1.6	1.1	59,003	245	11,042
Total		663	100.0	16,085.32	5	57,521	2.8	0.5	21,623	24,101	9,990

Note: mach. tractor – machinery and tractors; moto cultiv. – mechanized cultivators

Source: FADN – Friuli-Venezia Giulia database.

FADN farms in the Fruili-Venezia database were granted 1,964,723 euro of public subsidies from measure *a*, investments in agriculture, by the RDP in 2001 while 4,498,723 euro were actually allowed, a ratio of 43.7 per cent. This shows that less than half of the total public subsidies available in 2001 have been exploited by the sample of FADN farms considered.

Public Involvement in the Innovation Process

The economic literature emphasizes the importance of public support for R&D. R&D can be considered as having characteristics of a *public good* which allow social benefits to exceed private benefits from such investment (Tirole, 1988; Link and Scott, 2001). R&D costs rise if more than one innovating firm acts in the market (see Aghion and Howitt, 1998). This is mainly due to the duplication of efforts since more than one firm invests in R&D but in some markets only one firm (the leader) wins by getting the patent and the related benefits from the innovation. Without intervention, private innovation efforts may not match the desired (or necessary) social optimum and may exceed or fall short of the level bringing maximum social welfare. Since competition through patents in the agricultural sector is not as relevant as in other sectors, public support takes on a crucial role.

The following analysis is used to examine the strategic role of public policies and the importance of targeted subsidies where the direct involvement of the government is perceived to be of some usefulness. A basic model using concepts from modern innovation economics has been taken as a point of reference (Onofri and Giannakas, 2001). The firm level data is taken from the FADN regional database. Two sub-samples of farms have been considered: the innovative farms (leaders) and the non innovative ones, or follower group. The RDP gives information about the direct subsidies assigned to agri-food enterprises by local government. Since the majority of small agri-food enterprises do not have any R&D expenditure, in order to allow the empirical analysis on FADN data, the variable 'new investments' has been considered as an indicator of the farm's level of technological development.

This section examines the strategic role of the government in supporting enterprises' investment through two possible scenarios. In the first, the subsidies are targeted on the leader (FADN 1) whereas in the second scenario, they are addressed to the follower (FADN 2). It looks at the consequences of the two types of policy to assess which is the optimum strategy for government to reach its objectives and the best kind of firm to support, the leader or the follower.

To support followers and, in general, less efficient enterprises, will encourage market competition and enhance consumer welfare as the atmosphere of increased competition in which the leader would then operate would tend to induce it to invest. The leader's payoff would be reduced because it would not be able to increase prices and, in general, its costs would be rising. The main consequence would be a reduction in the price of the products, which represents a benefit for consumers. Supporting the follower in this way would help to give it the means to compete with the leader, which will invest further efforts to retain its competitive advantage. Supporting the leader will not encourage increased efforts by other firms but is likely to allow the leader group to reinforce its market position in terms of prices, increasing the producer's surplus to the detriment of the consumer.

In this study, the two groups of farms considered (FADN1 and FADN2) are characterized by the following elements. First, unit variable costs of production at time $t = 0$ of FADN1 and FADN2 are $c(1,0)$ and $c(2,0)$ respectively. Second, both types of farms are involved in investment activities which are assumed to produce innovations and allow them to reduce their variable unit costs of production, gaining a cost advantage over their competitors. Third, the price of goods (output) X depends on the farm's cost structure and on the results of the innovation process.

The farm's investment intensity is categorized as zero (0), low (L) or high (H). The intensity is linked to the different size of the innovation process and to the cost of investment (Figure 15.2). Assuming that FADN 1 is the leader group at time 0, it will have lower costs than FADN 2 $[c(1,0) < c(2,0)]$. This means that FADN 1 starts investments at time $t = -1$, while FADN 2 does not. Assuming that at $t = -1$ the two firms had the same cost structure $[c(1,-1) = c(2,-1)]$, the low investment effort by FADN 1 means λ (L) advantage over FADN 2. The costs of the two group of firms at time $t = 0$ will then be $c(1,0) = c(2,0)/ \lambda$ (L). The investment choices, beside the cost structure, will also affect the equilibrium price of X and the level of the firms' profits. If the investment efforts are zero, then the price of product X will be $P(X) = c(2,0)-\varepsilon$. With this price, FADN 1 gets positive profits, while FADN 2 will not produce any of product X.

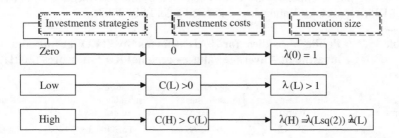

Figure 15.2 Sequential behaviour: strategies, costs and innovation

Starting from these considerations, the best government strategy will depend on the level of the government budget and on the importance that government attributes to consumer benefits when supporting producers – with respect to the impact of policy toward SMEs in this case. The results for the FADN data base taking FADN 1 as the leaders and FADN 2 as followers are shown in Tables 15.6 and 15.7.

**Table 15.6   Total public subsidies for leader and follower FADN farms –
regional RDP, measure *a* (2001)**

	RDP: Measure *a*		
FADN beneficiaries	Granted public subsidies (euro)	Allowed subsidies (euro)	Granted/ Allowed (%)
FADN 1	1,663,920	3,773,163	44.1
FADN 2	300,803	725,560	41.5
Total	1,964,723	4,498,723	43.7

Source: FADN – Friuli-Venezia Giulia database

The criteria used to obtain information about the innovative and non-innovative
group are based on the variables shown above (Table 15.5). The results of using
the available data to estimate the level of public subsidies show that government
tends to support the follower. Table 15.7 shows that only two of the ten TEO
groups considered take advantage of public subsidies for more than 50 per cent of
the total (TEO 2 and TEO 6) which are, as expected, those farms presenting the
higher values in terms of new investments. The last column of the table shows how
the subsidies granted are related to the amount of new investment. In interpreting
this data, it is necessary to take into account delays in the distribution of subsidies
that have often occurred in past years because of the local government procedures
adopted. This means that some investments have been carried out before obtaining
the subsidy – as, for example, in TEO 10. These difficulties in programming and
monitoring public expenses are clearly reported by the Intermediate Appraisal of
the RDP (Rapporto di Valutazione Intermedia del PSR, 2003).

**Table 15.7   Public subsidies for FADN farms by TEO group and new
investment – average values – regional RDP measures (2001)**

TEO groups	New investment (euro)	Granted public subsidies (euro)	Allowed subsidies (euro)	Granted/ allowed (%)	Granted/ new invest (%)
1	80,702	6,768	16,920	40.0	8.4
2	386,613	112,000	203,636	55.0	29.0
3	108,374	9,477	21,661	43.7	8.7
4	54,308	15,937	39,541	40.3	29.3
5	113,623	85,944	204,410	42.0	75.6
6	232,697	33,447	66,894	50.0	14.4
7	87,452	64,000	160,000	40.0	73.2
8	156,185	15,490	38,639	40.1	9.9
9	31,443	31,078	69,061	45.0	98.8
10	142,759	164,645	365,845	45.0	115.3

Source: FADN – Friuli-Venezia Giulia database

The results have to be interpreted with care because the data is drawn only from the FADN regional sample. Furthermore, the analysis considers only two scenarios as regards technological innovation. A number of points can be noted as far as the importance of public funds is concerned. First, the actual level of subsidies seems to be insufficient to promote innovation and development among SMEs. Second, the innovative farms are favoured, in terms of the exploitation of opportunities, rather than the non-innovative farms. This could be partly due to the delays in distribution of funds as non-innovative enterprises do not have the financial ability to carry out investments before receiving subsidies. Third, it suggests the crucial role of public involvement and the detrimental effect on development of any delay in granting subsidies.

A further development of the analysis could examine a third scenario, where FADN 1 is still the leader firm and the government would take the place of FADN 2. It would also be interesting to study the case where the government directly influences the game by acting as an independent player who invests and produces innovations that are made freely available to all firms that need them. In this scenario players have different objectives and different payoff functions where FADN 1 has to maximize profits while the government would have to maximize social welfare.

Conclusions

Innovation is necessary in the agri-food industry to meet the challenges of the new economic environment. This demands the development and adoption of new technologies and product diversification that need to be priorities for the whole sector. Firms are being forced by the market to engage in deep organizational change, involving the development of strategic objectives, changes in internal management, and new market relationships with clients and suppliers. The R&D function needs to be strengthened to assist in the pursuit of technological and product development. The more widespread diffusion of innovation and technical knowledge could help SMEs to improve their business performance. It emerges from this study that local investments in these fields are still not of great importance and that the diffusion of innovations is still restricted. The results of the case study analysis confirm that the inclination to innovate is linked with firm size and sub sector of activity as well as territorial location.

The study highlighted some problems related to SMEs and their owners and managers, and, in particular, the tendency to lack an innovation culture within the firm and a shortage of management skills. It also discussed the financial constraints and the need for external services given the problems of small size and associated lack of internal scale economies and R&D within this type of firm.

The Friuli-Venezia Giulia agricultural sector is characterized by a high fragmentation of land (farms with less than five hectares of land on average accounting for more than 70 per cent of the total), increasing ageing of agricultural entrepreneurs with associated difficulties of generation change and entry of new entrepreneurs, as well as an increase in part-time activities to supplement farm income from work in other sectors (tourism or industry).

Looking at the Interreg area within the Slovenian agricultural sector, it emerges that this border territory did not produce any virtuous circle of economic development in recent years. A possible development in this direction could be through adding value to common agricultural production (wine production, for instance) together with a combined approach in terms of quality, trade, marketing and promotion activities. The territorial area is, in fact, like a *continuum* in terms of environment and rural activities. The objective is to create an economic environment favourable to SMEs, which are widely spread throughout the Programme area, through a systematic approach to common problems, stimulating the introduction of process, product or service innovations as well as the creation and development of computer networks for technological transfer and co-operation. In this way, the distribution of information, the promotion and assistance services to enterprises (for instance, helping in the search for cross-border partners, market analyses and marketing or joint promotion) will be ensured. To this end, it would be necessary to foster entrepreneurial development and growth in competitiveness both through the strengthening of business-related services aimed at technological innovations based on quality systems, and through the acceleration of enterprises' internationalization process, especially by moves towards quality products with a low environmental impact. Such moves may produce higher incomes among the primary sector operators. The seeds of such intentions have already been sown thanks to local agreements already signed between the mayors of the two main cities in this region. These agreements are related to helping the most innovative enterprises to collaborate and public support is very important to facilitate such co-operation between enterprises.

Technological innovation is, by definition, a very risky and costly business and it is clear that strong public support is needed to foster the early stages of an innovation process. The EU, national authorities and industry all have their own ways of allocating funds to technology innovation and different processes to select areas of particular interest. The empirical results reported in this chapter suggest that local government supports the less efficient enterprises. The government's strategy can be defined as partially successful in the short run but it does not seem so in the long run. This is due both to the low percentage of publicly funded grants being taken up – only about 44 per cent of the total public subsidies have been exploited by farms (FADN farms, 2001) – and to the fact that such funds are employed by the most dynamic enterprises, which are those that are most likely to carry out investments. This raises a question about the less efficient enterprises. They appear to take less advantage of government policy, even though it is mainly directed towards them. So the results do not provide any evidence that supporting the follower group will provide competition to the leaders. Furthermore, the financial support provided does not take into account the TEO of farms, being a non-selective financing method. This leads to the following question: is it possible to follow a more targeted agri-food-technology policy? There are many different opinions on this issue. For such a policy to be successful, it is necessary for governments to have the capability of foreseeing not only which sectors will be the most profitable, but also which types of policies will have the most positive effects on innovation. In addition to this, the government must have access to the instruments necessary to implement the policy. There is, however, another area of policy research that warrants attention. Government can use its control of the public sector to develop modern and demanding users of technology. In addition, the development of new institutions can help enterprises in the agri-food sector to make full use of the potential of information and communications technology. This chapter has highlighted some of the main issues concerning the two types of actors/players involved in the process of innovation and development, the agri-food farms and the government. It tries to help identify the path which may lead to a virtuous circle of growth. Each player introduces some crucial elements that need to be linked to each other (Figure 15.3) and could supply a starting point for the future development of SMEs within the rural context examined in this study.

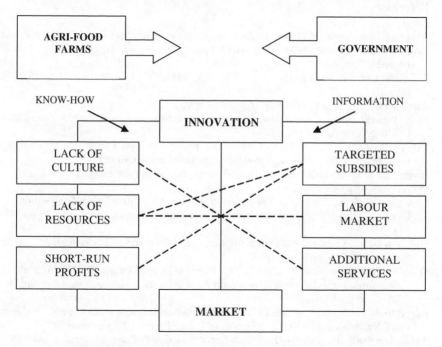

Figure 15.3 Main policies to enhance the development of SMEs' innovation processes

Notes

1 There have been various phases – Interreg I (1988-1993); Interreg II (1994-1999), and Interreg III (2000-2006). There are three kinds of Interreg co-operation – trans-frontier, trans-national and trans-regional.

2   The table does not include the slight changes approved by the first and the second Star and Mipaf auditing.
3   Farm Accountancy Data Network (FADN) was founded by Reg. (EC) n. 79/65 and Reg. CEE 797/85, 2328/91, 950/97. FADN is managed for Italy by the National Institute of Agricultural Economics (INEA).
4   The ESU limit in Italy has been > 2 ESU from 1985 to 2001 and > 4 ESU since 2002. The concept of standard gross margin used to determine the economic size of farms is also used in the Farm Structure Survey organized by Eurostat.
5   The sample was not completely representative because it was a non-probabilistic sample. The sample changed in 2003 and now follows a probabilistic design so that it is statistically representative. See Prot. INEA – ISTAT – Regions (2003) integrated REA survey (ISTAT) and RICA survey (INEA 2001/2002).

References

Aghion, P. and Howitt, P. (1998), *Endogenous Growth Theory*, MIT Press, Cambridge, MA.
European Commission (1999), Reg. (CE) No. 1257/1999, in GUCE. L214, 13/08/99, Brussels.
European Commission (2002), Reg. (CE) No. 445/2002, in GUCE. L74/1, 15/03/02. Brussels.
European Commission (2003), Reg. (CE) No. 1783/03.
Friuli-Venezia Giulia's Rural Development Plan (2000). Approved by EU Commission, DECE 2902/2000.
INEA (2001/2002), 'Le Politiche Comunitarie per lo Sviluppo Rurale – Il Quadro degli Interventi in Italia', *Osservatorio sulle Politiche Strutturali*, Roma.
Interreg III A. (2000-2006). Italy-Slovenia/Phare CBC Operational Programme.
ISTAT, various publications.
Link, A. and Scott, J. (2001), 'Public/private Partnerships: Stimulating Competition in a Dynamic Market', *International Journal of Industrial Organization*, Vol. 5, pp. 763-794.
OECD (various years), 'Small- and Medium-sized Enterprises: Local Strength, Global Reach', *OECD Observer*.
Onofri, A. and Giannakas, K. (2001), 'The Strategic Role of Public R&D in Agriculture', *Proceedings of the American Agricultural Economics Association, Annual Meeting, May* 2001, Chicago, Illinois.
Rapporto di Valutazione Intermedia del Piano di Sviluppo Rurale della Regione Autonoma Friuli-Venezia Giulia (2003), University of Udine, Faculty of Agricolture.
Tirole, J. (1988), *The Theory of Industrial Organization*, MIT Press, Cambridge, MA.

Chapter 16

Attitudes to Territorial Innovation Processes in Raia Central Ibérica

Maria Manuela Santos Natário, Paulo Alexandre Neto
and Felisberto Marques Reigado

Abstract

Innovation is not an individual firm process but rather results from the involvement of a large set of participants with the capacity to influence the territorial dynamics of innovation. The aim of this study is analyse the behaviour of participants in innovative initiatives promoting the competitiveness of the Raia Central Ibérica (RCI). The study looks at five sub regions of the RCI, three Portuguese and two Spanish. The sample for the quantitative analysis includes 166 companies and 46 educational, public and other institutions set up to offer support and assistance to firms. The attributes included in the analysis of firms relate to the general characteristics of the organization, the top manager's characteristics, sources of innovation, networking, financial support, obstacles to innovation, future attitudes towards innovation and the dynamics of collective learning. Three different types of behaviour were distinguished among the firms through cluster analysis and the institutions and associations were also classified into three different behaviours. The characteristics of each cluster were then examined statistically. The profiles drawn up in this way allowed some inferences to be drawn about the conditions encouraging the best innovative performance.

Introduction

Since the mid 1980s, the territorial dimension has assumed an important place in explanations of innovative activities. The notion of national systems of innovation has also been introduced and has become very influential. The systemic approach suggests that innovation is an interactive process with feedback loops and some empirical studies have confirmed this view of innovation. The economic performance of any given territory is now seen as depending on the activities, attitudes and interactions of the different actors, both public and private, toward promoting innovation and competitiveness. According to the OECD, 'The development of innovation and technology results from a complex set of relations between actors inside of the system, including companies, university and governmental institutes of investigation' (OECD, 1997, p. 7).

The purpose of this chapter is to analyse to what extent local actors have been involved in fostering innovation and competitiveness in the Raia Central Ibérica (RCI). Five sub-regions of RCI (three Portuguese and two Spanish) in the Portugal/Spain border area were considered. The work was based on a survey of a large set of local companies, public organizations and associations that, directly or indirectly, might be involved in the promotion of innovation and competitiveness of these areas. Altogether the study includes 166 companies and 46 institutional and associative organizations.

The methodology is based on the application of multivariate statistics. K-means clusters analysis allowed three different groups of companies to be distinguished in terms of behaviour and three different groups of institutional and associative actors were distinguished relative to their involvement in innovation activities. These groups were then compared statistically. The attributes considered were the general characteristics of the organization; the director's characteristics; sources of innovation; networking: cooperation; subcontracting and competitive relationships; financial support; obstacles to innovation; future attitudes toward innovation, and the dynamics of collective learning.

The next section comprises a brief discussion of the theoretical framework and describes the methodology used. The contribution of the different actors in the regions of the RCI, relative to their innovation activities, is then examined. Some final reflections are given in the conclusion.

Theoretical Approach

The treatment of innovation as a concept has been subject to many changes in the literature over time. It has come to encompass not only the perspective of Schumpeter (1934) that innovation exists when completely new elements are introduced (radical innovation), but also the adaptation, modification and improvement of existing products, processes or services (incremental innovation). In the last decades, moreover, the linear model of innovation which saw a direct relationship between 'pull' or 'push' factors and innovation has been abandoned. Today, innovation is seen as resulting from a system of feedbacks, both forward and backward linkages, between different functions and different actors in a network of cooperation. This view has been verified in the studies of Dosi (1988), Dosi et al. (1988), Barata (1992), Edquist (1997), Guinet (1999), Laranja (1999), Lopes (2001), Conceição and Ávila (2001) and Lundvall (1992), among others.

The study of regional systems of innovation (SRI) by Lundvall (1992), Nelson (1993) and Edquist (1997), of innovative milieu by Aydalot (1986), Maillat (1995, 1998) and Camagni et al (1999) and of learning regions (Florida, 1995; Asheim, 1996; Maillat and Kébir, 1999), are among the approaches taken to apply the new perspective of innovation in regional studies and to develop territorial models of innovation. In several respects, such as the inclusion of networks, knowledge, cooperation and interaction between different actors, the different perspectives do not differ very much but each one emphasizes different points.

The local and regional perspectives of systems of innovation are distinguished from the concept of innovative milieu because they relate to the analysis of the specificities of territorial processes of innovation and the definition of policies; they aim to specify the mechanisms and processes that promote innovation in certain regions. The concept of regional systems of innovation is therefore differentiated from other perspectives by having a more operational and policy related dimension.

The importance of these systems is related to the necessity, taking into account the specific characteristics of each region and, in particular, of border regions, to define and to coordinate policies and strategies for innovation. These require the involvement of the highest level of government as well as the local and border level of administration, working together with companies and the academic and research world to increase the innovative capacity of these regions. The aim of the regional systems of innovation is to strengthen the territorial platforms of competitiveness, encouraging a more innovative milieu and developing 'learning' regions (Santos, 2002, p. 308). This approach is required to stimulate innovation in border regions (for example Raia Central Ibérica) and to promote their competitiveness.

Figure 16.1 presents a framework including different elements that are now seen as important in promoting territorial innovation and competitiveness. In this diagram, the process of innovation, knowledge mechanisms, networks and the system of governance are seen as the four essential linked elements. These relate to the dynamic adjustment of economic agents, their organizational competences, their locational settings and their collective outcomes thus defining competitive territories.

The competitive capacity of territories does not depend only on their endowment of traditional resources (capital, labour and raw materials), but rather on their innovative dynamics. Territories with a positive attitude towards innovation (in intangible resources – knowledge and use of the ICT, for example) are more competitive in a world that is increasingly marked by internationalization and globalization.

Knowledge mechanisms are very important in this context. This includes the results of both collective learning, especially the accumulation of tacit knowledge through decades of experience, and individual learning which results from a spiral process that starts at the individual level and increases through a community of interactions, networking between companies, educational institutions, professional associations, interpersonal networks, etc., improving existing knowledge and allowing the production of new knowledge. Thus, initial levels of education are not enough in an economy where the changes are constant and rapid. Ongoing training and constant learning is of extreme importance for such economies if they are to become more competitive.

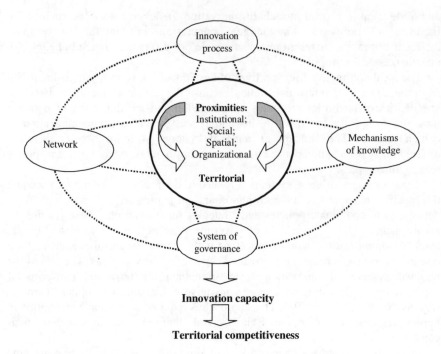

Figure 16.1 The influences on territorial competitiveness

Source: Adapted from de Natário, Reigado and Neto (2002); Bramanti (1999)

Networks can be very helpful in reducing the uncertainty and risks associated with the innovation process and in enriching the milieu (making it more innovative). A network seems to be a necessary but insufficient condition to transfer skills, knowledge and heterogeneous information and sources of innovation required in the region.

The ability to guide and to direct the organization and regulation of the territory to promote innovation and competitiveness depends on an efficient governance system. The governance system, the set of institutional actors with capacity to influence the territory, has a central role in this process through the projects that it promotes and also in the organization and regulation of local activities. It defines the rules of the game as regards decision procedures, the methods of commitment and the coordination actors. The governance[1] of a territory needs to be underpinned by the functioning of local cooperation networks (formal or informal). Taking a systemic perspective, this interaction, together with a shared culture and history, facilitates the development of trust based social capital in local and trans-territorial communities.

The complex interaction among these elements (knowledge, networks and governance) allows a potential innovation to become an effective innovation; it allows the ability to innovate to be improved and enables the territory to compete, to grow and to strengthen its internal cohesion. Thus, the territory benefits from using and harmonizing the four groups (visualized in Figure 16.1) to promote competitiveness and development.

Methodology

Selection of Actors and Data

The analysis was based on a survey which was used to collect information from a large set of actors that might be involved, directly or indirectly, in promoting the innovation and competitiveness of the Raia Central Ibérica. The main actors were identified following the approach of the National Innovation System of Guinett, (1999, p.68), and PRONOIV (Program Integrated of Support for Innovation (Rodrigues, 2000, p.22) in the Portuguese regions.

Four groups of actors in the RCI could have an important role in the process of innovation, namely:

A   Companies
B   Institutions offering support and assistance to enterprises: technological centres, enterprise and development associations
C   Education, training and R&D institutions: universities and polytechnics, Institutes of Employment and Professional Qualification (IEFP)
D   Public institutions: (central/regional administration, local administration and other public institutions (regional association of municipals, Institute of Commerce and Tourism of Portugal (ICEP), Institute of SME Support (IAPMEI)

The 2002 Portuguese database of establishments and companies (BELÉM) of INE (the Portuguese National Institute of Statistics) was used to identify the set of companies (group A) for the Portuguese NUTS III areas studied. That database supplies the name, the address, the Classification of Economic Activities (CAE) and the number of workers for each company. No similar database is available for the Spanish regions of the RCI. The database of the Official Chamber of Commerce and Industry of Salamanca was used to identify companies in the Province of Salamanca and this provided information on the name of the company, address and number of workers (among other variables). Database Árdan was used for companies of the Province of Cáceres, for the year 2002, that supply the same variables.

Groups B, C and D were contacted using a listing published for the Commission of Coordination of the Region Centre (2002), of the organizations of the border region, with name, address and telephone number and/or e-mail address.

Selection of the Region

The Raia Central Ibérica (RCI) is made up of sub-regions on the border of Portugal and Spain. The Raia Central Ibérica, in the scope of the INTERREG II,[2] covers the Portuguese sub-regions (NUTS III), of the Interior Central Region: Beira Interior Norte (BIN), Beira Interior Sul (BIS) and Cova da Beira (CB) within Raia Central Portuguesa (RCP), the Portuguese border of the interior region. It also includes the totality of the territories of Spanish provinces of Salamanca and of Cáceres, situated in Autonomous Communities of Castilla y Léon and Extremadura, in turn part of Raia Central Espanhola (RCE), the Spanish border interior central region.

These sub-regions are characterized by very similar social-economic features; the regions on both sides of the border have been losing population and have weak corporate sectors and poor economic capacity. In several studies (Reigado, 1995; 2000a; 2002; Santos and Caetano, 2002; Hernández, 2000; Lourenço, 1996; De La Fuente, 2002; López and Diéguez, 1994, among others), the border region of Portugal and Spain is shown to be disfavoured and depressed. It presents a geographic and political situation of periphery, a territory that is 'very marginal and distant from the national centres of decision' (Hernández, 2000, p. 17) and also from regional (in the case of Spain) and consumer centres.

Moreover, according to statistical data from INE of Portugal and Spain (BELÉM and DIRCE), service companies predominate in the RCI, with 68 per cent and 79 per cent in RCP and RCE respectively, and have most importance in the BIN and Cáceres. Civil construction represents 11 per cent of the companies in RCP and 13 per cent in RCE; manufacturing represents only 17 per cent of companies in RCP and 8 per cent of the total of companies of RCE. In comparison, agri-industries represent about 5 per cent of companies in the RCP and 3 per cent in RCE.

Companies with less than ten employees predominate in RCI, representing about 87 per cent of the companies in RCP and 95 per cent of the companies in RCE. There is an insignificant number of companies with more than 100 employees (0.5 per cent and 0.2 per cent respectively). Only 11.2 per cent of the companies of BIN, 12.9 per cent of the companies of BIS, 12.9 per cent of the companies of CB; 4.6 per cent of the companies of Salamanca and 5.6 per cent of the companies of Cáceres have more than ten employees.

The present interest in these peripheral regions is related to the possibility of evaluating the dynamics of innovation through an analysis of the participation of the different actors within them in promoting innovation. The chapter continues by discussing the data used in the attempt to perceive which environmental factors are associated with these dynamics.

Data Gathering and the Sample

The principal sources of fieldwork data resulted from two surveys. One inquiry was carried out with companies and the second inquiry was carried out with the different institutions and associations in these five regions.

In selecting the universe for the collection of company data, all legally constituted companies with headquarters in RCP and RCE and more than ten employees in all *sectors* were included.[3] The questionnaires were all addressed to the managers by name and were sent by post and by e-mail. The information was initially collected in January, February, March and April, 2003. However, given the lack of responses from the Spanish companies, the questionnaire was sent again in August by post to all the companies who had still not replied requesting a response by the end of September. The final structure of the sample by industrial classification and size of company is given in Appendix 16.1.

A listing published by the Commission of Coordination of the Region Centre (2002) was used (see Appendix 16.1).[4] Table 16.1 summarizes the RCI actors studied and compares the data used with the population fitting the criteria.

Table 16.1   Summary of actors studied in the RCI

		RCP		RCE	
		No.	Per cent of population	No.	Per cent of population
A	Companies	105	15	64	9,2
B	Institutions providing support and assistance to enterprise activity: technology centres, company and development associations	14	70	6	35
C	Education and training and R&D: polytechnics, universities and technology schools	7	100	2	33
D	Public institutions (local, regional/national public administration, other institutions – ICEP, IAPMEI, Regional Association of Municipals)	16	59	10	36
	Total (B+C+D)	37	71	18	47

Source: INE Portugal and Spain, CCRC (2002)

Innovation Variables

According to Cowan and Paal (2000, p. 4), the creation, adaptation or adoption of new or improved products, processes and services are innovative activities on which economic success depends, especially in the long run. Lundvall (1998) adds innovation in markets to this list, and Edquist (1997) stresses organizational innovations. Following Lundvall (1992, p. 46), innovation is taken to include the creation of something qualitatively different, new ideas and new knowledge. In this view innovation can take several forms: product innovation; process innovation;

organizational innovation; innovation of services; innovation of markets; institutional innovation; and environment innovation. In the study of innovation in small regions, such as the one analysed here, the adoption of a broad concept of innovation is advisable, including the diffusion and the imitation of technological, organizational, economic and cultural modifications and the training of human resources. The classification of innovation activities considered in the study is shown in Table 16.2. This follows the Community Innovation Surveys II and IIII and 14 variables are used to capture different dimensions of company innovation.

To characterize the attitude of the different actors in innovation activities, a methodology similar to the one developed in Project INNOVALOC was used (see Vaz and Cesário, 2005; and Vaz et al., 2006). The set of variables given in Table 16.2 was analysed to classify the behaviour of the companies as regards innovation and to classify the behaviour of institutional and associative actors.

Table 16.2   Variables used in the cluster analyses

Variables used to classify the behaviour of the companies	Variables used to classify the behaviour of the institutional and associative actors
R&D inside the company	R&D inside the organization
Acquisition of external services – R&D	Acquisition of external services – R&D
Acquisition of new technologies	Acquisition of new technologies
Acquisition of information technologies	Acquisition of information technologies
Acquisition of other external knowledge	Acquisition of other external knowledge
Training of human resources	Training of human resources
Introduction of innovation into markets	Management strategy/techniques
Management strategy/techniques	Changes in organizational structure
Changes in organizational structure	Marketing innovation
Marketing innovation	
Company introduced innovation	
Product innovation	
Process innovation	
Organizational innovation	

Source: Adapted from CIS III

K-means clusters, a multivariate statistical technique within the Statistical Package for the Social Sciences, was applied to these two sets of variables. The aim of this analysis was to detect groupings of companies within the company sample with respect to involvement in innovation activities and, similarly, to detect groupings within the institutions/associations in terms of their innovation activities.

The resulting clusters of companies and of institutional actors were analysed, in turn, to identify the set of attributes of each cluster and to investigate the differences between the groups as well as which factors were associated with the best performance. The attributes considered for the different actors were the general characteristics of the organization, the director's characteristics, the sources of innovation, cooperation, subcontracting, competitive relationships, financial support, the obstacles to innovation, the future attitude to innovation and the dynamics of collective learning. The results of this analysis are now presented, together with the findings concerning the factors that are associated with better performance.

Companies within RCI – Cluster Behaviour by Innovative Activities

Applying K-means clusters analysis to the group of variables previously defined for the companies resulted in three groups of companies. Table 16.3 summarizes the results of each group relative to each of the variables previously presented. Note that 0 corresponds to 'no' (the cluster is not involved in this innovation activity) and 1 corresponds to 'yes' (the cluster is involved in this innovation activity).

Table 16.3   Involvement of RCI companies in innovation activities – results of K-means analysis

Variables used in cluster analysis	Cluster one: medium involvement N=61	Cluster two: low involvement N=62	Cluster three: high involvement N=43
R&D inside the company	0	0	1
Acquisition of external services – R&D	0	0	1
Acquisition of new technologies	1	1	1
Acquisition of information technologies	1	0	1
Acquisition of other external knowledge	0	0	1
Training of human resources	1	1	1
Introduction of innovation into markets	0	0	1
Management strategy/techniques	0	0	1
Changes in organizational structure	0	0	1
Marketing innovation	0	0	1
Company introduced innovation	1	0	1
Product innovation	1	0	1
Process innovation	0	0	1
Organizational innovation	0	0	0

Source: Own elaboration

An ANOVA test was carried out and showed that the clustering of the selected variables was statistically significant – see Appendix 16.3. An F test ($p<0.05$) showed that each factor has a differentiated contribution in the three groups (see Pestana and Gageiro, 2000).

Cluster one groups together 61 companies which are characterized by medium involvement in innovation activities (innovation exists in the introduction of new products in the market, new technologies and ICT, in the qualifications of human resources and in introducing innovations). In this group of companies, innovation is unlikely to be radical but it is linked with the constant necessity to introduce new products to survive. The companies within this group belong largely to the BIN and CB (33 per cent and 23 per cent, respectively) while the remaining companies are distributed in the other three regions in the following way: 16 per cent in BIS; 15 per cent in Salamanca, and 3 per cent in Cáceres. Fifty-nine per cent of the companies making up this cluster are in manufacturing (CAE 15-37) and 28 per cent are engaged in commerce (CAE 50-54).

Cluster two contains 62 companies characterized by a very low involvement in innovation activities. Their attitude is very passive and the only evidence of innovation efforts is related to the acquisition of new technologies and the training of human resources. The companies within this group belong largely to Cáceres and to the BIS (29 per cent and 23 per cent respectively), the remainder being in Salamanca (19 per cent), CB (16 per cent) and BIN (13 per cent). Moreover, 34 per cent are in manufacturing industry and a much higher proportion is in the service sector with 32 per cent from commerce, 18 per cent from construction and 13 per cent from other services.

Cluster three groups together 43 companies and it is distinguished from the previous groups by its very considerable involvement in innovation activities and both radical and incremental innovation features. In this group, only organizational innovation is unimportant. The companies are located in Salamanca (28 per cent), CB (28 per cent) BIN (19 per cent) and BIS (16 per cent). Manufacturing industry accounts for 63 per cent of the cluster and commerce for 28 per cent.

Looking first at the location of the companies in the different clusters, it appears that 56 per cent of the companies based in BIN are in cluster one while 45 per cent of the companies in BIS belong to cluster two and 32 per cent to cluster one; in CB, 39 per cent of the companies belong to cluster one and 33 per cent to cluster three. Salamanca has a distinct situation; 36 per cent belong in the more innovative cluster and 36 per cent are in the less innovative group. In the province of Cáceres, the situation is reversed. Thirty-seven per cent of companies belong to each of cluster one and cluster two.

Second, the sectors can be distinguished according to the cluster in which they appear. More than 65 per cent of companies in construction and other services (excluding commerce) belong to cluster two. Forty-one per cent of commercial firms are in cluster two and 35 per cent in cluster one. About 75 per cent of manufacturing firms are in the more innovative two clusters with 32 per cent in cluster three. Looking at the breakdown of manufacturing industries, 68 per cent of firms in agri industries (CAE 15) are in cluster one, 50 per cent of textile manufacturers (CAE 17) belong to cluster three and 38 per cent to cluster one while in the clothes industry (CAE 18), 73 per cent of the firms belong to cluster one and 18 per cent to cluster two.

Characterization of the Companies by Cluster

Introduction

The three groups of companies previously identified in terms of their involvement in innovation activities can be characterized in terms of the attributes previously presented: general characteristics of the company, characteristics of the general manager, sources of innovation, networks in terms of cooperation, subcontracting, competitive relationships, financial support, obstacles to innovation and dynamics of collective learning. These attributes will help to analyse the profiles of innovative behaviour and highlight which factors or environmental variables are associated with the best performance in terms of innovation.

General Company Characteristics

The three clusters are mainly characterized by companies which operate one single establishment, with the ones that are the head-office being next in importance. However, while cluster one has a greater percentage of companies with a single establishment, cluster three has greater percentage of companies with a head office within Raia Central Ibérica, and curiously cluster two has a greater percentage of companies who have more than one establishment (branch business/network). Most companies in all the clusters have been in operation between 11 and 25 years.

About 90 per cent of companies in cluster one and two have sales of less than five million Euros, while about 34 per cent of cluster three companies have sales exceeding this value. Moreover, in 2002, sales in the two less innovative clusters averaged around 3,500,000 Euros, while the average in cluster three was about 8,700,000 euros. The exporting companies are most involved in innovation. In 2002, 50% of cluster three and 48% of cluster one were involved in exporting compared with only 32% of cluster two.

There are also size differences in terms of numbers of employees. While the two less innovative groups had less than 20 employees (about 45 per cent of cluster one and 52 per cent of cluster two), only 26 per cent of the companies within the most innovative group had less than 20 employees. It is also the more innovative cluster that has more employees with a higher education degree (an average of six) and more computers in the company (an average of 16) while in cluster two, these figures are two and eight respectively. Curiously cluster two, not involved in innovation, has higher averages for these variables than cluster one (three people with higher education degree and nine computers on average). Thus, 8 per cent of the employees in cluster one have higher education compared with 9 per cent in cluster two and 11 per cent in cluster three.

All the companies in cluster three have access to the Internet and computerize their data unlike the other clusters where less than 90 per cent of companies have Internet access and not all keep data in computerized form. Also 61 per cent of cluster three companies have a website, against 48 per cent in cluster one and 42 per cent in cluster two. Moreover, cluster three makes more use of the new information technologies for electronic commerce and in relationships with customers.

The most important geographic market in all clusters is the company's own region. Suppliers are localized in the region for 47 per cent of the companies in cluster two, compared with 34 per cent in cluster three and 44 per cent in cluster one. However, the more innovative clusters operate with suppliers from other parts of the EU and other countries (about 40 per cent of companies in cluster three have suppliers elsewhere in the EU and 14 per cent go further afield; in cluster one the corresponding figures are 36 per cent and 5 per cent respectively).

Some significant differences emerge as regards the attitude of the companies to the features of the region.[5] On average, cluster three valued the grouping concerned with human resources more, followed by the availability of inputs and the environment of the region; cluster one valued personal factors more and cluster two was most concerned about market proximity.

Characteristics of the Top Manager

The profile of the top manager was studied as this was expected to be an important element in the definition of company strategies. The top manager's personality can help or hinder innovation as it can promote a collective culture of innovation and encourage innovation initiatives and risk taking, or suffocate creativity through a rigid and conservative attitude.

Top managers with higher education predominated in cluster three, accounting for over half the firms (56 per cent as against 45 per cent in cluster two and 49 per cent in cluster one). In the latter two clusters, about one third of the top managers completed their education before the twelfth grade. These results confirm the findings of Kitchell (1997) who showed that the higher the level of education, the greater the capacity to generate creative solutions.

Sources of Innovation

Sources of information are important in innovation as they suggest innovative projects and contribute to the implementation of innovations. The importance of the sources of information for innovation has been shown in the three Community Innovation Surveys (CIS I, II and III). Thus, it was necessary to identify the main sources of information used by the companies and to determine the importance attributed to them. Using the terminology of the Community Innovation Survey (CIS III) and of Conceição and Ávila (2001) the main potential sources of information for innovation were grouped into the following – internal to the company; the market (suppliers, clients and competitors); institutional (institutions of higher education and R&D and public laboratories), and other sources (including conferences, meetings and publications, fairs and exhibitions).

The main sources of information for the sample companies were found to be internal sources and market sources (mainly from suppliers and clients). Less than 33 per cent of the companies consider institutional sources as an important source of information for innovation showing the absence of potentially important links between knowledge producers and the company sector. However, this situation is not only found in the RCI. According to Conceição and Ávila (2001), institutional sources (among others) are little used by Portuguese companies with more than 70 per cent of the companies studied claiming not to have used them. Thus, external information sources for the development of innovations essentially result from the relationship of the company with its customers and suppliers, and are often of a tacit, less codified nature.

There are some differences in information sources between the more innovative clusters one and three. All sources of information, except customers, are more important to cluster three than to cluster one. In cluster three, the main and most important source of innovation is the company, while customers are the main source of information in cluster one. However, relative to the institutional sources, these have a middle or high importance for 33 per cent of the cluster three companies compared with 21 per cent for cluster one. Moreover, cluster three values the other sources more than cluster one, including proceedings from scientific and professional conferences, meetings and publications (where the information has one more codified character), and information from consulting companies.[6]

Networks: Cooperation, Competition and Subcontracting

The importance of cooperation as a vehicle to promote territorial innovation and competitiveness has been emphasized in some studies (Lundvall, 1992; Bramanti, 1999; Edquist, 1997; OECD/Eurostat, 1997, among others). The innovation process, in the contemporary context, emerges as a result of endogenous capacities and networking between entrepreneurs, as well as between entrepreneurs and local institutions (Veltz, 1999; Ferrão, 2000). These networks, according to Camagni (1991), Planque (1991) and Maillat, Crevoisier and Lecoq (1993) among others, reduce the intrinsic uncertainties in the innovation process. They facilitate the production and transmission of knowledge, influence the territorial dynamics of innovation producing externalities through use of the local synergies and help to determine the innovative performance of companies (Courlet and Pecqueur, 1991).

First, as regards cooperation to access information and resources to help in the general functioning of the company, 74 per cent of the companies in the most innovative cluster (three), had established formal or informal cooperation agreements with other external entities. In cluster one, 57 per cent had these types of agreements while only 37 per cent of the companies in cluster two cooperate externally in this way to access information and other resources.

Second, as regards cooperation in innovation itself, there was little difference between the two more innovative clusters (in cluster one, 44 per cent of the companies cooperate to innovate and 48 per cent in cluster three) whereas companies in cluster two do not cooperate in this way.

Of the actors previously identified that might potentially cooperate with companies in their innovation efforts, cluster three has greater cooperation with suppliers and with enterprise/commercial associations (more than 50 per cent of the companies) and institutions of R&D and higher education (42 per cent), while cooperation with customers, development associations, central and local administration, and other institutions are found in about 20 per cent of the companies. Cluster one presents some differences. Suppliers are the main cooperation partners (44 per cent of companies) followed by customers (37 per cent), and other companies (33 per cent), while cooperation with R&D and higher education institutions and enterprise/trade associations is evident in only around 20 per cent of the companies.

Cooperation with several actors is established mainly at the level of the region for the two groups, except for the suppliers where the national level is more important in both of the clusters. Institutes of higher education assume equal importance at the national and regional level for cluster three (compared to cluster one, where the regional level predominates). Thus, cluster one entrepreneurs have a little more pronounced territorial dimension in their cooperation activities than those of cluster three.

The importance of subcontracting does not differ much between the clusters. 47 per cent of companies in cluster three have subcontracting arrangements compared with 44 per cent in cluster one and 39 per cent in cluster two.

Financial Support for Innovation Activities

Lack of finance is an obstacle to innovation and the study investigated the aid received by the sample companies from public sources. The results showed that the great majority of the companies (about 80 per cent) did not receive financial support for innovation activities from local or central administration irrespective of the type of innovative behaviour they represent, although central administration was more supportive than the local level, especially towards the more innovative clusters. The percentage of companies that benefited from EU support for innovation was 38 per cent, and 51 per cent respectively for clusters one and three (see Table 16.4).

Table 16.4   Financial support (per cent of companies)

Source of support	Cluster one	Cluster two	Cluster three
Local administration	8	7	12
Central administration	20	16	23
EU funds	38	10	51
EU initiatives	2		2

Source: Own elaboration

Other Obstacles to Innovation

The lack of public financial support was not an obvious impediment to cluster one which had an average involvement in innovation activities, but clearly other impediments to innovation exist. Thus it was important to analyse the other difficulties that companies had found and to see if these can be used to distinguish between the innovative profiles.

Factorial analysis was used to group the possible obstacles.[7] This showed that cluster one attributes greater importance to external economic and financial barriers (such as risks, costs, lack of sources of financing and lack of breadth in the market) while cluster three emphasized the internal obstacles within the company (lack of information on markets, on technology, organizational structure, lack of qualified staff, weak mobility of workers, lack of cooperation, as well as the impact of regulations, lack of acceptability of innovation to customers and their low requirements for innovation).

More detailed analysis showed that extreme risks, high costs and lack of sources of finance are not relevant for 1 per cent more of the cluster three companies than those in cluster one. This suggests that the most innovative companies do not ignore external obstacles but are more sensitive to internal constraints than cluster one companies, especially those concerning organizational structure, lack of qualified personnel, cooperation and the mobility of workers. Cluster three is more conscious of difficulties with respect to intangible resources, cooperation and also mobility of workers between companies of the region than cluster one. These factors are increasingly seen as important in promoting territorial innovation and competitiveness in a world with an increasingly knowledge based economy and marked by internationalization and globalization.

Future Attitudes to Innovation

The future is uncertain and the future of these regions and of their companies inevitably depends on attitudes with respect to innovation. The cluster analysis suggested that, the groups most involved in innovation in the short term are those that expect to innovate. Process innovations have the highest values in cluster three, which is predominantly made up of manufacturing industry. In cluster two, which is less involved in innovation, 85 per cent of the companies foresee organizational innovation (see Table 16.5).

Table 16.5   Future behaviour in innovation (per cent)

Type of innovation	Cluster one	Cluster two	Cluster three
Expect to innovate	62	23	67
Product innovation	61	23	69
Process innovation	32	23	48
Organizational innovation	45	85	48

Source: Own elaboration

Dynamics of Collective Learning

Collective learning and individual learning assume an important role in the process of territorial innovation. According to De Bernady (2000), collective learning is related to continuity (affected by the mobility of the work force and relationships between suppliers and consumers) and to dynamic synergies between local actors (affected by turnover of the work force; local innovation in cooperation with suppliers and consumers as well as spin-offs). Moreover, the accumulation of experience, culture and know-how throughout decades results in tacit knowledge that is difficult to imitate and to transmit and is a source of innovation and competitive advantage. Individual learning is also important if territories are to become more innovative and more competitive.

There was some difference between clusters in the responses to questions about the effect of collective learning and diffusion of know how. Seventy-six per cent of cluster two entrepreneurs did not acknowledge the existence of a learning effect or did not answer compared with lower proportions in cluster one (52 per cent) and cluster three (51 per cent).

The least innovative cluster depends more on national suppliers for human resources training carried out in the region. More companies in cluster one depend on the region for training human resources and cluster three gives most attention to the trainees whose place of origin is Raia Central Ibérica.

Sixty-one per cent of cluster three regards the mobility of employees between companies within the region as a source of learning compared with 82 per cent in cluster one and 69 per cent in cluster two. Similar results emerge for the mobility of employees between companies in the same sector. However, cluster three is the one that cooperates more with local suppliers and with customers to obtain the resources and information needed to innovate.

Summary

The innovative performance of the territories depends on the attitude of the different actors (public and private) to innovation. Quantitative methods allowed profiles of the entrepreneurs' involvement in innovation to be drawn up and greater or lesser similarities between the attitudes of the entrepreneurs to be revealed. The most important variables that distinguished these profiles were whether the company is involved in exporting, has employees with higher education degree and uses computers as well as new information technologies. Localization factors, the level of education of the top managers, use of institutional sources of innovation, and the extent of cooperative relationships were also important.

The most innovative companies have most links with R&D centres and higher education institutions and were more often in receipt of public financial support. They recognized the internal obstacles to innovation and the effect of collective and individual learning. The receipt of state financial support did not discriminate between the innovative profiles, but the more innovative cluster, the more it benefited from EU support. Furthermore the more innovative group of companies showed a greater predisposition to innovate in the future.

Institutional Actors within RCI – Cluster Behaviour by Innovative Activities

To be innovative, territories require the involvement not only of the companies located there but also of the different institutional and associative actors. The next sections report the results of the study of the behaviour of actors within RCI other than the companies themselves, which have been discussed above.

K-means clusters analysis was applied using the group of variables previously defined for these actors in Table 16.3. This resulted in three clusters, each representing a distinct behaviour as regards involvement in innovation. Table 16.6 summarizes the results by cluster for each of the variables previously presented. In this table, 0 corresponds to 'no' (the cluster is not involved in this type of innovation activities) and 1 corresponds to 'yes' (the cluster is involved).

Table 16.6   Involvement of RCI institutions/associations in innovation activities – results of K-means analysis

	Cluster one: high involvement N=10	Cluster two: low involvement N=23	Cluster three: medium involvement N=13
R&D inside the organization	1	0	0
Acquisition of external services – R&D	1	0	0
Acquisition of new technologies	1	0	1
Acquisition of information technologies	1	1	1
Acquisition of other external knowledge	1	0	1
Training of human resources	1	1	1
Management strategy/techniques	1	0	1
Changes in organizational structure	1	0	1
Marketing innovation	1	0	1

Source: Own elaboration

The results of an ANOVA analysis on the selected variables (Appendix 16.4 show that all the variables are statistically significant. The F test ($p<0.05$) shows that each factor has a differentiated contribution in the three groups.

Cluster one groups ten organizations characterized by involvement in all the innovation activities. In this group of organizations, innovation is a priority. Three are from Cáceres, two from each of BIN, CB, and Salamanca and one is located in BIS. The cluster is made up of four higher education institutions, three companies/commercial associations, two local administration organizations and one institute of central/regional administration.

Cluster two contains 23 organizations which are characterized by very little involvement in innovation. This relates only to the acquisition of information technologies and the development of human resources. Six of this group are located in BIN, and the same number are from CB, with the remaining organizations distributed over the three regions in the following way – five in BIS, two in Salamanca and four in Cáceres. The main types of organizations in this cluster are development associations and regional/central administration organizations (five each). It includes four company/commercial associations, three technological and training institutions and the same number of local public administration organizations.

Cluster three groups 13 organizations with a medium involvement in innovation. This group does not contemplate internal or external R&D. The cluster contains four organizations from Salamanca and four from BIN with two each from BIS and CB. Five of them are connected to regional/central administration, four are companies/commercial associations and three are organizations connected to local administration.

If the breakdown of the organizations in different regions in the cluster is analysed, it appears that the organizations in BIN largely fall into cluster two (six of the total of twelve), and cluster three (four). The majority of the organizations in BIS belong to cluster two (five out of a total of eight) and two to cluster three. In CB, six of the total of ten organizations belong to cluster two, two to cluster one with cluster three accounting for two. In Salamanca half of the total of eight organizations belong to cluster three, with a medium involvement in innovation and the rest are equally divided between the other two clusters. In the province of Cáceres, three of the total of seven organizations belong to the more innovative cluster (cluster one) and four to the less innovative cluster (cluster two).

Analysis of the distribution of the different groups of actors shows that four of the total of five institutions of higher education belong to cluster one, the most involved in innovation. Three quarters of the technological and training institutions are in cluster two, the least involved in innovation. All the development associations belong to cluster two. The companies/commercial associations are almost equally distributed between all the clusters. Nearly half the organizations connected with regional and central administration fall into cluster two and a similar amount are in cluster three. Three of the total of eight organizations involved with local administration belong to cluster two and three to cluster three, with the two remaining found in cluster one which is more involved in innovation activities. The group of other institutions (consisting of the Regional Association of Municipals, IAPMEI and ICEP) all belong to cluster two.

Characterization of Institutional/Associative Actors by Cluster

The three groups defined by organizational behaviour previously identified could be characterized in terms of the set of attributes considered for the companies: general characteristics of the organization and of the top manager; sources of innovation; cooperation; financial support for innovation activities; obstacles to innovation; future attitudes regarding innovation, and the dynamics of collective learning. These attributes were analysed to help draw profiles of innovation behaviour and to identify which environmental factors are associated with the best performance.

General Characteristics of the Institutions/Associations and the Top Manager

The percentage of employees with higher education qualifications relative to the total employees is higher in more innovative clusters. In the majority of cluster one organizations, more than half of the workers have higher levels of education compared with 47 per cent of cluster two and 40 per cent of cluster three. Curiously, cluster three (with medium involvement) has less than in cluster two, although cluster three presents a larger group of organizations (30 per cent) where more than three quarters of employees have a higher education degree.[8]

All the organizations studied had access to the Internet and all of those classified to the most innovative cluster have a website whereas only three quarters of cluster two members have a web site. The two more innovative clusters have the biggest percentage of organizations using computerized data and communicating with their users and associates with new ICT.

Some differences are also apparent as regards the characteristics of the top manager. All had a higher education degree in the most innovative cluster and in cluster two only one manager did not have this level of education. In cluster three which showed a reasonable level of involvement in innovation, 85 per cent of the directors have higher education.

Sources of Innovation

The most innovative cluster values all potential information sources, with internal sources of information identified as the most important. Cluster two places little value on different information sources except internal ideas, those coming from other companies, especially from users/partners and conferences, which are more valued than in cluster three.

Cooperative Relationships

Cooperation can be a very efficient way of reducing uncertainty and the high risks associated with the innovation process in peripheral regions. An innovation approach suggests that interaction, relationships and informal networks of cooperation between the actors involved in the development of innovation are fundamental in reaching high levels of innovation and competitiveness (Lundvall, 1992; Nelson, 1993; OECD, 1997; Edquist, 1997; Guimarães, 1998).

As Table 16.7 shows, a great majority of the entities in the previously defined clusters, especially those most involved in innovation, have established cooperative agreements – 78 per cent (cluster one), 62 per cent (cluster three), but only 52 per cent in cluster two. However, as discussed earlier, only half of the companies have established cooperation agreements and these were mainly with customers and suppliers rather than with institutional actors.

In general, more than half of the institutional/associative actors in RCI had established cooperative agreements with other actors to help in their innovation effort. Cluster three cooperated with all the other actors except the development associations and the most important cooperation was with companies/commercial associations. Cluster two companies had little cooperation with the R&D and higher education institutions, with companies, development associations and with public administration. Cluster one, while having average involvement in innovation, cooperated very little with companies, users/associates and did not have any cooperative arrangements with consultants.

Table 16.7   Cooperation of the associative and institutional actors in innovation (per cent)

	Cluster one	Cluster two	Cluster three
Does cooperate for innovation	78	52	62
Does not cooperate with companies	14	33	50
Does not cooperate with users/associates	43	68	88
Does not cooperate with consultants	29	58	100
Does not cooperate with R&D institutes	43	83	50
Does not cooperate with higher education institutes	14	67	25
Does not cooperate with development associations	86	83	63
Does not cooperate with comp/commercial assocs	43	58	38
Does not cooperate with public central administration	29	67	50
Does not cooperate with public local administration	43	58	50
Does not cooperate with other institutions	71	92	100

Source: Own elaboration

Cooperation was described as essentially formal although informal cooperation had the highest values in cluster two (47 per cent); only about 30 per cent of the organizations in the other two groups had established informal agreements.

It appears from these results that the system of innovation in RCI does not favour network cooperation. This could translate into a weak regional innovation dynamic and result in competitiveness problems.

Obstacles to Innovation and Financial Support

In terms of financial support for innovations, the organizations independently of the group they represent had received national and EU support. Cluster three benefited the least from assistance provided by local and central public administrations, although this was counterbalanced with the receipt of EU funds. Cluster two benefited from assistance from local and central administration more than cluster three and also benefited from EU funds (see Table 16.8).

Table 16.8   Financial support (per cent)

Institutions/associations	Cluster one	Cluster two	Cluster three
Local administration	33	25	15
Central administration	78	35	23
EU funds	67	40	77
EU initiatives	33	20	39

Source: Own elaboration

As regards the obstacles to innovation,[9] the main factors hindering cluster one are regulations and norms, the narrowness of the market and the lack of receptivity of users/associates. The main difficulties faced by cluster two are the lack of adequate sources of financing and relatively inflexible organizational structures whereas cluster three was impeded by heavy costs and the lack of financing sources.

Future Attitude Toward Innovation

In the short-term, different actors are concerned with innovating, both at the services and organizational level. The clusters most involved in innovation are those that express greater intention to innovate in the near future (see Table 16.9).

Table 16.9   Future innovation behaviour (per cent)

Institutions/associations	Cluster one	Cluster two	Cluster three
Expect to innovate	90	70	92
Innovation in services	89	69	83
Organizational innovation	67	63	58

Source: Own elaboration

Dynamics of Collective Learning

The local dynamics of collective learning will influence the development of innovation in a region (see Table 16.10). This will be affected by whether there is a feeling that such collective learning exists in the region. Also important will be the extent of the diffusion of know-how, sharing of experiences, cooperation between agents, diffusion of innovations, whether the promotion of services is organized at a regional level and whether qualified human resources and trainees are drawn from the region.

More than 55 per cent of the actors agreed that collective learning exists, irrespective of the cluster to which they belonged. However, only 25 per cent of the public institutions, in particular those at central level, agreed that this effect exists. In relation to the territorial scale of promotion of services, cluster one has the lowest percentage of actors that operate at a regional level, and its members tend to focus on providing services both nationally and to other countries. Much of the training is carried out in the region and even the trainers are drawn primarily from the region.

Table 16.10   Effect of collective learning (per cent)

Institutions/associations	Cluster one	Cluster two	Cluster three
Existence of collective learning	60	57	62
Promotion of services at regional level	50	90	83
Training human resources in region	80	75	75
Trainers drawn from of region	89	90	90
Worker rotation inside institution/association	60	44	69
Worker mobility between organization and other institutions	20	26	54

Source: Own elaboration

In terms of job flexibility inside the organization and the mobility of workers to other organizations in the region, there are distinct situations in the three clusters. Cluster two is the one that lists fewest organizations in which the employees move internally (44 per cent) and cluster three has the most movement of employees (69 per cent of organizations). Cluster three has the greatest mobility of workers to other organizations in the region (54 per cent) and this helped in innovation activities. In contrast, only a minor percentage of organizations in cluster one have such mobility.

Summary

Innovation is not an individual company process but instead results from the involvement of a large number of actors which have the capacity to decide and to influence the territorial dynamics of innovation; these include higher education and training institutes, associations of entrepreneurs, and local and central administrative organizations. Thus, after analysing the companies, an attempt was made to understand the behaviour of the institutional and associative actors in terms of their involvement in innovation activities. The analysis of the behaviour profiles of groups of organizations of RCI demonstrated which factors or variables of the environment were associated with the best performance. However, national and community financial support and the effect of collective learning did not prove to be distinguishing elements among the clusters.

Conclusions

The profiles drawn for companies and for institutions using quantitative methods suggest inferences about the conditions associated with the best innovative performance. The conditions in the cluster most involved in innovation include more employees with higher education, greater access to new ICTs and their use of electronic commerce, more relationships with users, consumers and associates, more qualified top managers, the highest use of diverse sources of information, extensive cooperation in both formal or informal relationships, with companies preferring to cooperate with R&D and higher education institutions and the institutions cooperating more with companies. Future attitudes toward innovation and the individual learning effect also influenced the most innovative profile.

The different actors (companies and institutions/associations) in BIS had the least innovative profile which potentially could bring disastrous consequences in terms of innovation and competitiveness. However, these also valued collective learning more highly, justifying its reduced participation in innovation activities in terms of the difficulties of forming joint innovation strategies. The different actors in BIN and CB present an intermediate situation; the companies are largely found in the two clusters most involved in innovation but the institutional and associative actors showed behaviour similar to those in BIS. Salamanca presents the most favourable situation in relation to both the institutions and to the companies. The opposite appears to be the case in Cáceres. Thus Cáceres and BIS are the two regions that present the least favourable situation as regards innovation.

Moreover, the development associations, the technical training institutions and training schools, such as CILAN, Encarnacion College (Spanish), Agricultural Professional School and IEFP, appear to have an insignificant role in the development of the territorial dynamics of innovation. The public administrative organizations have a modest role in promoting innovation activities and higher education institutions are the most dynamic group as far as this is concerned.

It appears necessary to foster regional politics of innovation and trans border innovation policies to promote innovation and competitiveness within RCI. In particular, it seems necessary to promote the territorial and trans-territorial process of innovation in this region by improving the functioning of the regional system of innovation, implementing a cross border system of innovation and constructing a culture of innovation in the region. A number of other measures are also important. These include improving the interaction, cooperation and relationships between R&D and higher education institutions, technological centres and companies intra and inter sub-regions of RCI and also taking a border perspective. In addition, the availability of information and services supporting innovation needs to be enhanced, encouraging the use of the new ICTs in particular. Technological research and technology transfer through the participation of companies needs to be promoted as well as the creation of joint ventures. From a longer term perspective, it is important to stimulate creativity and the enterprising spirit from childhood, taking a new approach to this in terms of education and training.

Notes

1 'Governance' takes a combination of different forms: hierarchy, sub-contract, partnership, public and non public agencies. For the reasons governance is emphasized, see Natário, Reigado and Neto, 2002.

2 However, the Cova da Beira only belonged to the border zone in INTERREG II. In INTERREG I and in INTERREG III (the current one), it is not part of the zone of intervention. Despite this, it was decided to include CB because the RCI included this NUTS III at the beginning of the study, and the data was available.

3 5559 companies in total in the Portuguese sub-regions were registered for INE in the year 2000. They were distributed as follows: 2119 were part of the BIN, 1500 of BIS and 1940 of the CB. Only companies with 10 or more employees were considered in this study. Thus the universe of companies that satisfied this condition were: 237 companies of BIN, 193 companies of BIS and 269 companies of CB. For the Spanish regions (RCE), the Database of the Official Chamber of Salamanca shows 450 companies in the Province of Salamanca with more than ten workers. The Árdan database identified 3339 companies in the province of Cáceres, of which 428 had more than ten workers. As it was not possible to collect the population of companies (699 of RCP and 696 of the RCE), a sample of 120 companies of each side of the RCI was analysed. This represents about 17 per cent of the population and gives a minimum of 30 cases in each NUTS III or Province which is sufficient to allow statistical work (Hill, 2002:252). The 120 companies of RCP (BIN+BIS +CB) and 120 companies of the RCE (Provinces of

Salamanca and Cáceres) were proportionally distributed to the number of companies of each NUTS III/province in study. Sector distribution was not carried out because the database for the companies of the Province of Salamanca did not make use of comparable industrial classifications.

4   Since the General and Direction Conselharias has headquarters in Valladolid and Mérida, respectively, of the Autonomous Region of Castilla y Léon and of Extremadura and is under leadership of the Junta of Castilla y Leon and the Junta Extremadura, with the same postal address, the Juntas were considered to be part of the sample.

5   Through factorial analysis, the localization variables were reduced to seven groups. These were the environment of the region (including image/prestige of the region; surrounding propitious to innovation; surrounding propitious for contacts/ visibilities, and information intensiveness of the environment); human resources (including availability of sufficient labour; availability of skilled labour; proximity of centres of teaching and research, and mobility of staff between companies of the same industrial sector); personal factors (including residence in the region; knowledge of home environment; origin, and ownership of property); market and accessibility to the market (including accessibility of the region to the rest of the EU, and accessibility of the region to the rest of the country); supply of inputs (including availability of input materials and accessibility); proximity of market (including proximity of potential customers; absence or existence of companies in the same industry, and creation of new markets), and enterprise relations (including existence of supplying companies; existence of companies' customers; existence of other companies owned by the proprietor; existence of support service companies, and access to subcontractors). The KMO was calculated to see if it was reasonable to carry out a factorial analysis (see Hill and Hill, 2002; Kaiser and Rice, 1974). The value here was 0.875 which is suitable. After the factorial analysis, averages were compared.

6   Factorial analysis with a KMO of 0.799 was used to reduce the sources of information into four groups classified as internal; market; institutional, and other sources (with the importance of these as discussed in the main text).

7   Factorial analysis was also used here to reduce and regroup the variables. The KMO was 0.897 when the obstacles were regrouped into internal obstacles and external obstacles to innovation.

8   The calculation of the average percentage of staff with higher education degree shows that cluster two (less involved in innovation) has a larger percentage of staff with higher education, following cluster one (most innovative). However, many of the higher education institutions did not supply data on their staff and 40 per cent of cluster one is made up of such institutions.

9   Through factorial analysis, the following three groups of factors were obtained: economic factors (perception of extreme risks; costs of innovation; lack of appropriate sources of financing; lack of qualified staff); internal factors (flexible organizational structure; lack of information technology; regulations and norms; lack of cooperation with other local agents; weak mobility of workers inside of the region); other factors (lack of information on markets; lack of receptivity of the users/associates to innovation; narrowing of the market). KMO = 0.717 and significant. Cluster three was hindered most by economic factors, while cluster one was most affected by the group of other obstacles and cluster two was most concerned with internal factors.

References

Asheim, B. (1996), 'Industrial Districts as Learning Regions: a Condition for Prosperity', *European Planning Studies*, Vol. 4 (4), pp. 379-400.

Aydalot, P. (ed), (1986), *Milieux Innovateurs en Europe*, Groupe de Recherche Européen sur les Milieux Innovateurs (GREMI), Paris.

Barata, J. (1992), 'Inovação e Desenvolvimento Tecnológico: Conceitos, Modelos e Medidas', *Pistas para a Investigação Aplicada, Estudos de Economia*, Vol. XII(2), pp.147-171.

Bramanti, A. (1999), 'From Space to Territory: Relational Development and Territorial Competitiveness', *Revue d'Economie Régionale et Urbaine* – RERU, No. 3, pp. 633-654.

Camagni, R. (ed.) (1991), *Innovation Network: Spatial Perspectives*, Belhaven Press, Bristol.

Camagni, R., Maillat, D., Matteccioli, A. and Perrin, J.C. (1999), 'Le Paradigme du Milieu Innovateur dans L'Économie Spatiale Contemporaine', *Revue d'Economie Régionale et Urbaine* – RERU, *No. 3*, pp. 425-428.

Conceição, P. and Ávila, P. (2001), *A Inovação em Portugal: II Inquérito Comunitário às Actividades de Inovação*; Celta Editora, Oeiras.

Courlet, C. and Pecqueur, B. (1991), 'Systèmes Locaux d'Entreprises et Externalités: Essai de Typologie', *Revue d'Economie Régionale et Urbaine* – RERU, No. 3/4, pp. 391-406.

Cowan, R. and Paal, G. (2000), '*Innovation Policy in a Knowledge-Based Economy*', A Merit Study Commissioned By the European Commission Enterprise Directorate General, Commission of the European Communities, Luxembourg, ECSC-EC-EAEC, Brussels-Luxembourg, June.

De Bernady, M. (2000), 'Système Local d'Innovation: Facteurs de Cohésion et de Pérennité', *Revue d'Economie Régionale et Urbaine* – RERU No.2, pp. 265-280.

De la Fuente, A.A.H. (ed.) (2002), 'La Cooperación Transfronteriza Hispano-Portuguesa en 2001', *Cuadernos del Instituto Rei Afonso Henriques de Cooperación Transfronteriza*, No. 1, Editorial Tecnos.

Dosi, G. (1988), 'Sources, Procedures and Microeconomic Effects of Innovation', *Journal of Economic Literature*, Vol. XXVI No.3, pp. 1120-1171, September.

Dosi, G. et al. (1988), *Technical Change and Economic Theory*, Pinter Publishers, London and New York.

Edquist, C. (1997), *Systems of Innovation: Technologies, Institutions and Organizations*, Pinter, London and Washington.

Ferrão, J. (2000), 'Innovative Milieux in Small Cities – an Attainable Utopia? The Case of Évora, Portugal', in O. Crevoisier and R. Camagni (eds), *Les Milieux Urbains: Innovation, Systèmes de Production et Ancrage*, IRER, EDES, Neuchâtel, pp. 245-266.

Florida, R. (1995), 'Toward the Learning Region', *Futures*, n° 27 (May-June), pp. 527-536.

Guimarães, R. A. (1998), *Política Industrial e Tecnológica e Sistemas de Inovação*, Celta Editora, Oeiras.

Guinet, J. (1999), 'Libertar o Potencial de Inovação: o Papel do Governo', *Revista Economia & Prospectiva*, No. 10, Jul/Sept, pp. 53-80.

Hernández, F.J.C. (ed.) (2000), *Cooperación Transfronteriza: Castilla y León y Portugal, Centro de Documentación Europea*, Universidad Salamanca, Editorial Tecnos.

Hill, M.M. and Hill, A. (2002), *Investigação por Questionário*, Edições Silabo,

Kaiser, H.F. and Rice, J. (1974), 'Little Jiffy, Mark IV', *Educational and Psychological Measurement*, Vol. 34, pp. 111-117.

Kitchell, S. (1997), 'CEO Characteristics and Technological Innovativeness: A Canadian Perspective', *Revue Canadienne des Sciences de L'Administration*, Vol. 14(2), pp. 111-125.

Laranja, M. (1999), 'Por uma Política de Apoio à Evolução Tecnológica da Economia Portuguesa', *Economia & Prospectiva*, No. 10, Jul/Sept, pp. 125-143.

Lopes, R. (2001), *Competitividade, Inovação e Territórios*, Celta Editora, Oeiras.

López, F.S. and Diéguez, V.C. (1994), *La Frontera Hispano-Portuguesa el Marco de la Nueva Europa: La Región Fronteriza de Salamanca*, Universidad Salamanca, Salamanca.

Lourenço, A. (1996), *Análise da Competitividade/cooperação entre o Concelho do Sabugal e a Comarca de Ciudad Rodrigo: Cooperação Transfronteiriça, Tese de Mestrado*, UBI, Covilhã, Fevereiro.

Lundvall, B.A. (ed.) (1992), *National Systems of Innovation: Towards a Theory of Innovation and Interactive Learning*, Pinter Publishers, London, 1st edition.

Lundvall, B.A. (1998), 'Why Study National Systems and National Styles of Innovation', *Technology Analysis & Strategic Management*, Vol. 10 (4), pp. 407-21.

Maillat, D. (1995), 'Milieux Innovateurs et Nouvelles Générations de Politiques Régionales', in J. Ferrão (ed.), *Políticas de Inovação e Desenvolvimento Regional e Local*, Encontro Realizado em Évora, Edição do ICSUN-ISCTE, pp. 13-30.

Maillat, D. (1998), 'Interactions between Urban Systems and Localised Productive Systems: An Approach to Endogenous Regional Development in Terms of Innovative Milieu', *European Planning Studies*, Vol. 6 (2), pp. 112-131.

Maillat, D. and Kebir, L. (1999), '"Learning Region" et Systèmes Territoriaux de Production', *Revue d'Economie Régionale et Urbaine* – RERU, No. 3, pp. 429-448.

Maillat, D., Crevoisier, O. and Lecoq, B. (1993), 'Réseaux d'Innovation et Dynamique Territorial: le cas de l'Arc Jurassien', in D. Maillat, M. Quévit and L. Senn (eds) (1993), *Réseaux d'Innovation et Milieux Innovateurs: un Pari pour le Développement Régional*, Irer, Gremi/Edes, Neuchâtel, pp. 17-51.

Natário, M., Reigado, F. and Neto, P.A. (2002), 'A Proximidade e a Competitividade: um Pré-estudo à Competitividade na Raia Central Ibérica', Paper Presented in IX Encontro da APDR 26-29 Junho, Lisboa.

Nelson, R. (ed.) (1993), *National Systems of Innovation: a Comparative Study*, Oxford University Press, Oxford.

OECD/Eurostat (1997), OECD Proposed Guidelines for Collecting and Interpreting Technological Innovation Data-Oslo Manual OCDE/EUROSTAT, Paris.

OECD (1997), National Innovation Systems, OECD Publications, Paris.

Pestana, M.J. and Gageiro, J.N. (2000), *Análise de Dados para as Ciências Sociais. A Complementaridade do SPSS*, 2nd edition, Edições Silabo, Lisboa

Planque, B. (1991), 'Note sur la Notion de Réseau D'innovation – Réseaux Contractuels et Réseaux Conventionnels', *Revue d'Économie Régionale et Urbaine*, No. 3/4, pp. 295-320.

Reigado, F.M. (1995), 'Ensino Superior, Investigação e Cooperação Transfronteiríça', Paper presented in Seminário *Dinamismos Sócio-Económico e (Re)Organização Territorial: Processo de Urbanização e de Reestruturação*, Produtiva, Covilhã.

Reigado, F.M. (2000), 'Actividades Emergentes e Recentralização da Raia Central Ibérica', in F.J.C. Hernández (ed.), *Cooperación Transfronteriza: Castilla y León y Portugal*, Centro de Documentación Europea, Universidad Salamanca, Editorial Tecnos, pp. 95-118.

Reigado, F.M. (2002), 'Desenvolvimento Regional Transfronteiriço', in J.S. Costa (ed.), *Compêndio de Economia Regional*, Colecção APDR, pp.571-596.

Rodrigues, M.J. (ed.) (2000), 'Pronoiv-Programa Integrado de Apoio à Inovação', Presidência do Conselho de Ministros, Versão para Consulta Pública.

Santos, D. (2002), 'Teorias de Inovação de Base Territorial', in Costa, J.S. (ed.), *Compêndio de Economia Regional*, Colecção APDR, pp. 285-359

Santos, J.L.A. and Caetano, L. (eds) (2002), *Modelos de Organización Territorial en la Raya Central Ibérica: Una Visión de Conjunto*, Ediciones Universidad de Salamanca.

Schumpeter, J.A. (1934), *The Theory of Economic Development*, Harvard University Press, Cambridge, MA (Reproduced New York 1961).

Vaz, M.T.N. and Cesário, M. (2005), 'Behavioural patterns towards innovation: The case of European rural regions', 16th ISPIM (International Society for Professional Innovative Management), INESC Porto, Portugal.

Vaz, M.T.N, Cesário, M. and Fernandes, S. (2006), 'Interaction between Innovation in Small Firms and their Environments: An exploratory study'. *Special Issue: Rural Development*, in *European Planning Studies*, no. 1/2006, Taylor and Francis.

Veltz, P. (1999), 'Territoires Innovateurs: De Quelle Innovation Parle-t-on?', *Revue d'Economie Régionale et Urbaine* – RERU, No. 3, pp. 607-616.

Appendix 16.1 Structure of sample by industrial classification and number of employees, 2002

CAE Rev.2	Total of RCP		Total of RCE	
	No. of companies	Per cent	No. of companies	Per cent
01 Agriculture, hunting, fishery, and others related services	0	0.0	2	3.1
14 Others extractives industries	3	2.9	0	0.0
15 Agro-food industries	16	15.2	5	7.8
17 Textiles industries	8	7.6	0	0.0
18 Clothes industries	11	10.5	0	0.0
19 Tanneries industries	0	0.0	1	1.6
20 Wood industries	2	1.9	1	1.6
21 Paper industries	1	1.0	0	0.0
22 Publication and print industries	1	1.0	4	6.3
24 Manufacture of chemical products	1	1.0	4	6.3
25 Manufacture of rubber and plastics products	1	1.0	1	1.6
26 Manufacture of glass	5	4.8	1	1.6
27 Metallurgy industries	0	0.0	1	1.6
28 Manufacture of metallic products	4	3.8	0	0.0
29 Manufacture of machines and equipment	4	3.8	0	0.0
31 Manufacture of machines and electric equipment	1	1.0	0	0.0
33 Manufacture of medical instruments	2	1.9	1	1.6
34 Manufacture of automobiles	1	1.0	1	1.6
36 Manufacture of furniture	3	2.9	4	6.3
45 Construction	7	6.7	11	17.2
50 Commerce of vehicles automobiles	8	7.6	8	12.5
51 Other commerce of wholesale	12	11.4	10	15.6
52 Commerce of retail	7	6.7	3	4.7
55 Accommodation and restaurants	2	1.9	2	3.1
60 Transports and storage	2	1.9	1	1.6
72 Informatics activities	1	1.0	0	0.0
74 Others services	1	1.0	3	4.7
80 Education services	1	1.0	0	0.0
93 Health and public hygiene services	0	0.0	0	0.0
Total	105	100.0	64	100.0
Number of Employees				
1-9*	6	5.7	2	3.1
10-19	41	39.0	22	34.4
20-49	31	29.5	26	40.6
50-99	17	16.2	10	15.6
100-249	7	6.7	4	6.3
250-499	3	2.9		
Total	105	100.0	64	100.0

Source: Own survey.

*The companies investigated in this study employed ten or more people when the sample was being selected. However, when the survey was undertaken, employment had fallen in these firms.

Appendix 16.2   Number of institutions and associations in RCI regions, 2002

	RCP	RCE
Bureau of Initiatives Transfronteiriças	1	2
Regional Services of Agriculture and of Environment	3	2
Culture and Patrimony	1	
Economic	2	
Professional Formation Institutions and Technological Schools	4	
Tourism	1	
Local Administration	16	9
Associations /Federations of Municipals	1	2
Enterprise Associations	9	6
Local Development Associations	8	9
Higher Education Institutions	3	4
Infra-structures Technological	1	2
Government Civil/Deputations	2	2
Total	52	38

Source: CCRC

Appendix 16.3   ANOVA applied to the three clusters of companies relative to the involvement in innovation

ANOVA

	Cluster		Error			
	Mean Square	df	Mean Square	df	F	Sig.
R&D inside the company	4.334	2	.123	163	35.174	.000
Acquisition of external services - R&D	3.244	2	.111	163	29.235	.000
Acquisition of new technologies	1.225	2	.186	163	6.581	.002
Acquisition of information technologies	2.451	2	.201	163	12.165	.000
Acquisition of other external knowledge	3.509	2	.164	163	21.442	.000
Training of human resources	1.942	2	.220	163	8.821	.000
Introduction of innovation into markets	6.439	2	.145	163	44.558	.000
Management strategy /techniques	6.500	2	.121	163	53.501	.000
Changes in organizational structure	6.497	2	.150	163	43.337	.000
Marketing innovation	4.984	2	.172	163	28.951	.000
Company introduced innovation	17.992	2	.023	163	777.032	.000
Product innovation	11.786	2	.110	163	107.309	.000
Process innovation	3.524	2	.146	163	24.106	.000
Organizational innovation	1.640	2	.123	163	13.369	.000

The F tests should be used only for descriptive purposes because the clusters have been chosen to maximize the differences among cases in different clusters. The observed significance levels are not corrected for this and thus cannot be interpreted as tests of the hypothesis that the cluster means are equal.

Appendix 16.4   ANOVA applied to the three clusters of institutions and associations relative to the involvement in innovation

ANOVA

	Cluster		Error			
	Mean Square	df	Mean Square	df	F	Sig.
R&D inside the organisation	3.104	2	.082	43	37.788	.000
Acquisition of external services - R&D	2.060	2	.099	43	20.852	.000
Acquisition of new technologies	1.593	2	.152	43	10.458	.000
Acquisition of information technologies	.809	2	.169	43	4.795	.013
Acquisition of other external knowledge	2.008	2	.172	43	11.675	.000
Training of human resources	.533	2	.113	43	4.703	.014
Management strategy /techniques	2.879	2	.109	43	26.469	.000
Changes in organizational structure	2.131	2	.156	43	13.684	.000
Marketing innovation	1.412	2	.200	43	7.066	.002

The F tests should be used only for descriptive purposes because the clusters have been chosen to maximize the differences among cases in different clusters. The observed significance levels are not corrected for this and thus cannot be interpreted as tests of the hypothesis that the cluster means are equal.

Index